K- Ref

KU-328-056

A CHRONOLOGY OF IRISH HISTORY SINCE 1500

by the same authors:

A Dictionary of Irish History 1800 – 1980

A CHRONOLOGY OF IRISH HISTORY SINCE 1500

J. E. DOHERTY

D. J. HICKEY

GILL AND MACMILLAN

KILKENNY COUNTY LIBRARY

Published in Ireland by
Gill and Macmillan Ltd
Goldenbridge
Dublin 8
with associated companies in
Auckland, Delhi, Gaborone, Hamburg, Harare,
Hong Kong, Johannesburg, Kuala Lumpur, Lagos, London,
Manzini, Melbourne, Mexico City, Nairobi,
New York, Singapore, Tokyo
© J. E. Doherty and D. J. Hickey, 1989
Index compiled by Helen Litton
Print origination in Ireland by Irish Typesetting and Publishing Ltd, Galway
Printed by Billing & Sons Ltd, Worcester

All rights reserved. No part of this publication may be copied,
reproduced or transmitted in any form or by any means,
without permission of the publishers.

British Library Cataloguing in Publication Data

Doherty, J.E. (James E)
A chronology of Irish history since 1500.
1. Ireland, history
I. Title II. Hickey, D.J. (Denis Joseph), *1937–*
941.5

ISBN 0–7171–1634–4
ISBN 0–7171–1705–7 pbk

KILKENNY COUNTY
LIBRARY
Acc. No. 354081
Class No. 941.5 REF.
Inv. No. 10197
Cat. 20.4.90

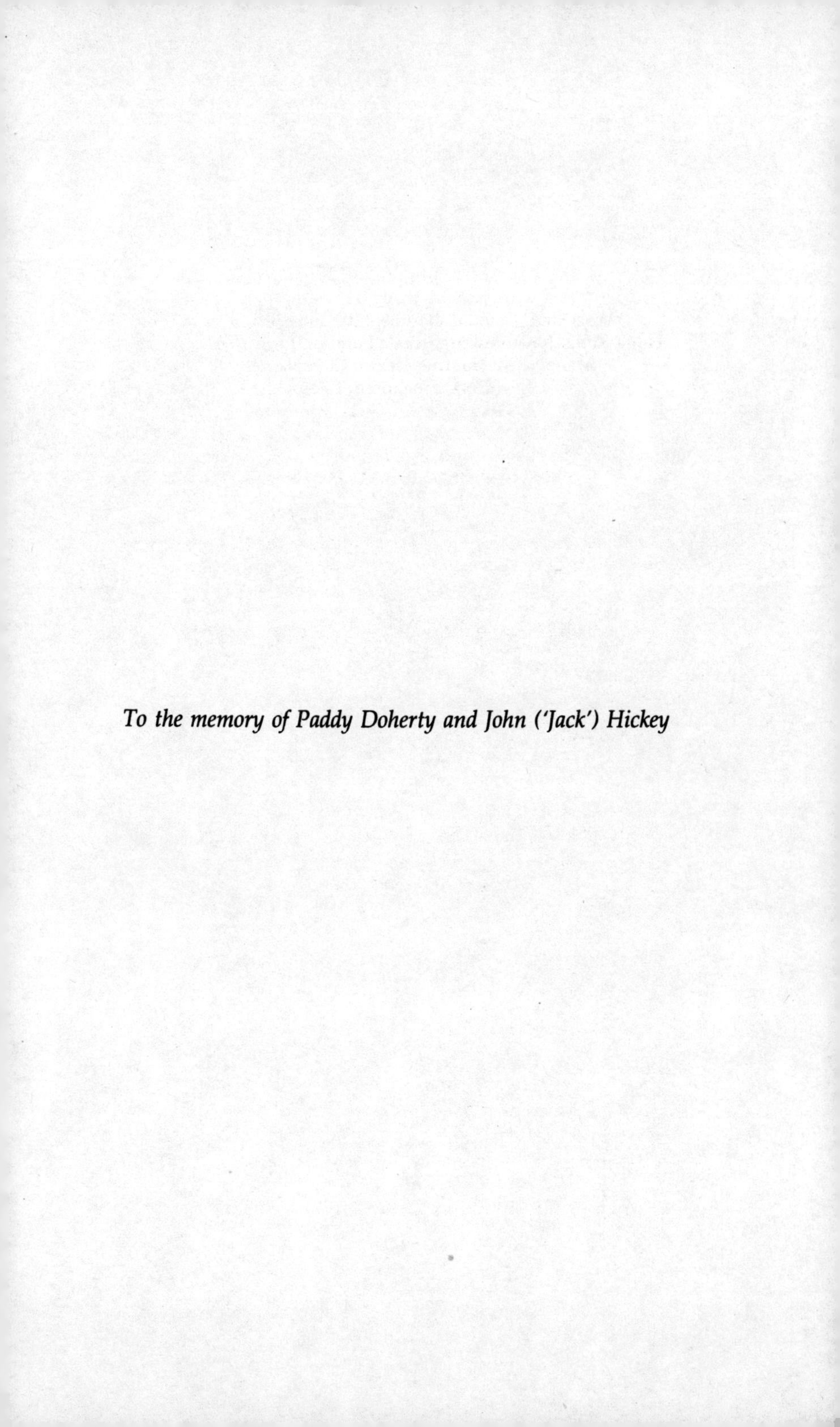

To the memory of Paddy Doherty and John ('Jack') Hickey

Contents

Preface

This is the first chronology of Irish history, designed for general readers and students, covering, in the main, modern Irish history. Other chronologies deal with either much longer or shorter periods. Availability of space placed constraints on the time-scale to be covered, posing some problems for the authors. While it is clear that there is a rising interest in all periods of Irish history, ancient, medieval and modern, we felt that a one-volume work must include the modern period and should provide, as far as possible, a broad perspective on Irish history. An obvious starting point, therefore, was 1534, generally taken to mark the beginning of early modern Irish history. However, we made the decision to start in 1500, not so much for the roundness of the date, as to give the reader an opportunity to observe the transition from the end of the medieval period, marked by the introduction and imposition of the Reformation on the Irish political and religious establishments, to the early modern.

As in our *Dictionary of Irish History since 1800* (1980: republished as *A Dictionary of Irish History 1800–1980* in 1987) we have viewed Irish history in the broadest possible terms. This inevitably posed problems of selectivity. The problems of selectivity are as great in a chronology as in any other work of history confined to limitations of space. Readers may query the inclusion of some events and personalities to the exclusion of others. Our main concern has been to balance the inevitable preponderance of political and military material with entries on religious, social, cultural and sporting events. An obvious problem arose in dealing with those years which are regarded as of particular significance in Irish history, such as 1534–41, 1594–1603, 1641–51, 1689–91, 1798, 1848, 1867, 1916–23 and from 1969 onwards. Here, we have been at pains to include as detailed a picture as possible to enable the reader to have a clear view of the development of events, and at the same time indicate that political and military incidents were not the only history of the time; to provide an impressionistic picture while preserving objectivity and accuracy.

It has not been possible in a book of this size to provide a bibliography which would, in any event, be of interest mainly to the specialist. The *Annals* and *Calendars of State Papers* have been used for the earlier material (where Old Style dating has been followed) and the most modern research available has been used throughout the work.

We have given extensive coverage to the modern period since the Famine. While this may result in an imbalance, we sought to provide a thorough chronology for the period in which there appears to be most interest among general readers and students. The period from 1969 may appear to be dominated by the recrudescence of violence in Northern Ireland but this is a fact of very recent Irish history which cannot be ignored.

Nomenclature: we have generally indicated people by the name by which they are best known. In the case of titled persons we have indicated them in the text by name as well as title. Until the plantation of Ulster, Derry refers to the city and its surrounding area; after the plantation Derry refers to the city and Londonderry to the county. For the very modern period, Northern Ireland (N.I.), Irish Free State (I.F.S.), Éire and Republic of Ireland (R.I.) have been used as appropriate to the times.

Acknowledgments

It would be invidious to single out individuals from among the many friends and colleagues who gave us support and encouragement while we were engaged on the work. The following people and institutions are acknowledged for the aid which they provided: John Killeen, Librarian, and the staff of the Linen Hall Library, Belfast; the Librarian and staff, Clare Co. Library (Ennis); the Librarian and staff, Limerick City Library, in particular the staff in Research; the Librarian and staff of the Limerick County Library; Librarian and staff of the University of Limerick; the Library staff at R.T.E. were as usual generous with their help as were the staff of the *Irish Times* library; *Irish Independent* Sports Department, particularly Tom Myler; Dr Lammey and staff at the Northern Ireland Public Record Office; Br Gill, Superior of the Christian Brothers, Mount Sion and Br Carroll who was especially helpful on the early history of the school; Iarnrod Éireann; the Blood Transfusion Service; Liam Nolan, Director General, National Olympic Council of Ireland; Wanda Ryan, Research Assistant, National Gallery of Ireland; Aer Rianta staff, Shannon airport; the U.S. Embassy; Estuary House, Limerick, Telecom Éireann staff, Clem Clear, Sean Bourke and Ger Mulcahy were of invaluable assistance; the Government Information Service. Special thanks are due to Robert Duffy for introducing the first-named of the authors to the intricacies of word-processing, and to Richard Tobin for his generosity in serving as technical consultant on the computer system and word-processing programme over the past eighteen months.

Our editor, Fergal Tobin, as always, was there with encouragement and advice and our warmest thanks and appreciation are due to our copy-editor Colm Croker, many of whose helpful suggestions we have incorporated.

Our families once more tolerated the sort of neglect and absent-mindedness which seem to go with research and writing of whatever form, so, yet again, our inadequate thanks are due to our families, Caithlin, Patrick and Carmel Doherty, and Anna, John, Michelle and Michael Hickey, for sustaining us with love and understanding during the course of this work.

J. E. Doherty
D. J. Hickey
September 1989

KILKENNY
COUNTY
LIBRARY

Abbreviations

A.C.A.	Army Comrades' Association
A.I.F.T.A.	Anglo-Irish Free Trade Area Agreement
B.O.A.C.	British Overseas Airways Corporation
C.I.	Church of Ireland
C.I.E.	Córas Iompair Éireann
C.I.U.	Congress of Irish Unions
C.S.	Chief Secretary
d.	death/died
D.I.	District Inspector
D.M.P.	Dublin Metropolitan Police
D.U.P.	Democratic Unionist Party
E.E.C.	European Economic Community
E.M.S.	European Monetary System
E.S.B.	Electricity Supply Board
F.C.A.	Fórsa Cosanta Áitiúil
F.F.	Fianna Fáil
F.G.	Fine Gael
F.U.E.	Federated Union of Employers
G.A.A.	Gaelic Athletic Association
G.O.C.	General Officer Commanding
G.P.O.	General Post Office
I.C.T.U.	Irish Congress of Trade Unions
I.D.A.	Industrial Development Authority
I.E.R.	*Irish Ecclesiastical Record*
I.F.S.	Irish Free State
I.L.S.C.	International Labour and Socialist Conference
I.M.F.	International Monetary Fund
I.N.L.A.	Irish National Liberation Army
I.N.T.O.	Irish National Teachers' Organisation
I.R.A.	Irish Republican Army
I.R.B.	Irish Republican Brotherhood
I.R.S.P.	Irish Republican Socialist Party
I.S.R.P.	Irish Socialist Republican Party
I.T.G.W.U.	Irish Transport and General Workers' Union
I.T.U.C.	Irish Trade Union Congress
L.A.W.	Loyalist Association of Workers
L.D.	Lord Deputy
L.J.	Lord Justice
L.L.	Lord Lieutenant
M.E.P.	Member of the European Parliament
M.P.	Member of Parliament
N.A.T.O.	North Atlantic Treaty Organisation
N.I.	Northern Ireland
N.I.A.	Northern Ireland Assembly
N.I.C.R.A.	Northern Ireland Civil Rights Association
N.I.H.E.	National Institute for Higher Education
N.U.D.L.	National Union of Dock Labourers
N.U.I.	National University of Ireland
O.E.E.C.	Organisation for European Economic Co-operation
O.U.P.	Official Unionist Party

P.D.	Peoples' Democracy
P.M.	Prime Minister
P.O.	Post Office
P.P.	Parish Priest
P.R.	Proportional Representation
Pub.	Publication/published
R.A.F.	Royal Air Force
R.C.	Roman Catholic
R.D.S.	Royal Dublin Society
R.H.A.	Royal Hibernian Academy
R.I.	Republic of Ireland
R.I.A.	Royal Irish Academy
R.I.C.	Royal Irish Constabulary
R.N.L.I.	Royal National Lifeboat Institution
R.T.E.	Radio Telefís Éireann
R.U.C.	Royal Ulster Constabulary
S.A.S.	Strategic Air Services
S.D.L.P.	Social Democratic and Labour Party
S.E.A.	Single European Act
S.F.	Sinn Féin
T.C.D.	Trinity College, Dublin
T.D.	Teachta Dála (Member of the Dáil)
T.U.C.	Trades Union Congress
U.C.D.	University College Dublin
U.D.A.	Ulster Defence Association
U.D.R.	Ulster Defence Regiment
U.F.F.	Ulster Freedom Fighters
U.K.	United Kingdom
U.N.	United Nations
U.N.E.S.C.O.	United Nations Educational, Scientific and Cultural Organisation
U.S.A.	United States of America
U.U.A.C.	Ulster Unionist Action Council
U.U.U.C.	United Ulster Unionist Council
U.V.F.	Ulster Volunteer Force
U.W.C.	Ulster Workers' Council
V.A.T.	Value Added Tax
V.C.	Victoria Cross
V.U.P.P.	Vanguard Unionist Progressive Party
W.U.I.	Workers' Union of Ireland

1500
Aug. Charter renews the privileges of Cork city.

Galway city partly destroyed by fire.

O'Briens of Thomond defeat the Butlers at Moyaliff, near Kilnamanagh, Co. Tipperary.

Hugh Ruadh O'Donnell invades Tyrone, burning Dungannon and the crannóg at Loch Laoghaire.

L.D. Gearóid Mór FitzGerald, ('The Great Earl'), 8th Earl of Kildare, besieges Kinard Castle (Caledon), Co. Tyrone, which he restores to Turlough O'Neill.

Book of Lismore written about this time for Fineen MacCarthy Reagh.

1501
17 Mar. The O'Neills defeat the Scots near Armagh.

5 July d. Donal Fallon, Bishop of Derry since 1485.

Turlough O'Brien of Thomond raids Limerick county and burns the city.

Thomas Maguire slain by the McMahons at the battle of Sliabh Betha.

O'Connors capture Sligo Castle.

O'Briens and O'Loughlins of the Burren, Co. Clare, defeat the O'Flahertys in Killary Bay, Co. Galway, but are driven back into Clare.

1502
Fighting between factions of the O'Boyles in Co. Donegal at Tullaghfin leads to the death of Niall Buidhe O'Boyle and his two sons.

d. Donough O'Brien of Thomond.

O'Donnells and Maguires invade Co. Cavan at Dartry, burning and pillaging before retreat.

Inclement weather and disease in cattle leads to famine and plague.

1503
Apr. d. Seán Maguire, ruler of Fermanagh, at Enniskillen.

30 Apr. L.D. Kildare sails for England; returns in Aug. with eldest son, Gerald or Gearóid Óg, who has been in the King's custody and is now married to Elizabeth, daughter of Sir John Zouche.

Sept. Campaigning in Ulster, L.D. Kildare sacks Belfast Castle.

Theobald Burke of Clanwilliam, Co. Tipperary, slain by Donough O'Carroll and Conor O'Dwyer.

Ulick Burke of Clanricard, Co. Galway, defeats the O'Kellys.

1504
26 Feb. Gearóid Óg FitzGerald appointed Lord High Treasurer.

19 Aug. L.D. Kildare and allies defeat Ulick Burke in a major battle at Knockdoe, Co. Galway, taking possession of Galway and Athenry.

Outbreak of plague which continues into 1505.

1505
11 July d. Hugh Ruadh O'Donnell of Tyrconnell (78), founder of the monastery of Friars of Strict Observance in Donegal; Hugh Dubh O'Donnell inaugurated as king of the territory on 2 Aug.

O'Donnells invade Tyrone, burn Dungannon and recover Castlederg from the O'Neills.

1506
Turlough Donn O'Brien of Thomond builds a bridge three hundred paces long, later fortified, across the Shannon (O'Brien's Bridge) at Portcrusha, in Stradbally parish, north of Limerick city (*see* 1510).

Maurice O'Fihely appointed Archbishop of Tuam by Pope Julius II (*see* 1512).

1507
c. 17 Mar. Monastery of Clogher burned.

6 May d. John Payne, Dominican Bishop of Meath since 1483.

30 Oct. d. Giolla Brighde Mac Con Midhe, hereditary poet to the O'Neills.

Monastery of Ballindoon founded by Thomas O'Farrell.

Hugh Maguire slain by the O'Rourkes.

Hugh Óg O'Donnell defeated by Niall O'Neill; later O'Donnell captures the castle of Carrickfergus and recovers the hostages which he had been forced to abandon.

Church of Aghavea, Co. Fermanagh, burned.

1508
6 Oct. Parliament opens; subsidies renewed for 10 years.

1509
21 Apr. d. Henry VII; succeeded by his son Henry VIII (crowned on 24 June).

28 July L.D Kildare does not answer summons to attend at London.

L.D. Kildare invades Tyrone on behalf of the O'Neills and demolishes Omagh.

Nicholas St Lawrence, Baron Howth, appointed Lord Chancellor.

1510
8 Nov. L.D. Kildare confirmed in his appointment; receives royal patent granting him in tail of all possessions he can recover from any rebel in Ireland.

Campaigning in Munster, L.D. Kildare takes the castles of Kanturk, Co. Cork, and Castlemaine, Co. Kerry.

O'Briens of Thomond defeat L.D. Kildare and his O'Donnell allies at Móin na mBráthar, Limerick, where they destroy O'Brien's Bridge at Portcrusha.

Hugh Dubh O'Donnell makes a pilgrimage to Rome.

1511
13 Feb. Hugh Dubh O'Donnell knighted in England by Henry VIII.

14 May d. Walter FitzSimons, Archbishop of Dublin since 1484; the first to be consecrated in St Patrick's Cathedral.

L.D. Kildare leads an expedition to the midlands against the O'Mores and the O'Reillys.

1512
28 Jan. William Rokeby appointed Archbishop of Dublin; appointed Lord Chancellor of Ireland on 21 May (d. 1521).

Apr. L.D. Kildare makes foray into Ulster, again destroying Belfast Castle and attacking Glenarm. Having wasted the surrounding territory, he raids Roscommon, capturing Roscommon and Cavetown castles.

Archbishop O'Fihely of Tuam and Thomas Halsey (appointed Bishop of Leighlin in 1513) attend the Fifth Lateran Council in Rome under Pope Julius II.

O'Neill acknowledges O'Donnell's authority in Fermanagh and Inishowen, Co. Donegal.

1513
25 Mar. d. Maurice O'Fihely, Franciscan Archbishop of Tuam since 1506, noted scholar (writing under the pseudonym 'Flos Mundi') and editor of the works of Duns Scotus.

3 Sept. d. L.D Kildare at Athy from gunshot wounds; his son, Gearóid Óg becomes 9th Earl of Kildare and is appointed L.D. on the same terms (26 Nov.; confirmed on 24 Mar. 1516).

24 Oct. John Kite, close friend of Wolsey, appointed Archbishop of Armagh (until 1521).

1514

July L.D. Kildare campaigns against Hugh O'Reilly, who is killed, and lays waste Cavan. In a campaign against the O'Mores of Leix he destroys Abbeyleix Castle. Campaigning against James FitzGerald of Connolloe, Co. Clare, he is halted by Turlough O'Brien.

1515

Apr. L.D. Kildare sets out for London to answer allegations before the King's Council (returns in Sept., confirmed as L.D.).

24 June Sir William Darcy submits papers to the English council suggesting need for political reform in Ireland and indicting Kildare's government.

3 Aug. d. Thomas Butler, 7th Earl of Ormond, leaving succession struggle between cousins, the Boleyns of England and the Butlers of Ormond (*see* 1516).

College for secular priests established at Maynooth by L.D. Kildare.

1516

24 Mar. L.D. Kildare confirmed in his appointment with power to appoint his own nominees as Lord Chancellor and Chief Justice.

Piers Ruadh Butler recognised as Earl of Ormond (*see* 23 Feb. 1528).

Hugh Dubh O'Donnell captures castles in Co. Sligo.

1517

L.D. Kildare campaigns with Ormond against O'Carrolls, destroying Garrycastle. Campaigning against Felim MacGuinness in Co. Cavan, he destroys Dundrum Castle.

1518

Turlough O'Melaghlin, having killed his brother, succeeds to kingship of Meath.

1519

12 Jan. L.D. Kildare, summoned to London to answer charges of maladministration, appoints kinsman Sir Thomas FitzGerald of Laccagh as deputy in his absence.

Outbreak of plague which continues into 1520.

1520

10 Mar. Thomas Howard, Earl of Surrey, appointed L.L., instructed by Henry VIII to win Ireland over by 'sober waies, politique drifts and amiable persuasions'; arrives at the head of over 1,000 soldiers on 23 May.

July – Aug. Surrey forces submission of O'Carrolls in Leinster and O'Neills in Ulster.

21 Sept. Cormac Láidhir MacCarthy of Muskerry defeats the Earl of Desmond at Mourneabbey, near Mallow, Co. Cork.

1521

July L.L. Surrey avenges a confederation against the Pale by O'Connors, O'Mores and O'Carrolls of the midlands by scorched earth campaign.

29 Nov. d. William Rokeby, Archbishop of Dublin and Lord Chancellor since 1512; succeeded in both offices by Hugh Inge.

21 Dec. Piers Ruadh Butler declared 'true and lawful heir' to the Earl of Ormond by act of parliament (*see* 23 Feb. 1528)

1522

26 Mar. Earl of Ormond sworn in as L.D.

11 June Con Bacach O'Neill captures Ballyshannon from the O'Donnells, burns it and devastates their territory.

Aug. O'Donnells defeat O'Neill at Knockavoe, near Strabane, Co. Tyrone.

Irish Privy Council appeals to Wolsey for six ships of war to cruise between Scotland and Ireland to stem the tide of Scottish 'invasion' into Ulster. Four are sent.

1523

1 Jan. Kildare returns to Ireland.

May Campaigning in Ulster, Kildare captures Belfast Castle and Carrickfergus.

Oct. Truce declared between O'Neills and O'Donnells.

1524

13 May Kildare reappointed L.D.

20 June Arrival of commissioners, Sir Ralph Egerton, Sir Anthony Fitzherbert and James Denton, Dean of Lichfield, to investigate complaints against Kildare, for whom they find and who is confirmed as L.D.

28 July Indenture between Kildare and Ormond to keep the peace. Ormond marries Kildare's sister.

Niall Garbh and Owen, sons of Hugh Dubh O'Donnell, kill each other in battle.

James FitzGerald, Earl of Desmond, refuses to appear at court to answer charges of high treason for entering into treaty with Francis I of France; Kildare, ordered to arrest him, makes token foray into Munster, but does not confront Desmond (*see* 5 Nov. 1526).

1525

Maurice O'Dorran, Bishop of Leighlin, killed on the orders of Maurice MacMurrough, archdeacon of the diocese; Kildare has those involved flayed.

Registry of the Antiquities of Clogher completed by Patrick Cullen, Bishop of Clogher, and Archdeacon Roderick Cassidy.

Summer drought followed by autumn floods leads to disastrous harvest.

1526

5 Nov. Kildare leaves for London to answer charges arising out of his failure to arrest his cousin, the Earl of Desmond (*see* 1524); leaves his brother, Sir Thomas FitzGerald, as deputy *pro tem*. Kildare, committed to the Tower by Wolsey, is freed on the bail of several influential dukes and restored to royal favour.

1527

O'Neill and O'Donnell enter into peace.

Charges not pressed after Kildare examined by the council in London.

1528

23 Feb. Sir Thomas Boleyn receives title of Earl of Ormond, and Piers Ruadh Butler becomes Earl of Ossory, in a solution to the dispute over the inheritance of Thomas Butler, 7th Earl of Ormond.

24 Mar. Con Bacach O'Neill offers 'to serve the king against the rebels in Ireland'.

12 May Vice-deputy Richard Nugent, 12th Baron Delvin, seized by Brian O'Connor at Rathin Castle, Co. Meath; Nugent released when O'-Connor's pension is restored on 25 Feb. 1529.

19 Sept. John Alen, Archbishop-elect of Dublin, appointed Lord Chancellor.

Oct. Earl of Ossory sworn in as L.D.

Conor O'Brien succeeds as King of Thomond.

1529
24 Feb. Gonzalo Fernandez commissioned by Emperor Charles V to treat with the Earl of Desmond (arrives at Dingle, Co. Kerry, on 21 Apr.).

18 June d. James FitzGerald, 11th Earl of Desmond.

22 June Henry Fitzroy, Duke of Richmond and Somerset, natural son of Henry VIII, appointed L.L.

4 Aug. Earl of Ossory loses office of L.D. through the artifice of Archbishop Alen and others.

24 Aug. William Skeffington arrives as King's special commissioner in Ireland.
Aug. – Sept. Synod of Limerick convened by Archbishop Butler of Cashel decrees that ecclesiastics may be arrested for debt; unpopular with lower clergy who consider it contrary to ecclesiastical privilege.

3 Sept. Edward Staples appointed Bishop of Meath (*see* 29 June 1554).

18 Oct. Cardinal Wolsey dismissed as Chancellor of England.

1530
22 June Kildare returns to Ireland with Skeffington, the new L.D.

L.D. Skeffington and Kildare attack the O'Mores of the midlands.

1531
11 Feb. King Henry VIII recognised by convocation of Canterbury as 'Supreme Head of the Church of England'.

L.D. Skeffington lays waste much of Ulster, including Donegal and Tyrone.

6 May Hugh Dubh O'Donnell submits to L.D. Skeffington at Drogheda to sue for peace terms.

O'Donnells attack and capture Beleek Castle, Co. Fermanagh.

15 Sep. Parliament opens; renews subsidy for 10 years.

1532
7 Feb. John Alen, Archbishop of Dublin, following Wolsey's fall from power, granted general pardon as Lord Chancellor and as Wolsey's commissioner.

Kildare again in England.

Skeffington, campaigning against the O'Neills of Tyrone, destroys Dungannon.

5 July Kildare appointed L.D.; George Cromer, Archbishop of Armagh, replaces Alen as Lord Chancellor.

James Butler, son of the Earl of Ossory, marries Joan FitzGerald, daughter of James, Earl of Desmond.

1533
15 Jan. L.D. Kildare convenes parliament; confirms supremacy of the archiepiscopal see of Armagh over Dublin.

25 Jan. Marriage of Henry VIII to Anne Boleyn, cousin of the Butlers of Ormond.

19 May Parliament opens; renews subsidy for three years.

5 July John Alen (not to be confused with Archbishop John Alen) appointed Master of the Rolls.

11 July Henry VIII excommunicated by Pope Clement VII.

Sept. Following representations from the Irish council to the King, Kildare is summoned to England.

Nov. L.D. Kildare sends his wife to London to answer charges against him.

1534

Feb. L.D. Kildare, recalled to England, leaves his son, 'Silken' Thomas, Lord Offaly, as his deputy; on arrival in London, Kildare is arrested on King's orders and lodged in the Tower.

8 May Appointment of Sir Patrick Finglas as Chief Justice of the King's Bench, over Kildare's protests, signals Thomas Cromwell's direction of constitutional reform in Ireland.

11 May Piers Butler, Earl of Ossory, and his son James (created Viscount Thurles) adopt the Protestant faith and are charged with the government of Kilkenny, Waterford and Tipperary.

31 May Earl of Ossory binds himself and his heirs to resist 'the abuse and usurped jurisdiction of the Bishop of Rome'.

11 June Silken Thomas surrenders the sword of state, denounces the King as a heretic and declares himself no longer in allegiance to the Crown.

29 June Kildare imprisoned in the Tower of London; rumours of his ill-treatment circulate in Dublin.

21 July Conor O'Brien of Thomond writes to Emperor Charles V asking for help and offering submission.

27 July Silken Thomas enters Dublin at the head of 140 horse and besieges the Castle (abandons it on 4 Oct.).

28 July Archbishop Alen murdered by followers of Silken Thomas at Artane.

30 July Sir William Skeffington appointed L.D. (*see* 24 Oct.), superseding Silken Thomas, who is commanded to appear before the King's Council.

26 Aug. William Brabazon knighted and appointed Vice-Treasurer; appointed Receiver-General in Oct.

2 Sept. d. Kildare in the Tower of London; Silken Thomas succeeds as 10th Earl of Kildare.

24 Oct. Skeffington lands with an army of 2,300.

28 Oct. Skeffington marches to the relief of Drogheda, where he proclaims Silken Thomas a traitor.

15 Nov. Skeffington takes Trim, Co. Meath.

18 Nov. Act of Supremacy passed by English parliament.

1 Dec. Kildare Castle taken by the government (both Trim and Kildare castles are subsequently retaken by Silken Thomas).

19 Dec. Truce between Skeffington and Silken Thomas (ends on 6 Jan. 1535).

Coinage for Ireland, displaying the harp, struck in London.

1535

23 Mar. In one of the first recorded uses of siege guns in Ireland, Skeffington takes Maynooth Castle after a week's siege and bombardment; in the 'Pardon of Maynooth' puts the garrison to the sword: 'We thought it expedient to put them to execution as an example to others.'

9 June Commission issued suppressing Graney, Co. Kildare (Augustinians) the first religious house in Ireland to be suppressed.

14 June Envoy from Silken Thomas arrives in Spain to seek help from the Emperor Charles V.

26 July Con Bacach O'Neill surrenders himself and his lands to the King, promising to be a faithful subject.

28 July Lord Leonard Grey arrives as marshal of the army to suppress the rebellion.

c. 18 Aug. Silken Thomas surrenders (sent to England c. 6 Oct.; *see* 3 Feb. 1537).

31 Dec. d. L.D. Skeffington at Kilmainham Priory, Dublin.

1536

14 Feb. Five uncles of Silken Thomas sent as prisoners to England.

23 Feb. Lord Leonard Grey appointed L.D.

19 Mar. George Browne consecrated Archbishop of Dublin by Cranmer (without sanction from Rome) in London; arrives in Ireland in July.

28 Apr. King forbids any Irish usages and customs in the town of Galway.

1 May 'Reformation parliament' meets; passes Act of Supremacy, act for the attainder of the FitzGeralds, and act resuming to the Crown the lands of absentee landowners.

6 May Commission issued suppressing religious houses and stripping them of their property in Baltinglass, Co. Wicklow; Bective, Co. Dublin; Dunbrody, Duiske and Tintern, Co. Wexford.

12 May Treaty between L.D. Grey and MacMurrough Kavanagh of Wicklow.

19 May Anne Boleyn executed.

July Publication of the 'Ten Articles', the confession of faith of the Anglican Church, as approved by Henry VIII (*see* Aug.).

18 July Parliament at Westminster passes an act of attainder against Silken Thomas and his five uncles (*see* 3 Feb. 1537).

31 July Lough Gur Castle, Co. Limerick, taken by government forces.

2 Aug. Carrigogunnell, Co. Limerick, surrenders to the government and is presented to Donough O'Brien as payment.

5–6 Aug. L.D. Grey destroys O'Brien's Bridge over the Shannon in Co. Clare; forced to abandon his campaign through the mutinous behaviour of his troops who are ill-fed and unpaid.

Aug. Publication of 'Injunctions to the Clergy' by Thomas Cromwell, to enforce the 'Ten Articles' (*see* July).

15–28 Sept. Parliament in session in Dublin.

1537

20 Jan. Parliamentary session opens; House of Commons refuses to pass taxation bills and bills for the suppression of certain monastic houses.

3 Feb. Silken Thomas and his five uncles executed at Tyburn (*see* 17 Mar. 1540).

25 Feb. Henry demands that Ireland be made self-supporting; savings to be made by reducing expenditure on the army.

5 June L.D. Grey, having ravaged the territory of the O'Connors in Offaly, takes Dangan Castle, Co. Meath.

5 July d. Hugh Dubh O'Donnell, lord of Tyrconnell; succeeded by his son Manus.

8 July Earl of Desmond offers his loyalty to the King, to reduce Munster to obedience to the Crown (L.D. Grey campaigns in Munster during the winter).

31 July Commission headed by Anthony St Leger appointed by the King to inquire into the deputyship of Grey (arrives on 8 Sept.).

26 Sept. St Leger commission of inquiry begins tour of inspection of areas close to the Pale (recalled on 17 Jan. 1538).

13 Oct. Parliament in session; act 'against the authority of the Bishop of Rome'; act also for the provision of parish schools to teach English.

1538

22 Feb. Earldom of Ormond returned to Piers Butler, Earl of Ossory.

6 Mar. Brian O'Connor of Offaly submits to L.D. Grey

5 May Clergy in Dublin refuse to read 'form of the beads' as directed by Archbishop Browne.

12 June Indenture between King and the O'Carrolls of Ely O'Carroll.

mid-Aug. Public burning in Christ Church Place, Dublin, of religious objects of great antiquity, including the Bacall Iosa (the Staff of Jesus) or St Patrick's Staff and an ancient statue of Our Lady of Trim, Co. Meath (*see* 3 Feb. 1539).

5 Sept. Pub. Thomas Cromwell's 'New Injunctions to the Clergy'.

18 Nov. Augustinian house of All Hallows handed over to the King's commissioners, the first religious house in Dublin to be suppressed (later provides the site for Trinity College, Dublin; *see* 13 Mar. 1592).

1539

3 Feb. Commission issued to Dublin government to take the surrender of and suppress all monasteries, and also to destroy images which were objects of popular honour and pilgrimage (*see* mid-Aug. 1538).

26 Feb. Proclamation orders clergy to instruct laity in the 'right use and effect' of religious ceremonies.

early May L.D. Grey in an expedition against Con Bacach O'Neill pillages Armagh and surrounding countryside.

May Papal brief to excommunicate all who accept King's religious supremacy in Ireland.

Aug. L.D. Grey routs O'Neill and O'Donnell, who have been attacking the Pale, at Bellahoe, near Carrickmacross, Co. Monaghan.

Many chiefs, including O'Regan of Owney, O'Dwyer of Kilnamona, MacCarthy Reagh, the White Knight and Lord Barry, submit.

26 Aug. d. Piers Ruadh Butler, Earl of Ormond and Ossory.

28 Oct. Dissolution of the convent of the Benedictine nuns at Gracedieu, the only girls' school in the Pale.

18–30 Nov. Surrender and dissolution of monastic communities at Kells, Louth, Dundalk, Fore and Tristeragh.

d. Conor O'Brien, last independent King of Thomond.

1540

17 Mar. Gerald FitzGerald, heir to the earldom of Kildare, taken in disguise to France, *en route* to Rome (*see* 13 May 1554).

23 Apr. Suppression of the Augustinian priory of Greatconnell, Co. Kildare, the last of 34 monastic communities to be voluntarily suppressed during 1539–40.

c. 1 May L.D. Grey leaves for England, recalled to answer charges including that of allowing his nephew, Gerald FitzGerald, to escape from Ireland (*see* 17 Mar.). Sir William Brereton becomes L.J. (acting deputy) and in a three-week campaign destroys the property, stock and crops of the O'Connors of Offaly.

20 May Commission issued to survey and value rents and revenues of dissolved monastic houses and to grant estates on leases for 21 years.

10 June Thomas Cromwell, Earl of Essex, falls from power as Lord Great

Chamberlain of England (executed on 28 July).

12 Aug. Sir Anthony St Leger sworn in as L.D. (his predecessor, Lord Leonard Grey, executed on 28 June 1541). L.J. Brereton becomes Earl Marshall, but dies at Kilkenny *en route* to seek submission of the Earl of Desmond.

mid-Aug. L.D. St Leger campaigns against the MacMurroughs, who eventually submit and adopt name Kavanagh.

Brief issue of fourpenny, twopenny and penny pieces emblazoned with Irish harp.

Sept. King authorises L.D. St Leger to make grants upon surrender 'to such Irishmen as shall come in and acknowledge their duties towards us' (policy known as 'surrender and regrant').

15 Sept. L.D. St Leger invades O'Neills' territory and enforces submission.

1541

16 Jan. James FitzGerald, 13th Earl of Desmond, submits to L.D. St Leger at Cahir, Co. Tipperary.

27 Jan. Turlough O'Toole approved by Henry VIII for terms of 'surrender and regrant' (*see* Sept. 1540).

5 Feb. Parliament summoned for which 'electors in counties must have a freehold worth 40s per annum'.

1 Mar. Promulgation of order of 6 Feb. officially establishing Protestantism as the religion of Ireland.

13 June Parliament opens, the first attended by Irish chiefs (proceedings are translated into Irish).

18 June Parliament enacts that the new title for the King and his heirs is 'King of Ireland' instead of the customary 'Lord of Ireland': 'the King's highness, his heirs and successors, be always kings of this land of Ireland.' It will be high treason to impeach the new title.

L.D. St Leger states to the King that 'There were made in the city great bonfires, wine was set in the streets and there were great feastings in the houses.'

6 Aug. Manus O'Donnell submits to L.D. St Leger, recognising Henry as King of Ireland and Supreme Head of the Church.

14 Aug. Bernard McMahon submits to the Crown.

24 Oct. Henry assents to papal appointment of Roland Burke as Bishop of Clonfert (appointed by the Pope in 1534 and subsequently opposed by Henry's nominee, Richard Nangle, who was driven out of the diocese in 1538).

28 Dec. Following campaign by L.D. St Leger, Con Bacach O'Neill submits.

1542

20 Feb. Franciscan friars vacate their Limerick house, but remain in the city until the reign of Edward VI.

Alfonso Salmeron and Paschasius Broet, two Jesuits, arrive in Ireland on a mission from Rome to O'Neill, but discover that he has submitted.

13 May Rory O'More of Leix submits to the Crown.

18 May MacDonnells submit to the Crown.

19 May Con Bacach O'Neill recognises Henry as Supreme Head of the Church.

4 July The O'Byrnes of Wicklow submit.

Aug. FitzGerald of Desmond renews his allegiance to the King in London and is admitted by order to the Irish Privy Council.

1 Oct. Con Bacach O'Neill created Earl of Tyrone, and his illegitimate son, Matthew, created Baron of Dungannon.

Oct. Oath of Renunciation, to be taken by all bishops, abjuring papal authority (no recorded acceptor).

1543

16 Mar. d. George Cromer, Archbishop of Armagh since 1521.

29 Apr. George Dowdall appointed Archbishop of Armagh and Primate of All Ireland by the King (approved by the Pope on 1 Mar. 1533; *see* Mar. 1545 *and* Oct. 1550).

7 May Con Bacach O'Neill, Earl of Tyrone, admitted Privy Councillor.

29 May Pub. *The King's Book or A Necessary Doctrine and Erudition for Any Christian Man* (a compendium of beliefs to be adopted by adherents of the reformed religion).

1 July Murrough O'Brien created Earl of Thomond, and Ulick Burke Earl of Clanricard. Although O'Donnell is granted the title Earl of Tyrconnell, the title is not conferred until 1603.

14 July Con Bacach O'Neill, Earl of Tyrone, and Manus O'Donnell, lord of Tyrconnell, indenture to keep the peace, following arbitration in their dispute over Inishowen, Co. Donegal, which is granted to O'Donnell.

1544

Feb. – 11 Aug. L.D. St Leger in England (Sir William Brabazon acts for him as L.J.).

1545

Mar. Pope grants pallium of archbishopric of Armagh to Robert Wauchop.

Sept. English mint issues debased coinage for Ireland.

1546

1 Apr. Sir William Brabazon again L.J. in absence of L.D. St Leger, in England with the Earl of Ormond.

20 Apr. Donal, son of Hugh Dubh O'Donnell, slain by Owen O'Gallagher at Ballyshannon, Co. Donegal.

July Brabazon campaigns against Brian O'Connor of Offaly and MacGillapatrick of Leix.

28 Oct. James Butler, 9th Earl of Ormond, poisoned at Ely House, London; succeeded by his son Thomas ('Black Tom').

16 Dec. L.D. St Leger returns to Dublin.

1547

28 Jan. d. Henry VIII; succeeded by his son Edward VI.

31 Jan. Storm blows down western wing of the cathedral at Clonmacnoise, Co. Offaly.

7 Apr. King confirms St Leger as L.D.

31 July Royal 'Injunctions' issued by English parliament, to apply also to Ireland, defining form of ceremony to be used in religious services.

1548

7 Feb. Manus O'Donnell defeats his son Calvagh and Manus O'Cahan at Ballybofey, Co. Donegal.

8 Mar. 'Order of Communion' issued in England, to apply also to Ireland.

21 May Sir Edward Bellingham sworn in to replace St Leger as L.D., who is recalled to answer charges drawn up by Sir William Brabazon.

c. 19 Aug. L.D. Bellingham routs the O'Connors who had invaded the

KILKENNY COUNTY LIBRARY

Pale; O'More and O'Connor submit and are sent to England.

1549

7 Feb. Statute ordains that no poet or any other person shall make or compose any poems or anything which is called 'auran' (song) to any person except the King, on penalty.

14 Mar. First Act of Uniformity prescribes the use of the Book of Common Prayer (second act issued on 14 Apr. 1552).

Dec. L.D. Bellingham recalled; temporary L.J. Sir Francis Bryan governs in his absence.

1550

2 Feb. d. L.J. Sir Francis Bryan; Sir William Brabazon appointed L.J. and governs in absence of L.D. (until 10 Sept.).

11 Mar. Agreement between Earls of Thomond and Desmond at Limerick.

June English Privy Council decides upon plantation of Leix and Offaly.

5 Aug. Sir Thomas Cusack appointed Lord Chancellor (until 3 July 1555).

10 Sept. Sir Anthony St Leger sworn in as L.D., with instructions to survey and lease Leix and Offaly; also issues proclamation against Catholic religious ceremonies.

Oct. George Dowdall, Archbishop of Armagh, loses title 'Primate of All Ireland', which is transferred to Archbishop Browne of Dublin; Dowdall retires (*see* 2 Feb. *and* 12 Mar. 1553).

Con Bacach O'Neill summoned to Dublin, where, with his wife, he is held captive by the L.D.

1551

Feb. L.D. St Leger instructed to introduce Book of Common Prayer in Ireland; first book printed in Ireland.

15 Mar. Order issued that none of the O'Mores are to hold land in Leix.

6 Apr. Robert Wauchop, Archbishop of Armagh, appointed papal legate (d. in Paris on 10 Nov.).

Easter Sunday Liturgy in English first read in Christ Church, Dublin.

23 May Sir James Croft, a military expert sent to fortify southern ports, sworn in as L.D.

June – July Campaigning in Munster, L.D. Croft secures submission of MacCarthy Mór.

16 Sept. O'Donnells and MacSweeneys slain by Scots at Tory Island, Co. Donegal.

L.D. Croft campaigns against the MacDonnells in Ulster, attacking Rathlin Island, Co. Antrim.

35Y081

1552

16 Apr. L.D. Croft reports famine.

9 July d. Sir William Brabazon, at various times L.J.

6 Nov. L.D. Croft recalled (leaves on 4 Dec.); L.J.s Sir Thomas Cusack and Sir Gerald Aylmer govern in his absence.

Clonmacnoise, Co. Offaly, plundered by religious reformers, who take the large bells from the clocktower (O'Rourke's Tower').

1553

2 Feb. Hugh Goodacre consecrated Archbishop of Armagh by royal appointment (George Dowdall deemed to have resigned; *see* Oct. 1550).

1 Mar. George Dowdall appointed Archbishop of Armagh by the Pope in succession to Robert Wauchop (*see* 6 Apr. 1551). Queen Mary later restores the primacy to Armagh.

6 July d. Edward VI; succeeded by his half-sister Mary, who is proclaimed monarch on 19 July.

KK139231

18 Aug. Queen Mary proclaims that no compulsion will be used on any of her subjects until the religious question has been settled by parliament.

19 Nov. Sir Anthony St Leger once more sworn in as L.D. with instructions to restore the old religion, establish council in Munster and lease lands of Leix and Offaly.

1554

14 Apr. Royal commission to Archbishop Dowdall of Armagh and others to deprive married clergy.

13 May Title and lands of the earldom of Kildare restored to Gerald FitzGerald, 11th Earl, by Mary.

29 June Edward Staples deprived of bishopric of Meath as a married man.

25 July Marriage of Queen Mary and Philip, son of the Holy Roman Emperor Charles V (King Philip II of Spain from 16 Jan. 1556).

1555

18 Feb. Charter of St Patrick's Cathedral, Dublin, issued.

7 June Papal bull reconciles the kingdom and people of Ireland with Rome, absolving Mary and Philip of all censure.

13 June Mary and Philip ban attacks on the papacy.

8 Sept. Hugh Curwin, nominated to archbishopric of Dublin by the Queen and papally appointed on 21 June, consecrated in London; appointed Lord Chancellor on 13 Sept.; arrives in Dublin on 20 Oct.

Manus O'Donnell of Tyrconnell held prisoner by his son Calvagh.

Hugh O'Neill of Clandeboye killed fighting the Scots.

1556

28 Apr. L.D. St Leger instructed to prepare for plantation of Leix and Offaly.

26 May Sir Thomas Radcliffe, Lord Fitzwalter (Earl of Sussex from 17 Feb. 1557) sworn in as L.D. with instructions to advance the Catholic religion, punish heretics, prepare for a parliament and plant Leix and Offaly.

1 July L.D. Radcliffe marches north to expel Scots from Antrim.

18 July L.D. Radcliffe defeats Shane O'Neill near Maghera (Co. Londonderry) and enforces submission.

Shane O'Neill submits in Dublin.

1557

17 Feb. L.D. Radcliffe succeeds to earldom of Sussex.

1 June – 2 July Parliament in session; acts for plantation of Leix and Offaly as King's and Queen's Counties and for repealing laws made against the see of Rome.

July L.D. Sussex campaigns in Offaly against the O'Connors.

22 Oct. L.D. Sussex marches to Ulster against Shane O'Neill; burns Armagh (27 Oct.) and ravages Tyrone.

30 Nov. L.D. Sussex returns to Dublin.

5 Dec. Archbishop Curwin and Sir Henry Sidney sworn in as L.J.s in absence of L.D. Sussex (returns on 27 Apr. 1558).

1558

10 Mar. Parliament dissolved at Drogheda.

20 June L.D. Sussex in Limerick, where he proclaims Donal O'Brien an outlaw and reinstates Conor O'Brien, who renounces his Irish titles.

15 Aug. d. George Dowdall (71), papal Archbishop of Armagh and Primate of All Ireland.

14 Sept. L.D. Sussex sails for Scotland to subdue the Isles; then ravages Antrim; returns to Dublin on 8 Nov.

18 Sept. Sir Henry Sidney sworn in as L.J. in absence of L.D. Sussex.

17 Nov. d. Queen Mary; succeeded by her half-sister Elizabeth I.

28 Nov. Gerald FitzGerald, 15th Earl of Desmond, does homage before Sussex at Waterford.

Matthew O'Neill, Baron of Dungannon, slain on the orders of his half-brother Shane, claimant to leadership of the O'Neills.

13 Dec. L.D. Sussex leaves for England; Sir Henry Sidney sworn in as L.J.

14 Dec. Queen Elizabeth confirms Archbishop of Dublin, Hugh Curwin, the first occupant of an Irish see to change his religion, as Lord Chancellor.

1559

8 May Acts of Supremacy and Uniformity passed by English parliament.

14 May Calvagh O'Donnell taken prisoner by Shane O'Neill, who, upon the death of Con Bacach shortly afterwards, becomes chief of the O'Neills.

3 June Dissolution of the priory of St John of Jerusalem at Kilmainham, Dublin.

22 June Gerald FitzGerald, 15th Earl of Desmond, confirmed in his holdings by the Queen. A dispute with the Earl of Ormond brings him to London, where he is held in the Tower.

30 Aug. Earl of Sussex again sworn in as L.D. to implement Elizabeth's religious policies.

Hugh O'Neill, heir to Matthew, taken to England by Sir Henry Sidney to protect him from Shane O'Neill.

1560

12 Jan. – 1 Feb. Parliament in session; Act of Supremacy restores spiritual supremacy of the Crown and demands from all ecclesiastics, judges and all other temporal officers an oath of recognition; Act of Uniformity demands attendance at the parish church on pain of a fine of 12d (recusancy fine), and provides for the use of the Book of Common Prayer; laws against heresy repealed; Queen's title to the Crown of Ireland recognised.

4 Feb. R.C. bishops Walsh of Meath and Leverous of Kildare deprived of their sees for refusing to take the Oath of Supremacy.

7 Feb. Pope appoints Donat O'Teige Archbishop of Armagh; not recognised by Crown, nor is his successor Richard Creagh (*see* 22 Feb. 1565).

15 Feb. Sir William Fitzwilliam sworn in as L.J. in absence of L.D. Sussex.

22 May L.D. Sussex ordered by Queen to 'reduce' Shane O'Neill 'to his duty', by force if necessary, and to proceed with the plantation of Leix and Offaly.

24 June 'Act for the uniformitie of common prayer and service in the Church, and the administration of the sacraments' comes into force, prescribing the form of prayer and religious rites to be used throughout the kingdom.

25 June Sussex sworn in as L.L.

2 Aug. David Wolfe, S.J., appointed papal nuncio to Ireland (arrives in Jan. 1561).

15 Aug. L.L. Sussex ordered to reduce Shane O'Neill by force after

Shane makes what Queen regards as preposterous demands.

1561

30 Jan. – 5 June L.L. Sussex in England; Sir William Fitzwilliam L.J. in his absence.

31 Mar. Shane O'Neill postpones visit to London demanded by the Queen (*see* 3 Jan. 1562).

14 May Calvagh O'Donnell and his wife captured by Shane O'Neill (Calvagh released in 1564, but his wife held by Shane).

5 June Earl of Sussex upon return from England sworn in as L.L.

12 June L.L. Sussex marches to Ulster, garrisons Armagh and lays waste O'Neill's lands in Tyrone.

7 July Publication of proclamation of 8 June declaring Shane O'Neill a traitor.

1562

3 Jan. – 26 May Shane O'Neill in London; submits to the Queen on 6 Jan.; signs articles of agreement on 30 Apr. (*see* Nov.).

16 Jan. – 24 July L.L. Sussex in England (returns on 24 July); Fitzwilliam again deputises.

12 Apr. Brian O'Neill, son of late Matthew, Baron of Dungannon, slain in the feud with Shane O'Neill, by Turlough Luineach O'Neill.

3 July Order issued for establishment of Court of Castle Chamber for Ireland (*see* 15 Apr. 1581).

11 Sept. Shane O'Neill agrees to a treaty with Con O'Donnell at Drumcree, Co. Westmeath.

21 Sept. L.L. Sussex asks to be relieved of office (*see* 25 May 1564).

Nov. Shane O'Neill in rebellion; lays waste Maguire's country of Fermanagh.

1563

9 Feb. d. Manus O'Donnell, lord of Tyrconnell, at Lifford, Co. Donegal.

2 Mar. Adam Loftus consecrated Archbishop of Armagh.

3 Apr. L.L. Sussex leads government hosting against Shane O'Neill; disbands the army at Dundalk on 25 Apr.

1 June L.L. Sussex marches from Armagh to Dungannon; defeats Shane O'Neill at Tullaghogue.

11 Sept. Shane O'Neill submits.

Oct. Queen establishes a commission to investigate allegations of corruption against L.L. Sussex.

8 Nov. Shane O'Neill considers peace terms at Benburb, Co. Tyrone.

7 Dec. Papal nuncio David Wolfe, S.J., unable to enter the Pale, delegates jurisdiction for Dublin vicinity to Thady Newman.

1564

Feb. O'Connors and O'Mores of Leix and Offaly in rebellion.

22 Mar. Richard Creagh appointed Archbishop of Armagh and Primate of All Ireland by the Pope.

25 May L.L. Sussex, permitted to resign office, leaves Ireland; Sir Nicholas Arnold sworn in as L.J.

1 July Thomas Butler ('Black Tom') Earl of Ormond, forbids exactions of Irish custom within his territories.

6 Aug. King Philip II of Spain orders his London ambassador to break off contacts with Irish representatives.

Sept. Shane O'Neill campaigns against the MacDonnells of Antrim.

1565

18 Jan. R.C. Archbishop of Armagh, Richard Creagh, lodged in the Tower of London (*see* 22 Feb.).

1 Feb. Earl of Desmond invades territory of Sir Maurice FitzGerald, Viscount Decies, who seeks support from the Earl of Ormond; Desmond defeated by Ormond at Affane, Co. Waterford, where he is also wounded (*see* May).

22 Feb. Archbishop Creagh questioned in the Tower about his Irish activities; escapes at the end of April and returns to Ireland c. Aug.

2 May Shane O'Neill defeats the MacDonnells of Antrim at Glenshesk, near Ballycastle, Co. Antrim.

May Earls of Desmond and Ormond summoned to London, where in Sept. they enter into recognisances (£20,000) to abide by Queen's commands.

24 June MacCarthy Mór created Earl of Clancarty.

4 July Queen orders Sir Henry Sidney to punish recusants.

1 Oct. Commission for ecclesiastical causes appointed, led by Archbishop Adam Loftus.

12 Oct. Miler Magrath appointed Bishop of Down and Connor by the Pope (conforms to the Established Church two years later; *see* 3 Feb. 1571).

1566

20 Jan. Sir Henry Sidney sworn in as L.D.

17 Feb. Rory Óg O'More pardoned.

3 Aug. Shane O'Neill proclaimed traitor; burns the cathedral at Armagh.

Sept. – Nov. L.D. Sidney campaigns in Armagh, Tyrone and Tyrconnell.

20 Oct. Calvagh O'Donnell submits to Crown (d. 26 Oct.; succeeded by his brother Hugh).

24 Oct. O'Connor Sligo recognises the Queen's authority (enters indenture with the Crown on 20 Jan. 1568).

Nov. Col. Edward Randolph killed when Shane O'Neill attacks Derry.

1567

Mar. Earl of Desmond taken prisoner by L.D. Sidney at Kilmallock, Co. Limerick; sent to Tower of London in Dec.

21 Apr. Explosion at Derry ruins the cathedral and destroys English camp, driving garrison to Carrickfergus, Co. Antrim.

8 May Shane O'Neill defeated by Hugh O'Donnell at Farsetmore, near Letterkenny, Co. Donegal.

Richard Creagh, R.C. Archbishop of Armagh, arrested in Connaught, charged with high treason, acquitted but held in the Tower of London.

2 June Shane O'Neill, seeking aid from the MacDonnells, killed at Cushendun, Co. Armagh; Turlough Luineach succeeds him as chief of the O'Neills.

June Hugh O'Neill returns from England.

4 June Maurice MacGibbon appointed Archbishop of Cashel by the Pope.

30 June Commission established to inquire into causes of the differences between Thomas Butler, Earl of Ormond, and Gerald FitzGerald, Earl of Desmond.

27 June L.D. Sidney begins tour of Munster.

8 Aug. Robert Weston sworn in as Lord Chancellor of Ireland.

9 Aug. Adam Loftus, Archbishop of Armagh, translated by Queen to Dublin.

9 Oct. Sidney leaves for England (replaced by Robert Weston and Sir William Fitzwilliam, L.J.s, on 14 Oct.), accompanied by Hugh O'Neill to be invested with title Baron of Dungannon.

27 Nov. Sorley Boy MacDonnell lands at Marketon Bay from Scotland with 600–700 Redshanks; returns to Scotland shortly afterwards.

Papal nuncio, David Wolfe, S.J., imprisoned.

1568

1 Mar. Hugh O'Neill recognised as Baron of Dungannon.

13 June Thomas Lancaster, royal nominee to archbishopric of Armagh, consecrated.

12 July Earl of Desmond surrenders his palatinate into the Queen's hands, leaving his lands liable to the depredations of adventurers.

29 July James FitzMaurice FitzGerald defeated by Lord Lixnaw while raiding.

28 Oct. Sir Henry Sidney again sworn in as L.D.

7 Dec. Sir Peter Carew, English adventurer, granted claim to the barony of Idrone, Co. Carlow, traditional territory of the Kavanaghs; appointed captain of Leighlin Castle (*see* June 1569).

1569

17 Jan. Parliament opens; Sir Christopher Barnewall denounces it as illegal (21 Jan.).

29 Jan. Bill to suspend Poynings' Law defeated (48–44).

12 Feb. English adventurers offer to plant Munster (approved by L.D. on 30 June).

14 Feb. L.D. Sidney learns that James FitzMaurice FitzGerald and his Munster allies plan contact with Spain through Archbishop MacGibbon of Cashel.

11 Mar. Act for attainder of Shane O'Neill.

1 June Sir Edward Fitton appointed first Lord President of Connaught; government declares Thomond, hitherto part of Munster, united with Connaught for administrative purposes (*see* Feb. 1570 *and* 31 Mar. 1579).

June Sir Edmund Butler, brother of the Earl of Ormond, invades the barony of Idrone, Co. Carlow, claimed by Sir Peter Carew (*see* 7 Dec. 1568).

c. 17 June FitzMaurice and Lord Clancarty slaughter garrison at Abbeycastle, Tracton, Co. Cork.

3 July Authorities in Kilmallock, Co. Limerick, report to L.D. Sidney that FitzMaurice has exacted an oath that no service other than that 'used by the Church of Rome' will be used.

8 July Conor O'Brien, Earl of Thomond, enters into league with FitzMaurice.

12 July FitzMaurice orders the Mayor of Cork to ensure that only R.C. form of worship is practised.

Earl of Desmond submits.

24 July Commission for shiring Connaught.

Sept. Sir Humphrey Gilbert defeats FitzMaurice.

10 Oct. Earl of Kildare, his brothers and sisters restored in blood by repeal of act of attainder of Henry VIII.

4 Dec. Earl of Clancarty surrenders to Sir Humphrey Gilbert.

1570

20 Jan. Turlough Luineach O'Neill agrees peace with the government and his neighbours.

9 Feb. James FitzMaurice FitzGerald sacks Kilmallock, Co. Limerick.

Feb. Conor O'Brien, Earl of Thomond, rebels against the inclusion of Thomond in Connaught; attacks Fitton at Ennis, driving him into Galway; submits to Ormond a few weeks later (*see* 18 July *and* 21 Dec.).

25 Feb. Pope Pius V signs bull *Regnans in excelsis* excommunicating Queen Elizabeth and releasing her Catholic subjects from their obedience.

1 Mar. Earl of Ormond ordered to 'parley, protect or prosecute' FitzMaurice (ignores order).

26 June Act orders establishment of a free grammar school in chief town of each diocese (a failure, as clergy would not undertake the financial burden).

Act for attainder of Munster rebels unless they surrender.

18 July Earl of Thomond in Paris; offers loyalty to Sir Henry Norris (*see* 21 Dec.).

13 Dec. Sir John Perrot appointed first Lord President of Munster, with mandate to suppress FitzMaurice's rebellion (*see* 27 Feb. 1571).

21 Dec. Earl of Thomond surrenders castles in Clare to the Queen (*see* Apr. 1571).

1571

20 Jan. Turlough Luineach O'Neill agrees to a temporary peace.

3 Feb. Miler Magrath appointed Archbishop of Cashel and Emly by the Queen while holding papal appointment as Bishop of Down and Connor (until 1580) (*see* 14 Mar. 1580).

27 Feb. Sir John Perrot, President of Munster, arrives at Waterford.

13 Mar. L.D. Sidney leaves office; Sir William Fitzwilliam sworn in as L.J. on 1 Apr.

15 Mar. Indenture between the Crown and Brian Kavanagh.

Apr. Conor O Brien, Earl of Thomond, surrenders his lands to the Queen (restored in June 1573).

21 June Sir John Perrot besieges Castlemaine, Co. Kerry (raises siege five weeks later).

5 Oct. Crown signs indenture with Messrs Malby, Smith and Chatterton to colonise privately lands in Down, the Ards peninsula and Armagh (only Smith in the Ards enjoyed any success.)

Pub. *Aibidil Gaoidheilge & Caiticiosma* ('Gaelic Alphabet and Catechism'), by John Kearney; first book in Irish printed in Ireland.

Edmund Campion writes his 'History of Ireland' (*see* 1577).

1572

13 Jan. Sir William Fitzwilliam sworn in as L.D.

June Sir John Perrot again besieges Castlemaine, Co. Kerry, and takes it three months later.

18 July Nicholas White appointed Master of the Rolls (until Apr. 1578).

26 Aug. Fiach MacHugh O'Byrne invades and plunders Wexford (pardoned in Feb. 1573).

Nov. L.D. Fitzwilliam defeated by a Butler force of galloglass near Kilkenny.

1573

23 Feb. James FitzMaurice FitzGerald submits at Kilmallock, Co. Limerick, to Sir John Perrot.

25 Mar. Gerald FitzGerald, Earl of Desmond, a prisoner in England since 1567, returns to Ireland and is immediately arrested.

20 May d. Robert Weston, Lord Chancellor; succeeded by Adam Loftus, Archbishop of Dublin.

Aug. Walter Devereux, Earl of Essex, lands at Carrickfergus with an army.

16 Nov. Earl of Desmond escapes from Dublin; affirming his loyalty, he refuses to give himself up unconditionally.

27 Dec. d. James Stanihurst, Recorder of Dublin and politician; his books and manuscripts placed at the disposal of Edmund Campion.

1574

30 Mar. Essex instructed to crush Turlough Luineach O'Neill as 'the principal maintainer of rebellion' (O'Neill submits by the end of Apr.).

18 July Earl of Desmond, refusing terms, enters into confederacy.

2 Sept. Desmond surrenders to L.D. Fitzwilliam.

10 Sept. Desmond makes over his lands to Lords Dunboyne and Power and Sir John FitzEdmund FitzGerald with provision for his wife and son.

Oct. Some 200 Irish killed by Essex when they respond to his invitation to a banquet at Belfast; Brian O'Neill of Clandeboye is captured and sent to Dublin for execution, together with his wife and brother.

1575

28 Feb. James FitzMaurice FitzGerald sails from Glin, Co. Limerick, for the continent, to seek aid from the Pope and continental Catholic monarchs to uphold the Catholic religion in Ireland (*see* 25 Feb. 1577).

8 Apr. William Walsh, R.C. Bishop of Meath since 1554, empowered by Pope to act for the Archbishops of Armagh and Dublin in their absence.

22 May Elizabeth informs Essex that his scheme for Ulster is ended and orders him to evacuate.

27 June Treaty between Turlough Luineach O'Neill and the Earl of Essex.

26 July Capt. John Norris, in response to Essex's orders, massacres the MacDonnells on Rathlin Island, where they have been placed for safe-keeping by Sorley Boy MacDonnell.

18 Sept. Sir Henry Sidney again sworn in as L.D.

c. 19 Oct. Sorley Boy MacDonnell submits.

27 Nov. d. Sir Peter Carew, the adventurer whose claim to the Desmond and MacCarthy lands sparked off the insurrection in Munster in 1569.

1576

9 Mar. Essex appointed Earl Marshal of Ireland.

Apr. During visit to Connaught Sidney receives submission of Irish chiefs, including Grace O'Malley.

23 Apr. William Gerrard appointed Lord Chancellor.

4 June Rory Óg O'More again pardoned.

20 June Sir William Drury appointed Lord President of Munster.

23 July Capt. Nicholas Malby (knighted on 7 Oct.) appointed military governor of Connaught.

22 Sept. d. Essex in Dublin.

4 Oct. Malby lays waste territory of John and Ulick Burke, sons of the Earl of Clanricard.

Grace O'Malley visits Queen Elizabeth in England.

1577
4 Jan. d. William Walsh, R.C. Bishop of Meath since 1554.

25 Feb. Papal brief issued, commending James FitzMaurice FitzGerald's proposal to defend Catholicism in Ireland.

O'Mores and O'Connors massacred at Mullaghmast, Co. Kildare, while meeting with English under pledge of safety.

Pub. Holinshed's *Chronicles of England, Scotland and Ireland*, containing sections by Richard Stanihurst incorporating material from Edmund Campion's 'History of Ireland'.

1578
3 Feb. Papal force under Sir Thomas Stukeley sails from Civita Vecchio, Italy, to link up with FitzMaurice at Lisbon and proceed to Ireland. Stukeley makes a detour to Morocco and dies at battle of Alcazar on 4 Aug.

30 June d. Rory Óg O'More in battle.

12 Sept. L.D. Sidney leaves Ireland; Sir William Drury sworn in as L.J. in his absence on 14 Sept.

21 Sept. Fiach MacHugh O'Byrne submits to Sir William Drury at Dublin.

7 Oct. Brian na Murtha O'Rourke of Leitrim comes to terms with L.D. at Athlone (rebels again in 1580).

1579
26 Mar. Government ships raise siege of Carraighooley Castle, near Newport, Co. Mayo, home of Grace O'Malley.

31 Mar. Sir Nicholas Malby appointed Lord President of Connaught; Clare united with Connaught for administrative purposes (*see* 1 June 1569).

12 Apr. Malby receives grant of manor and lordship of Roscommon.

Apr. Sir William Pelham takes possession of Desmond's last two castles, at Askeaton and Ballyloughan, Co. Limerick.

18 July FitzMaurice arrives in Smerwick harbour, Co. Kerry, establishing base at Dún an Óir with a Spanish–Italian force; accompanied by Nicholas Sanders, papal legate, he bears letters from the Pope to the Irish lords, absolving them from allegiance to Elizabeth and calling on them to rise in support of the Catholic religion.

24 July Sir Humphrey Gilbert commissioned to attack FitzMaurice.

1 Aug. Sir John and Sir James FitzGerald of Desmond kill Henry Davells and Arthur Carter in a Tralee tavern.

18 Aug. FitzMaurice killed in a skirmish with the Burkes of Castleconnell, Co. Limerick, at Barrington's Bridge; leadership of rebellion falls to Sir John FitzGerald, brother of the Earl of Desmond.

Sept. (second week) Sir John FitzGerald defeats English force at Springfield, near Lough Gur, Co. Limerick, but is shortly afterwards defeated by Sir Nicholas Malby at Enabeg, near Croom, Co. Limerick.

3 Oct. d. Sir William Drury, L.J. and President of Munster, in Waterford; succeeded as L.J. by Sir William Pelham on 11 Oct. (until 7 Sept. 1580).

Thomas Butler ('Black Tom'), Earl of Ormond, arrives in Ireland.

FitzGeralds defeated by Sir Nicholas Malby at Monasternenagh, about five miles from Bruff, Co. Limerick.

10 Oct. Malby, having sacked Askeaton, Co. Limerick, withdraws to Limerick city.

2 Nov. Earl of Desmond proclaimed a traitor; assumes command of the Munster rebel forces.

A section of the defensive wall of Youghal, Co. Cork, collapses.

15 Nov. Desmond sacks Youghal, Co. Cork.

29 Nov. Desmond takes up position in Newcastle, Co. Limerick.

6 Dec. Ormond, making for Newcastle, begins policy of scorched earth in Co. Limerick.

1580

17 Feb. Sir Nicholas Malby establishes a garrison at Burrishoole, Co. Mayo, in campaign against Richard-in-Iarann Burke, husband of Grace O'Malley.

10 Mar. L.J. Pelham and the Earl of Ormond meet at Rathkeale, Co. Limerick, and arrange a scorched earth policy from Limerick into Kerry.

14 Mar. Pope Gregory XIII deposes Miler Magrath, C.I. Archbishop of Cashel, from the bishopric of Down and Connor.

c. 17 Mar. Admiral Sir William Winter instructed to search the Irish coast for Spanish ships.

27–29 Mar. L.J. Pelham lays waste the Limerick countryside and slaughters the garrison of the Desmond castle at Carrigafoyle, Co. Limerick; Askeaton surrenders, and he takes Ballyloughan.

c. 15 July Rising in Wicklow: Fiach MacHugh O'Byrne joins James Eustace, Viscount Baltinglass, in rebellion.

4 Aug. Cormac MacCarthy captures Sir James FitzGerald of Desmond, brother of the Earl; FitzGerald hanged, drawn and quartered by Sir Warham St Leger and Sir Walter Raleigh.

12 Aug. Lord Grey de Wilton arrives in Ireland; sworn in as L.D. on 7 Sept.

25 Aug. Grey defeated in Glenmalure, Co. Wicklow, by the O'Byrnes.

Sept. Turlough Luineach O'Neill in revolt, supported by some of Hugh's family, while Hugh himself remains aloof; Turlough Luineach later agrees peace with government at Benburb, Co. Tyrone.

8 Sept. O'Connors of the midlands in revolt.

12 Sept. Sebastiano di San Giuseppe arrives at Smerwick, Co. Kerry, with some 600 papal troops; takes up position at Dún an Óir (*see* 10 Nov.).

15 Sept. Baron of Lixnaw advises government of the arrival of three Spanish ships at Smerwick, Co. Kerry on 12–13 Sept.

22 Sept. Ormond reports arrival of eight ships off Kerry.

19 Oct. Fiach MacHugh O'Byrne burns Rathcoole, Co. Dublin.

10 Nov. L.D. Grey, accompanied by Sir Walter Raleigh and the Earl of Ormond, massacres the Spanish–Italian force at Smerwick. On 12–13 Nov. Fr Lawrence Moore, Oliver Plunkett and William Walsh, a servant of Nicholas Sanders, have their legs broken at a forge and are hanged, drawn and quartered next day.

1581

12 Jan. Fiach MacHugh O'Byrne fails to dislodge Wicklow garrison.

Jan. d. Conor O'Brien, 3rd Earl of Thomond; succeeded by his son Donough.

4 Apr. Government fails to capture Fiach MacHugh O'Byrne.

15 Apr. First commission for the Court of Castle Chamber (*see* 3 July 1562).

16 Apr. Queen recognises Richard-in-Iarann Burke of Mayo as chief of the MacWilliam Burkes in return for his promise to accept English customs (knighted in Sept.).

Apr. d. Nicholas Sanders, papal legate, in Clonlish Wood, Kylemore, Co. Limerick.

15 June Desmond evades capture near Kilmallock, Co. Limerick.

4 July Con O'Donnell, assisted by Turlough Luineach O'Neill, defeats his uncle Hugh MacManus O'Donnell in battle at Kiltole.

12 Aug. L.D. Grey de Wilton reports peace with Turlough Luineach O'Neill.

16 Aug. Adam Loftus, C.I. Archbishop of Dublin, reappointed Lord Chancellor.

11 Sept. Dermot O'Hurley appointed R.C. Archbishop of Cashel (*see* 20 June 1584).

Pub. *The Image of Irelande* by John Derricke.

1582

3 Jan. Sir John FitzGerald of Desmond killed in an ambush laid by John Zouche near Castlelyons, Co. Cork.

Jan. Outlawed William Nugent, brother of Baron of Delvin, aided by Turlough Luineach O'Neill, escapes by way of Scotland to the continent (d. 30 June 1625).

28 Jan. Nicholas Nugent and Edward Cusack committed to Castle on information of John Cusack for role in William Nugent's rebellion (*see* 6 Apr.).

24 Feb. Pope Gregory XIII orders reform of the calendar: 4 Oct. is to be followed by 15 Oct., and year is to begin on 1 Jan.; this New Style (N.S.) calendar replacing the Julian or Old Style (O.S.) does not become legal in Ireland and England until 2 Sept. 1752 (*see* 22 Mar. 1584.)

14 Mar. L.D. Grey de Wilton reports that 'in Munster the famine prevails everywhere' (mainly due to his scorched earth policy).

6 Apr. Nicholas Nugent executed (*see* 27 Aug. 1584).

20 Apr. Sir Warham St Leger reports 'plague and famine' in Munster.

23 Apr. Reports from Munster indicate '30,000 dead of famine in half a year, besides numbers that are hanged and killed'.

27 Apr. Cornelius (Conor) O'Devany appointed R.C. Bishop of Down and Connor (*see* 1 Feb. 1612).

22 June Sir Christopher Nugent, Baron of Delvin, suspected of involvement in Baltinglass revolt, examined by Lord Chancellor in London and released.

10 July L.D. Grey de Wilton informed by the Queen of his recall (leaves Ireland on 31 Aug., when Archbishop Adam Loftus and Sir Henry Wallop are sworn in as L.J.s).

July Turlough Luineach O'Neill foments unrest in Connaught.

25 Sept. Earl of Desmond attainted.

29 Sept. Donough O'Brien, Lord Inchiquin, hanged at Limerick for insurrection.

Oct. Grace O'Malley suspected of plotting with the Earl of Thomond and others.

13 Nov. Household cess remitted.

1583

21 Jan. Earl of Ormond, military governor of Munster, arrives in Waterford from England.

Feb. Earl of Desmond, almost totally deserted, takes refuge in the Sliabh Luachra region on Cork–Kerry border.

May Hugh O'Neill inaugurated as The O'Neill at Tullaghogue, Co. Tyrone, although the title is held by Turlough Luineach (*see* May 1593).

11 June John FitzGerald, seneschal of Imokilly, Co. Cork, last of Desmond's adherents, submits.

14 June John FitzEdmund FitzGerald surrenders.

11 Nov. Earl of Desmond killed by Daniel Kelly, a servant of the O'Moriartys, at Glenageenty, near Tralee, Co. Kerry, where he has been hiding in a cave; end of Desmond rebellion.

1584

4 Mar. d. Sir Nicholas Malby, Lord President of Connaught; succeeded by Sir Richard Bingham.

22 Mar. O'Neill, O'Donnell and Maguire of Fermanagh adopt the Gregorian calender (*see* 24 Feb. 1582).

9 June Sir John Perrot arrives in Ireland; sworn in as L.D. on 21 June.

19 June Queen's commission to examine escheated lands in Munster.

20 June Dermot O'Hurley, R.C. Archbishop of Cashel since 1581, executed following torture.

22 June L.D. Perrot orders general hosting at Tara, Co. Meath, for 10 Aug.

24 June John Norris (knighted in 1586) appointed Lord President of Munster.

8 July Commission appointed under Sir Richard Bingham to implement martial law in Connaught.

26 Aug. L.D. Perrot sets out for Athlone, Co. Westmeath.

27 Aug. Ellen, widow of Nicholas Nugent (*see* 6 Apr. 1582), granted his estate for life with reversion to her son Richard.

1 Sept. Commissioners of survey for plantation of Munster arrive in the province.

14 Sept. L.D. Perrot besieges Dunluce, Sorley Boy MacDonnell's castle, which surrenders within days.

18 Sept. Turlough Luineach O'Neill renews his pledge of peace to the Crown.

20 Sept. Indenture between Turlough Luineach O'Neill and Hugh O'Donnell.

Pub. *De Rebus in Hibernia Gestis* by Richard Stanihurst.

1585

3 Jan. L.D. Perrot instructed not to proceed with plans to convert St Patrick's Cathedral in Dublin into a courthouse.

20 Apr. Fr Maurice MacKenraghty executed in Clonmel for attempting to say mass.

26 Apr. Parliament meets after an interval of 16 years; Hugh O'Neill sits as Earl of Tyrone; Viscount Baltinglass attainted; bill for suspension of Poynings' Law again rejected.

23 May Act of Oblivion provides for ignoring of or surceasing of suits and complaints concerning anything occurring before 1 May 1583.

29 May Parliament prorogued to 26 Apr. 1586.

15 July Commission issued for the Composition of Connaught (agreements with the main landowners of the province).

17 Aug. Clare constituted as a county; O'Brien of Thomond indentures with Perrot.

13 Sept. Majority of the Connaught chiefs accept the Composition of Connaught, proposed by Sir John Perrot, under which English customs and usages are to be introduced.

3 Oct. Survey for plantation of Munster presented to the L.D.

14 Oct. d. in the Tower of London of Richard Creagh, R.C. Archbishop of Armagh since 1564, confined since 1567.

16 Nov. d. Gerald FitzGerald, 11th Earl of Kildare.

Dec. 'Plot of Her Majesty's Offer for the Peopling of Munster' drawn up.

14 Dec. Nicholas Walsh, C.I. Bishop of Ossory, stabbed to death by James Dallard, whom he had cited for adultery.

1586

26 Apr. Last session of parliament opens (dissolved on 14 May); act for the attainder of the late Earl of Desmond and supporters.

1 Mar. Mahon O'Brien's Clanowen Castle, Co. Clare, taken by Sir Richard Bingham after three weeks' siege; O'Brien killed and garrison massacred.

May Alexander MacDonnell, chief of the Ulster Scots, slain.

18 June Indenture between Sir John Perrot and Sorley Boy MacDonnell, who is granted pardon for his role in the rebellion.

21 June Abstract of the articles for repeopling and inhabiting the province of Munster.

27 June Articles binding the government and the undertakers to carry out their respective obligations in Munster approved by Queen and promulgated by letters patent in England.

12 July Bingham starts campaign against the Burkes of Mayo.

22 Sept. Bingham massacres Scots supporters of the Mayo Burkes on the River Moy at Ardnaree in modern Ballina, Co. Mayo.

Start of inquisitions by commissioners for plantation of Munster, at Youghal.

1587

1 Feb. Sir George Carew appointed Master of the Ordnance in Ireland (until 22 Aug. 1592).

8 Feb. Mary Stuart, Queen of Scots, executed.

28 Feb. Sir Walter Raleigh granted some 40,000 acres in Counties Cork and Waterford by Queen; tobacco planted at his Youghal estate.

26 Apr. Commission issued for passing of lands to the undertakers in Munster; commission to pronounce on disputes between undertakers; draft of a grant to the undertakers in Munster.

10 May Hugh O'Neill granted patent conferring title Earl of Tyrone.

21 June Edmund Magauran, R.C. Bishop of Ardagh, translated to Armagh in succession to Richard Creagh (*see* 23 June 1593).

c. 22 Sept. Red Hugh O'Donnell kidnapped on ship at Rathmullan, Co. Donegal, and lodged in Dublin Castle (*see* 30 Sept. 1588 *and* 26 Dec. 1591).

Pub. *Almanack for Ireland* by William Farmer in Dublin; earliest known Irish almanac.

1588

1 May Hugh O'Neill routed by Turlough Luineach O'Neill and Niall Garbh O'Donnell at Carricklea.

May Grace O'Malley seeks and receives Queen's pardon from L.D.

28–30 May Spanish Armada, commanded by the Duke of Medina Sidonia, sails from Lisbon to attack England.

23 June Richard Boyle, an English adverturer, arrives in Ireland (*see* 7 Dec. 1602).

30 June Sir William Fitzwilliam sworn in as L.D. (until 10 Aug. 1594).

2 July Special commission under Edward Anderson established to hear and decide controversies within Munster arising out of the plantation.

July Fiach MacHugh O'Byrne submits to L.D. Fitzwilliam.

5 Sept. Seven ships of the Spanish Armada in Shannon estuary, anchor at Carrigaholt, Co. Clare; leave when refused aid by the natives, who fear Sir Richard Bingham.

10 Sept. Spanish ship wrecked off Doonbeg, Co. Clare; 60 of the 300 who come ashore are slaughtered by the O'Briens and followers who plunder the wreck; remainder executed by Clancy, the high sheriff.

12–13 Sept. Storm damages *La Trinidad Valencera* in Kinnagoe Bay, eastern tip of Malin Head, north Donegal.

15 Sept. Spanish ship *San Juan Bautista* off Blasket Islands, joined by *San Juan of Portugal*, finds haven between Great Blasket and Beginish, where they are joined by *Santa Maria de la Rosa* (sinks on 21 Sept.); later joined by *San Bernado* and a second *San Juan Bautista;* escape on 23–24 Sept.

17 Sept. *La Rata Sancta Maria Encoronada* enters Blacksod Bay, Co. Mayo; driven aground.

19 Sept. Sir Geoffrey Fenton, Secretary of State, reports to Lord High Treasurer Burghley that 16 ships of the Armada have been wrecked on the coast of Ireland, with 5,394 men drowned, killed or taken.

20 Sept. Ships, *Juliana, La Livia* and *Sancta Maria de Vision,* destroyed in storm at Streedagh Strand, Co. Sligo.

22 Sept. L.D. Fitzwilliam orders execution of all Spaniards found in Ireland.

30 Sept. L.D. Fitzwilliam rejects plea for liberty on behalf of Red Hugh O'Donnell.

4 Nov. – 23 Dec. L.D. Fitzwilliam marches through Connaught.

10 Nov. English Privy Council rejects request from L.D. Fitzwilliam and Irish Privy Council for release of Red Hugh O'Donnell.

1589

c. 7 Feb. Burkes revolt in Mayo; sheriff John Browne and his retinue are attacked and slain at Corraun by Richard Burke ('The Devil's Hook').

10 Feb. Florence (Fineen) MacCarthy Reagh committed to Tower of London on suspicion that he is intriguing with Spain (freed on 19 Jan. 1591; returns to Ireland in Nov. 1593).

5 Apr. Commission appointed to examine and deal with disturbance in Connaught.

2 June L.D. Fitzwilliam sets out to pacify Connaught.

12 June Burkes of Mayo submit a 'Book of Complaints' to L.D. Fitzwilliam, concerning the administration of Sir Richard Bingham (*see* 5 Dec.).

17 June Hugh Maguire becomes chief of Fermanagh.

June Sir Brian O'Rourke of Leitrim defeated by Sir Richard Bingham at Dromore; flees to Scotland, where he is betrayed (*see* 3 Nov. 1591).

19 Oct. Sir Edward Woodhouse appointed Chancellor of the Irish Exchequer.

24 Oct. d. Sir Christopher St Lawrence, Baron Howth, probable owner of the Book of Howth; leader in anti-cess agitation in the Pale, 1577–78.

5 Dec. Sir Richard Bingham, President of Connaught, cleared of charges by the Burkes, returns to office; instructed to prosecute Burkes and other rebels in Connaught (12 Dec.).

Pub. *Brief Description of Ireland* by Robert Payne.

1590

Jan. Sir Richard Bingham, President of Connaught, aided by the Earls of Clanricard and Thomond, defeats the Burkes of Mayo.

28 May Hugh O'Neill, Earl of Tyrone, agrees to maintain English law (repeated on 17 June and accepted at Greenwich).

25 Aug. Sir George Carew appointed Irish Privy Councillor.

Dec. Red Hugh O'Donnell recaptured after escaping from Dublin Castle.

Pub. *The Faerie Queene* (Pt I: Pt II 1596) by Edmund Spenser.

1591

3 Aug. Hugh O'Neill, Earl of Tyrone, elopes with and marries Mabel, sister of Sir Henry Bagenal, marshal of the Queen's forces.

3 Nov. Sir Brian O'Rourke executed for treason at Tyburn.

26 Dec. Red Hugh O'Donnell and Art O'Neill escape from Dublin Castle; rescued in the Dublin mountains by Fiach MacHugh O'Byrne; O'Donnell eventually reaches Donegal; O'Neill dies of exposure.

d. Tadgh Dall Ó hUiginn (41), poet.

1592

13 Mar. Foundation stone of College of the Holy and Undivided Trinity (Trinity College, University of Dublin), laid by the Mayor, Thomas Smith, on the site of the former priory of All Hallows (*see* 18 Nov. 1538).

3 May Red Hugh O'Donnell inaugurated as The O'Donnell at Kilmacrenan, Co. Donegal.

30 May Memorandum of Miler Magrath, C.I. Archbishop of Cashel, calls for a more intensive campaign against Catholic clergy and for universal enforcement of the Oath of Supremacy.

30 June Tibbot na Long Burke and allies repulsed in attack on Cloonagashel Castle.

16 July d. Donough MacNamara, musician and poet, at Moyreask, Co. Clare.

2 Aug. Hugh O'Neill, Earl of Tyrone, brings Red Hugh O'Donnell to the church in Dundalk, where O'Donnell submits to L.D.

8 Sept. Tibbot na Long Burke submits to Sir Richard Bingham, President of Connaught, at Aghagower, Co. Mayo, ending rebellion (influenced by the news that O'Donnell, who has promised him aid, has submitted).

Irish College founded at Salamanca by King Phillip II.

1593

12 Feb. Issue of order for the apprehension of Catholic bishops.

May Confederacy of bishops and laymen led by the R.C. Archbishop of Armagh, Edmund Magauran, and Red Hugh O'Donnell takes arms against the government.

May Turlough Luineach O'Neill resigns as The O'Neill in favour of Hugh O'Neill, Earl of Tyrone (*see* 28 June).

20 June Tyrone assures L.D. Fitzwilliam of his loyalty.

23 June Edmund Magauran, R.C. Archbishop of Armagh, killed in action between Maguire and Sir Richard Bingham.

June Red Hugh O'Donnell defeats Sir Richard Bingham at Tulsk, Co. Roscommon.

28 June L.D. Fitzwilliam brings about peace between Earl of Tyrone and Turlough Luineach O'Neill: Turlough receives life interest in Strabane, while Tyrone's supremacy is recognised over all of the O'Neill territory.

Sept. Grace O'Malley meets with Elizabeth; secures release (in Nov.) of her son Tibbot na Long Burke, held by Sir Richard Bingham, President of Connaught.

10 Oct. Earl of Tyrone aids Sir Henry Bagenal to victory over the Maguires at Beleek, Co. Fermanagh.

Irish College founded at Lisbon.

1594

9 Jan. T.C.D. opens; Abel Walsh the first student enrolled, and James Ussher, later C.I. Archbishop of Armagh, the second.

2 Feb. Hugh Maguire's castle at Enniskillen, Co. Fermanagh, taken by Conor Roe Maguire ('The Queen's Maguire'), Hugh's half-brother, with Captains John Dowdall and George Bingham.

23 Feb. Proclamation issued in England ordering the removal from the kingdom of certain Irish peasants who cannot be identified as having good cause for their presence in England.

4 Mar. Archbishop Adam Loftus, Sir Robert Gardiner and Sir Anthony St Leger appointed to deal with Earl of Tyrone and Hugh O'Donnell.

14 Mar. Tyrone, hands a list of grievances to the government at Dundalk and concludes a truce of sorts.

18 Mar. Walter Reagh FitzGerald, son-in-law of Fiach MacHugh O'Byrne, and his sons attack home of the sheriff of Kildare at Athy, killing sheriff's family; O'Byrne held responsible (*see* 10 Mar. 1595).

7 June Archbishop Adam Loftus resigns as Provost of T.C.D.; succeeded by Walter Travers.

8 June – 10 Aug. Red Hugh O'Donnell and Hugh Maguire besiege Enniskillen Castle.

7 Aug. George Bingham, coming to the relief of Enniskillen Castle, defeated by Hugh Maguire at the 'Ford of the Biscuits' on River Arny.

11 Aug. Sir William Russell sworn in as L.D. (until 21 May 1597).

15 Aug. Tyrone attends Council of State to claim that he was not involved in recent events.

17 Aug. Tyrone submits to L.D. Russell when charges are preferred against him by Sir Henry Bagenal; decision to charge Tyrone deferred.

30 Aug. L.D. Russell relieves Enniskillen Castle.

Irish College founded at Douai.

1595

3 Jan. Ulick Burke, son of the Earl of Clanricard, mutinies in Sligo Castle, kills Capt. George Bingham, and places castle at O'Donnell's disposal.

16 Jan. L.D. Russell enters Wicklow but fails to capture Fiach MacHugh O'Byrne.

20 Jan. Tyrone and O'Donnell meet with Sir Henry Wallop and Sir Robert Gardiner, representing the government, and renew truce until 1 May.

30 Jan. Followers of Fiach MacHugh O'Byrne raze the village of Crumlin, near Dublin.

16 Feb. Art O'Neill, Tyrone's brother, attacks and destroys fort on the Blackwater.

2 Mar. d. John Garvey, C.I. Archbishop of Armagh since 1589.

10 Mar. Walter Reagh FitzGerald, ally of Fiach MacHugh O'Byrne, hanged in chains.

19 Mar. Henry Norris arrives at Waterford with forces from Brittany; his brother Sir John arrives at Waterford as military commander for the country on 4 May.

5 May Grace O'Malley petitions for the return of her husband's lands.

30 May Fiach MacHugh O'Byrne surprised by government forces; escapes wounded.

13 June Tyrone defeats Sir Henry Bagenal, whose forces are saved from rout by O'Neill's lack of ammunition, at Clontibret, Co. Monaghan.

23 June Tyrone declared to be 'the principal traitor and chief author of this rebellion'.

17 Sept. Tyrone and O'Donnell write to King Philip II of Spain seeking aid; letter falls into government hands.

Sept. d. Turlough Luineach O'Neill.

18 Oct. Tyrone and O'Donnell submit and seek pardon; promise no more communication with foreign powers.

27 Oct. Tyrone and O'Donnell enter into 'articles agreed into in the cessation of arms'.

Nov. L.D. Russell removes responsibility for Connaught from Sir Richard Bingham.

Fiach MacHugh O'Byrne submits, but then enters alliance with Tyrone.

1596

19 Jan. Meeting government representatives in a field near Dundalk, Tyrone and O'Donnell demand dismissal of all English officials in Ulster, liberty of conscience and restoration of church lands to Catholics.

22 Jan. King Philip II of Spain writes to O'Neill, complimenting him on his defence of Catholicism and offering any assistance required (letter received in May).

26 Jan. Articles agreed extending cessation of war in Ulster.

11 Mar. Queen displeased with commissioners for manner in which negotiations with Tyrone and O'Donnell have been conducted; she considers their demands 'presumptuous and disloyal petitions'.

Gunpowder explosion in Winetavern Street, Dublin, kills more than 100 people and destroys 20 houses.

12 May Tyrone pardoned.

18 May Owney O'More defeats garrison at Stradbally Bridge, Queen's County, where Alexander Cosby and his son Francis are killed in action.

6 July Tyrone calls on Munster chieftains to rise and 'assist the Catholic religion, and join in confederacy and make war with us'.

17–18 Sept. Spanish ships with arms and munitions at Killybegs, Co. Donegal.

6 Oct. Tyrone and O'Donnell meet with Alonso Cobos, who has letters from Philip II of Spain, at the monastery in Donegal.

2 Dec. Sir Conyers Clifford appointed chief commissioner of Connaught; appointed Lord President of Connaught on 4 Sept. 1597.

4 Dec. Tyrone claims that 'promise was not kept with us.'

1597

6 Feb. Order prohibits trade between Ireland and Spain.

7–8 May L.D. Russell in Wicklow; Fiach McHugh O'Byrne killed when taken by surprise by a Sergeant Milborne.

20 May Commission to inquire into abuses in the government of Ireland.

22 May Thomas, Lord Burgh, sworn in as L.D.

18 June Shane MacBrien O'Neill takes Belfast Castle and slaughters the garrison.

Tibbot na Long Burke signs a covenant with Sir Conyers Clifford, chief commissioner of Connaught, receives pardon for past transgressions, and gives his son Miles as a hostage.

11 July Sir John Chichester recovers Belfast.

14 July L.D. Burgh takes fort on the Blackwater.

c. 1 Aug. O'Donnell defeats Sir Conyers Clifford at Ballyshannon, Co. Donegal.

c. 9 Sept. d. Sir John Norris at Mallow, Co. Cork; succeeded as Lord President of Munster by his brother Sir Thomas on 20th.

2 Oct. L.D. Burgh relieves Portmore fort on the Blackwater.

13 Oct. 'Second Armada' sets sail, but is dispersed by gales four days later.

L.D. Burgh dies of 'ague' at Newry.

29 Oct. Earl of Ormond appointed military commander.

4 Nov. Sir John Chichester, governor of Carrickfergus, defeated and killed by James MacSorley MacDonnell.

15 Nov. Archbishop Loftus and Richard Gardiner appointed L.J.s in the L.D.'s absence.

7 Dec. Government forces defeated attacking Richard Tyrrell at Philipstown, King's County.

10 Dec. Tyrone and the Earl of Ormond in talks near Dundalk; Tyrone submits on 22 Dec., agreeing a truce to run for eight weeks (later extended to 7 June 1598, and on 11 Apr. 1598 'his pardon passed the great seal').

1598

4 Apr. d. Rory O'Cahan, chieftain of Coleraine area, principal vassal of Tyrone; succeeded by Donal Ballagh (knighted on 20 June 1607).

10 July O'Mores of Leix (Queen's County) defeat Ormond's forces.

14 Aug. Tyrone, O'Donnell and Maguire decisively defeat Sir Henry Bagenal (killed in action) at the Yellow Ford, one of the major battles in Irish history.

13 Sept. d. Philip II of Spain; succeeded by Philip III.

4 Oct. Outbreak of rebellion in Munster, incited by Rory O'More, dispatched south by Tyrone.

8 Oct. James FitzThomas FitzGerald assumes title of Earl of Desmond and leads rebellion against the plantation in Munster, where his opponents dub him 'Iarla an tSúgáin' ('the Straw-rope Earl').

16 Oct. MacSheehys destroy Kilcolman Castle, Co. Cork, home of Edmund Spenser, who escapes with his wife to Mallow.

Oct. Edmund Butler, Viscount Mountgarrett, and Thomas Butler, Lord Cahir, join Tyrone in rebellion (*see* 20 May 1599).

1599

18 Jan. d. Sir Richard Bingham, former President of Connaught.

14 Apr. d. Sir Henry Wallop, former L.J.

15 Apr. Robert Devereux, 2nd Earl of Essex, sworn in as L.L.

9 May L.L. Essex leaves Dublin for a campaign in the south; Kildare surrenders to him on 11 May.

16–17 May Owney O'More of Leix defeats L.L. Essex at the Pass of the Plumes, near Maryborough (now Portlaoise).

20 May Essex receives submissions of Lords Mountgarrett and Cahir.

29 May Phelim MacFeagh O'Byrne defeats government force at Deputy's Pass, near Wicklow; Essex orders decimation of Sir Henry Harrington's troops for cowardice.

30 May Sir Thomas Norris, President of Munster, wounded in skirmish around Kilteely, Co. Limerick (d. in Aug.).

4 June L.L. Essex in Limerick.

June Philip III of Spain sends Tyrone a consignment of arms (1,000 arquebuses and 1,000 pikes).

21 June L.L. Essex defeated in skirmish at Arklow, Co. Wicklow.

30 July Queen orders L.L. Essex not to leave Ireland.

15 Aug. Sir Conyers Clifford, President of Connaught, defeated and slain by Brian Óg O'Rourke ('Brian of the Battle-axes') in the Curlew Mountains, Co. Roscommon.

Donough O'Brien, 4th Earl of Thomond, appointed governor of Clare.

6–7 Sept. Tyrone and L.L. Essex meet on opposite sides of the River Lagan at the ford of Aclint, on Louth–Monaghan border; truce starts on 9 Sept. pending the Queen's reply to Tyrone's terms (she disavows the treaty on 17 Sept.).

24 Sept. Essex appoints Archbishop Loftus and Sir George Carey as L.J.s (until 28 Feb. 1600) and leaves for England, contrary to the Queen's express command.

17–18 Oct. Sir William Warren on behalf of the government meets with Tyrone for the second time (first met c. 29 Sept.); meet again at Dungannon on 8 Nov.

21 Oct. Commencement of truce which government requested (to end in Dec.).

16 Nov. Tyrone's manifesto 'To the Catholics of the towns of Ireland', requesting them 'to come and join with me against the enemies of God and of our poor country', meets with little response.

30 Nov. – 1 Dec. Tyrone and Ormond parley and agree to extend truce for another month.

15 Dec. Tyrone further complains of treachery and cessation of truce.

1600

24 Jan. Tyrone terminates truce and raids Westmeath, where Lord Delvin and Thomas Dillon submit; plunders as far south as Cashel, where he is joined by the Súgán Earl, and lays waste the lands of Lord Barry in Cork; returns to Ulster in March.

28 Feb. Lord Mountjoy sworn in as L.D. with an army of 20,000 to suppress the insurrection.

6 Mar. Sir George Carew appointed Lord President of Munster.

10 Apr. Owney O'More captures Earl of Ormond while parleying at Ballyraggett, Co. Kilkenny (releases him on 12 June).

mid-Apr. Spanish arms arrive for Tyrone with Mateo de Oviedo, Archbishop-designate of Dublin, who also brings from Pope Clement VIII indulgences for those defending the Catholic faith.

c. 25 Apr. Sir Henry Docwra and his army arrive at Carrickfergus.

11 May Mountjoy marches to the southern border of Ulster.

15 May Docwra lands at Lough Foyle and fortifies Culmore fort.

22 May Edmund FitzJohn FitzGibbon, the White Knight, surrenders to Carew.

1 June Docwra receives submission of Art O'Neill.

21 June Earl of Thomond forces O'Donnell out of Clare, where he has been plundering.

28 June Docwra in battle with the O'Dohertys at Elogh.

1 July Don Martin de la Cerda presents Tyrone's case for aid at the Spanish court.

Docwra seizes Dinnalong on the Foyle and fortifies it.

7–8 July Glin Castle, Co. Limerick, besieged and taken by Sir George Carew; O'Connor Kerry shortly afterwards surrenders Carrigafoyle Castle.

29 July Red Hugh O'Donnell defeats Docwra, who is wounded.

17 Aug. d. Owney O'More in battle against Mountjoy.

20–26 Aug. Carew lays waste the area around Kilmallock, Co. Limerick, seeking surrender of the Súgán Earl.

2–5 Oct. Battle of Moyry Pass, Co. Armagh, as Tyrone denies passage through to Mountjoy; Tyrone leaves the pass on 13 Oct, and Mountjoy leads his forces through on 17th (builds a fort at Mount Norris, between Newry and Armagh).

3 Oct. Niall Garbh O'Donnell switches to the government side in the war; captures Lifford Castle on 9th.

14 Oct. James, son of the 15th Earl of Desmond, arrives in Youghal to set up in opposition to the Súgán Earl (but loses support when he attends an Established Church service at Kilmallock, Co. Limerick).

29 Oct. Florence MacCarthy submits to government (*see* 29 May 1601).

13 Nov. Fynes Moryson arrives in Dundalk and becomes chief secretary to L.D. Mountjoy.

7 Dec. d. Sir Hugh O'Donnell, father of Red Hugh.

24–25 Dec. Two Spanish ships arrive at Killybegs, Co. Donegal, with money and arms for Tyrone and O'Donnell.

25 Dec. – 20 Jan. 1601 Mountjoy plunders the O'Byrnes' territory around Glenmalure, Co. Wicklow.

John Dymmok writes 'Treatise of Ireland' (pub. 1842) around this time.

Peter Lombard writes 'De Regno Hiberniae Commentarius'.

1601

15 Mar. Redmund O'Gallagher, Bishop of Derry, killed by government forces.

20 May New coinage proclaimed only legal tender after 10 July.

26–27 May Sir Henry Docwra checks Red Hugh O'Donnell's attempts to secure Inishowen.

Niall Garbh O'Donnell defeats Tyrone.

29 May Súgán Earl, hiding out in cave at Coolagarraunroe, near Mitchelstown, Co. Cork, captured by the White Knight for reward of £1,000; convicted in Cork of high treason, he, along with Florence

MacCarthy, is confined in the Tower of London until death (1607).

29 June Pope appoints Peter Lombard Archbishop of Armagh and Primate of All Ireland in succession to Edmund Magauran (d. 1593).

19 July Sir Oliver Lambart appointed governor of Connaught; fortifies Galway.

July Franciscan Mateo de Ovideo consecrated Archbishop of Dublin (d. in Valladolid in 1610).

2 Aug. Niall Garbh O'Donnell takes Donegal Abbey, where he is besieged by Red Hugh O'Donnell; forced to vacate on 26 Sept. following explosion of gunpowder, he retreats to Magherabeg monastery, which he fortifies and holds.

21 Sept. Don Juan del Águila lands at Kinsale, Co. Cork, which he fortifies for his force of c. 3,500.

27 Sept. Mountjoy reaches Cork from Kilkenny; reconnoitres Kinsale on 29th.

23 Oct. Red Hugh O'Donnell assembles his force at Ballymote, Co. Sligo, and begins his march to Munster.

27 Oct. Mountjoy's full troop of 15,000, of whom half are Irish, assembles; hunger and disease effectively reduce it to 6,600.

30 Oct. Tyrone leaves Dungannon for Munster.

1 Nov. Del Águila surrenders Rincurran fort (now Charles Fort) to Mountjoy.

10 Nov. Mountjoy repulses Spanish attack.

21 Nov. Mountjoy opens fire on Kinsale.

22–23 Nov. O'Donnell and army avoid Sir George Carew, President of Munster, by marching in freezing conditions across Slieve Phelim mountains, from Holy Cross Abbey, Co. Tipperary, to Croom, Co. Limerick.

28 Nov. Del Águila rejects Mountjoy's call to surrender.

29–30 Nov. Mountjoy attacks Kinsale but fails to take it; Red Hugh O'Donnell at Castlehaven.

1 Dec. Spanish reinforcements (621) under Pedro de Zubiar land southwest of del Águila's Kinsale fort and take ports of Castlehaven, Baltimore and Berehaven; Mountjoy fails to storm a breach at Kinsale.

2 Dec. Spanish attack on Mountjoy repulsed.

5 Dec. Tyrone links up with Red Hugh O'Donnell near Inishannon on the Bandon river, Co. Cork.

6 Dec. English fleet under Sir Richard Levison repulsed in attack on Berehaven.

8 Dec. Tyrone, approaching from Coolcarron Wood, closes in on Mountjoy.

11 Dec. Del Águila repulses attempted breach by Mountjoy.

21 Dec. Tyrone moves camp to Coolcarron, on the Cork side of Mountjoy's army besieging Kinsale.

24 Dec. Battle of Kinsale: Tyrone and O'Donnell attack and are defeated by Mountjoy in an engagement lasting less than three hours.

27–28 Dec. O'Donnell sails from Castlehaven for Spain; Tyrone begins retreat to Ulster.

1602

2 Jan. Del Águila surrenders on terms to Mountjoy; sails from Kinsale on 16 Mar.; arrested on return to Spain and dies shortly afterwards.

25 Mar. Niall Garbh O'Donnell takes Ballyshannon Castle.

5 June Sir George Carew lands forces on Bere Island to begin attack on Donal Cam O'Sullivan Beare's castle at Dunboy; besieges and captures castle, 11–18 June; hangs survivors.

c. 20 June Tyrone burns Dungannon, where Docwra and Mountjoy link up on 26th.

22 June Dunboy Castle blown up by Carew, who begins a scorched earth policy; Donal Cam O'Sullivan Beare, his castle at Dursey Island also having fallen, retreats to Glengarriff, Co. Cork.

June Owen MacEgan, vicar apostolic of Ross, arrives in Spanish ship at Kilmakilloge in Kenmare Bay with £12,000, which renders the Irish 'for a while more sturdy after the siege of Dunboy than before' (*see* 5 Jan. 1603).

29 June Mountjoy begins scorched earth policy around Tyrone.

27 July Donal O'Cahan in Ulster submits to Sir Henry Docwra.

31 Aug. Red Hugh O'Donnell dies in Simancas, Spain.

Sept. Sir Edmund Pelham appointed Chief Baron of the Exchequer in Ireland.

7 Dec. Richard Boyle signs agreement with Sir Walter Raleigh to buy Raleigh's 42,000 acres for £1,500.

14 Dec. Rory O'Donnell, brother of Red Hugh, and O'Connor Sligo surrender to Mountjoy at Athlone.

27 Dec. Donal Cam O'Sullivan Beare defeated by Sir Charles Wilmot at Glengarriff, Co. Cork.

31 Dec. – 14 Jan. 1603 Donal Cam O'Sullivan Beare marches to Leitrim with 1,000 of his followers (arrives at O'Rourke's Castle with about 35; *see* 3 Jan. 1603).

d. Maoilín Óg Mac Bruaideadha, genealogist and poet to the O'Briens of Thomond, *ollamh* to the O'Gradys and O'Gormans; exponent of the *dán díreach*.

1603

3 Jan. O'Sullivan Beare defeats Sir Thomas Burke and Capt. Henry Malby at Aughrim, Co. Galway.

4 Jan. Tibbot na Long Burke knighted.

5 Jan. Owen MacEgan, vicar apostolic of Ross, slain in skirmish at Cladach in Carberry, west Cork.

17 Feb. Elizabeth authorises Mountjoy to offer Tyrone pardon if he surrenders (warrant of pardon issued on 12 Sept.).

24 Mar. d. Elizabeth I.

30 Mar. Tyrone submits to Mountjoy at Mellifont, Co. Louth; hears of Queen's death on 5 Apr.; pledges loyalty to the King on 7th; submits before L.D. and Council on 8th.

5 Apr. James I proclaimed King of Ireland in Dublin.

11 Apr. Cork city refuses to recognise James as monarch and remains in a state of insurrection until Mountjoy enters on 10 May.

19 Apr. Sir Arthur Chichester appointed to Privy Council.

4 May Mountjoy at Waterford refuses to allow open practice of Catholic religion but permits mass in private houses.

26 May King James issues protection to Tyrone and Rory O'Donnell, who accompany Mountjoy to London on 30th; Mountjoy remains in London with title of L.L.

1 June Sir George Carey appointed L.D.

25 July Richard Boyle marries Katherine Fenton, daughter of the Secretary of State and Privy Councillor.

KILKENNY COUNTY LIBRARY

4 Sept. Sir Cahir O'Doherty, chieftain of Inishowen, confirmed in his possessions.

17 Sept. James I authorises minting of new silver coins for Ireland (*see* 11 Oct.).

27 Sept. Rory O'Donnell created Earl of Tyrconnell.

11 Oct. Irish currency revalued when Elizabethan coinage is devalued by one-third (*see* 3 Dec.).

20 Nov. Sir John Davies assumes office as Solicitor-General (*see* 29 May 1606).

3 Dec. Proclamation fixes rates of Irish money *vis-à-vis* sterling.

5 Nov. Sir Arthur Chichester granted Belfast Castle and surrounding land.

Pub. *Tiomna Nuadh,* Irish translation of the New Testament by William O'Donnell, C.I. Archbishop of Tuam (*see* also 1608).

1604

28 Jan. d. Sir Brian Óg O'Rourke, who fought on both sides during the war of 1594–1603; driven from his Leitrim lands by Rory O'Donnell, Earl of Tyrconnell.

11 July Charter for the incorporation of the town of Derry (*see* 29 Mar. 1613).

14 Aug. Sir Henry Brouncker, Lord President of Munster, issues proclamation commanding all regular and secular R.C. clergy to quit the province before 30 Sept. (*see* 4 July 1605).

15 Oct. Sir Arthur Chichester appointed L.D. (sworn in on 3 Feb. 1605).

d. Catherine FitzGerald, Countess of Desmond, her age variously estimated between 100 and 140.

1605

11 Mar. Amnesty issued 'against reviving questions and challenges for offences committed during the late rebellion and against the continuance of oppressions and unlawful exactions usurped by the chief lords of the country'. All the inhabitants of Ireland are admitted without distinction to the protection of the law.

5 Apr. d. Adam Loftus, Archbishop of Dublin and Lord Chancellor.

6 Apr. – 8 Nov. James Ley, Commissioner of the Great Seal, endeavours to force Catholics to attend church on penalty of appearing before English Court of Star Chamber; refuses defendants copies of indictments against them.

16 Apr. Grant of Upper Clandeboye and the Ards to Con O'Neill, Sir Hugh Montgomery and James Hamilton.

4 July Proclamation issued against toleration in religion, commanding attendance of laity at services of the Established Church on pain of recusancy fines and banishing 'all Jesuits, seminary priests, or other priests whatever' by 10 Dec.

9 July Commission of Surrenders established.

5 Nov. Discovery of the Gunpowder Plot at Westminister.

2 Dec. Sir Patrick Barnewall, refusing to recognise the King's authority in religion, imprisoned in Dublin Castle (released in Mar. 1607, and proceedings eventually dropped).

6 Dec. Landowners in the Pale imprisoned after claiming their right to 'private use of their religion and conscience'.

30 Dec. First sitting of the Commissioners of Arrears.

Irish College founded in Paris by John Lee.

1606

12 Feb. Richard Boyle appointed to Privy Council of Munster.

3 Apr. d. L.L. Mountjoy in England.

29 May Sir John Davies appointed Attorney-General.

22 July Commission for remedying defective titles enables native occupiers to secure clear title under English law in return for promise of allegiance to the Crown.

St Anthony's College, Louvain, founded by Franciscan order.

1607

17 Feb. Tyrone and Donal Ballagh O'Cahan enter land bond at Dungannon.

Apr. Earl of Tyrone summoned to answer charges laid against him by Donal Ballagh O'Cahan before the Irish Privy Council.

2 May Donal Ballagh O'Cahan presents a 'humble petition' to L.D. Chichester seeking protection from the Earl of Tyrone's demands; Tyrone rejects O'Cahan's complaints on 23 May.

18 May Christopher St Lawrence, Baron Howth, claims, without corroboration, that Rory O'Donnell, Earl of Tyrconnell and Cúchonnacht Maguire are involved in conspiracy to seize Dublin Castle.

26 May Tyrone dispatches a memorial to the King seeking new letters patent for all his claimed territory.

20 June L.D. Chichester and Council find against Tyrone in dispute with Donal Ballagh O'Cahan; O'Cahan knighted and later appointed commissioner to administer justice in Ulster in place of Tyrone and Tyrconnell; Tyrone and O'Cahan summoned to London on 16 July.

4 Sept. 'Flight of the Earls': Tyrone and Tyrconnell with allies and dependants sail from Lough Swilly, Co. Donegal, for the continent; both denounced by royal proclamation on 15 Nov.

7 Sept. L.D. Chichester proclaims that natives of lands governed by Tyrone and Tyrconnell will remain undisturbed in their holdings if they behave as dutiful subjects.

4 Nov. Sir Cahir O'Doherty complains to L.D. Chichester of treatment by governor of Derry, Sir George Paulet; Paulet informs L.D. that O'Doherty is in rebellion.

6 Nov. Sir Richard Nugent, 15th Baron Delvin, confesses to conspiracy; escapes two weeks later from Dublin Castle to Cloughoughter, Co. Cavan (*see* 5 May 1608).

Dec. Grand Juries in Tyrone and Donegal bring in bills charging the absent Earls of Tyrone and Tyrconnell with high treason and their properties forfeit.

1608

23 Jan. Project for the plantation of escheated lands in six Ulster counties (Tyrone, Coleraine, Donegal, Fermanagh, Armagh and Cavan); commission for survey issued on 19 July, which finds for the King (*see also* 1609).

18–19 Apr. Sir Cahir O'Doherty seizes Culmore fort, on Lough Foyle; captures and burns Derry, killing governor Sir George Paulet; proclaimed a traitor on 23 Apr.

5 May Sir Richard Nugent (*see* 6 Nov. 1607) submits to the Irish Privy Council; forgiven by the King; restored to favour in Jan. 1614; created Earl of Westmeath on 4 Sept. 1621.

20 June Sir Henry O'Neill slain in action against Sir Cahir O'Doherty.

5 July Sir Cahir O'Doherty shot dead at Kilmacrenan, Co. Donegal, and his head sent to Dublin; his lands confiscated and granted to L.D. Chichester.

18 July d. Rory O'Donnell, Earl of Tyrconnell, in Rome.

14 Oct. L.D. Chichester instructs Sir James Ley and Sir John Davies in 'Certain Notes of Remembrance touching the Plantation and Settlement of the Escheated Lands in Ulster'.

Oct. Niall Garbh O'Donnell, who had surrendered with his son Naughten and his two brothers on 14 June, suspected of supporting O'Doherty's rebellion, committed to Tower of London, where he dies in 1626.

8 Dec. Sir Humphrey Winche appointed Lord Chief Justice of the King's Bench in Ireland (until Nov. 1611).

Pub. *Leabhar na nVrnaightheadh gComhchoidchiond*, Irish translation of the Book of Common Prayer by William O'Donnell. (*See* also 1603.)

1609

Jan. Conditions and plan for the plantation of Ulster completed in detail.

May 'Articles of Plantation', a final plan, issued; some 500,000 acres thrown open to settlers.

21 July New commission issued to Sir Thomas Ridgeway for an inquisition into the forfeited lands in Ulster because the first was defective.

31 July Commission sets out to survey Ulster lands (survey completed by early Oct.).

14 Nov. Sir William Temple appointed Provost of T.C.D.

1610

28 Jan. Articles agreed between the English Privy Council and the city of London for the plantation of the city of Derry, the county of Coleraine and the Tyrone barony of Loughinsholin; the whole area when planted to be known as the county of Londonderry.

Feb. Inquisitions drawn up in legal forms and maps prepared for the Ulster plantation.

23 Aug. Proclamation issued in each of the six counties to be planted, explaining that the law now requires native inhabitants of the land allotted to British undertakers to remove to the lands of servitors, native freeholders and of the Church; date of removal subsequently deferred to 1 May 1611, then to 1 May 1612 (*see* 1 Oct. 1618).

Pub. *A New Description of Ireland* by Barnaby Rich.

1611

13 July Proclamation reissued against regular and secular R.C. clergy.

Pub. *The Theatre of the Empire of Great Britaine* by John Speed, containing earliest surviving large-scale cartographic representation of Dublin city.

1612

1 Feb. Execution of octogenarian Cornelius (Conor) O'Devany, Franciscan Bishop of Down and Connor, suspected of association with Earl of Tyrone.

12 Feb. Richard Boyle appointed to Irish Privy Council.

30 Sept. Liberties of any town or city without magistracy through municipal officials refusal to take Oath of Supremacy to be seized and governors appointed by the government.

25 Nov. Letter to the King 'from six Catholic lords of the Pale'.

27 Nov. Dungannon becomes first of 40 new boroughs to be incorporated by May 1613.

Irish College founded at Seville.

Pub. *A Discovery of the True Causes Why Ireland Was Never Entirely Subdued until the Beginning of His Majesty's Happy Reign* by Sir John Davies (Irish Attorney-General).

1613

29 Mar. Derry incorporated as the city of Londonderry and the new county of Londonderry.

27 Apr. Belfast incorporated by charter.

8 May Christopher Hampton consecrated C.I. Archbishop of Armagh and Primate of All Ireland (d. 3 Jan. 1625).

18 May Opening of first Irish parliament since 1585: 232 members (125 Protestants, 101 Catholics, 6 absentees); Catholic M.P.s elect Sir John Everard Speaker of the House of Commons, while the Protestants elect Sir John Davies; Everard forcibly removed from the Speakership and Catholics withdraw and send a deputation to the King; parliament prorogued on 5 June.

24 May First national convocation of Church of Ireland, summoned by the King, meets in St Patrick's Cathedral, Dublin (until 1615).

23 July Irish customs farmed for almost ten years from 30 Sept. 1612 at an annual rent of £6,000 to an English syndicate headed by Arthur Ingram.

27 Aug. Commission established to inquire into R.C. accusations of irregularities and illegalities in elections to parliament (reports 12 Nov.).

1614

31 May Proclamation against toleration of popery: '. . . all titular archbishops, bishops, deans, vicars-general, Jesuits, friars, seminary priests, and other priests, depart the realm of Ireland before the 30th of September'.

5 June L.D. Chichester ordered to renew the policy of driving the Irish into practice of Protestantism.

11 Oct. – 29 Nov. Parliament in session; acts attaint the Earls of Tyrone and Tyrconnell and confirm the King's title to escheated lands in Ulster.

15 Nov. d. Giolla Brighde (Bonaventure) O'Hussey, Franciscan priest and scholar of Irish language and literature, in Louvain.

22 Nov. d. Thomas Butler ('Black Tom') (82), 10th Earl of Ormond, who helped capture Armada survivors.

29 Nov. L.D. Chichester recalled.

1615

18 Apr. L.D. Chichester reports existence of a 'pack of dangerous conspirators in Ulster, centring on Con O'Neill, whom Alexander MacDonnell and Brian O'Neill intend to steal from Charlemont fort'.

Third session of parliament opens; ends on 16 May with mutual concessions; votes to meet again on 24 Oct., but is dissolved.

25 Apr. Convocation of the Church of Ireland closes, having adopted the 104 articles known as the 'Confession of Faith' (*see* 10 Dec. 1634).

6 May Donough O'Brien, 4th Earl of Thomond, appointed Lord President of Munster.

21 July King's letter states intention to give legal titles to persons on certain lands.

Pub. *Reports of Cases* by John Davies.

1616
22 Jan. Robert Stewart becomes Marquis of Londonderry (d. 8 Apr. 1621).

10 Feb. Sir Arthur Chichester vacates office of L.D.; receives additional lands and is created Baron Belfast.

20 July d. Hugh O'Neill (c. 66), 2nd Earl of Tyrone, in Rome.

30 Aug. Sir Oliver St John sworn in as L.D.; very active in prosecution of recusants.

24 Sept. L.D. St John commissioned to aid in the settlement of British undertakers in Ulster.

29 Sept. Sir Richard Boyle created Lord Boyle and Baron of Youghal (*see* 6 Oct. 1620).

1617
4 Oct. d. William Lyon, C.I. Bishop of Cork, Cloyne and Ross (united since 1587), noted for devotion to spread of the reformed religion.

25 Oct. Proclamation against harbouring Jesuits.

16 Dec. d. Aengus O'Daly, poet, stabbed to death near Roscrea, Co. Tipperary.

Proclamation for expulsion of R.C. clergy.

Pub. *An Itinerary* (3 parts) by Fynes Moryson, including a treatment of Ireland.

1618
18 July Donal Cam O'Sullivan Beare (58) killed in Madrid by John Bathe.

1 Oct. L.D. and Council proclaim that natives must either leave lands of British undertakers before 1 May 1619 or pay fines of 10s each.

1619
10 Apr. d. Thomas Jones, C.I. Archbishop of Dublin and Lord Chancellor since 1605.

13 May Sir Adam Loftus appointed Lord Chancellor.

30 Sept. Commissioners appointed for the plantation of the county of Longford and Ely O'Carroll.

Pub. *Pathologia Haereditaria Generalis* by Dermot O'Meara, first work in Latin published in Ireland.

Pub. *De Processu Martyriali,* part III of *Analecta Sacra* by David Rothe (Cologne) (parts I and II pub. 1616–17).

1620
6 Oct. Richard Boyle created Earl of Cork (*see* 9 Nov. 1631).

Seathrún Céitinn (Geoffrey Keating) starts his *Foras Feasa ar Éirinn,* first narrative history of Ireland in Irish; completed by 1634.

Pub. *Discoverie of Ireland* by Luke Kiernan.

1621
20 Jan. Plantations authorised in Leitrim, King's and Queen's Counties and Westmeath.

1622
8 Sept. Henry Cary, Viscount Falkland, sworn in as L.D.

14 Nov. d. Miler Magrath (approaching his 100th birthday), C.I. Archbishop of Cashel, Catholic and Anglican bishop at various times.

18 Dec. d. Robert Rothe (72), antiquary.

1623
20 June Oath of Supremacy to be administered to all officers in cities and corporate towns.

23 Dec. Franciscan Thomas Fleming consecrated R.C. Archbishop of Dublin (d. 2 Aug. 1651).

1624
21 Jan. Proclamation orders all titular archbishops and bishops, Jesuits and

seminary priests to leave Ireland within 40 days (not enforced).

3 Sept. Mícheál Ó Cléirigh starts composition of *Réim Ríograidhe* ('The Royal List') with others; completed on 4 Nov. 1630.

5 Sept. d. Donough O'Brien, 4th Earl of Thomond.

24 Sept. King approves revised programme for plantation of Londonderry.

c. 1624 Beginnings of religious revival among Ulster Scots, known as the Sixmilewater Revival (until 1631), mainly in south Antrim.

1625

21 Mar. James Ussher appointed C.I. Archbishop of Armagh.

27 Mar. d. King James I; succeeded by his son Charles I.

13 Oct. L.D. Falkland instructed by King to discontinue collection of recusancy fines.

30 Nov. Sir George Carew's will bequeathes his papers to Thomas Stafford (the Carew Papers, including the material on which the *Pacata Hibernia* is probably based; *see* 1633).

Pub. *Annales Minorum* (Vol. I) by Luke Wadding (Rome) (history of the Franciscan order, completed in 8 vols in 1654); the largest work ever written by an Irishman.

1626

28 May Franciscan Hugh McCaghwell consecrated R.C. Archbishop of Armagh (d. 12 Sept. in Rome).

22 Sept. L.D. Falkland lays before the Catholic lords the King's offer of 'Graces' or concessions to his Catholic Irish subjects in return for subsidies to maintain his army.

15 Nov. Assembly of Catholic Old English lords meets in Dublin to consider King's offer of 'Graces'.

22 Nov. L.D. Falkland rejects Old English demands for permission to send delegates to represent grievances before the King.

26 Nov. Archbishop Ussher and 12 Protestant bishops condemn toleration for Catholics, declaring that 'to grant the papists a toleration or to consent that they freely exercise their religion and profess their faith and doctrines, was a grievous sin' (*see* 19 Apr. 1627).

8 Dec. d. Sir John Davies, former Attorney-General.

Pub. *Archiepiscoporum Casseliensium et Tuamensium Vitae* by James Ware.

1627

28 Feb. Roger Boyle, son of the Earl of Cork, created Baron Broghill.

19 Apr. 'Great assembly' meeting in Dublin rejects proposed toleration for Catholics; adjourns on 22 Apr., publicly attacking the proposals; reconvenes on 30 Apr.

2 May L.D. Falkland dismisses the assembly in Dublin when he fails to secure support for government measures.

21 June Tibbot na Long Burke created Viscount Mayo.

26 June L.D. Falkland agrees to conventions to select delegates to meet the King.

30 June Conell Mageoghagan completes translation into English of *The Annals of Clonmacnoise*.

July Sir William St Leger returns to Ireland as Lord President of Munster (until 1642).

16 Aug. William Bedell appointed Provost of T.C.D.

1628

20 Feb. Sir John Temple succeeds Sir Christopher Wandesford as Master of the Rolls.

[...]NNY COUNTY LIBRARY

20 Mar. Old English petition King for favourable consideration for a number of requests in return for which they will contribute to the upkeep of the army in Ireland for three years.

14 May Concessions to Irish Catholics negotiated by Old English delegation approved by royal commissioners and formed into 51 'Instructions and Graces', in return for delegates' promise to provide three annual subsidies of £40,000 each; sent to government in Ireland on 24 May.

5 June Undertakers in Ulster permitted on certain conditions to take native Irish tenants on one-quarter of their estates.

20 Oct. Proclamation indefinitely postpones meeting of parliament.

1629

30 Jan. Sir Matthew Renzy claims existence of a plot among Leinster Catholics to massacre the English.

1 Apr. L.D. Falkland issues proclamation directing all R.C. convents, monasteries and churches to close and no priests to officiate in public.

26 Oct. L.D. Falkland leaves Ireland; Earl of Cork and Adam, Viscount Loftus, sworn in as L.J.s.

26 Dec. Rioting follows attempts to suppress religious houses in Dublin; congregation in Cook Street prevent C.I. Archbishop Bulkeley and the Mayor and troops from breaking up a mass service at the Franciscan chapel, forcing the Archbishop to seek refuge.

Beginning of a series of harvest failures lasting until 1633.

1630

19 Apr. Mícheál Ó Cléirigh completes his *Félire na Naomh nÉrennach* ('Calendar of Irish Saints', also known as Martyrology of Donegal).

1631

19–20 June Algerines, led by Capt. Matthew Rice and guided by one Hackett (subsequently hanged in Cork), sack the coastal town of Baltimore, Co. Cork; over 107 taken into captivity and 47 killed.

10 Oct. Malachy O'Queely consecrated R.C. Archbishop of Tuam (killed on 26 Oct. 1645 by troops of Sir Charles Coote).

9 Nov. Earl of Cork becomes Lord High Treasurer (*see* 28 June 1640).

22 Dec. Mícheál Ó Cléirigh completes a revised edition of *Leabhar Gabhála* ('The Book of Invasions').

1632

12 Jan. Thomas Wentworth, Viscount Wentworth, nominated L.D.

22 Jan. Franciscan laybrother Mícheál Ó Cléirigh, assisted by Fearfeasa Ó Maoil Chonaire, Cúchoigcríche Ó Cléirigh and Cúchoigcríche Ó Duibhgeannáin, begins compilation of *Annála Ríoghachta Éireann* ('Annals of the Kingdom of Ireland', better known as the Annals of the Four Masters) at Donegal Abbey (completed on 10 Aug. 1636).

14 Apr. Charles I approves reimposition of recusancy fines to aid Irish government finances.

11 June Government instructs bishops to initiate proceedings for presenting names of recusants.

28 June Jurors called to presentment sessions for collecting names of recusants refuse to co-operate; fined £50–£100 and given into custody of sheriff.

11 July Names of recusants presented when presentment session reopens.

c. 25 Oct. Destruction of St Patrick's Purgatory on Lough Derg, Co. Donegal, by C.I. Bishop of Clogher in accordance with government instruction of 8 Sept.

6 Nov. Recusants petition L.D. Wentworth to refrain from rigorously enforcing Act of Uniformity of 1560.

17 Nov. Earl of Cork refuses to allow delegation of Old English to see copy of the King's letter of 14 Apr.; letter read to delegation two days later.

12 Dec. King instructs L.J.s to discontinue recusancy proceedings when Old English promise to pay £20,000.

1633

17 May Christopher Wandesford appointed to Irish Privy Council.

25 July Viscount Wentworth (later Earl of Strafford) sworn in as L.D.

Pub. *A View of the State of Ireland* by Edmund Spenser.

Pub. *Pacata Hibernia: Ireland Appeased and Reduced, or An Historie of the Late Warres in Ireland, especially within the Province of Munster under the Government of Sir George Carew,* most likely written by Thomas Stafford (*see* 30 Nov. 1625).

Pub. *The History of Ireland,* ed. by Sir James Ware.

1634

26 May John Bramhall consecrated C.I. Bishop of Derry.

26 June L.D. Wentworth decides dispute between Dublin and Armagh over episcopal primacy of Ireland in favour of Armagh.

29 June Commission issued for remedying defective land titles.

14 July – 2 Aug. Parliament in session; six subsidies of £50,000 each voted (18 July).

22 July *Ad hoc* committee of grievances established, including five Catholics; report endorsed by House of Commons on 1 Aug.

18 Aug. Charles Moore, 2nd Viscount Moore of Drogheda, appointed commissioner for regranting escheated lands in Ulster.

24 Sept. King orders Court of Castle Chamber to sit as often as possible.

4 Nov. – 14 Dec. Parliament in session.

27 Nov. Wentworth declares to parliament that 10 of the 'Graces' will become law, but does not include statute of limitations guaranteeing land titles of 60 years' standing or a confirmation of land titles in Connaught.

10 Dec. Convocation of the Church of Ireland adopts the 39 Articles of the Church of England under pressure from L.D. Wentworth, and under the influence of Archbishop Laud enacts the English canons of 1604.

1635

Commission of 'defective titles' issued for Connaught, designed to confiscate properties to the Crown; Sir Gerald Lowther, Chief Justice of the Common Pleas, receives 4s in the £ of first year's rent raised under the commission.

26 Jan. – 21 Mar. Parliament in session.

28 Feb. Court of Star Chamber in London fines corporation of London £70,000 and withdraws its charter for Londonderry plantation.

18 Apr. Act forbids 'ploughing by the tail' and pulling the wool off live sheep.

11 July Jury in Boyle, Co. Roscommon, admits King's title to the whole county; similar decision reached in Mayo (13 July) and in Sligo (20 July).

17 Aug. Jury in Portumna, Co. Galway, refuses to find for the King on land title (*see* 27 May 1636).

4 Oct. Henry Leslie, leading anti-Dissenter, consecrated C.I. Bishop of Down and Connor.

12 Dec. Baron Mountnorris sentenced to death by court martial for publicly expressing contempt for L.D. Wentworth; imprisoned from 12 Dec. to 16 Apr. 1637, he accepts pardon and is stripped of all government offices.

1636

27 May Jury which refused to find for the King on land titles in Galway put on trial; fined £4,000 each and imprisoned (*see* 17 Aug. 1635 *and* 9 Feb. 1637).

3 July Christopher Wandesford and Lord Chancellor Adam, Viscount Loftus, sworn in as L.J.s.

11 Aug. Meeting between C.I. bishops Bramhall and Leslie and Presbyterian leaders in Ulster led by Edward Brice; Brice refuses to compromise and is imprisoned and on 12 Aug. sentenced to perpetual silence.

10 Dec. d. Randal MacDonnell, 1st Viscount Dunluce and 1st Earl of Antrim.

1637

9 Feb. Galway landholders admit justice of the King's title to their lands (*see* 27 May 1636); corroborated by a new inquisition in Apr.

25 July Christopher Wandesford acquires Castlecomer, Co. Kilkenny, where he initiates exploitation of coal resources.

1638

1 Apr. Lord Chancellor Adam, Viscount Loftus, suspended by L.D. Wentworth and arrested (sentence quashed by English House of Lords on 3 May 1642).

11 Apr. Robert Stewart appointed governor of Culmore fort on Lough Foyle.

26 Sept. C.I. Bishop of Down and Connor, Henry Leslie, attacks the National Covenant (taken on 1 Mar. in Edinburgh by opponents of the King's ecclesiastical policy).

1639

27 Apr. 'Black Oath' (swearing allegiance, obedience on ecclesiastical conformity and abjuration of all other oaths) enforced on all persons of the Scottish nation aged 16 and upwards holding property in Ireland.

12 Sept. Christopher Wandesford and Lord Robert Dillon sworn in as L.J.s.

21 Sept. L.D. Wentworth arrives in London, where he remains as chief adviser to the King.

Publication of the works of Duns Scotus, ed. by Luke Wadding *et al.* (Lyons).

Pub. *Catechismus seu Doctrina Christiana Latino-Hibernica: An Teagasc Críostuí* by Theobald Stapleton (Teabóid Gálldubh) (Brussels); text in Latin and Irish.

1640

12 Jan. Wentworth created Earl of Strafford; appointed L.L. on 13th.

15 Jan. Sir Richard Bolton appointed Lord Chancellor of Ireland (until 11 May 1641, when relieved by Sir William Ryves) (*see* 23 Aug. 1642).

16 Mar. Parliament meets but is postponed for two days until L.L. Strafford arrives.

23 Mar. Under pressure from L.L. Strafford, Irish House of Commons votes four subsidies (£200,000 over three years) to the King, to aid suppression of Scottish rebellion.

2 Apr. Murrough O'Brien, 6th Baron Inchiquin, appointed Vice-President of Munster (becomes governor on 2 July 1642).

3 Apr. Strafford leaves Ireland, having raised an army of 8,000 foot and 1,000 horse for use against the Scots; Christopher Wandesford sworn in as L.D.

13 June Parliament declares sole right to assess the subsidies required by the King.

28 June Earl of Cork appointed to the English Privy Council.

20 Aug. d. Brian Ó Cearnaidh (Barnabas Kearney), Jesuit missioner in Ireland, having successfully eluded all attempts to capture him since 1603.

30 Oct. Old English peers seek reduction in contribution of nobility to the subsidies.

3 Nov. Long Parliament convenes at Westminster.

7 Nov. House of Commons' petition of remonstrance against Strafford viceroyalty adopted over government's objections.

11 Nov. House of Lords appoints commission to take remonstrance to England; provides Pym with much of his case for impeachment of Strafford for high treason.

30 Nov. Petition of remonstrance comes before the English House of Commons.

3 Dec. d. L.D. Wandesford; Sir William Parsons and Sir John Borlase, sworn in as L.J.s on 10 Feb. 1641.

5 Dec. John Atherton, C.I. Bishop of Waterford since 1636, executed for homosexual behaviour.

1641

26 Jan. – 5 Mar. Parliament in session.

13 Feb. Commons appoints committee to consider legality of recent administrative practices (the 'Queries', adopted on 16 Feb.; *see* 28 May).

16 Feb. Protestants under the protection of Miles Burke, 2nd Viscount Mayo, massacred at Shrule, Co. Mayo, by Edward Burke.

18 Feb. Grievances drawn up by the Irish Lords for the King.

27 Feb. Commons appoints committee to prepare articles of impeachment against the Lord Chancellor, Lord Chief Justice, Bishop of Derry and Sir George Radcliffe; the King, denying parliament's competence, orders proceedings to be discontinued (May).

May Niall O'Neill arrives as emissary of titular Earl of Tyrone (John, son of Hugh O'Neill) in Spain, with promise of money and arms from Cardinal Richelieu.

3 May King renews promises of the 'Graces' of 1628.

11 May – 17 Nov. Parliament in session.

12 May Strafford, attainted by the English parliament, executed.

17 May Ormond commissioned to command the army in the absence of the L.L., the Earl of Leicester (who never came over).

25 May Strafford's Irish army disbanded.

28 May Judges' answers to the 'Queries' of February rejected by the Commons.

9 June Patrick Darcy presents the case of the Irish Commons before the judges in the House of Lords, arguing, in an attempt to unravel the constitutional relationship of the

English and Irish parliaments and the King, that the Irish parliament is the sole legislative authority for Ireland.

26 June d. Anthony Hickey (55), definitor (sub-head) of Franciscan order; collaborated with Luke Wadding on several publications, including 3 folio vols of Wadding's edition of the works of Duns Scotus (1639).

16 July King grants 30 concessions in return for additional subsidies.

28 Aug. English parliament declares its opposition to levying men in Ireland to serve in armies of major Catholic powers.

5 Oct. Conor Maguire, Hugh Óg MacMahon and Sir Phelim O'Neill at Loughross, Co. Armagh, plan an insurrection for 23 Oct.

22 Oct. Owen O'Connolly betrays the plans for the insurrection to Sir John Borlase; Sir Phelim O'Neill, unaware that the plans have been betrayed, takes Charlemont fort and other key Ulster centres.

23 Oct. Arrests of Conor Maguire and Hugh Óg MacMahon (*see* 17 Aug. 1644); government proclaims the insurrection 'a conspiracy intended by some evil-affected Irish papists'; six days later another proclamation states that 'We did not intend or mean . . . any of the Old English lords of the Pale, nor of any other parts of this kingdom, we being well assured of their fidelity to the Crown.'

24 Oct. Sir Phelim O'Neill, having captured Charlemont fort and the town of Dungannon, proclaims that the insurrection is in 'the defence and liberty of ourselves and the Irish natives of this kingdom'.

31 Oct. Insurgents appear before Dundalk, Co. Louth, which surrenders; Newry, Co. Down, Fermanagh, Castleblayney, Co. Monaghan, and Carrickmacross, Co. Monaghan, all held by insurgents.

1 Nov. English parliament appoints 26 Lords and 52 M.P.s as 'commissioners for Irish affairs'.

Rebels kill some 80 Protestants at Portadown bridge.

4 Nov. Sir Phelim O'Neill publishes a commission purporting to be from the King, dated 1 Oct., authorising use of arms in his defence.

Sir Henry Tichborne, governor of Drogheda, Co. Louth, sets about fortifying the town.

6 Nov. Philip MacHugh O'Reilly heads remonstrance detailing rebels' grievances (he joins rebels on 27 Nov.).

10 Nov. English parliament decrees that no Irishman can leave England for Ireland without a licence.

11 Nov. Proclamation orders everyone who has no reason to be in Dublin to leave; non-residents banished on 28 Oct.

12 Nov. O'Byrnes of Wicklow lay siege to Carysfort.

13 Nov. Insurrection now reported to have spread to Roscommon and Sligo in Connaught.

16 Nov. Parliament, having adjourned on 7 Aug., meets under armed guard (prorogued next day); Christopher Plunkett, 2nd Earl of Fingall, appointed commissioner to confer with all persons in arms to secure peace (declared an outlaw the next day and helps to bring about alliance between Ulster insurgent leaders and Old English lords; *see* 3 Dec.).

17 Nov. Commons committee appointed to confer with the insurgents to discover their reasons.

Insurrection by now has spread to Carlow, Kilkenny and Wexford;

Protestants are burnt to death in a church at Blackwatertown, Co. Armagh.

21 Nov. Mellifont, Co. Louth, taken and looted by insurgents; Drogheda besieged by insurgents.

29 Nov. Rory O'More defeats government forces at Julianstown, near Drogheda; Sir Charles Coote relieves Wicklow Castle, subjecting inhabitants of town to great cruelty.

1 Dec. O'Tooles defeated by Coote at Kilcoole, Co. Wicklow.

2 Dec. Coote appointed governor of Dublin city.

3 Dec. Old English lords of the Pale meet at Knockcrofty, near Drogheda, with Ulster leaders; further meeting at Tara (7 Dec.) leads to alliance in defence of their common religion.

8 Dec. English parliament resolves that Catholics should not be tolerated in any part of the King's dominions.

9–10 Dec. Appropriation of corn belonging to Protestants ordered by the Earl of Fingall (Co. Meath) and Lord Louth (Co. Louth).

12 Dec. Ormond informs King that the Old English lords have treated with the insurgents.

13 Dec. Old English lords of the Pale summoned to attend a conference in Dublin and, as they distrust Coote, are given pledges of safety.

15 Dec. Coote burns all the boats in Clontarf and much of the town, including the home of the landlord, George King, who was promised safety on 13 Dec.

23 Dec. English parliamentary commission appointed to take depositions on events since 23 Oct.

31 Dec. Tipperary in rebellion; spreads to Limerick in Jan. 1642.

1642

1 Jan. King issues proclamation against the 'Irish rebels'.

9 Jan. Massacre at Island Magee: large numbers of Catholics killed by Scottish garrison and English settlers from Carrickfergus, Co. Antrim.

11 Jan. Coote sacks Swords, Co. Dublin; Sir Phelim O'Neill again repulsed at Drogheda, which he now tries to starve into submission, but government ships bring food into the harbour the next day (O'Neill raises siege in early Mar.).

18 Jan. Second commission to collect information from refugees from the 1641 rising.

1 Feb. Ormond (Royalist) burns Newcastle and marches on Naas, Co. Kildare, which is abandoned; his troops loot the surrounding area.

3 Feb. 'Demands of the Irish' issued.

7 Feb. d. William Bedell (71), C.I. Bishop of Kilmore since 1629; as Provost of T.C.D. (1627) he ordered that divinity students should learn Irish (*see* 1685).

8 Feb. L.J.s issue proclamation asserting that the insurrection has failed and offering rewards for the Ulster leaders (£1,000 for Sir Phelim O'Neill).

11 Feb. In England 'divers worthy and well-affected persons' offer to raise a loan on the security of Irish land to aid in the defeat of the Irish rebellion (*see* 19 Mar.).

12 Feb. Lord Lambert defeats the Wicklow insurgents five miles south of Dublin.

20 Feb. Government reinforcements commanded by Lt-Col. George Monck (1,500 foot) and Sir Richard Grenville (400 cavalry) arrive.

Mar. *A Remonstrance of Divers Remarkable Passages concerning the Church and*

Kingdom of Ireland by Dean Henry Jones includes depositions from refugees in Dublin but places greater reliance on rumour than on fact.

5 Mar. Ormond leaves Dublin to lay waste the Boyne valley.

9 Mar. Patrick Barnewall surrenders to Ormond, as does Lt-Col. Reade, soon followed by other prominent Old English leaders.

19 Mar. Adventurers' Act provides that 2,500,000 acres of land in Ireland will be used to repay those who provide £306,718 for the English government to suppress the insurrection in Ireland (*see* 14 July 1643).

23 Mar. Sir Henry Tichborne (Royalist) defeats insurgents at Ardee, Co. Louth.

26 Mar. Sir Henry Tichborne takes Dundalk from Sir Phelim O'Neill; Carrickmines Castle, main outpost of Wicklow insurgents, taken by government and destroyed.

Conor Maguire confesses to his role in the rising (*see* 17 Aug. 1644).

15 Apr. Ormond, having laid waste Co. Kildare, defeats Viscount Mountgarrett and Rory O'More at Kilrush, near Athy, Co. Kildare; English parliament votes £500 for purchase of a jewel to be presented to Ormond as mark of esteem.

Major-Gen. Robert Monro lands at Carrickfergus with advance force of 2,500 Scottish royalist troops to aid the Ulster planters.

7 May Sir Charles Coote the elder shot dead at Trim, Co. Meath, which insurgents unsuccessfully try to recapture.

12 May Sir Henry Tichborne and Sir John Borlase sworn in as L.J.s (until 21 Jan. 1644).

10–13 May Catholic clergy meet in synod at Kilkenny, presided over by Hugh O'Reilly, Archbishop of Armagh; 'Confederation of Kilkenny' mooted (*see* 7 June).

12 May Galway surrenders to Sir Charles Coote the younger (later Lord Mountrath), now provost-marshal of Connaught.

7 June Meeting of the Confederate Catholics at Kilkenny chooses a Supreme Council which begins to function on 11 June (*see* 24 Oct.).

10 June First formal presbytery in Ireland established at Carrickfergus by soldiers of the Scottish army in Ulster.

16 June Alasdair MacDonnell and Sir Phelim O'Neill defeated at Glenmacquin near Raphoe by Sir Robert and Sir William Stewart.

20 June Sir Phelim O'Neill defeated by Hugh Montgomery on the Blackwater.

22 June 41 Catholics expelled from parliament.

26 June Fort Mountjoy captured from the insurgents by Col. James Clotworthy.

2 July Lord Castlehaven (Confederate) defeated by Murrough O'Brien, 6th Baron Inchiquin (Royalist), who becomes notorious as 'Murchadh na dTóitean' ('Murrough of the Burnings').

d. Sir William St Leger, Lord President of Munster; succeeded as governor of Munster by his son-in-law Inchiquin.

July Petition of R.C. nobility and gentry to the King.

8 or 9 July Owen Roe O'Neill arrives from continent at Sheephaven Bay, Co. Donegal; commands Confederate army in Ulster (*see* mid-Sept.); Sir Phelim O'Neill nominated Lord President of Ulster, having resigned command of the Catholic army in Ulster to Owen Roe O'Neill.

7 Aug. Lord Forbes arrives in Ireland with fleet fitted out by London adventurers.

23 Aug. Sir Richard Bolton reappointed Lord Chancellor of Ireland.

3 Sept. Inchiquin's army (Royalist) defeats Parliamentary army at Liscarroll, Co. Cork.

16 Sept. Ormond becomes Lieutenant-General under the Crown.

mid-Sept. Col. Thomas Preston arrives at Waterford from the continent with a man-of-war, two frigates, siege guns, field guns and ammunition; receives command of Confederate army in Leinster (14 Dec.).

5 Oct. Thomas Preston (Confederate) defeats Col. Monck (later Duke of Albemarle) (Parliament) at Timahoe.

23 Oct. Battle of Edgehill in England; inconclusive first battle of the English Civil War.

24 Oct. General Assembly of the Confederate Catholics at Kilkenny assumes the powers of a parliament and establishes a government; Nicholas Plunkett elected Speaker; Lord Mountgarrett elected President; adopt motto 'Pro Deo, rege et patria Hiberni unanimes' ('For God, King and country, the Irish united').

Control of the Confederate armies is vested in Owen Roe O'Neill (Ulster), Thomas Preston (Leinster), Gerald Barry (Munster); John Burke in Connaught is appointed Lieutenant-General, but the chief command is reserved for the Earl of Clanricard should he join the Confederation.

6 Dec. Fr Luke Wadding appointed Vatican agent to the Supreme Council of the Confederation of Kilkenny.

1643

11 Jan. King authorises Ormond to confer with the Confederation (meeting occurs on 17 Mar. at Trim, Co. Meath).

20 Jan. Thomas Preston (Confederate) captures Birr Castle.

16 Mar. L.J.s and Council report to the King that 154,000 Protestants have been killed by insurgents (a gross exaggeration).

18 Mar. Ormond (Royalist) defeats Preston (Confederate) at Old Ross.

23 Apr. King instructs Ormond to secure cessation of arms with the Confederates (*see* 24 June).

20 May – 19 June Second meeting of the General Assembly of Confederation at Kilkenny.

13 June Owen Roe O'Neill (Confederate), having defeated Monro in successive encounters at Charlemont, Co. Armagh, is defeated by Sir Robert Stewart (Royalist) at Clones; shortly afterwards O'Neill is victorious at Portlester Mill, some five miles from Trim, Co. Meath, when Lord Moore (Parliament) is killed.

17 June Heber MacMahon appointed R.C. Bishop of Clogher (*see* 21 June 1650).

24 June Negotiations between Ormond and the Confederation begin.

14 July English Parliament offers double portions of land to adventurers (*see* 19 Mar. 1642) who pay an additional quarter to raise more finance for the war in Ireland.

July Papal envoy Piero Scarampi arrives in Kilkenny with stores and money.

O'Neill, forced out of Ulster by the Scots, retires to Connaught.

Aug. Sir William Parsons and Sir John Temple, members of the Irish

Privy Council, arrested, together with other prominent supporters of Parliament.

6 Aug. Galway joins the Confederation.

3 Sept. d. Richard Boyle, Earl of Cork.

15 Sept. Ormond and the Confederation sign truce to run for one year at Sigginstown, near Naas, Co. Kildare.

25 Sept. Solemn League and Covenant between English Parliament and the Scots; ordered to be taken throughout Ireland.

9 Oct. King declares against the Solemn League and Covenant.

Nov. – 1 Dec. Third meeting of the General Assembly of the Confederation at Kilkenny.

13 Nov. Ormond appointed L.L. (sworn in on 21 Jan. 1644).

18 Dec. L.J.s condemn the Solemn League and Covenant, which Gen. Robert Monro and the Scots army in Ulster have ordered to be generally taken.

Pub. *Vindiciae Regum, or The Grand Rebellion* by Griffith Williams, C.I. Bishop of Ossory (d. 29 Mar. 1672).

Pub. *Foclóir no Sanasán Nua* ('A New Vocabulary') by Mícheál Ó Cléirigh (Louvain).

Pub. *Argument* by Patrick Darcy (containing his arguments on Ireland's constitutional position; *see* 9 June 1641).

1644

2 Jan. Sir Robert Stewart and other Royalist commanders refuse to take the Covenant.

24 Mar. Seven Confederate delegates arrive at Oxford to see the King.

4 Apr. Robert Monro and his Scottish officers take the Covenant at Carrickfergus; soon spreads throughout Ulster.

15 Apr. L.L. Ormond condemns the Covenant.

17 Apr. Protestant delegation arrives at Oxford to see the King.

14 May Belfast falls to Monro (Scots army).

24 June Confederate representatives return from meeting the King; Ormond authorised by King to enter into negotiations with the Confederation.

20 July – 31 Aug. Fourth meeting of the General Assembly of the Confederation at Kilkenny; discusses violations of cease-fire.

17 Aug. Conor Maguire and Hugh Óg MacMahon escape; recaptured on 19 Sept. (*see* 11 Nov.).

25 Aug. Inchiquin informs Ormond that he will support the Parliamentary forces; appointed Lord President of Munster by English Parliament in Jan. 1645.

6 Sept. Negotiations again open between Ormond and the Confederation, but are broken off in Oct. (renewed in Apr. 1645).

18 Oct. English Parliament accepts that the war in Ireland will be a charge on the English public purse.

24 Oct. English Parliament orders that any Irishman taken in arms in England or Wales is to be executed.

11 Nov. Trial of Hugh Óg MacMahon and Conor Maguire (MacMahon executed on 22 Nov. in London; Maguire executed in 1645).

12 Nov. Ormond tenders his resignation as L.L., which is declined by King.

31 Dec. Richard Bellings leaves to seek help for Confederation from the continent.

1645

12 Feb. Sir Henry Tichborne imprisoned in Tower of London (released in Sept.).

12 Mar. Lord Glamorgan, son-in-law of the Earl of Thomond, commissioned by King to treat with the Confederation.

10 Apr. Truce expires.

16 Apr. Castlehaven (Confederate) draws up army in front of Youghal, defended by Lord Broghill (Parliament).

12 May Sir Charles Coote appointed Lord President of Connaught by English Parliament.

15 May – 31 Aug. Fifth meeting of the General Assembly of the Confederation of Kilkenny.

1 June Convocation of regular and secular R.C. clergy states that in any treaty with the Protestant party there must be provision for keeping 'in our hands such churches, abbeys, monasteries and chappels now in our possession'.

1 July English Parliament appoints new committee of the House of Commons and the House of Lords for Ireland.

25 Aug. Lord Glamorgan enters into secret treaty with Confederation.

12 Oct. Papal nuncio extraordinary Giovanni Battista Rinuccini, Archbishop of Fermo, arrives at Kenmare, Co. Cork, with aid from Cardinal Mazarin and the Pope.

17 Oct. Sir Charles Coote routs Confederates at Ballysadare, Co. Sligo.

26 Oct. d. Malachy O'Quealy, R.C. Archbishop of Tuam, in skirmish outside Sligo; leads to discovery of terms of Glamorgan's treaty with Confederates.

20 Dec. Glamorgan and Rinuccini (acting for Confederates) enter into second secret treaty.

26 Dec. L.L. Ormond arrests Glamorgan for high treason (released on 22 Jan. 1646 on bail of £40,000 secured by Clanricard and Kildare).

1646

29 Jan. King disavows Glamorgan treaty (*see* 18 Mar.).

Feb. – 4 Mar. Sixth meeting of the General Assembly of the Confederation of Kilkenny; agrees to extend truce to 1 May.

18 Mar. King disowns Glamorgan (*see* 28 Sept.).

28 Mar. L.L. Ormond concludes peace with the Confederation (*see* 12 Aug.).

5 May Charles I surrenders to Scots near Newark.

c. 5 June Thomas Preston (Confederate) takes Roscommon.

5 June Owen Roe O'Neill (Confederate) defeats Monro (Scots army) at Benburb, Co. Tyrone.

7 June Owen Roe O'Neill marches to Clones, Co. Monaghan, driving Sir Robert Stewart back to Derry.

14 July Confederates take Bunratty Castle, Co. Clare, from the Parliamentarians.

30 July Thirty-article proclamation of peace between Ormond (acting on behalf of the King) and the Confederation.

12 Aug. Having condemned the Ormond peace on 6 Aug., Rinuccini now declares perjured all who adhere to it; announces their excommunication on 1 Sept.

18 Sept. Rinuccini arrests and imprisons his opponents on the Supreme Council; Confederation disbands and Rinuccini presides over a new one, consisting of four bishops and eight laymen (inaugurated on 26 Sept.).

28 Sept. Lord Glamorgan (Royalist) takes oath of allegiance to Rinuccini and the Confederation.

9 Nov. Preston, Owen Roe O'Neill and Rinuccini meet at Lucan in an attempt to settle differences.

Pub. *The Irish Rebellion* by Sir John Temple, claiming a general massacre of Protestants in 1641.

1647

10 Jan. – 4 Apr. Seventh meeting of the General Assembly of the Confederation of Kilkenny, now dominated by Rinuccini.

2 Feb. Confederation declares against the Ormond peace (288–12).

21 Feb. L.L. Lord Lisle arrives with army at Kinsale on Parliament's behalf but with commission expiring on 15 Apr.

1 Mar. Terence Albert O'Brien appointed R.C. Bishop of Emly (Co. Tipperary) by the Pope (*see* 31 Oct. 1651).

15 Apr. L.J.s replace Lord Lisle for administration of civil government while a body of commissioners administers the military.

7 June English Parliamentary army of 2,000 commanded by Col. Michael Jones lands near Dublin.

19 June L.L. Ormond negotiates treaty with Parliamentary commissioners; he agrees to surrender Dublin and the sword of state and to leave the country (28 July; returns on 30 Sept. 1648).

24 June Parliamentary commissioners order that Book of Common Prayer is not to be used in churches.

9 July C.I. clergy issue declaration of reasons for not abandoning Anglican liturgy.

8 Aug. Jones (Parliament) defeats Preston (Confederate) at Dungan's Hill, near Trim, Co. Meath.

13–14 Sept. Inchiquin (Parliament) sacks Cashel, Co. Tipperary, slaughtering military, civilians and clergy.

Munster Confederates mutiny against Glamorgan's command; leadership is vested in Lord Muskerry, who transfers it to Lord Taaffe.

12 Nov. – 24 Dec. Eighth meeting of the General Assembly of the Confederation of Kilkenny.

13 Nov. Inchiquin (Parliament) routs the Munster Confederates under Lord Taaffe at Knockanuss, near Kanturk, Co. Cork; Alasdair MacColkitto MacDonnell, galloglass leader, killed.

1648

3 Apr. Inchiquin breaks with Parliament and again declares for the King.

May – Aug. Second Civil War in England.

20 May Supreme Council of the Confederation enters truce with Inchiquin.

27 May Rinuccini issues excommunication of those involved in peace with Inchiquin; large-scale desertions from Confederation.

31 May Supreme Council appeals to Rome against Rinuccini's decrees and is supported by majority of the clergy; Rinuccini flees to Galway.

2 Aug. Eight C.I. bishops refuse to forgo the power of the keys over Catholics.

30 Aug. R.C. bishops pronounce it 'a deadly sin against the law of God and of his Church' to observe the truce with Inchiquin.

4 Sept. – 17 Jan. 1649 Last meeting of the General Assembly of the Confederation of Kilkenny.

30 Sept. Ormond arrives at Cork from France and is met by Inchiquin.

General Assembly of the Confederation declares Owen Roe O'Neill, who has treated with the Scots, a traitor.

2 Nov. 'Derby House Committee' for Irish affairs calls upon English Parliament to enact that after the 2,500,000 acres has been disposed of (*see* 19 Mar. 1642) all the residue of lands forfeited by rebels be disposed of for the further prosecution of the war in Ireland and to advance the revenues of the Crown.

21 Nov. Confederate envoys Bishop Nicholas French and Nicholas Plunkett land at Waterford.

1649

17 Jan. Ormond concludes peace with Confederates.

30 Jan. Charles I executed.

15 Feb. Belfast Scots Presbyterians denounce Parliament's edict in favour of toleration, stating that 'universal toleration of all religions' is 'directly repugnant to the word of God'.

17 Feb. Charles II (in exile) declares Ormond L.L.

23 Feb. Rinuccini leaves Galway for the continent in his frigate the *San Pietro* (d. 4 Dec. 1653).

29 Mar. Cromwell accepts command of the Parliamentary army in Ireland.

8 May Gen. Monck (Parliament) enters into three-month armistice with Owen Roe O'Neill (Confederate).

22 June Oliver Cromwell commissioned Governor-General of Ireland with civil and military authority.

7 July Sligo Castle surrenders to Earl of Clanricard (Royalist).

11 July Inchiquin (Royalist) takes Drogheda; after seven-day siege garrison surrenders on terms.

24 July Monck (Parliament) surrenders Dundalk to Inchiquin (Royalist); most of the garrisons in Drogheda and Dundalk go over to Inchiquin.

28 July Royalists take Rathfarnham Castle from Parliamentarians.

2 Aug. Col. Michael Jones (Parliament) defeats Ormond (Royalist) at Rathmines, Dublin, establishing a bridgehead for Cromwell (the last battle fought in the city until Easter 1916); Ormond does not again take the field.

8 Aug. Ulster Scots lift siege of Derry (where Sir Charles Coote has been under siege since 1 Apr.).

15 Aug. Cromwell lands at Ringsend, Dublin.

16 Aug. Charles II annuls the peace of 1648.

23 Aug. Cromwell issues proclamation forbidding 'profaning, swearing, drinking, cursing, which were said to be the daily practice'.

Henry Ireton lands in Ireland with his army.

9 Sept. Charles II asks Philip MacHugh O'Reilly to secure peace between Confederates and Royalists.

9–11 Sept. Cromwell besieges Drogheda and massacres the garrison under Sir Arthur Aston and civilian population.

27 Sept. Cromwellian general Col. Robert Venables starts four-day siege of Belfast which ends with the city's surrender.

11 Oct. Wexford falls to Cromwell; massacre of garrison and civilians.

16 Oct. Incited by Lord Broghill, son of the Earl of Cork, garrison in Cork deserts to Cromwell and drives Irish out of the town.

19 Oct. New Ross surrenders to Cromwell.

20 Oct. L.L. Ormond and Owen Roe O'Neill enter into treaty.

5 Nov. Cromwell abandons attempt to take Duncannon fort.

6 Nov. d. Owen Roe O'Neill (c. 59) at Cloughoughter, Co. Cavan.

20 Nov. Cromwell takes Carrick-on-Suir.

24 Nov. Having taken the fortified town of Passage without a struggle, Cromwell besieges Waterford, defended by Farrell, one of O'Neill's most able officers; Cromwell raises the siege after a few days and sets up winter quarters, his troops for the most part having to shift for themselves.

4 Dec. R.C. bishops hold synod at Clonmacnoise where they call for unity between Catholics and King against Cromwell.

Pub. first issue of *Irish Monthly Mercury* in Cork; Ireland's first newspaper.

1650

4 Jan. Henry Ireton appointed Lord President of Munster.

Jan. Cromwell publishes a declaration 'for the undeceiving of deluded and seduced people'.

8 Mar. Ormond meets with bishops at Limerick; receives their loyalty on 28th.

27 Mar. Cromwell takes Kilkenny.

28 Mar. Certain prelates are empowered by the Pope to absolve those who disobeyed Rinuccini.

10 Apr. Lord Broghill (Parliament) defeats Confederates led by Boetius MacEgan, Bishop of Ross, outside Macroom, Co. Cork; MacEgan hanged on 11 May.

27 Apr. Having accepted the bloodless surrender of Cashel, Co. Tipperary, Cromwell meets heaviest resistance of his campaign at Clonmel, defended by Hugh O'Neill; town surrenders on favourable terms only when O'Neill has left (10 May).

26 May Cromwell leaves for England; Ireton in command.

21 June Confederates under Heber MacMahon, R.C. Bishop of Clogher, defeated in battle at Scariffhollis, near Letterkenny; MacMahon executed on 17 Sept.

28 June Charles II lands in Scotland.

2 July Parliament approves Cromwell's appointment of Edmund Ludlow as second-in-command to Ireton.

8 July Sir Charles Coote (Parliament) takes Athlone.

24 July Carlow surrenders to Ireton.

6 Aug. Waterford surrenders to Ireton.

Sir Phelim O'Neill capitulates, then escapes (captured in Feb. 1653).

12 Aug. Catholic bishops at Jamestown, Co. Leitrim, release people from their allegiance to Ormond as L.L. and excommunicate those who follow him.

16 Aug. Charles II, in alliance with the Scots at Dunfermline, denies all terms to 'Irish rebels' and revokes peace terms of 1649.

17 Aug. Duncannon fort surrenders to Parliament.

4 Oct. Parliamentary commissioners (Edmund Ludlow, Miles Corbet, John Jones and John Weaver) appointed for civil administration of Ireland (*See* 24 Jan. 1651.).

26 Nov. Catholic laity meet at Loughrea, Co. Galway.

11 Dec. Ormond, accompanied by Inchiquin and others, leaving the Earl of Clanricard as deputy, sails for Saint-Malo, Brittany, from Galway Bay, losing vessel containing personal effects *en route.*

c. 1650 Composition of *Páirlimint Cloinne Thomáis,* a parody, mainly in prose, which satirises those rising on the social scale as a result of changes in landholding in the Munster plantation; most likely composed by a hereditary poet or historian of the MacCarthys of south Munster.

1651

24 Jan. Parliamentary commissioners arrive at Duncannon, Co. Wexford.

May Thomas Preston erects fortress on the island of Inishbofin, off Connemara, and becomes governor of Galway (*see* 14 Feb. 1653).

2 June Ireton forces the passage of the Shannon at Killaloe.

4 June Ireton invests Limerick (*see* 27 Oct.).

18 June Thomas Dillon agrees terms for surrender of Athlone Castle with Sir Charles Coote.

26 July Lord Broghill (Parliament) defeats Lord Muskerry at Knockbrack or Knocknaclashy, Co. Cork.

3 Sept. In last pitched battle of the English Civil War Cromwell decisively defeats Charles II at Worcester; Charles flees to France.

9 Oct. Navigation Act stipulates that all goods imported into Ireland and England and other lands belonging to the English Commonwealth can only be carried in English ships.

27 Oct. Limerick surrenders to Ireton as plague rages within the city; Sir Hardress Waller appointed governor.

31 Oct. Terence Albert O'Brien, Dominican Bishop of Emly, is among those hanged by Ireton in Limerick.

5 Nov. Clare Castle surrenders to Ludlow.

Nov. Offices of Lord Lieutenant and Lord Deputy abolished by Parliament; parliamentary commissioners now receive responsibility for military as well as civilian administration.

26 Nov. d. Henry Ireton of plague in Limerick; Edmund Ludlow succeeds as C.-in-C. until the arrival of Charles Fleetwood (Sept. 1652).

1652

3 Apr. Roscommon surrenders.

12 Apr. Galway surrenders.

21 Apr. Articles of agreement between Sir Hardress Waller and Col. Murtagh O'Brien, C.-in-C. of the Confederate forces in Clare.

11–12 May Parliamentary committee issues proposals to the 'adventurers', including threat that if land is not inhabited and cultivated by 29 Sept. 1655 it will be forfeit to the Commonwealth.

12 May Richard Nugent, 2nd Earl of Westmeath, surrenders with the Leinster Confederate army under terms known as the 'Articles of Kilkenny'.

May Pub. *An Abstract of Some Few of those Barbarous, Cruell Massacres and Murthers of the Protestants and English in Some Parts of Ireland, Committed since the 23 of October, 1641* by Henry Jones, propagandist; receives widespread attention and provides moral justification for expropriation of those deemed to be rebels.

17 May Loghlen O'Mara defeats Cromwellians at Nenagh, Co. Tipperary.

26 May Ballyshannon, Co. Donegal, surrenders.

22 June Lord Muskerry surrenders Ross Castle, Co. Kerry, to Ludlow; last mainland garrison to surrender.

28 June Earl of Clanricard surrenders to Sir Charles Coote; Clanricard goes to England (d. Summerhill, Kent, 1657).

9 July Charles Fleetwood assumes offices of C.-in-C. and parliamentary principal commissioner of government (arrives on 11 Sept.).

12 Aug. 'Act for the Settling of Ireland' divides the whole population into six categories according to purported guilt and sets out treatment for all not pardoned.

11 Oct. Orders issued for the publication of the Act of Settlement.

17 Dec. Sir Charles Coote appointed Commonwealth commissioner in Connaught.

Pub. by Samuel Hartlib of *Ireland's Natural History* by Gerard Boate.

1653

6 Jan. Parliamentary commissioners order the expulsion of all Catholic priests.

8 Jan. General order issued to the commissioners of precincts to press ships for the transportation of 8,000 Irish to 'tobacco islands' (*see* 16 May).

14 Feb. Inishbofin, last military stronghold in the British Isles where royal flag still flew, surrenders to Parliamentary soldiers.

19 Feb. Orders issued enforcing declaration for the expulsion of Jesuits and seminary priests.

10 Mar. Sir Phelim O'Neill executed in Dublin.

27 Apr. Philip MacHugh O'Reilly surrenders at Cloughoughter, Co. Cavan; last formal surrender of the war.

16 May Order to commissioners for the relief of the poor directs them to hand over incorrigible vagrants for transportation to the Caribbean (*see* 8 Jan.).

22 June Council of state orders three surveys; (1) by inquisition ('Civil Survey'); (2) by measurement and mapping ('Down Survey'; *see* 11 Dec. 1654); (3) 'Gross Survey' to determine how much land is available to the government to satisfy its debts to soldiers and adventurers.

29 June District commissioners ordered to appoint days for hunting wolves under bounty (£6 for bitch, £5 for dog, and £2 for cub); published on 1 July 1656.

2 July Parliamentary commissioners order that any Irish who are to be settled (*see* 12 Aug. 1652) must be settled in Connaught, provided that they leave for there before 1 May 1654.

4 July – 12 Dec. Barebones Parliament at Westminster; Ireland represented by six M.P.s.

15 July Parliamentary commissioners require all persons who possess any right or title to lands in Ireland on 23 Oct. 1641 to put in a statement of their claims for commissioners' satisfaction.

1 Aug. Appointment of standing committee to work out details of plan for transplanting Irish into Connaught.

26 Sept. 'Act of Satisfaction' proclaims the rebellion in Ireland to be at an end and states that the counties of Waterford, Limerick, Tipperary,

Queen's County, King's County, Meath, Westmeath, Armagh, Down and Louth are to answer all claims of adventurers and arrears of the army since 5 June 1649.

16 Dec. Cromwell named Lord Protector (proclaimed in Dublin on 30 Jan. 1654); Commissioner Ludlow resigns.

Commissioners in Ireland estimate debts at £1,750,000, but amount of land available to satisfy them is only £800,000; remainder will have to be repaid from some other source than Irish land.

Piaras Feiritéir (53), soldier and poet, captured after the fall of Ross Castle, executed at Killarney, Co. Kerry.

1654

6 Jan. Commissioners appointed to sit at Loughrea, Co. Galway, to allot land to transplanters on strength of certificates granted by the commissioners of revenue (commission terminates on 30 Sept. 1657).

24 Jan. Drawing of lots to decide which baronies will belong to the army and which to adventurers, at Grocers' Hall, London.

14 Apr. Benjamin Worsley authorised to appoint fit and able persons to survey lands in the ten counties allotted for the satisfaction of the claims of soldiers and adventurers (*see* 11 Dec.).

3 Sept. – 22 Jan. 1655 First Protectorate parliament at Westminster; Ireland represented by 30 M.P.s.

6–7 Sept. Fr Edmund O'Reilly found guilty of murder but pardoned (*see* 6 Apr. 1657).

3 Nov. Commission appointed to hear and determine all claims to forfeited land in Ireland (*see also* 28 Dec.).

30 Nov. Government orders all 'transplantable persons' to be in Connaught by 1 Mar. 1655.

11 Dec. William Petty takes over mapping forfeited land in 22 counties (*see* 14 Apr.); survey to be completed inside 13 months (known as the 'Down Survey').

18 Dec. Order published forbidding the observance of Christmas (repeated on 21 Dec. 1655).

28 Dec. Commissioners appointed to hear and determine all claims on the part of transplanters to Connaught to compensatory grants of land in Connaught or Clare ('Athlone Commission').

1655

19 Mar. Courts martial established with power to impose death sentence for refusal to transplant.

13 Apr. Order forbids observance of Easter holidays.

7 May Order issued that Dublin should be cleared of 'papists' and that 'cabins and other noisome places' should be destroyed.

1 June Commissioners revoke all former dispensations for English proprietors to plant with Irish tenants.

16 June Commissioners of 6 Jan. 1654 instructed to proceed to a final instead of a conditional settlement.

22 June Petition of Erasmus Smith 'contemplates the establishment of five free schools' (*see* 1 Dec. 1657).

23 July Inhabitants of Galway ordered to quit the town by 1 Nov.; owners of houses to be compensated by eight years' purchase.

17 Dec. Order given that all Quakers should be arrested; further orders of 21 and 30 Jan. 1656 direct that Quakers from Dublin and Waterford should be transported to England.

Pub. *The Great Case of Transplantation Discussed* by Vincent Gookin.

1656
21 Mar. d. James Ussher (75), C.I. Archbishop of Armagh since 1625; his 10,000-volume library later goes to T.C.D. on orders of Charles II.

15 Apr. Order that no 'tories' or wood-kerne are to be shown any mercy.

13 June Sir John Temple appointed commissioner for determining settlement of differences among adventurers concerning land.

7 July William Petty, Vincent Gookin and Miles Symner appointed to apportion to the soldiers the land alloted to them in payment of arrears.

20 Aug. William Steele appointed Lord Chancellor (arrives in Sept.).

17 Sept. – 4 Feb. 1658 Second Protectorate parliament at Westminster.

1657
6 Apr. Edmund O'Reilly appointed Archbishop of Armagh by the Pope (visits Ireland briefly in Oct. 1659).

9 June 'Act for the assuring, confirming and settling of lands and estates in Ireland'.

26 June 'Act for the attainder of the rebels in Ireland' attaints all 'rebels' and 'papists' but pardons those who have transplanted; those not transplanted by 24 Sept. will forfeit all claims.

Act requires suspected Catholics to abjure supremacy of the Pope under oath and deny the doctrine of transubstantiation under pain of losing two-thirds of their property.

17 Nov. Henry Cromwell appointed L.D.

18 Nov. d. Luke Wadding (69), Franciscan scholar.

1 Dec. By indenture Erasmus Smith establishes five grammar schools, having bursaries at T.C.D., and five elementary schools.

1658
3 Sept. d. Oliver Cromwell (59), Lord Protector of the Commonwealth; succeeded by his son Richard (proclaimed Lord Protector on 11 Sept.).

1659
27 Jan. – 22 Apr. Third Protectorate parliament at Westminster.

24 May Richard Cromwell resigns Protectorate.

7 June Long Parliament appoints three commissioners to govern Ireland (Robert Goodwin, John Jones and William Steele; *see* 7 July); Henry Cromwell recalled (leaves Ireland on 27 June).

7 July Miles Corbet and Matthew Tomlinson appointed to join commissioners for Ireland.

26 Aug. Mayor of Dublin ordered to put the laws for the observance of the Lord's Day into execution.

26 Oct. Army in England expels the Long Parliament and establishes a Committee of Safety.

13 Dec. Group of army officers under Sir Hardress Waller seize Dublin Castle, arrest Jones and other commissioners and declare for the restoration of the Long Parliament (*see* 15 Feb. 1660).

31 Dec. Edmund Ludlow arrives to suppress Waller rebellion, but is forced to return to England.

1660
Jan. Lord Broghill, Sir Charles Coote and Major William Bury appointed commissioners for the government of Ireland.

6 Feb. Robert Stewart reappointed governor of Derry (until 17 Sept. 1661).

7 Feb. Convention of 'old' and 'new' Protestants meets in Dublin; Lord Broghill and Sir Charles Coote persuade majority that their interests will best be served by restoration of the monarchy.

15 Feb. Sir Hardress Waller seizes Dublin Castle (*see* 13 Dec. 1659) in defence of republican principles; surrenders within a few days.

16 Mar. Long Parliament dissolves itself.

14 Apr. Declaration of Breda: King Charles II declares that none of his subjects 'of what degree of guilt soever' should suffer; exceptions were regicides.

8 May Restoration: Charles II proclaimed King of England; enters London on 29th.

14 May Charles II proclaimed King of Ireland in Dublin.

25 May Lord Broghill and Sir Charles Coote and others appointed by Convention to present Irish desires to the King.

1 June Royal proclamation orders all Irish rebels in England or Ireland to be proceeded against as traitors.

25 July John, Lord Robartes, appointed L.D.; does not come over (*see* 18 Sept. 1669).

30 July Sir Charles Coote reappointed Lord President of Connaught; created Earl of Mountrath on 6 Sept.

29 Aug. 'Act of free and general pardon, indemnity, and oblivion' excludes persons concerned in the Irish rebellion.

13 Sept. Navigation Act to control England's external trade treats Ireland and England as a single economic unit.

30 Nov. Charles issues declaration on the settlement of Ireland which becomes the basis for the Act of Settlement (*see* 31 July 1662); confirms Cromwellian settlers in their possessions (church lands excepted) and provides for the restoration to their estates of 'innocent papists'.

31 Dec. Earl of Orrery (Roger Boyle, formerly Lord Broghill), Earl of Mountrath and Sir Maurice Eustace (Lord Chancellor) sworn in as L.J.s in absence of L.D.

1661

1 Jan. Franciscan Peter Walsh empowered by R.C. hierarchy to plead the Catholic case with the King.

18 Jan. John Bramhall appointed C.I. Archbishop of Armagh.

27 Jan. Church of Ireland re-established when two archbishops and 10 bishops are consecrated in St Patrick's Cathedral, Dublin.

30 Mar. James Butler, Marquis of Ormond, created Duke of Ormond in Ireland and Lord High Steward of England (*see* 4 Nov.).

8 May – 31 July Parliament in session (first Irish parliament for 20 years); 260 members vote £30,000 to the Duke of Ormond.

27 Aug. d. Francis Kirwan (72), ascetic R.C. Bishop of Killala since 1645.

6 Sept. – 22 Mar. 1662 Parliament in session.

4 Nov. Duke of Ormond declared L.L. (arrives on 27 July 1662).

6 Nov. Committee appointed by L.J.s to prepare and transmit bill for suppression of Irish Catholic hierarchy.

COUNTY LIBRARY

18 Dec. d. Charles Coote, 1st Earl of Mountrath.

Dec. Catholic 'Remonstrance' drawn up, declaring allegiance to the King, denying Pope's authority to absolve Catholics from said allegiance.

1662

17 Apr. – 16 Apr. 1663 Parliament in session.

19 May Act of English parliament makes export of Irish wool a felony.

27 July Duke of Ormond sworn in as L.L.

31 July Act of Settlement provides for the immediate restoration of 'innocents' and for the compensation of Cromwellian holders with equivalent land elsewhere; names individual Catholics whose loyalty recommends them for special consideration.

20 Sept. Court of Claims under the Act of Settlement opens.

27 Sept. Act 'for encouraging Protestant strangers to inhabit and plant in the kingdom of Ireland'.

Oct. Smock Alley Theatre, Dublin, opens under John Ogilby.

1663

13 Jan. Court of Claims begins to hear claims, although sitting since 20 Sept. 1662 (*see* 21 Aug.).

21 May Date set for insurrection led by Col. Thomas Blood to defend Protestant land interests in Ireland; plans made known to government, and insurrectionists flee.

27 July English parliament restricts Irish trade with colonies and the importation of Irish cattle into England.

21 Aug. First Court of Claims under Act of Settlement closes, having issued over 500 decrees of innocence to Catholics; over 3,000 Catholic estates declared forfeit when Ormond refuses to extend sitting.

1664

1 July First Cattle Act comes into force.

Pub. *Rerum Hibernicarum Annales (1485–1558)* by Sir James Ware.

1665

23 Dec. Act of Explanation confirms all decrees of innocency already issued, but stipulates that no more claims will be heard; estates are to be restored to certain named persons, lands to be provided by the surrender by adventurers and soldiers of one-third of what they have received.

1666

4 Jan. Second Court of Claims under the Act of Settlement opens (last sitting begins on 2 Jan. 1669).

1 Apr. Robert Mossom consecrated C.I. Bishop of Derry (d. 21 Dec. 1679).

22 May Soldiers mutiny at Carrickfergus; suppressed by Lord Arran, who executes those responsible.

11–25 June Edmund O'Reilly, R.C. Archbishop of Armagh, who receives special permission to re-enter the country from exile, attends synod of clergy to consider drawing up loyal 'Remonstrance' (*see* Dec. 1661); Remonstrance rejected by L.L. Ormond, who dissolves the synod, arrests the bishops and expels O'Reilly on 25 Sept. (d. at Louvain 1669).

18 June Act of Uniformity orders use of revised Book of Common Prayer; schoolmasters to be licensed by bishop of Established Church; all holders of public office, civil and military, to take the Oath of Supremacy (comes into force on 29 Sept. 1667).

7 Aug. Parliament dissolved.

1 Dec. d. Sir James Ware (72), antiquary.

1667

18 Jan. English act excludes Irish cattle, sheep, beef and pork from the English market; Scotland follows suit.

3 Mar. Dudley Costello, tory, killed in skirmish with soldiers in Mayo.

8 Aug. College of Physicians incorporated by charter (assumes title Royal College of Physicians of Ireland in 1890).

13 Aug. d. Jeremy Taylor, C.I. Bishop of Down and Connor since 1661, noted preacher and writer.

Pub. *Treatise on Miracles* by Richard Archdekin, S.J., believed to be the first book printed jointly in Irish and English.

1668

22 Oct. Richard Jones appointed Chancellor of the Exchequer.

English Treasury commission is set up to investigate Irish financial administration.

1669

14 Feb. King announces that L.L. Ormond is to be removed from office (*see* 18 Sept.).

29 Apr. Peter Talbot consecrated R.C. Archbishop of Dublin at Antwerp (d. 15 Nov. 1680).

May – Aug. George Fox, founder of Quakers, organises Quaker meetings in Ireland.

9 July Oliver Plunkett appointed R.C. Archbishop of Armagh; consecrated at Ghent on 21 Nov.; arrives in Ireland in mid-Mar. 1670 (*see* 6 Dec. 1679).

27 July Molly Malone christened at St Werburgh's Church, Dublin; later a fishmonger, she is the subject of a ballad which becomes the city's anthem (*see* 13 June 1699).

18 Sept. John, Lord Robartes, sworn in as L.L.

1670

21 Apr. John, Lord Berkeley of Stratton, sworn in as L.L.

17 June Synod of Catholic bishops called by Archbishop Oliver Plunkett declares loyalty to the King.

30 July New peal of six bells for Christ Church in Dublin first rung; new peal of eight bells for St Patrick's first rung on 23 Sept.

6 Dec. Duke of Ormond kidnapped in London by Col. Thomas Blood and held for a short time before rescue.

1671

22 Apr. English Navigation Act prohibits direct importation of colonial produce to Ireland (expires on 18 Jan. 1681, but renewed on 2 July 1685).

July Dublin apprentices riot, attacking unfinished wooden bridge linking Ussher's Quay to Oxmanstown; 30 arrested and three killed attempting to rescue them (bridge becomes known as 'Bloody Bridge').

4 Aug. 'Ranelagh Undertaking': Richard Jones, Earl of Ranelagh, enters into agreement with King whereby Jones and a consortium will receive all payments due to the Crown from the revenue farmers and will pay all charges on the Irish treasury.

8 Sept. d. John Leslie, C.I. Bishop of Clogher since 1661; as Bishop of Raphoe (since 1633) one of the last Royalists to submit and the only C.I. bishop to stay at his post during the interregnum.

Pub. *Praecipuae Controversiae Fidei* by Richard Archdekin, S.J. (Louvain) (13 editions by 1718).

1672

15 Mar. Declaration of Indulgence: King announces intention to suspend all legislation restricting Catholics and Dissenters (withdrawn on 7 Mar. 1673).

5 Aug. Arthur Capel, Earl of Essex, sworn in as L.L.

Aug. Presidencies of Munster and Connaught abolished.

c. Oct. *Regium donum* (royal bounty) first paid to Presbyterians (£600 initially, doubled by William III; *see* 19 June 1690).

Sir William Petty conducts statistical inquiry into the economic state of Ireland (*Political Anatomy of Ireland*, pub. 1691).

1673

29 Mar. Test Act effectively excludes all but Anglicans from public life by demanding office-holders to receive sacrament in accordance with usage of Church of England.

27 Oct. Proclamation banishes Catholic bishops and priests and orders closure of religious houses and schools (*see* 16 Oct. 1678).

1674

17 May Andrew Sall, provincial superior of the Society of Jesus, announces at Cashel his adherence to the Church of England; repeats it in Christ Church, Dublin, on 5 July.

9 Sept. d. Murrough O'Brien (60), 1st Earl of Inchiquin, soldier.

1675

22 Sept. Commission established on King's orders to inquire into cases of transplanters in Connaught.

1676

Pub. *Lucerna Fidelium: Lóchrann na gCreidmheach* by Francis Molloy (Ó Maolmhuaidh), Irish agent at papal court (Rome).

1677

24 Aug. Duke of Ormond again sworn in as L.L.

Pub. *Grammatica Latino-Hibernica* by Francis Molloy (Ó Maolmhuaidh), grammar of the Irish language in Latin (Rome).

1678

28 Sept. Titus Oates reveals 'a damnable and hellish [popish] plot' to the English Privy Council; his story accepted by the House of Lords (31 Oct.); Oates names Peter Talbot, Archbishop of Dublin, who dies imprisoned in Dublin Castle on 15 Nov. 1680 (*see* 6 Dec. 1679).

14 Oct. L.L. Ormond orders all officers and soldiers to take up positions until further notice.

16 Oct. L.L. Ormond proclaims closure of all religious houses and schools and the banishment of all R.C. bishops and secular and regular clergy before 20 Nov.

1679

23 Mar. Edward Wetenhall consecrated C.I. Bishop of Cork and Ross (translated to Kilmore and Ardagh on 18 Apr. 1699).

6 Dec. Oliver Plunkett, R.C. Archbishop of Armagh, arrested in connection with the 'Popish Plot' (*see* 23–24 July 1680).

1680

29 Apr. First stone laid for the Royal Hospital, Kilmainham, Dublin, by the Duke of Ormond, for soldiers of the Irish army; architect William Robinson (*see* 28 Mar. 1686).

23–24 July Trial of Archbishop Oliver Plunkett at Dundalk; ends without indictment when chief prosecution witness fails to appear (*see* 3 May 1681).

24 Aug. d. Col. Thomas Blood (62), adventurer.

1681

25 Apr. Count Redmond O'Hanlon, tory, shot dead at Eightmilebridge, Co. Down.

3 May Oliver Plunkett arraigned in London; found guilty on false evidence of Florence MacMoyer (*see* 12 Feb. 1713); executed on 1 July (beatified on 23 May 1920, canonised on 12 Oct. 1975).

1682

5 Jan. d. Henry Jones, C.I. Bishop of Meath since 1661; collected evidence on 1641 rising; played leading role in destruction of Archbishop Oliver Plunkett (1681).

9 Nov. L.L. Ormond created a duke in the English peerage.

1683

23 July Patrick Russell appointed R.C. Archbishop of Dublin (d. in prison on 14 July 1692).

1684

Jan. Dublin Philosophical Society, known also as Dublin Society, founded by William Molyneux, modelled on Royal Society of London; Sir William Petty first president (*see* 25 June 1731).

18 Feb. 'Court of grace' established under 'commission of grace' for securing defective titles and disposing of land still in the King's possession.

1685

6 Feb. d. Charles II; succeeded by his brother, James, Duke of York (James II).

20 Mar. L.L. Ormond leaves Ireland; Michael Boyle, C.I. Archbishop of Armagh, and the Earl of Granard sworn in as L.J.s (*see* 9 Jan. 1686).

20 June Richard Talbot created Earl of Tyrconnell.

21 July R.C. bishops petition James to confer on the Earl of Tyrconnell authority to protect them in the exercise of their ministry.

4 Aug. d. Thomas Price, C.I. Archbishop of Cashel since 1667; promoted Irish as the language of the Established Church in Ireland.

Pub. *Hiberniae Delineatio* by Sir William Petty, containing first effective map of Ireland.

Pub. *Leabhuir na Sein-Tiomna* (Old Testament in Irish) translated by James Nangle and Murtagh King, started in 1629 under direction of Bishop William Bedell (d. 1642).

Pub. *Ogygia,* scholarly history of Ireland in Latin by Roderic O'Flaherty.

1686

9 Jan. Henry Hyde, Earl of Clarendon, sworn in as L.L.

22 Mar. By royal warrant R.C. archbishops and bishops to receive payments from the Exchequer.

28 Mar. First pensioners admitted to the Royal Hospital, Kilmainham (*see* 29 Apr. 1680).

16 Apr. Sir Charles Porter appointed Lord Chancellor (*see* 4 Jan. 1687).

5 June Earl of Tyrconnell returns as Lieutenant-General of the army with Justin MacCarthy, Lord Mountcashel, as Major-General and proceeds to pack army with Catholics; Tyrconnell returns to England on 26 Aug. (*see* 6 Feb. 1687).

Pub. *Sciotherium Telescopicum* by William Molyneux, his first book.

1687

4 Jan. Lord Chancellor Sir Charles Porter recalled; replaced by Sir Alexander Fitton, a Catholic, on 12th

(Porter reappointed in Dec. 1690 by William III).

6 Feb. Earl of Tyrconnell returns from England; sworn in as L.D. on 12 Feb.

8 Mar. L.D. Tyrconnell issues proclamation promising protection in their rights and properties to the King's subjects of whatever religious persuasion.

16 Dec. d. Sir William Petty (64), pioneer statistician, author of Down Survey.

1688

18 June James orders that Jesuits are to be appointed masters in government-controlled schools wherever vacancies occur.

21 July d. James Butler (78), Duke of Ormond, in retirement in England.

5 Nov. William Henry de Nassau, Prince of Orange, James II's son-in-law, arrives at Torbay, in Devon.

24 Nov. John Churchill (later Duke of Marlborough) deserts James for William.

7 Dec. Apprentice boys close the gates of Derry against Lord Antrim's Catholic regiment.

8 Dec. L.D. Tyrconnell issues proclamation promising protection to loyal subjects and denouncing reports of impending massacres.

21 Dec. Robert Lundy becomes governor of Derry (*see* 19 Apr. 1689).

23–24 Dec. James II flees from England for France; deemed to have abdicated.

1689

8 Jan. Lt-Gen. Richard Hamilton arrives in Dublin from William to negotiate with Tyrconnell and deserts to Tyrconnell.

Feb. Starvation and epidemic rife in Ulster.

13 Feb. William and Mary ascend the throne after accepting a Bill of Rights.

20 Feb. Sir Lawrence Parsons surrenders Birr Castle, King's County, to Col. Heward Oxburgh (Parsons found guilty of high treason but sentence deferred; released after battle of the Boyne, 1690).

22 Feb. William issues proclamation calling on Jacobites to surrender by 10 Apr., promising security of property and toleration of religion; offer not availed of.

2 Mar. Justin MacCarthy, Lord Mountcashel, reduces the Protestant town of Bandon, Co. Cork, and imposes fine of £1,000 for an attack by its citizens on Jacobite garrison on 25 Feb.

12 Mar. James lands at Kinsale, Co. Cork, with a force commanded by English and French officers.

Thomas Southwell and other anti-Jacobites in Galway sentenced to be hanged, drawn and quartered (reprieved and released on 2 Jan. 1690).

14 Mar. Richard Hamilton (Jacobite) defeats Ulster Protestant force under the Earl of Mountalexander at the 'Break of Dromore' in Co. Down, a severe blow to Protestant morale in Ulster.

James meets Tyrconnell in Cork; creates him Duke of Tyrconnell on 30th.

24 Mar. James enters Dublin, accompanied by Comte d'Avaux (ambassador from France); on 25th summons a parliament for 7 May.

18 Apr. James at Derry, refused admittance and fired on; siege begins (*see* 28 *and* 31 July).

19 Apr. Governor Lundy, who advocates surrender of the city to James, escapes from Derry; replaced by Rev. George Walker.

1 May English and French in naval battle off Bantry Bay; English sustain heavier casualties.

7 May – 18 July 'Patriot Parliament' at King's Inns, Dublin; 46 peers, 228 commoners and 7 bishops (no R.C. prelates summoned); James attends (last monarch to attend an Irish parliament until 1921).

7 May Thomas Lloyd defeats the Jacobites on the River Erne at Beleek, Co. Fermanagh.

England declares war on France.

14 June William arrives at Carrickfergus.

18 June James issues proclamation providing for circulation of 'brass money': bells, gun-metal and ultimately pewter used; the Jacobite government pledges to make good the value of the coinage at a future date (*see* 10 July 1690).

19 June William in Belfast promises that all loyal subjects will 'enjoy their liberties and possessions under a just and equal government'.

22 June Act repeals land settlement, vesting in the King the land of absentees.

28 July Williamite ships break the boom on the Foyle to relieve Derry.

31 July Relief of Derry after an investment of 105 days; Jacobites lift the siege and make for Lifford, Co. Donegal.

Battle of Newtownbutler: Justin MacCarthy, Lord Mountcashel (Jacobite) defeated (and captured but escapes) by Enniskilleners under William Wolseley (Williamite) whose password is 'No Popery'.

13 Aug. Marshal Schomberg arrives at Bangor Bay in Belfast Lough with army of Dutch, French Huguenots and English levies; besieges Carrickfergus, Co. Antrim (20–28 Aug.), which is surrendered on terms by Col. Charles MacCarthy More.

7 Sept. Schomberg pitches camp at Dundalk, Co. Louth, and begins to fortify the town.

19 Sept. Charles O'Kelly and Patrick Sarsfield (Jacobites) defeated by Thomas Lloyd (Williamite).

21 Sept. James and his forces arrive at Dundalk; his camp beset by outbreak of dysentery, Schomberg rejects James's challenge to fight.

27 Sept. Christ Church Cathedral, Dublin, handed over to the Catholic Church by the Jacobites.

6 Oct. James moves his army back from Dundalk to Ardee, Co. Louth.

c. 4 Nov. James moves from Ardee to winter quarters in Dublin.

9–10 Nov. Schomberg leaves Dundalk.

25 Nov. Christopher Plunkett takes Newry from Schomberg's troops.

1690

12–14 Mar. French fleet of 41 men-of-war at Cork carrying French regiments under Antoine, Comte de Lauzun.

21 Mar. Sir John Temple (jun.) appointed Attorney-General (until 1695).

18 Apr. Justin MacCarthy, Viscount Mountcashel, leads Irish regiments to France.

14 May Charlemont fort surrenders to Schomberg, who treats garrison and families humanely.

14 June William III arrives at Carrickfergus from Chester.

[K]ENNY COUNTY LIBRARY

19 June William orders collector of customs at Belfast to authorise payment of £1,200 p.a. to Ulster Presbyterian clergy (*regium donum;* later made payable from Exchequer).

22 June William reviews his army, 36,000 strong, of English, Irish, Dutch, Danish, Prussian, French Huguenots, Swiss and Norwegians at Loughbrickland, Co. Down.

29 June James's army crosses the Boyne at Drogheda and Oldbridge.

30 June William's army reaches the Boyne and camps at Tullyallen; William grazed by six-pound shot, and rumour spreads on Jacobite side that he is mortally wounded.

1 July William (36,000 strong) defeats James (25,000) at the Boyne in the largest military engagement in Irish history (Schomberg killed in action); James flees to Dublin.

2 July James flees from Dublin for Duncannon, Co. Wexford; sails for France from Kinsale on 4th.

Drogheda submits.

6 July William enters Dublin and camps at Finglas.

7 July William declares pardon for all Jacobites except the leaders of the rebellion, who will have to convince him of their entitlement to mercy.

9 July William marches from Finglas for Limerick.

10 July Proclamation by William orders that the crown pieces issued by James – 'brass money' (*see* 18 June 1689) – should pass as equal in value to one penny.

16 July Kilkenny submits.

17–25 July Williamites fail to take Athlone from Col. Richard Grace; Lt-Gen. Douglas raises siege after seven days.

19 July William at Kilkenny; dines with Ormond.

20 July Williamites enter Clonmel.

25 July Waterford surrenders to Williamites.

9 Aug. William invests Limerick when it refuses to surrender.

11 Aug. Patrick Sarsfield, guided by 'Galloping' Hogan, sets out from Limerick to intercept Williamite siege train; overtakes the convoy at Ballyneety, Co. Limerick, on 12th and destroys it, evading Williamite cavalry under Sir John Lanier.

17–27 Aug. Limerick bombarded by Williamites; general attack fails (27th); William calls off siege (29th) and leaves for Waterford (30–31 Aug.).

5 Sept. William sails for England, leaving command to Count de Solms, who is succeeded by Baron von Ginkel.

12 Sept. Tyrconnell and Lauzun sail from Galway for France, taking French troops with them.

15 Sept. Thomas Coningsby and Henry, Viscount Sidney, sworn in as L.J.s (Williamite).

21 Sept. Duke of Marlborough arrives at Cove in Cork harbour.

22 Sept. Cork invested; surrenders to Marlborough on 28th.

3 Oct. Williamites under Duke of Marlborough take James Fort in Kinsale harbour; garrison killed or taken prisoner.

15 Oct. Williamites take Charles Fort in Kinsale harbour; Sir Edward Scott and his command allowed to march with their baggage to Limerick.

Sarsfield and Duke of Berwick (natural son of James II) foil Williamite attempts to cross the Shannon at

Lanesborough, Jamestown and Banagher during the winter.

1691

14 Jan. Duke of Tyrconnell (Jacobite L.L.) arrives at Limerick from France, bringing money and patent creating Sarsfield Earl of Lucan, Viscount of Tully and Baron of Rosberry.

25 Jan. William King consecrated C.I. Bishop of Derry (*see* 11 Mar. 1703).

c. 24 Feb. Duke of Berwick leaves Limerick for France (*see* 16 Jan. 1698).

2 Mar. Henri Massue, Marquis de Ruvigny, created Baron Portarlington and Viscount Galway by William (created Earl of Galway on 12 May 1697); leader of the Huguenot colony in Ireland.

8 May Marquis de St Ruth's French army sails up the Shannon; in Limerick on 9th, accompanied by Major-Generals d'Usson and de Tessé.

8 June Ginkel takes fort at Ballymore, outpost to Athlone.

17 June Williamites sack Tipperary town.

19 June Ginkel and Würtemberg with 18,000 advance on Athlone and besiege it; Jacobite defenders forced to destroy the bridge across the Shannon and retreat into the Irishtown on the Connaught bank on 20th; falls to Williamites on 30th; Tyrconnell strikes camp and repairs to Limerick.

9 July Ginkel issues proclamation offering terms to Jacobites (who surrender within three weeks) and raises a storm of Protestant protest; extends period by eight days on 16 Sept.

12 July Williamites defeat St Ruth, who is killed in action, at Aughrim, Co. Galway; last battle of the war and the last major battle fought in Ireland between professional armies.

19 July Ginkel besieges Galway, which surrenders on 21st; its governor, d'Usson, departs for Limerick with 2,300 followers on 26th.

14 Aug. d. Richard Talbot (61), Duke of Tyrconnell and Jacobite L.L., in Limerick.

25 Aug. Ginkel besieges Limerick.

14 Sept. Sligo surrenders.

15–16 Sept. Williamites cross the Shannon above Limerick on pontoon bridge.

22 Sept. Ginkel crosses the Shannon and attacks fort on Thomond Bridge at Limerick.

24 Sept. Truce agreed in the siege of Limerick.

26 Sept. Jacobites and Williamites at Limerick exchange hostages as preliminary to negotiations.

27 Sept. Jacobites at Limerick send proposals for a settlement to Ginkel.

28 Sept. Full conference between Jacobites and Williamites at Limerick.

3 Oct. Articles of the Treaty of Limerick signed.

12 Oct. Sarsfield and 'Wild Geese' leave Limerick to sail from Cork (22 Dec.) for France.

20 Oct. French fleet arrives in Shannon estuary.

23 Dec. d. Robert Boyle (64), scientist, enunciator of 'Boyle's Law'.

24 Dec. English act of parliament substituting new oath and an anti-Catholic declaration for the Oath of Supremacy effectively bars Catholics from public office in Ireland (*see* 4 Mar. 1704).

1692

11 Jan. Proclamation calls on any person claiming benefit of the Treaty of Limerick to prefer claim (first hearings on 6 Apr.).

24 Feb. Terms of the Treaty of Limerick enrolled in Chancery; letters patent ratify the treaty and declare taht the 'missing clause' ('and all such as are under their portectin in the said counties') should be part of the articles (*see* 25 Sept. 1697).

4 Sept. Henry, Viscount Sidney, sworn in as L.L.

5 Oct. Parliament meets, completely Protestant and predominantly Anglican; Sir Richard Levinge elected Speaker of the House of Commons; parliament hostile when informed that members are required to ratify, and not discuss, the articles of the Treaty of Limerick in the extended form in which William has ratified them, and that the Act of Settlement will be re-enacted with further concessions to Catholics.

3 Nov. 'Act for encouragement of Protestant strangers to settle in this kingdom of Ireland' allows such people to worship in their accustomed manner; Irish landholders outlawed for supporting James, involving forfeiture of 3,921 estates (total acreage of 1,060,792).

Parliament prorogued (dissolved on 26 June 1693).

1693

13 June L.L. Sidney recalled (*see* 28 July).

19 July Patrick Sarsfield, Earl of Lucan, mortally wounded at the battle of Landen (d. 23rd).

28 July Lord Capel, William Duncombe and Sir Cyril Wyche sworn in as L.J.s.

31 Aug. d. Richard Archdekin (75), Jesuit author.

16 Nov. d. Francis Marsh, C.I. Archbishop of Dublin since 1682.

1694

3 Dec. Triennial Act passed by English parliament; fixes three years as maximum duration of parliament.

28 Dec. d. Mary II; William III becomes sole monarch.

1695

27 May Henry, Lord Capel, sworn in as L.D.

6 June Robert Rochfort appointed Attorney-General (until 1707).

27 Aug. – 14 Dec. Parliament in session; Robert Rochfort elected Speaker of the House of Commons (until 1703); parliament passes laws directly contravening Treaty of Limerick (*see* 7 Sept. *and* 22 Oct.); M.P.s use their expanded financial role to investigate and audit Treasury accounts for the first time (9 Sept.).

7 Sept. Act prohibits Catholics from educating their children abroad or opening schools at home; Catholic gentlemen forbidden to bear arms without a licence; Catholics forbidden to be recruited into the army or to own a horse worth more than £5.

22 Oct. Act imposes a fine of 2s or a whipping on labourers and servants who refuse to work on any day other than Sunday or statutory holiday; sets number of holidays at 29.

Pub. *Ireland's Case Briefly Stated* by Hugh Reily (Louvain).

1696

27 Apr. Duties removed from Irish plain linen entering England.

30 May d. L.D. Capel; Irish government administered by Lords Justices until 1701.

8 Dec. d. Sir Charles Porter, Lord Chancellor since Dec. 1690.

Pub. *Account of the Irish Elk* by Thomas Molyneux.

1697

11 Mar. John Methuen appointed Lord Chancellor (until 1703).

23 Apr. William III rules that the articles of the surrender of Galway only extend to those in the town when it surrendered (*see* 19 July 1691).

16 June Thomas Southwell appointed a Commissioner of Revenue in Ireland (until 1712; reappointed on 9 Oct. 1714); encourages the linen industry.

25 Sept. 'Act for banishing all papists exercising any ecclesiastical jurisdiction and all regulars of the popish clergy out of the kingdom' by 1 May 1698.

Act confirming articles of the Treaty of Limerick, but with the 'missing clause' still excluded.

Act forbidding burial in any suppressed monastery, abbey or convent not used for divine service.

Act for suppression of tories and rapparees.

Nov. William invites Samuel-Louis Crommelin to Ireland, leading to the establishment of a Huguenot settlement at Lisnagarvey (Lisburn) and the rise of the linen industry under Crommelin, who becomes overseer of the royal linen manufactory (*see* 14 Feb. 1700).

1698

Jan. d. Dáithí Ó Bruadair (c. 73), poet in the traditional Gaelic style.

16 Jan. d. Honora de Burgh, widow of Patrick Sarsfield, after whose death she married Duke of Berwick, natural son of James II.

Apr. Pub. *The Case of Ireland's being bound by Acts of Parliament in England Stated* by William Molyneux (his last work); condemned by English parliament for being 'of dangerous tendency to the Crown and people of England' on 27 June.

May Commencement of transportation of the religious (by year's end Paris alone has in excess of 400 members of banned Irish religious).

1–3 June Subscription to the Westminster Confession of Faith ruled to be a necessary condition for entry to ministry by the General Synod of Ulster.

30 June Address of the Irish House of Commons on Molyneux's *Case of Ireland* (*see* Apr.) and on the Irish woollen trade.

11 Oct. d. William Molyneux (42), philosopher, scientist and political writer.

1699

26 Jan. – 14 June Parliament in session; act imposing duties on woollens exported from Ireland, heralding the destruction of the Irish woollen trade (*see* 4 May).

Act prohibiting Catholics from becoming solicitors.

1 Feb. Act of English parliament authorises the Crown to maintain a 12,000-strong standing army in Ireland (continues at this level until 1769, when it is raised to 15,235).

4 May English parliament prohibits export of Irish woollens to foreign ports other than English.

13 June Burial of Molly Malone (29), a Dublin fishmonger, subject of a famous ballad.

15 Dec. Francis Annesley presents the complete record of the commission of inquiry into Irish forfeitures to the English House of Commons.

KILKENNY COUNTY LIBRARY

1700
16 Jan. – 11 Apr. Sir Richard Levinge imprisoned in the Tower of London for speaking ill of his fellow-commissioners inquiring into forfeited land in Ireland.

14 Feb. Samuel-Louis Crommelin granted subsidy to establish linen manufacture in Ireland.

June Forfeiture trustees arrive to hear all claims on 620,000 (Irish) acres still deemed confiscated and to sell those lands which were clearly forfeit by 24 June 1703.

1701
16 Sept. d. James II (68) at Saint-Germains, France.

18 Sept. Laurence Hyde, Earl of Rochester, sworn in as L.L.

Five-year economic recession starts; Irish government lowers exchange rate of the guinea coin within Ireland by more than 11 per cent.

Central block of the Royal Barracks (later Collins Barracks) built; architect Thomas Burgh (completed in 1708).

Building starts on Marsh's Library, first public library in Ireland (regulated by act on 30 Oct. 1707).

1702
1–3 Feb. Cremona saved by the Irish Brigade.

8 Mar. d. William III (52) as a result of a fall from his horse; succeeded by Anne.

24 May Royal assent for bill confirming titles to all leases held by Irish Huguenots in Portarlington.

Pub. first issue of *Dublin Intelligence* (runs until 1767).

1703
22 Feb. Sir Toby Butler and others protest at breach of the articles of the Treaty of Limerick.

27 Feb. Abjuration Act passed by English parliament; imposes stricter oath for all M.P.s, clergymen and office-holders in Ireland to recognise Queen Anne as the rightful monarch.

11 Mar. William King translated from Derry to be C.I. Archbishop of Dublin in succession to Narcissus Marsh, who is translated to Armagh; King inaugurates reforms.

4 June James Butler, 2nd Duke of Ormond, sworn in as L.L.

6 Aug. Sir Richard Cox appointed Lord Chancellor (until 30 June 1707).

21 Sept. – 4 Mar. 1704 First session of new parliament; Alan Brodrick elected Speaker of the House of Commons.

29 Sept. Parliament votes address to the Queen protesting against suspicion that it wishes to make Ireland independent and declaring that it believes Ireland's welfare depends on maintenance of connection with England.

22 Oct. House of Commons implores the Queen to consider their wrongs and grant a 'firm and strict union' between Ireland and England (Crown ignores the appeal).

Pub. first issue of *Pue's Impartial Occurrences*, first regular Irish newspaper; appears thrice weekly until 1773.

1704
1 Jan. Act imposing penalties on native R.C. clergy extended to every R.C. clergyman entering the country.

4 Mar. 'Act to prevent the further growth of popery' restricts Catholics, prohibiting them from buying land, taking a lease for longer than 31 years or acting as guardians; gavelkind provision leads to the division of Catholic estates between all the sons upon death of the father, but the eldest inherits the entire estate if he conforms to the Established Church (*see* 14 Aug. 1778 *and* 4 May 1782).

'Test Act' (i.e. section 17 of the above act) requires all persons holding public office to take communion in the Established Church within three months of taking up office, thus excluding Catholics and Protestant Dissenters (*see* 18 Apr. 1792 *and* 9 Apr. 1793).

Registration Act requires every Catholic priest in Ireland to register in court from 23 June and to furnish two securities of £50 each, to be of good behaviour, and not to leave the county for which registered (*see* 30 Aug. 1709).

12 Oct. Foundation stone laid for the Dublin City Workhouse (later known as the Foundling Hospital).

Pub. *A Tale of a Tub* and *The Battle of the Books* by Jonathan Swift.

1705

10 Feb. – 16 June Parliament in session.

14 Mar. English act permits direct export of Irish linen to British colonies.

Arthur Upton promotes petition of the Irish House of Commons to repeal the Test Act (*see* 4 Mar. 1704).

June English parliament declares illegal saying or hearing mass by anyone who has not taken the Oath of Abjuration.

Pub. *Prayers and Meditations* by Dr Cornelius Nary, P.P., St Michan's, Dublin, the first of his religious works for the use of parishioners.

Pub. *Essay on Linen Manufacture in Ireland* by Samuel-Louis Crommelin.

1706

d. Tadhg Ó Rodaighe, scholar.

23 May Battle of Ramillies in the War of the Spanish Succession: victory for Marlborough's Protestant force over Villeroy's mainly Catholic force; Lord Clare's Irish regiment captures Marlborough's colours.

'Cill Cais', anonymous poem written in the Irish language.

1707

1 May Act of Union between Scotland and England; Irish House of Lords expresses hope for such a union between Ireland and England (9 May 1709).

24 June Thomas Herbert, Earl of Pembroke, sworn in as L.L.

30 June Alan Brodrick appointed Attorney-General.

Robert Rochfort appointed Chief Baron of the Irish Exchequer (until Oct. 1714).

1 July – 30 Oct. Parliament in session.

24 Oct. Dublin Ballast Office established.

1708

25 Mar. Registry of Deeds opens.

25 Apr. Belfast Castle destroyed by fire in which three of the Earl of Donegall's sisters are burnt to death.

Christ Church Cathedral, Lisburn, completed.

Very poor harvest.

1709

21 Apr. Thomas, Earl of Wharton, sworn in as L.L.

5 May – 3 Aug. Parliament in session.

30 Aug. Registered priests required to take Oath of Abjuration, renouncing claims of the exiled Stuarts to the thrones of England and Ireland (act fails when only 33 of 1,089 registered clergy comply).

Sept. Sir Thomas Southwell brings (German) Palatines to settle in Ireland, mainly around Rathkeale, Co. Limerick.

Pub. *Essay towards a New Theory of Vision* by George Berkeley.

1710

Agrarian unrest in Connaught directed against the extension of pasture (*see* 11 Sept.).

19 May – 28 Aug. Parliament in session.

20 June Catholics of Co. Kerry complain about piracy to the L.L., who puts a barracks on Valentia Island.

28 Aug. Establishment of trustees for linen manufacture.

11 Sept. Houghing (maiming) of cattle, sheep and horses made a felony punishable by death.

15 Oct. d. Dr Richard Steevens (57), whose property eventually is used to build 'an hospital for maintaining and curing from time to time sick and wounded persons whose distempers and wounds are curable' (*see* 23 July 1733).

Dublin Mansion House built by Joshua Dawson and sold to Dublin Corporation for £3,500. (The Declaration of Independence (1919) and the Anglo-Irish truce (1921) are signed in its Round Room.)

Smithwick's, Ireland's oldest surviving brewery.

1711

22 Jan. Constantine Phipps appointed Lord Chancellor and sworn in as L.J.

15 Apr. State papers destroyed by fire in the Surveyor-General's office in Essex Street, Dublin.

3 July 2nd Duke of Ormond again sworn in as L.L.

9 July – 9 Nov. Parliament in session.

16 Aug. Opening of medical school, laboratory and anatomical theatre at T.C.D.

c. Oct. Wave of agrarian unrest associated with the 'Hougher' movement in west Galway.

10 Oct. Linen board appointed for the extension of linen manufacture meets.

30 Nov. Government proclamation prompted by Hougher activities reminds the public of the penalties for maiming cattle etc. (*see* 11 Sept. 1710).

13 Dec. Government proclamation notes that persons responsible for maiming cattle are levying money on occupants of houses, offers rewards and enjoins sheriffs and magistrates to search suspected houses for arms.

Church of Ireland Board of First-Fruits established.

1712

Jan. Houghers now active in Mayo; by Feb. they have spread to Sligo, Leitrim, Roscommon, Fermanagh and Clare, with several thousand cattle and sheep killed.

8 Feb. Proclamation offers reward of £100 for information leading to apprehension or discovery of Houghers.

20 Mar. Proclamation states that all priests in Galway, Mayo, Roscommon, Sligo, Leitrim, Clare and Fermanagh are to surrender to the authorities by 28 Mar., having neglected to acquaint their laity with the heinousness of the crime of houghing animals.

29 Mar. *Dublin Intelligence* notes the last recorded instance of cattle-houghing.

12 May Building starts on the library of T.C.D., designed by Thomas Burgh, costing £15,000.

20 Sept. Proclamation issued directed against unregistered non-juring Catholic priests.

13 Nov. d. Sir William Robinson, architect of the Royal Hospital, Kilmainham (1680–84), Marsh's Library and James and Charles Forts in Kinsale harbour.

Pub. *A Proposal for the Conversion of the Popish Natives of Ireland* by Rev. John Richardson, advocating Irish-speaking ministries in the Established Church.

Pub. Irish translation of the Book of Common Prayer.

1713

4 Feb. Proclamation offers pardon to anyone involved in the Hougher movement in Connaught (except for leaders) provided that they surrender before 31 Mar.

12 Feb. d. Florence MacMoyer, keeper of the Book of Armagh, which he pledged in 1680 for £5 to give evidence against Archbishop Oliver Plunkett in London (*see* 3 May 1681). (The book is not redeemed, and in 1707 comes into the possession of Arthur Brownlow, from whose descendants it is bought by Bishop William Reeves, who sells it for £200 to T.C.D.)

13 June Jonathan Swift installed as Dean of St Patrick's, Dublin.

27 Oct. Charles Talbot, Duke of Shrewsbury, sworn in as L.L.

2 Nov. d. Narcissus Marsh (75), C.I. Archbishop of Cashel (1691–94), Dublin (1694–1703) and Armagh since 1703; endowed the first public library in Ireland (*see* 1701).

25 Nov. – 24 Dec. Parliament in session.

1714

3 June Pilgrimage to Glendalough dispersed; crosses destroyed by militia.

5 June L.L. Shrewsbury leaves Ireland; succeeded by Earl of Sunderland (21 Sept. 1714 – 23 Aug. 1715), who does not come over.

1 Aug. d. Queen Anne (49); succeeded by Prince George Louis Guelph, Elector of Hanover, proclaimed King of England (George I).

30 Sept. Constantine Phipps removed from office of Lord Chancellor.

11 Oct. Alan Brodrick (created Lord Midleton on 13 Apr. 1715) appointed Lord Chancellor (resigns on 25 May 1725).

Regium donum suspended.

1715

23 Aug. L.L. Sunderland resigns; Earl of Galway and Duke of Grafton sworn in as L.J.s on 1 Nov.

6 Sept. Jacobite rebellion in Scotland.

11 Oct. Sir Robert Walpole appointed First Lord of the Treasury and Chancellor of the Exchequer in England (*see* 4 Apr. 1721).

12 Nov. Parliament opens; Speech from the Throne recommends 'such unanimity as might end all distinction, save that between Protestant and papist'; William Conolly elected Speaker of the House of Commons (until 12 Oct. 1729).

1716

20 June James Butler, 2nd Duke of Ormond, leading Jacobite, attainted for high treason (20 Aug. 1715), has his estates confiscated and his palatinate in Tipperary abolished.

d. Garrett Morphey, earliest known Irish portraitist, known for his painting of Archbishop Oliver Plunkett.

1717

13 Feb. Viscount Townshend appointed L.L., but does not come over; dismissed on 9 Apr.; Lord Midleton and Speaker Conolly sworn in as L.J.s on 20 Mar. (joined by Archbishop King on 20 July).

7 Aug. Charles Powlett, Duke of Bolton, sworn in as L.L.

3 Nov. Col. Henry Luttrell assassinated (shot dead while being conveyed by sedan chair to his home in Stafford Street, Dublin); suspected of having sold information contributing to the Jacobite defeat at Aughrim (12 July 1691); despite reward of £1,000 his killer(s) never apprehended.

1718

27 Feb. d. St George Ashe (60), C.I. Bishop of Derry, teacher (T.C.D.) and close friend of Jonathan Swift; reputed to have officiated at the alleged marriage of Swift and Stella (1716).

8 Apr. d. Roderic O'Flaherty (89), historian, author of *Ogygia* (*see* 1685).

1 June Edmund Byrne, R.C. Archbishop of Dublin, arrested by John Garzia, a noted 'priest-hunter' or 'priest-catcher' (*see* 13 Nov. 1719).

21 July d. John MacBride, Presbyterian writer, Moderator of the General Synod of Ulster (1697–98).

Charitable Infirmary founded at Cork Street, Dublin; the oldest voluntary hospital in Ireland (located at Jervis Street from 1786).

1719

10 Aug. House of Commons proposes that every unregistered priest or friar found in Ireland after 1 May 1720 be branded on the cheek (proposal does not succeed).

22 Aug. Irish Privy Council advises the British government that unless foreign priests are prevented from entering Ireland the country will 'never be quiet or well affected to the Crown'.

19 Sept. Rev. John Abernethy delivers his sermon 'Religious Obedience founded on Personal Persuasion' which inaugurates the Non-Subscription Presbyterian controversy.

20 Oct. Irish House of Lords protests against outcome of appeals in *Sherlock v. Annesley* case when British House of Lords reverses decision of the Irish House of Lords; leads to the Declaratory Act denying all appellate competence to the Irish House of Lords (*see* 7 Apr. 1720).

2 Nov. Toleration Act recognises the educational and religious liberties of Protestant Dissenters, exempting them from penalties which previously applied in common with Roman Catholics.

13 Nov. Trial of Archbishop Byrne (*see* 1 June 1718) ends in discharge when John Garzia fails to appear as witness.

Pub. first issue of *Dublin Evening Post* (runs until 1875).

1720

7 Apr. 'Act for the better securing the dependency of Ireland . . . upon the Crown of Great Britain' (6 George I, c. 5) or Declaratory Act (also known as the 'Sixth of George I') asserts the supremacy of the British parliament over the Irish; the British House of Lords becomes court of final appeal in all Irish litigation (repealed in 1782).

Cork Harbour Water Club (later Royal Cork Club) founded by Lord Inchiquin; the world's first yacht club.

Pub. *A Proposal for the Universal Use of Irish Manufactures* and *Proposal for National Bank of Ireland* by Jonathan Swift.

1721

4 Apr. Sir Robert Walpole becomes 'Prime Minister' (until 11 Feb. 1742).

24 June British act prohibits import to Ireland of East Indian goods except through Great Britain.

28 Aug. Charles Fitzroy, Duke of Grafton, sworn in as L.L.

19 Nov. d. George Walter Story, Dean of Limerick since 1705, historian of the Williamite war (*An Impartial History*, 1691; 2nd ed. with 'continuation', 1693).

1722

18 Jan. Act makes it a felony punishable by death to enlist in or recruit for a foreign power without a licence.

12 July Patent grants to William Wood, ironmaster, 'full, free, sole, and absolute power, privilege, licence, and authority' for fourteen years to coin copper halfpence and farthings for Ireland to the amount of £100,800 (patent originally granted to the Duchess of Kendal, mistress of George I, and sold by her to Wood; Treasury warrant signed by Sir Robert Walpole on 23 Aug.).

19 Sept. Irish Commissioners of Revenue call on the Lords Commissioners of His Majesty's Treasury 'to represent the ill effects of Mr Wood's patent' to the King (no reply received).

Work starts on Castletown House, Celbridge, Co. Kildare, owned by William Conolly, Speaker of the House of Commons.

Pub. first issue of *Dublin Mercury* (runs until 1775).

1723

10 May Walpole's bill for raising £100,000 by special tax on estates of Catholics extended to include non-jurors.

13 Sept. House of Commons seeks from L.L. copy of the patent to William Wood; L.L. replies that he has neither the patent nor any other papers relating to the issue (14th); Commons orders an examination of the matter for 16 Sept., on which day L.L. provides a copy of the patent.

20 Sept. House of Commons resolves itself into a committee 'to take into consideration the state of the nation, particularly in relation to the importing and uttering of copper halfpence and farthings in this kingdom'.

23 Sept. House of Commons resolves that Wood's patent is 'highly prejudicial to His Majesty's revenue and is destructive of trade and commerce, and most dangerous to the rights and properties of the subject'; address to this effect adopted on 27th; similar address voted by House of Lords on 28th.

1724

17 Jan. d. John Whalley (81), astrologer and almanac-maker.

Feb. Start of Jonathan Swift's campaign against Wood's halfpence with publication of the first Drapier Letter: *A Letter to the Shopkeepers, Tradesmen, Farmers, and Common People of Ireland, concerning the Brass Half-pence coined by Mr Wood* by M. B. Drapier.

27 Apr. Assayists (Sir Isaac Newton, Edward Southwell and Thomas Scroope) report that the coins issued by Wood are correct in both weight and quality.

13 July d. Thomas Lindsay, C.I. Archbishop of Armagh and Primate since 1714.

24 July Committee of inquiry of English Privy Council on Wood's halfpence recommends amount to be coined to be reduced from £100,800 to £40,000 (reported in Ireland by John Harding, Swift's publisher, on 1 Aug.).

4 Aug. Second of Swift's Drapier Letters: *A Letter to Mr Harding the Printer upon Occasion of a Paragraph in his Newspaper of August 1 relating to Mr Wood's Half-pence.*

25 Aug. Third of Swift's Drapier Letters: *Some Observations upon a Paper, call'd The Report of a Committee of the Most Honourable the Privy Council in England relating to Wood's Half-pence.*

31 Aug. Hugh Boulter appointed C.I. Archbishop of Armagh.

13 Oct. Swift's fourth Drapier Letter: *A Letter to the Whole People of Ireland.*

22 Oct. John, Lord Carteret, sworn in as L.L.

27 Oct. L.L. Carteret issues proclamation offering £300 reward for discovery of the author of 'this wicked and malicious pamphlet' (the fourth Drapier Letter).

11 Nov. Swift issues *Seasonable Advice to the Grand Jury concerning the Bill preparing against the Printer of the Drapier's Fourth Letter*; the bill against John Harding is thrown out.

14 Dec. Swift's fifth Drapier Letter: *A Letter to the Right Honourable the Lord Viscount Molesworth.*

Jonathan Swift writes *The Truth of Some Measures in State and Government Examined with reference to Ireland.*

Pub. *The Case of the Roman Catholics of Ireland* by Rev. Cornelius Nary.

Pub. *A Collection of the Most Celebrated Irish Tunes* by John and William Neale, containing 20 tunes by Turlough Carolan.

1725

5 Jan. Dominic Edward Murphy, R.C. Bishop of Kildare, translated to Dublin.

27 Mar. Pub. first issue of *Faulkner's Dublin Journal* (runs until 1825).

23 Oct. Dr Edward Synge, Chancellor of St Patrick's, preaches to the House of Commons, urging the principle of religious toleration and liberty of conscience.

3 Dec. House of Commons resolves 'that the most probable way to restrain popish priests and regulars from coming into the kingdom, would be to allow a competent number of secular priests to exercise their functions under such regulations as might be for the security of the civil state'.

George Berkeley, later C.I. Bishop of Cloyne, receives as legacy half the estate of Hester Vanhomrigh (Swift's 'Vanessa').

Pub. *A Discourse on Danish Forts* by Thomas Molyneux.

1726

1 Mar. Quaker school opened at Ballitore, Co. Kildare, by Abraham Shackleton.

5 Apr. d. Rev. Eoghan O'Keeffe (70), Gaelic poet.

21–25 June Non-Subscribing Presbyterians form the Presbytery of Antrim following expulsion from juridical communion with the General Synod.

d. Aodhagán Ó Rathaille (56), Gaelic poet.

Oct. Pub. *Gulliver's Travels* by Jonathan Swift.

1727

11 June d. George I (67); succeeded by his son George II.

14 July d. Samuel-Louis Crommelin, Huguenot refugee and founder of linen manufacture in Lisburn, Co. Antrim.

19 Nov. John, Lord Carteret, again sworn in as L.L.

Start of a series of bad harvests leads to famine lasting until 1730.

1728
27 Jan. d. Esther Johnson (c. 47), 'Stella', friend of Jonathan Swift.

6 May Catholics lose the franchise through an act for further regulating the election of M.P.s.

Act requires occupiers of 100 or more acres to put 5 per cent under the plough (largely unsuccessful).

14 Nov. Dublin Linen Hall opens near North King Street.

Act prevents Catholics from becoming solicitors.

Pub. *A Short View of the State of Ireland* by Jonathan Swift.

1729
3 Feb. Foundation stone laid for new parliament building in College Green (now Bank of Ireland), designed by Edward Lovett Pearce; work supervised by Pearce and Arthur Dobbs (*see* 27 Feb. 1792).

13 Feb. Jonathan Swift receives freedom of the city of Dublin.

26 Feb. Disturbances in Cork occasioned by potato failure.

8 May d. William King (79), C.I. Archbishop of Dublin since 1703; encouraged teaching of Irish in T.C.D. and supported Swift in the agitation against Wood's halfpence.

12 Oct. William Conolly resigns as Speaker of the House of Commons; Sir Ralph Gore elected Speaker on the following day.

30 Oct. d. William Conolly, former Speaker of the House of Commons; at funeral the wearing of linen scarves (to encourage the trade) was first observed.

Pub. *A Modest Proposal* by Jonathan Swift.

1730
7 Sept. Rev. Samuel Madden submits scheme to T.C.D. for encouragement of learning through establishment of premium, towards which he contributes £600.

22 Oct. Robert Jocelyn appointed Attorney-General.

Permission to export coarse Irish linen to the colonies renewed (*see* 14 Mar. 1705), in return for which British linens are allowed into Ireland without duty.

1731
7 May Removal of prohibition on imports from America.

25 June 'Dublin Society for Improving Husbandry, Manufactures and Other Useful Arts' founded by Thomas Prior and Thomas Molyneux in the rooms of the Philosophical Society, T.C.D. (*see* Jan. 1684); 'and Sciences' added to their aims a week later (prefix 'Royal' received in June 1820 when George IV becomes patron).

11 Sept. Lionel Cranfield Sackville, Duke of Dorset, sworn in as L.L.

5 Oct. First meeting of parliament in the new Parliament House in College Green.

Construction starts on the Newry Canal.

1732
Pub. *A Proposal for the General Encouragement of Learning at Dublin College* by Dr Samuel Madden.

Pub. *An Examination of Certain Abuses, Corruptions, and Enormities in the City of Dublin* by Jonathan Swift.

Pub. *English–Irish Dictionary* by Aodh Buidhe Mac Cruitín and Fr Conor Begley (Paris).

1733

Feb. d. Séamus Dall Mac Cuarta, Gaelic poet.

17 May Act prohibits direct importation to Ireland of sugar, molasses, or rum (other than British rum).

23 July Eight men and two women are admitted as the first patients to Dr Steevens' Hospital.

4 Oct. Henry Boyle (later Earl of Shannon) succeeds the late Sir Ralph Gore as Speaker of the House of Commons (until 1756).

24 Oct. Incorporated Society for Promoting English Protestant Schools established by charter (the schools, known as 'Charter Schools', are widely viewed among Catholics as proseletysing agencies).

16 Nov. d. Sir Edward Lovett Pearce, architect who designed the Parliament House (now Bank of Ireland) in College Green, Dublin.

Dublin Society's Gardens opened at Summerhill, Dublin; Society later sponsors the Botanic Gardens at Glasnevin (1795).

Pub. *A Serious and Useful Scheme to Make an Hospital for Incurables* by Jonathan Swift.

1734

29 Apr. Converts from the Catholic Church whose wives are Catholic are prohibited from educating their children as Catholics or from acting as magistrates.

c. 10 May Mob of weavers from the Dublin Liberties riot in protest at Dublin shops selling goods of English manufacture.

19 May George Berkeley consecrated C.I. Bishop of Cloyne.

17 Aug. Ten-bed hospital opened by Mary Mercer in Dublin.

1735

3 May Jonathan Swift signs his will settling his 'whole fortune in the city in trust for building and maintaining an hospital for idiots and lunatics' (*see* 9 Apr. 1748).

'Hell-Fire Club' founded at the Eagle Tavern, Cork Hill, Dublin by the Earl of Rosse, Col. Jack St Leger and James Worsdale.

Pub. *The Querist* by George Berkeley; continues in 1736 and 1737.

1736

18 Mar. Resolution by House of Commons against attempts by C.I. clergy to collect the tithe of agistment (tithe on pasturage for dry and barren cattle); from now on this tithe is not paid.

6 Apr. British House of Lords rejects motion for repeal of the Test Act.

24 Apr. Dublin merchants petition government against lowering the value of gold.

25 May L.L. Dorset takes to London an application for lowering the value of gold and raising the value of foreign silver (*see* Aug.–Sept. 1737).

Aug. – Sept. Anti-Irish riots in London.

Pub. 'The Legion Club', satirical poem by Jonathan Swift, denouncing bills for commuting the tithe due to the C.I. clergy.

Pub. first issue of *Dublin Daily Advertiser*; first daily newspaper in Ireland.

1737

12 Apr. Margaret ('Peg') Woffington plays Ophelia, her first serious acting role, at Smock Alley Theatre, Dublin.

Aug. – Sept. Currency revalued: value of guinea reduced from 23s to £1 2s 9d.

1 Sept. First issue of the *Belfast News-Letter and General Advertiser*, published by Francis Joy; Ireland's oldest surviving newspaper and one of the oldest provincial newspapers in the world.

7 Sept. William Cavendish, Duke of Devonshire, sworn in as L.L.

1738

3 Mar. d. Rev. Cornelius Nary, P.P., St Michan's, Dublin (from 1703); writer and religious controversialist.

23 Mar. Act makes Presbyterian marriages legal provided that persons marrying and the officiating minister take oaths as required under Toleration Act of 1719.

25 Mar. d. Turlough Carolan (68), musician, last of the traditional Irish bards, at Kilronan, Co. Roscommon.

1739

26 Feb. 'Address of the Roman Catholics of Ireland' thanks the King for such toleration as they have and professes loyalty.

7 Sept. Robert Jocelyn appointed Lord Chancellor (created Baron Newport on 29 Nov. 1743).

winter 1739–40 Unprecedented frost causes famine which lasts until 1741 and kills an estimated 400,000 (about one-eighth of the population).

1740

18 Feb. House of Commons describes attempts by former owners of Irish land to recover their forfeited lands through the courts as 'highly prejudicial to the Protestant interest of this kingdom'.

31 Mar. Act directs that new roads should run in direct lines between towns.

1 May Duties removed from Irish woollen and worsted yarn, excluding worsted yarn of two or more threads twisted, thrown or 'cruel'.

May – June Bread riots in Dublin.

3 Aug. George Stone consecrated C.I. Bishop of Ferns and Leighlin (*see* 19 Mar. 1743).

Nov. – Dec. Severe frost.

1741

Continuation of the famine accompanied by outbreaks of fever and disease.

23 July d. Edward Synge, C.I. Archbishop of Tuam since 1716 (he was the son and the nephew of bishops and had two sons who were later bishops).

2 Oct. The Charitable Musical Society opens the New Music Hall in Fishamble Street, Dublin; popularly known as Neale's Music Hall, it remains for long the biggest public hall in Dublin (*see* 13 Apr. 1742).

Completion of Ireland's first major canal from Newry to Lough Neagh (its stone lock designed by Richard Cassels).

1742

11 Feb. P.M. Walpole, his ministry defeated, resigns; succeeded by Spencer Compton, Earl of Wilmington (*see* 2 July 1743).

13 Apr. George Frideric Handel, in Dublin since 18 Nov. 1741, conducts the first performance of his *Messiah*, with the choirs of St Patrick's and Christ Church, Dublin, at the New Music Hall in Fishamble Street; proceeds of £400 go to the relief of

[KILKE]NNY COUNTY LIBRARY

prisoners, Mercer's Hospital and the Charitable Infirmary.

27 Sept. d. Hugh Boulter, C.I. Archbishop of Armagh and Primate since 1724.

Pub. *An Teagasg Críosduidhe*, a bilingual catechism of Christian doctrine by Dr Andrew Donlevy (Paris).

1743
19 Mar. George Stone, C.I. Bishop of Ferns and Leighlin, translated to Kildare (*see* 11 May 1745).

2 July d. P.M. the Earl of Wilmington (70); succeeded by Henry Pelham, who heads a Tory–Whig coalition until 6 Mar. 1754.

1744
Feb. – Mar. Reports of an intended French invasion of England or Ireland provokes strong anti-Catholic measures (England and France at war from 4 Mar.).

Magistrates are instructed 'strictly to put in execution' all penal laws relating to ecclesiastics and firearms; clergy are arrested and places of worship closed down: those suspected of Jacobite sympathy among the laity are persecuted.

23 May Royal Hospital for Incurables opened in Donnybrook.

Potato crop rots in the north.

1745
15 Mar. Dr Bartholomew Mosse opens lying-in hospital in George's Lane, Dublin (*see* 9 July 1751).

30 Apr. Battle of Fontenoy: Irish Brigade assists French army in defeat of British army.

11 May George Stone, C.I. Bishop of Kildare, translated to Derry (*see* 13 Mar. 1747).

25 July Prince Charles Edward Stuart arrives in Scotland to lead Jacobite rising; some Irishmen among his followers.

31 Aug. Philip Dormer Stanhope, Earl of Chesterfield, sworn in as L.L.

17 Oct. d. David Digues La Touche, Huguenot founder of the La Touche banking business in Dublin.

19 Oct. d. Jonathan Swift (*see* 19 Sept. 1757).

Building starts on Kildare House, later Leinster House, home of the Duke of Leinster; designed by Richard Cassels.

1746
19 Mar. Act prohibits Irish glass exports and imports except from Britain.

11 Apr. Act annuls future marriages between a Protestant and a Catholic or between two Protestants if performed by a Catholic priest.

16 Apr. Collapse of the Jacobite cause with the defeat of Prince Charles at Culloden by Duke of Cumberland.

25 Apr. L.L. Chesterfield recalled; government of Ireland controlled by L.J.s Archbishop Hoadly, Lord Chancellor Newport and Speaker Boyle.

1747
19–21 Jan. 'Kelly riots' at Smock Alley Theatre in Dublin destroy most of the theatre when proprietor Thomas Sheridan assaults a Galway rake named Kelly for frightening actresses during a performance.

13 Mar. George Stone, C.I. Bishop of Derry, appointed Archbishop of Armagh and Primate of All Ireland; enthroned on 26 Sept. 1752.

10 Apr. Archbishop Stone appointed a member of the Privy Council and L.J. in succession to Hoadly (d. 16 July 1746); takes seat in House of Lords on 6 Oct.

9–24 Aug. John Wesley's first visit to Ireland; between 1747 and 1789 visits the country on a total of 43 occasions, spending a total of 6½ years in it (*see* 14 Aug. 1752).

9 Sept. d. Rev. John Richardson, C.I. clergyman who advocated Irish-speaking ministries in the Established Church.

13 Sept. William Stanhope, Earl of Harrington, sworn in as L.L.

29 Nov. John O'Brien appointed R.C. Bishop of Cloyne and Ross (d. 1769); author of *Focalóir Gaoidhilge–Sax-Bearla, or An Irish–English Dictionary* (Paris 1768).

Pub. *Citizen's Journal*, weekly paper edited by Charles Lucas.

1748

7 Feb. d. Rev. David Malcolme, Presbyterian preacher and antiquary; author of *An Essay on the Antiquities of Great Britain and Ireland* (anon., 1738).

9 Apr. Governors of Dr Steevens' Hospital agree to lease a site upon which to build Swift's hospital for 'idiots and lunatics' (*see* 19 Sept. 1757).

'Newtown Act' makes residence of burgesses and freemen unnecessary, clearing way for creation of large numbers of honorary freemen who use their influence to guide elections.

1749

16 Oct. Charles Lucas, editor of the *Censor*, condemned by the House of Commons, which seeks his commital to Newgate; Lucas flees the country.

Building starts on Swift's hospital, St Patrick's; architect George Semple (*see* 19 Sept. 1757).

1750

29 Aug. d. Laetitia Pilkington (38), whose *Memoirs* (1748) provides the chief source concerning Swift's last days.

1751

9 July First stone laid for Dr Bartholomew Mosse's lying-in hospital (known as the Rotunda from 1767), built with grants from parliament; designed by Richard Cassels (*see* 8 Dec. 1757).

19 Sept. Duke of Dorset again sworn in as L.L.

21 Oct. d. Thomas Prior (69), co-founder of the Dublin Society.

19 Dec. Act authorising use of surplus revenue for reduction of the national debt, provokes long-running dispute between British and Irish parliaments over appropriation of revenue surplus (*see* 17 Dec. 1753).

1752

16 Apr. First regular stage-coach, Dublin to Belfast; drawn by six horses, it covers the 100-mile journey in three days (mail first carried on contract basis on 15 Aug. 1789).

14 Aug. John Wesley's first Irish conference held in Limerick.

2 Sept. Gregorian or New Style calendar (introduced by Pope Gregory XIII in 1582) legally replaces the Julian or Old Style calendar in Ireland and Britain; the day following becomes 14 Sept.

First steeplechase, ridden by Edward Blake and Mr O'Callaghan 'from the church of Buttevant to the spire of the St Leger Church' (Doneraile Co. Cork), some 4½ miles distant.

Building starts on the west front (main entrance) of Trinity College, Dublin; architects Henry Keene and John Sanderson (completed in 1759).

1753

14 Jan. d. George Berkeley (68), philosopher, C.I. Bishop of Cloyne since 1734.

2 Mar. Meath Hospital opens in a house in the Coombe, Dublin.

Nov. Arthur Nevil Jones, M.P., the Surveyor-General, held responsible for building defective military barracks, is expelled from the House of Commons.

17 Dec. Surplus revenue dispute continues; bill for appropriation of surplus Irish revenue to the Crown defeated by 122 votes to 117.

1754

2 Mar. Riots at Smock Alley Theatre when proprietor Thomas Sheridan attempts to censor Voltaire's *Mahomet the Imposter,* which contains implied criticism of political corruption by L.L. Dorset; ruins Sheridan's career in Ireland (he leaves on 15 Sept.).

6 Mar. d. P.M. Henry Pelham; succeeded by his brother, Thomas, Duke of Newcastle, on 16th.

d. Seán Clárach Mac Domhnaill, Gaelic poet.

1755

5 May William Cavendish, Marquis of Hartington, sworn in as L.L. (succeeds as Duke of Devonshire on 5 Dec.); leaves Ireland in May 1756.

1756

26 Apr. John Ponsonby elected Speaker of the House of Commons (on resignation of Henry Boyle, who is created Earl of Shannon and is granted a £2,000 pension).

22 July Bread riots break out in Belfast and continue sporadically into the next month.

26 Oct. P.M. the Duke of Newcastle resigns; succeeded by Duke of Devonshire (L.L.).

Work starts on the Grand Canal linking Dublin with the River Barrow (completed in 1791) and with the Shannon (completed in 1805).

1757

19 Sept. Opening of St Patrick's Hospital, built with bequest from Jonathan Swift, to care for mentally ill.

25 Sept. John Russell, Duke of Bedford, sworn in as L.L.

8 Dec. First patients (52) admitted to Dr Bartholomew Mosse's 'Hospital for Poor Lying-in Women' (known as the Rotunda from 1767).

Government makes additional £20,000 available for relief of poverty.

1758

29 Apr. Act empowers 'Wide Streets Commissioners' to supervise making street from Essex Street Bridge to Dublin Castle (commission survives until 1840 when its functions are taken over by Dublin Corporation).

10 May Archbishop Stone, the Earl of Shannon and Speaker Ponsonby sworn in as L.J.s.

20 June British act permits export from Ireland of salted meats and butter.

20 Sept. d. Charles Tottenham (73), origin of the patriot toast 'Tottenham in his boots'.

John Bowes, Lord Chancellor, declares during the Saul case that the law does not presume a Catholic to exist except for the purposes of punishment.

1759

16 Feb. d. Dr Bartholomew Mosse (47), founder of the Rotunda Maternity Hospital, Dublin (*see* 9 July 1751 *and* 8 Dec. 1757).

5 Apr. Cattle acts suspended and British market opened to Irish cattle and beef; leads to levelling of villages and enclosure of commons for pasture, and to the rise of the Whiteboy movement (*see* Oct. 1761).

3 Dec. Rumours of a legislative union with Britain lead to rioting.

31 Dec. Arthur Guinness leases brewery at St James's Gate, Dublin.

Responsibility for roads vested in Grand Juries.

1760

21–25 Feb. François Thurot enters Belfast Lough with three ships and 700 men and occupies Carrickfergus before retiring; Thurot killed in action off the Isle of Man when his ships are captured on 28th.

28 Mar. d. Margaret ('Peg') Woffington (c. 46), noted actress and celebrated beauty.

c. 31 Mar. Catholic Committee founded by Dr John Curry, Charles O'Conor and Thomas Wyse at a meeting at The Elephant, Essex Street, Dublin.

17 May Act abolishes statutory obligation of local inhabitants to give six days' unpaid annual service on roads.

27 Aug. Philip Tisdall appointed Attorney-General.

25 Oct. d. George II (77); succeeded by his grandson George III.

17 Nov. Henry Mossop reopens Smock Alley Theatre as a rival to Crow Street Theatre, managed by Spranger Barry (*see* 7 Dec. 1767).

d. Mícheál Coimín (72), Gaelic poet, whose 'Laoi Oisín' (1750) is believed to have inspired Macpherson's Ossianic poems (1760).

1761

Oct. First appearance of 'Whiteboys' in Counties Tipperary, Cork, Limerick and Waterford, directed against tithes and other grievances.

6 Oct. George Montague-Dunk, Earl of Halifax, sworn in as L.L.

22 Oct. Parliament opens; M.P.s include the 'patriot group' led by Charles Lucas, Henry Flood and Sir Lucius O'Brien.

19 Dec. Performance of Scolari's *La Cascina* at Smock Alley Theatre marks first appearance of Italian opera in Ireland.

1762

Feb. Catholic gentry offer services to the King.

Apr. Several Ulster-recruited regiments move into Munster areas marked by Whiteboy activity, to reinforce the local garrisons and strengthen the execution of magisterial authority.

30 Apr. Act gives converts from the Catholic religion immunity from prosecution for failure to observe requirements of conformity.

26 May P.M. the Duke of Newcastle resigns; succeeded by the Earl of Bute.

21 June Work starts on the Poolbeg lighthouse (completed in 1768).

1763

Rise of peasant agitation in Ulster led by 'Hearts of Oak' or 'Oakboys' or 'Greenboys'.

16 Apr. George Grenville appointed P.M.

10 Sept. Pub. first issue of the *Freeman's Journal* (runs until 1924).

22 Sept. Hugh Percy, Duke of Northumberland, sworn in as L.L.

Irish national debt stands at £650,000.

1764

12 May Act provides magistrates and police officers with indemnification for action taken while suppressing riots.

27 Sept. d. Henry Boyle (82), Earl of Shannon, Speaker of the House of Commons from 1733 to 1756.

19 Dec. d. George Stone (56), C.I. Archbishop of Armagh since 1747.

Building starts on Rotunda concert hall.

1765

Severe drought continues through most of the year.

22 Mar. British Stamp Act imposes duties on American colonists (repealed on 18 Mar. 1766).

July Marquis of Rockingham forms coalition ministry in Britain.

19 Oct. Francis Seymour-Conway, Earl of Hertford, sworn in as L.L.

31 Dec. d. Samuel ('Premium') Madden (79), co-founder of the Dublin Society (*see* 7 Sept. 1730).

1766

15 Mar. Fr Nicholas Sheehy hanged at Clonmel; his trial in Dublin on charges of 'high treason and rebellion' collapsed when a key witness failed to appear, and he was tried again before a packed jury in Tipperary (*see* 6 Sept. 1770).

16 Mar. James FitzGerald, Earl of Offaly and Marquis of Kildare (since 3 Mar. 1761), created Duke of Leinster, the only Irish duke.

18 Mar. Declaratory Act asserts the right of British parliament to legislate for American colonies.

27 Mar. Pub. *The Vicar of Wakefield* by Oliver Goldsmith.

7 June Tumultuous Risings Act passed to deal with Whiteboys.

Historian Thomas Leland purchases the manuscript which becomes known as the *Annals of Loch Cé* and presents it to T.C.D.

Hibernian Society set up to establish Hibernian Academy, with schools of English, Classics, French and Mathematics.

Pub. first issue of the *Limerick Chronicle*, founded by John Ferrar; oldest surviving newspaper in the Republic of Ireland (*see* 1 Sept. 1737).

1767

14 Oct. George, Viscount Townshend, sworn in as L.L.; the first fully resident viceroy, he breaks the power of the L.J.s (who governed in absence of L.L.).

20 Oct. Parliamentary session opens.

7 Dec. Henry Mossop opens as Richard III in Crow Street Theatre, which he now owns along with Smock Alley Theatre (resigns Crow Street in 1770).

1768

9 Jan. James Hewitt appointed Lord Chancellor; created Baron Lifford.

16 Feb. Octennial Act limits life of parliament to eight years (previously limited by life of a monarch).

18 Feb. Frederick Augustus Hervey, C.I. Bishop of Cloyne since Feb. 1767, translated to Derry (succeeds as 4th Earl of Bristol on 23 Sept. 1779).

28 May Parliament dissolved in accordance with Octennial Act (16 Feb.).

14 Oct. Earl of Chatham resigns as P.M. and is succeeded by the Duke of Grafton.

16 Oct. Pub. first letter in collection *Baratariana* directed against L.L. Townshend.

1769

c. 3 Apr. d. Peadar Ó Doirnín (87), Gaelic poet.

July Further outbreak of agitation by 'Hearts of Steel' or 'Steelboys', peasant Presbyterian movement in Counties Antrim and Down.

17 Oct. Parliament opens.

21 Nov. House of Commons rejects the Supply Bill because it does not originate in the House.

26 Dec. Protesting against rejection of the Supply Bill, L.L. Townshend rebukes the House of Commons and prorogues parliament (until 26 Feb. 1771).

1770
28 Jan. Lord North appointed P.M.

23 May Pub. *The Deserted Village* by Oliver Goldsmith (goes into five editions immediately).

6 Sept. After performing an execution, the hangman (who had hanged Fr Nicholas Sheehy on 15 Mar. 1766) is stoned to death by a mob at Philipstown, King's County.

Potato crop fouled by curl.

23–24 Dec. Some 1,200 farmers calling themselves 'Hearts of Steel', protesting at evictions in Templepatrick, march from Templepatrick meeting-house to Belfast barracks to release David Douglas (held on charge of maiming cattle); five killed and nine wounded when military fire; agitation continues during 1771–72.

Trinity College Historical Society founded.

£40 p.a. pension offered to any 'popish priest duly converted to the Protestant religion'.

1771
25 Jan. L.L. Townshend issues proclamation condemning the agitation which led to rioting in Belfast on 23–24 Dec. 1770.

24 Feb. Government defeats the parliamentary opposition led by the Ponsonbys (132–107).

26 Feb. John Ponsonby, Speaker of the House of Commons, resigns office after refusing to present the customary address to the King; Edmund Sexton Pery elected in his place on 7 Mar.; riots ensue, quelled by military.

1 Aug. First stone laid for Clifton House (Belfast Poorhouse), designed by Robert Joy (opens in Dec. 1774).

10 Oct. Benjamin Franklin, in Ireland since 5 Sept., visits the House of Commons.

4 Nov. d. Charles Lucas (58), politician, one of the earliest campaigners against abuses in sale of drugs (1735).

Army Augmentation Act requires that not less than 12,000 soldiers supported by the Irish revenue should be permanently stationed in Ireland (amendment of 1775 reduces figure to 8,000 to allow 4,000 to be made available for fighting in the American War of Independence).

Pub. first issue of the *Hibernian Magazine* (runs until 1812).

1772
19 Feb. Edmund Sexton Pery, Speaker of the House of Commons, uses casting vote to favour motion censuring increase in the number of Irish Commissioners of Revenue.

6 Mar. 'Battle of Gilford': driven from his home by Oakboys, Richard Johnston of Gilford secures military assistance and arrests three of his attackers.

28 Mar. Act introduced to suppress Steelboy agitation in Ulster.

2 June 'Bogland Act' enables Catholics to secure leases for up to 61 years of holdings under 50 acres of reclaimable bog.

Woodward Act permits Grand Juries to establish 'houses of industry' for infirm and able-bodied beggars (leads to the Dublin House of Industry, opened on 8 Nov. 1773).

30 Nov. Simon, Earl Harcourt, sworn in as L.L.

1773

4 May Art O'Leary killed in an encounter with soldiers near Millstreet, Co. Cork, after refusing to sell his horse for £5 to Abraham Morris, a Protestant; inquest on 4 Sept. acquits Morris of the charge of murdering O'Leary, whose death is the subject of a lament by his wife, Eibhlín Dhubh Ní Chonaill ('Caoineadh Airt Uí Laoghaire').

16 June First stone laid for King's Hospital in Black Hall Place, Dublin (Blue Coat Hospital); designed by Thomas Ivory.

18 Nov. d. Henry Mossop (45), actor-manager, one-time owner of both Smock Alley and Crow Street Theatres.

19 Nov. d. James FitzGerald (51), 1st Duke of Leinster; succeeded by his son William Robert (d. 20 Oct. 1804).

26 Nov. House of Commons rejects resolution promoted by Henry Flood and others of the 'patriot party', for a tax of 2s in the £ on absentee landowners of more than six months' annual non-residence.

16 Dec. 'Boston Tea-Party': American colonists protest against duty on tea by boarding three ships in Boston harbour and dumping the cargo of tea into the water (*see* 19 Apr. 1775).

Pub. *History of Ireland from the Invasion of Henry II* by Thomas Leland (3 vols).

Penny post established in Dublin.

1774

4 Apr. d. Oliver Goldsmith (46), author and poet.

2 June Act enables Catholics to testify allegiance to the monarch.

Act establishes 'paving board' for paving, cleaning, lighting and improving the streets.

22 June 'Quebec Act' establishes permanent government for Canada and provides for religious toleration for Catholics.

George Faulkner, printer, completes his *Ancient Universal History* (7 vols), one of the great printing achievements of the time.

Estate duty imposed in Ireland for the first time.

Pub. *Ierne Defended* and *General History of Ireland* by Sylvester O'Halloran.

1775

Whiteboy activity in Counties Kildare, Kilkenny and Queen's County.

19 Apr. American War of Independence starts at Lexington.

30 Aug. d. George Faulkner (76), printer and owner of the *Dublin Journal*.

31 Aug. d. Seán ('An Ghrinn') Ó Tuama (67), Gaelic poet.

28 Sept. Owen Carroll and John Duggan, leading Whiteboys, executed at Newtownbarry, Co. Wexford.

24 Oct. In an address to the King some 3,000 freemen of Dublin urge a conciliatory policy towards the American colonists.

27 Oct. Henry Flood abandons opposition by accepting government office as Vice-Treasurer (£3,500 p.a.); his role as opposition leader is assumed by Henry Grattan, who enters the House on 11 Dec. (maiden speech on 15 Dec.) and describes Flood as having 'a metaphor in his mouth and bribe in his pocket'.

23 Nov. Chief Secretary to the L.L. requests removal of 4,000 troops from Ireland for use in America; House of Commons reluctantly accedes on 28th (*see* 1771).

1776

3 Feb. British Treasury prohibits exports of Irish beef, butter, pork and other provisions to all places except Britain and colonies still under British control (remains in force for three years with disastrous effect on the Irish economy).

4 Apr. Anti-Whiteboy Act (made perpetual in 1800).

5 Apr. Parliament dissolved.

20 June Arthur Young commences his tour of Ireland.

4 July Second Continental Congress in Philadelphia approves the Declaration of Independence drafted by Thomas Jefferson.

Pub. *Hibernian Atlas* by Bernard Scalé.

1777

10 Jan. d. Spranger Barry (58), actor-manager of Crow Street Theatre, Dublin.

25 Jan. John Hobart, Earl of Buckinghamshire, sworn in as L.L.

1 Nov. John Scott (later Earl of Clonmell) appointed Attorney-General (*see* 4 May 1782).

25 Dec. Opening of school and convent to cater for the female poor in Cork, founded by Nano Nagle of the Order of the Presentation of the Blessed Virgin Mary (*see* 9 Apr. 1805).

Arthur Young becomes land agent to Lord Kingsborough in Co. Cork.

Cotton-spinning introduced into Belfast (employing over 60,000 within a century) (*see* 19 May 1779).

1778

7 Feb. Henry Grattan defeated (143–66) when he moves parliamentary address to the Crown stating that the condition of Ireland is no longer endurable.

17 Mar. Volunteer companies started in Belfast, with Lord Charlemont as commander of Northern Volunteers and the Duke of Leinster commanding in Leinster.

13 Apr. John Paul Jones, American privateer, having raided the coasts of Scotland and England, sails the *Ranger* into Belfast Lough and captures H.M.S. *Drake*; L.L. Buckinghamshire makes it clear that Belfast will have to defend itself.

16 Apr. As a result of the incursion into Belfast Lough by John Paul Jones, Volunteer movement is expanded in Belfast at meeting in the Donegall Arms; this example followed elsewhere; by Dec. Volunteers number some 40,000.

28 May British act provides that commodities can be exported from Ireland to British colonies provided that Irish parliament imposes same export duties as are payable by British importers.

14 Aug. Luke Gardiner's Catholic Relief Act enables Catholics to take leases for 999 years and to inherit land on the same terms as other religious denominations (*see* 4 May 1782).

1779

8 Jan. Rev. Robert Fowler, C.I. Bishop of Killaloe and Kilfenora, translated to Dublin.

17 Mar. First St Patrick's Day Parade in New York, includes parade by the

COUNTY LIBRARY

Volunteers of Ireland under their colonel, Lord Rawdon.

28 Mar. Rev. William Steel Dickson advocates enrolment of Catholics in the Volunteers.

26 Apr. Meeting of Dublin citizens at the Tholsel resolves that 'We will not directly or indirectly import or use any wares, the produce or manufacture of Great Britain which can be produced or manufactured in this kingdom.'

19 May Belfast Charitable Society decides to establish a cotton manufacturing business in the poorhouse (*see* 1777).

July L.L. Buckinghamshire authorises release of light arms for use by Volunteers.

13 Oct. Thomas Conolly and Duke of Leinster successfully carry motion of thanks to the Volunteers to accompany traditional vote of thanks to the viceroy in parliament.

14 Oct. Duke of Leinster leads Volunteer Corps in lining the streets of Dublin from College Green to the Castle when the Speaker carries the amended address.

4 Nov. Volunteers parade the streets of Dublin; in College Green King William's statue bedecked with 'A free trade – or else', 'Relief to Ireland' and 'The Glorious Revolution'.

24 Nov. Henry Grattan carries resolution 'that at this time it would be inexpedient to grant new taxes'.

1 Dec. Lord Shelburne defeated when he calls for vote of censure on the British administration for its neglect of Ireland.

Proposals to lift restrictions on export of wool, woollen goods and glass from Ireland announced in the British House of Commons.

Pub. (anon.) *The Commercial Restraints of Ireland* by John Hely Hutchinson.

1780

24 Feb. Act of British parliament grants Ireland the right to trade freely with the colonies, freedom to export wool and linen, a part in trade with the Levant, and restoration of bounty on coarse linen sent into England.

Act of British parliament allows import of English gold and silver, and also foreign (as opposed to English) hops. Sole remaining trade barrier is exclusion from the East India Company's market.

23 Mar. Belfast Volunteers instruct Belfast M.P.s to work for 'the privilege of being bound only by laws enacted by the King and parliament of Ireland'.

19 Apr. Henry Grattan introduces declaration of rights of the Irish parliament (indefinitely postponed after marathon debate).

2 May Act abolishes sacramental test, rendering Protestant Dissenters eligible for office.

2–9 June Gordon riots in London; attacks on Catholics.

11 July Earl of Charlemont and Henry Grattan present at review of Volunteer corps.

12 July Volunteers fight mock battle involving some 3,000 men in arms before a reported 30,000 spectators.

19 Aug. Revenue act prescribing minimum revenue for stills leads to expansion of illicit distillation.

Perpetual Mutiny Act places government of the army beyond the power of parliament.

16 Dec. John Beresford appointed First Commissioner of the Revenue.

23 Dec. Frederick Howard, Earl of Carlisle, sworn in as L.L.

Pub. *A Tour in Ireland* by Arthur Young (2 vols).

Brian Merriman writes *Cúirt an Mheáin Oíche* ('The Midnight Court'; pub. 1800).

1781

26 Apr. Architect James Gandon arrives in Dublin to build the Custom House, amid great opposition; first stone laid on 8 Aug. (opens on 7 Nov. 1791, having cost almost £400,000).

20–22 July Volunteer manoeuvres in Belfast, attended by some 230,000 spectators.

19 Oct. Lord Cornwallis surrenders at Yorktown, marking the virtual end of the American War of Independence, freeing large numbers of troops for service in Ireland, if required.

7 Dec. Henry Grattan attacks the disbursement of pensions among the Irish nobility.

18 Dec. Motion for introduction of Barry Yelverton's bill for repeal of Poynings' Law carried unanimously.

28 Dec. Meeting of Volunteers in Armagh, presided over by Lord Charlemont, deplores the lack of attention paid to constitutional rights, demands the elimination of corruption and court influence in the legislature, and calls for a convention to be held in Dungannon on 15 Feb. 1782 to seek legislative independence.

Number of Volunteers now around 80,000.

1782

5 Feb. Speaking in favour of the Catholic Relief Bill, John Hely Hutchinson urges payment of Catholic clergy and recommends establishment of an institution for their education.

12 Feb. Bradstreet's Act clarifies the right of *habeas corpus*.

15 Feb. 242 delegates from 148 corps attend Volunteer convention at Dungannon; resolve that 'the claims of any other than the King, Lords and Commons of Ireland to make laws to bind this kingdom is unconstitutional'; only two oppose Henry Grattan's resolution expressing approval of the relaxation of the penal laws.

22 Feb. Grattan asserts that there is no legal basis for legislative supremacy of the British over the Irish parliament; his motion for repeal of Declaratory Act of 1720 defeated.

1 Mar. Corps of Dublin Volunteers, presided over by the Duke of Leinster, resolves 'that we will not obey or give operation to any laws, save only those enacted by the King, Lords, and Commons of Ireland'.

20 Mar. Lord North's ministry resigns.

27 Mar. Marquis of Rockingham appointed P.M. and forms a Whig administration, including Charles James Fox and Lord Shelburne (who succeeds Rockingham as P.M. on 14 July).

14 Apr. William Bentinck, Duke of Portland, sworn in as L.L.

4 May Gardiner's Second Catholic Relief Act permits Catholics to purchase and bequeath freehold land on the same terms as Protestants (except in parliamentary boroughs) (*see* 27 July).

Attorney-General John Scott dismissed from office for claiming that Great Britain has no right to bind Ireland by acts of parliament (*see* 10 May 1784).

Parliament establishes the Bank of Ireland, which acts as government banker and performs many of the functions of a central bank (opens on 25 June 1783).

17 May Charles James Fox in the British House of Commons and Lord Shelburne in the Lords secure leave for repeal of the Declaratory Act (*see* 21 June).

27 May L.L. Portland informs parliament that the King is giving his unconditional assent 'to acts to prevent the suppression of bills in the Privy Council of this kingdom, and the alteration of them anywhere'; also will limit the Mutiny Act to two years' duration; these measures erroneously perceived by many as conceding legislative independence to the Irish parliament (does not occur until 1783); Grattan moves address of gratitude to the King.

31 May House of Commons votes £50,000 to purchase lands to be settled on Grattan.

21 June Repeal of the Declaratory Act of 1720 on initiative of Charles James Fox and Lord Shelburne.

27 July Gardiner's Third Relief Act permits Catholics to become schoolmasters and private tutors, own horses with a value of more than £5, and acquire freehold land.

Yelverton's Act amends Poynings' Law: any bill passed by both Houses of the Irish parliament will be transmitted by the L.L. under the Great Seal of Ireland; if returned under Great Seal of Great Britain, L.L. will declare the royal assent.

Irish Mutiny Act, limited to two years' duration, regulates raising of army in Ireland.

Forbes's Act 'for securing the independence of judges, and the impartial administration of justice'.

15 Sept. George Grenville, Earl Temple (later Marquis of Buckingham), sworn in as L.L.

24 Nov. King's Speech refers to 'what further benefits and advantages may be extended to Ireland'.

1783

22 Jan. Rev. Henry Ussher appointed first Andrews Professor of Astronomy at T.C.D. (director of Dunsink Observatory from 1786 until d. 8 May 1790).

24 Feb. Earl of Shelburne resigns as P.M.; succeeded by Duke of Portland (2 Apr.), whose coalition collapses on 19 Dec.

17 Mar. First installation of 'the Knights of the Most Illustrious Order of St Patrick' in St Patrick's Cathedral, Dublin. Thereafter the L.L. (*ex officio* Grand Master) annually entertains the knights at Dublin Castle on 17 Mar.; originally 15 knights, then increased to 22 (1833); ribbon sky-blue in colour, with motto 'Quis separabit?'; order is third in precedence of chivalry.

17 Apr. British Renunciation Act recognises Irish parliament's right to legislate exclusively for Ireland and recognises the exclusive jurisdiction of the Irish courts.

28 Apr. Foundation stone laid for the Belfast White Linen Hall (opens for business in Sept. 1784).

3 June Robert Henley, Earl of Northington, sworn in as L.L.

8 Sept. Volunteer convention held in Dungannon, the first of the provincial assemblies held to prepare for fight for parliamentary reform.

10–12 Nov. 300 delegates representing 150,000 Volunteers attend convention chaired by Lord Charlemont at the Rotunda in Dublin to seek parliamentary reform. Without any authority to do so, Sir Boyle Roche, purporting to speak on behalf of Lord Kenmare of the Catholic Committee, informs the convention that Catholics do not desire the franchise.

James Napper Tandy leads Dublin artillery past the Parliament House, guns bedecked with ribbons and scrolls reading: 'O Lord, open thou our lips, and our mouths shall show forth thy praise.'

29 Nov. Henry Flood's bill for reform defeated (157–77) by House of Commons, which refuses, as M.P.s view it, to be intimidated by Volunteers.

19 Dec. William Pitt (the younger) appointed P.M.

Henry Flood enters British parliament but retains his Irish seat.

1784

11 Feb. Charter incorporates the Dublin Society of Surgeons separately from the Company of Barbers, following petition by surgeons to the L.L.

24 Feb. Charles Manners, Duke of Rutland, sworn in as L.L., with Thomas Orde as C.S.

2 Mar. First meeting of the College of Surgeons, Samuel Croker-King presiding (*see* 17 Mar. 1806).

20 Apr. d. Nano Nagle (56), founder of the Order of Presentation Sisters.

23 Apr. John Foster appointed Chancellor of the Irish Exchequer.

10 May John Scott appointed Chief Justice of the King's Bench (created Viscount Clonmell on 18 Aug. 1789 and Earl of Clonmell on 20 Dec. 1793).

13 May Belfast 1st Volunteer Company becomes the first in Ireland to invite Catholics to join—'We invite to our ranks persons of every religious persuasion.'

14 May Foster's Corn Law regulates price of corn by providing subsidies when prices are low and prohibits export when prices are high (leads to increase in Irish tillage and boom in construction of mills).

Irish Post Office established by statute.

30 May Belfast Volunteer companies' collection to build a 'new mass-house' leads to the erection of St Mary's Chapel for about £170, of which £84 is collected by Protestants.

7 June Reform meeting called by High Sheriff Reilly of Dublin resolves that the Irish people have right to frequent elections and equal representation; also recognises right of Catholics to suffrage, but wishes to maintain Protestant government; similar resolutions reached at meeting held in Belfast.

June d. Eoghan Ruadh Ó Súilleabháin (36), poet, following a brawl in a tavern.

21 June Reformers led by James Napper Tandy petition the King to dissolve parliament; organise another national delegate meeting (*see* 25–27 Oct.).

4 July 'Peep o' Day Boys', Protestant peasant movement, formed at Markethill, Co. Armagh.

14 Aug. d. Nathaniel Hone (66), portraitist.

c. 25 Aug. Soldiers fire on Dublin mob which attempts to prevent whipping of Garrett Dignam for 'patriotic' tarring and feathering.

25–27 Oct. Reform convention in Dublin, again called by High Sheriff Reilly and led by Napper Tandy, fails to attract support.

1785

19 Jan. Balloonist Richard Crosbie makes the first flight from Irish soil

KILKENNY COUNTY LIBRARY

from Ranelagh Gardens, near Dublin, to North Strand, Dublin.

20 Jan. Parliamentary session opens; Speech from the Throne looks forward to closer commercial co-operation between Great Britain and Ireland.

7 Feb. C.S. Orde lays Pitt's 'commercial propositions' to permit free trade between Ireland and Britain before the Irish House of Commons.

22 Feb. Pitt introduces amended commercial propositions to British House of Commons (later accepted).

3 May Irish Academy (granted title Royal Irish Academy on 28 Jan. 1786) meets for the first time.

12 Aug. Grattan denounces Pitt's commercial propositions as fatal to the Irish constitution when C.S. Orde moves for leave to introduce his bill; first reading on 15 Aug. gives government majority of only 19 (127–108) and the propositions are withdrawn.

4 Sept. Edmund Sexton Pery resigns as Speaker of the House of Commons; John Foster unanimously elected Speaker on the following day.

22 Sept. Sir John Parnell appointed Chancellor of the Irish Exchequer.

Sept. Rise of 'Rightboy' peasant movement in Munster.

'Defender' peasant movement originates among Catholics in Armagh and quickly extends throughout Ulster and beyond.

James Gandon adds the pillared portico of the House of Lords to the Parliament House in College Green.

1786

3 Mar. First stone laid for the new Four Courts at Inns Quay, moved from beside Christ Church; architect James Gandon (*see* 3 Nov. 1796).

1 May Belfast Academy opens (becomes Belfast Royal Academy in 1887).

8 May Act empowers L.L. to appoint three police commissioners for Dublin to form and direct a constabulary force some 700 strong (*see* 21 May 1787).

12 June George Robert ('Fighting') FitzGerald executed at Castlebar for murder.

3 Dec. John Thomas Troy, R.C. Bishop of Ossory, translated to Dublin.

Pub. *Monasticon Hibernicum; or An History of the Abbeys, Priories, and Other Religious Houses in Ireland* by Mervyn Archdall (based on forty years of research and writing).

1787

Tithes, church rates and rack-rents provoke upsurge in Whiteboy activity (denounced by R.C. clergy).

26 Mar. Tumultuous Risings Act ('Whiteboy Act') introduces into Ireland provisions of the British Riot Act of 1716; directed against people administering or accepting illegal oaths or interfering with collection of tithes.

21 May Act empowers L.L. to appoint a chief constable in each barony and the Grand Juries (of the counties) to appoint up to 16 subconstables (these tend to be Protestants).

24 Oct. d. L.L. the Duke of Rutland (33).

16 Dec. George Grenville, Marquis of Buckingham (formerly Earl Temple), sworn in as L.L. (his three-year term of office is marked by considerable political bribery and corruption, adding some £13,000 to the pension list).

King's Inn Library, Dublin, founded, maintained by Benchers (moved to present site in 1827).

Pub. *Transactions of the Royal Irish Academy* (first bound volume).

1788

25 Feb. Memorial from the Catholic Committee presented to P.M. Pitt by William Fermor.

13 May Belfast Reading Society formed (later known as the Belfast Library and Society for Promoting Knowledge, with Robert Carey as its first librarian; moves to the Linen Hall in 1802).

14 Aug. d. Thomas Sheridan (69), actor and one-time manager of Theatre Royal, Smock Alley; father of Richard Brinsley Sheridan.

22 Sept. Thomas ('Buck') Whaley sets out to walk to Jerusalem for a bet (said to have been £20,000); travels some 7,000 miles to play handball against the walls of Jerusalem and returns in June 1789.

25 Oct. News of the King's illness reaches Ireland; his apparent insanity from 5 Nov. provokes the 'Regency Crisis'.

4 Dec. British parliament decides there is need for a regency during illness of George III; question does not arise in Ireland until 1789.

1789

16 Feb. Grattan's motion for an address to the Prince of Wales declaring him Regent of Ireland passes both Houses.

17 Feb. Recovery of the King announced in London, but doubts remain as to its permanence (L.L. Buckingham informed of King's recovery on 20 Feb.).

18 Feb. In an attempt to underline the legislative independence of Ireland, the Lords and Commons resolve to invite the Prince of Wales to become Regent of Ireland; L.L. Buckingham refuses to transmit invitation (19th).

20 Feb. Parliament censures the conduct of the L.L. and appoints delegates led by the Duke of Leinster and the Earl of Charlemont to carry invitation to the Prince of Wales; arrive in London on 25 Feb., after King's recovery, and are thanked by the Prince of Wales.

3 Mar. Grattan introduces resolutions against absentees holding high offices of state and the pension list and seeks the repeal of the police bill (defeated).

20 June John Fitzgibbon appointed Lord Chancellor (created Earl of Clare on 12 June 1795).

26 June Whig Club formed in Dublin by the Earl of Charlemont, Henry Grattan and John Ponsonby, to fight for internal reform and to resist a legislative union.

3 July John Magee tried for libel on Francis Higgins; found guilty (*see* 3 Sept.).

14 July Attack on the Bastille in Paris; revolution in France.

3 Sept. John Magee again arrested, for organising a *Bra Pleasura* lampooning the Dublin Castle legal establishment; bailed on 29 Oct., but imprisoned from 5 to 27 Nov; committed again on 2 Dec. (*see* 8 Feb. 1790).

24 Oct. Start of the Royal Canal to link Dublin and the River Shannon.

12 Dec. d. John Ponsonby (76), politician, former Speaker of the House of Commons.

Pub. *Reliques of Irish Poetry* by Charlotte Brooke.

1790

5 Jan. John Fane, Earl of Westmorland, sworn in as L.L.

8 Feb. John Magee sentenced to six months' imprisonment and fined £50 (*see* 3 Sept. 1789).

20 Feb. Grattan's motion for a select committee to inquire into corrupt agreements for the sale of peerages and purchases of votes in the House of Commons rejected (144–88).

11 Mar. Proclamation issued against the Volunteers.

15 Mar. Charitable Society for the Relief of Sick and Indigent Room-keepers of All Religious Persuasions founded in Dublin.

8 May d. Rev. Henry Ussher (49), Professor of Astronomy, T.C.D., mainly responsible for erection of Dunsink Observatory.

2 July Parliament opens; John Foster re-elected Speaker of the House of Commons (145–105) on 9th; parliament votes the King support for the war against Spain and a sum of £200,000 for putting the country into a state of defence.

5 July Post Office inaugurates mail-coach service.

Aug. Richard Burke, son of Edmund, appointed adviser to the Catholic Committee (until 1792, when he is replaced by Theobald Wolfe Tone).

Wide Streets Commissioners adopt the functions of a planning authority when it is specified that all private street proposals in Dublin must be vetted by them.

Pub. *Antiquities of Ireland* by Edward Ledwich.

1791

Jan. Daniel O'Connell and his brother Maurice are smuggled to Saint-Omer, France, to continue their education (restricted in Ireland by penal laws); fees, 25 guineas p.a.; move to Douai in Aug. 1792; return to Ireland after execution of Louis XVI in 1793.

Feb. Catholic Committee petitions the King and parliament to 'relieve them [Catholics] from their degraded situation and no longer suffer them to continue like strangers in their native land'.

5 Mar. Work starts on building Carlisle Bridge, Dublin (O'Connell Bridge from 1880 when rebuilt); designed by James Gandon (opens in July 1795).

1 Apr. Samuel McTier holds a meeting in Barclay's tavern in Crown Entry, Belfast, where those present resolve 'to form ourselves into an association to unite all Irishmen to pledge themselves to our country' (*see* 14 Oct.).

1 May Inhabitants of Merrion Square, Dublin, begin payment of an annual sum for a period of 147 years to enclose and improve the square (*see* 1 May 1938).

1 July d. Charles O'Conor (81) of Belanagare, Co. Roscommon, antiquary.

14 July Northern Whig Club in Belfast celebrates the second anniversary of the fall of the Bastille. In Dublin James Napper Tandy leads a Volunteer commemoration: 'We do not rejoice because we are slaves; but we rejoice because of the French being free.'

July William Ritchie (later to be called 'father of Belfast shipbuilding'), shipbuilder from the Clyde, settles in Belfast with his brother John and a team of skilled labourers (*see* 7 July 1792).

6 Aug. d. Mervyn Archdall (68), antiquary and genealogist.

c. 22 Aug. Pub. (anon.) *An Argument on Behalf of the Catholics of Ireland* by

Theobald Wolfe Tone, seeking Catholic Emancipation, electoral and parliamentary reform and elimination of English influence in Ireland.

11 Oct. Theobald Wolfe Tone visits Belfast as secretary of the Catholic Committee.

14 Oct. Society of United Irishmen founded in Belfast by Samuel McTier and Robert Simms (*see* 1 Apr.).

18 Oct. First general meeting of the United Irishmen seeks 'complete and radical reform of the representation of the people in parliament' (*see* 9 Nov.).

9 Nov. First meeting of the Dublin Society of the United Irishmen at the Eagle Tavern in Eustace Street adopts the resolutions of the Belfast Society; secretary James Napper Tandy.

26 Nov. First convicts from Ireland arrive in New South Wales on board the *Queen*.

2 Dec. d. Henry Flood (59), politician.

27 Dec. Aristocratic element in the Catholic Committee led by Lord Kenmare secedes and presents a separate address to the L.L. seeking relief for Catholics at the discretion of parliament; the more radical main body is now dominated by John Keogh.

Pub. *The Rights of Man* by Thomas Paine; widely read in Ireland.

1792

4 Jan. Samuel Neilson and Robert and William Simms launch the *Northern Star*, organ of the Belfast United Irishmen.

19 Jan. Parliamentary session opens.

20 Feb. Napper Tandy is gratuitously insulted on his facial appearance by Solicitor-General John Toler; Tandy voted guilty of breach of privilege for challenging Toler to a duel; Tandy imprisoned but escapes on 23rd; surrenders on 18 Apr., held for a few hours, then released.

27 Feb. Fire guts the chamber of the House of Commons in the Parliament House in College Green.

18 Apr. Langrishe's Catholic Relief Act enables Catholics to practise as solicitors and barristers and hold legal positions below the rank of K.C.; repeals laws against intermarriage of Catholics (*see* 9 Apr. 1793).

7 July William Ritchie launches *Hibernia*, first ship built in his Belfast yard.

14 July Some 800 Volunteers meet at the Linen Hall to commemorate the fall of the Bastille; attended by Napper Tandy and Wolfe Tone; Rev. William Steel Dickson opposes resolution for gradual removal of Catholic disabilities and secures unanimous pledge for total and immediate emancipation.

25 July Wolfe Tone appointed agent of the Catholic Committee, holding the paid title of assistant secretary.

3–8 Dec. Meeting of Catholic Convention, the so-called 'Back Lane Parliament', in Dublin (first Catholic elected assembly since the parliament of James II in 1689); appoints delegates to petition the King on franchise and other matters (*see* 2 Jan. 1793).

9 Dec. Lord Chancellor Fitzgibbon issues proclamation against unauthorised bodies assembling in arms.

16 Dec. Volunteers meeting in Dublin resolve that their aim is to defend the country from internal and external foes.

Association for Discountenancing Vice and Promoting the Knowledge and Practice of the Christian Religion founded; grant-aided, it is regarded by Catholics as a proselytising agency.

1793

2 Jan. Delegates of the Catholic Convention, including Wolfe Tone and John Keogh, received by the King.

10 Jan. Parliamentary session opens; Speech from the Throne urges Catholic relief.

21 Jan. Louis XVI executed in Paris.

31 Jan. House of Commons thanks L.L. for prohibiting parade by National Guard (*see* 9 Dec. 1792).

1 Feb. France declares war on England and Holland.

15–16 Feb. Convention of Volunteers at Dungannon demand parliamentary reform ('Reform Convention').

25 Feb. Act to prevent importation of arms and gunpowder.

Feb. Napper Tandy flees when he learns that he is to be charged with taking Defenders' oath (reaches Philadelphia in 1795).

9 Mar. Riot in Belfast when fighting breaks out between soldiers of the 17th Dragoons in Belfast and Volunteers.

23 Mar. John Foster, Speaker of the House of Commons, opposes Catholic relief.

29 Mar. d. Charlotte Brooke (c. 53), author.

9 Apr. Hobart's Catholic Relief Act permits Catholics to vote as 40s freeholders in the counties and in the open boroughs, to act as Grand Jurors, bear arms, take degrees at T.C.D., become members of the corporations and advance to minor offices in the state service.

Militia Act establishes standing militia; units to be raised and maintained by counties and cities; initial strength 14,948 (increased to 21,660 in 1795); annual training period of 28 days in peacetime.

16 Apr. Catholic Convention meets in Dublin and votes thanks to the King and to Robert Hobart and sums of money to prominent activists in the Catholic Committee.

17 June Act of British parliament permits the importation into Great Britain from Ireland of colonial goods imported legally into Ireland.

11 July Confrontation at Taghmon, Co. Wexford, between peasant agitators and 56th Regiment of Infantry, results in deaths of over 80 rioters and a major of the 56th (Valotton).

16 Aug. Convention Act outlaws meeting of assemblies purporting to represent any large section of public opinion; prohibits meetings of elective or representative assemblies for the purpose of preparing petitions.

Place Act requires M.P.s to vacate their seats on acceptance of government office, by relinquishing seat upon acceptance of office of escheator of one of the provinces (sinecure worth 30s p.a.).

1 Oct. St Patrick's College, Carlow, opens; first institution of higher education for Catholics.

1794

4 Mar. Second reading (moved by George Ponsonby) of bill for parliamentary reform rejected (142–44).

1 Apr. Rev. William Jackson, agent of the French government, arrives in Dublin accompanied by British spy, John Cockayne, and meets with leading United Irishmen, including Wolfe Tone.

28 Apr. Rev. William Jackson arrested and charged with high treason (*see* 23 Apr. 1795).

2 May Archibald Hamilton Rowan, United Irishman (held on charges of distributing seditious material, for which he is fined £500 and imprisoned for two years), escapes from Newgate Jail and makes his way to America *via* France.

12 May d. Richard Woodward, C.I. Bishop of Cloyne since 1781; noted campaigner for better treatment of the poor.

23 May Police raid Tailors' Hall during meeting of the Dublin Society of the United Irishmen, seize papers and suppress the Society.

25 June William Drennan of the United Irishmen acquitted on charge of seditious libel after defence by John Philpot Curran.

4 Sept. d. John Hely Hutchinson, politician and Provost of T.C.D. since 1774.

10 Oct. d. Richard Robinson, C.I. Archbishop of Armagh and Primate since 1765; founder of Armagh Observatory (1793).

Meteorological observations commence at Armagh Observatory.

Pub. *Catalogus Systematicus Plantorum Indigenarum in Comitatu Dublinensi ... pars prima* by Walter Wade.

1795

4 Jan. William Earl Fitzwilliam, sworn in as L.L.; privately committed to Catholic Emancipation; dismisses all leading officials except for John Fitzgibbon, Lord Chancellor.

22 Jan. Parliamentary session opens.

25 Jan. William Newcome appointed C.I. Archbishop of Armagh and Primate (d. 11 Jan. 1800).

2 Feb. Belfast Protestants petition parliament for repeal of penal laws restricting Catholics.

12 Feb. Grattan introduces Catholic Relief Bill.

14 Feb. Government wins vote for funds to establish a new militia, designed to displace the Volunteers.

17 Feb. British cabinet objects when told of Grattan's Relief Bill and holds L.L. Fitzwilliam responsible for its introduction.

23 Feb. L.L. Fitzwilliam dismissed (leaves Ireland on 25 Mar.).

31 Mar. John Pratt, Earl Camden, sworn in as L.L. (amid rioting from those supporting Catholic Emancipation), with Thomas Pelham as C.S.

9 Apr. Meeting of Catholics at Francis Street, Dublin, resolves regret at removal of Fitzwilliam, expresses desire for a new relief bill, and opposes any surrender of the liberties of the country.

21 Apr. Grattan moves for a commission to inquire into the state of the nation and deprecates the return of 'the pernicious and profligate system which had made Ireland a disgrace before the world' (proposal rejected by 158 votes to 48).

23 Apr. Trial of Rev. William Jackson for high treason begins; he commits suicide by taking poison in the dock on 30th.

5 May Grattan's Catholic Relief Bill defeated in House of Commons (155–84).

10 May United Irishmen reconstituted as a secret, oath-bound society, dedicated to the establishment of an Irish republic and complete political separation from Britain; local organisations set up under a national Executive Directory.

5 June 'Act for the better education of persons professing the popish or Roman Catholic religion' provides for a state-aided (annual grant of £8,000) Catholic seminary at Maynooth, Co. Kildare (the Royal College of St Patrick) (*see* 25 June).

12 June John Fitzgibbon created Earl of Clare.

13 June Wolfe Tone and his family board the *Cincinnatus* at Belfast for Philadelphia (arrive at Wilmington on 1 Aug.).

25 June Rev. Thomas Hussey appointed President of St Patrick's College, Maynooth; 10 professorships instituted; college opens for matriculation on 30 June (*see* 1 Oct.).

1 Aug. Lord Clare lays the first stone for the King's Inns, designed by James Gandon.

14 Sept. Defenders assemble in Tentaraghan, Co. Armagh, and begin looting Protestant farms; Protestants attack homes of Defenders.

18 Sept. Shots exchanged between Defenders (Catholic) and Peep o' Day Boys (Protestant) across the Diamond, near Loughgall, Co. Armagh (*see* 21 Sept.).

21 Sept. 'Battle of the Diamond': Protestants, including Peep o' Day Boys, rout the Catholic Defenders who attack Winter's inn at the Diamond, a cross-roads near Loughgall, Co. Armagh; Peep o' Day Boys form the Orange Society (later 'Order') at the home of James Sloan, innkeeper in Loughgall.

1 Oct. St Patrick's College, Maynooth, formally opened (first lectures delivered on 6th; first stone of new building laid on 20 Apr. 1796).

1796

21 Jan. – 15 Apr. Parliament in session.

1 Feb. Wolfe Tone arrives in France at Havre de Grace from U.S.A.; meets Carnot, President of the Directory (5 May); Tone is joined by his family on 7 May 1797.

24 Mar. Insurrection Act (to deal with Defenders) provides magistrates with sweeping powers to proclaim a district and makes it a capital offence to administer illegal oaths (replaced in 1807).

23 Apr. Ringsend Docks, Dublin, open.

June – Oct. Lord Edward FitzGerald and Arthur O'Connor in Germany, Switzerland and France.

12 July First Orange Order 'Twelfth' demonstration, several thousand strong; a soldier in Lurgan kills a marcher who has struck him. (There are now some 90 lodges in the Order.)

29 July Commercial Buildings in Dublin started, designed by Robert Parke (or Sparks).

8 Aug. Robert Stewart created Earl of Londonderry; his son Robert becomes Lord Castlereagh.

Sept. As French war drains country of regular troops L.L. Camden agrees to establishment of yeomanry (armed Protestant volunteer units recruited by landlords).

16 Sept. Leaders of the Belfast United Irishmen, including Samuel Neilson, Thomas Russell and Charles Hamilton Teeling, arrested and charged with high treason.

10 Oct. Henry Joy McCracken arrested and imprisoned (released on 8 Dec. 1797).

13 Oct. – 3 July 1797 Parliament in session.

Oct. District corps and volunteer yeomanry formed.

26 Oct. *Habeas corpus* suspended until 1 June 1799 in order to deal with unrest caused by Orange Order, Defenders and the United Irishmen.

3 Nov. First sitting at the new Four Courts (started on 3 Mar. 1786).

15 Dec. Admiral Lazare Hoche's expedition (43 ships with 15,000 troops) with Wolfe Tone on board the *Indomptable* sails from Brest for Ireland.

22–29 Dec. Hoche's expedition broken up by storms, fails to make land and returns to France.

1797

7 Jan. Lord Edward FitzGerald (brother of the Duke of Leinster) joins the United Irishmen.

26 Feb. Bank of Ireland follows Bank of England in suspension of gold payments (gold payments resumed on 1 June 1821).

13 Mar. Gen. Gerard Lake issues proclamation in Ulster imposing martial law; all those not serving the Crown in some capacity ordered to bring in their arms (prelude to a reign of terror by military engaged in disarming Ulster).

3 May Edward John Newell, informing on the United Irishmen, examined before secret session of the House of Commons.

8 May Meeting in Ballymena, Co. Antrim, petitions King for relief of grievances and dismissal of his ministers in Ireland.

15 May Grattan and leaders of the parliamentary opposition in the House of Commons withdraw from parliament when defeated on Ponsonby's resolution for reform (117–30).

17 May L.L. Camden and Irish Privy Council place the whole country under martial law and proclaim the United Irishmen.

19 May Monaghan militia raid offices of the *Northern Star* and smash the plant.

21 May Masters of the Orange lodges meet at Armagh under chairmanship of James Sloan (secretary of the Orange Order since 1795).

29 May Declaration of the principles of the Orange Order appears in the *Belfast News-Letter*, pledging support to the Crown, the constitution, the Protestant Ascendancy and the Established Church and denying that members are sworn to destroy Catholics.

4 June Dublin Orange Lodge founded; Thomas Verner master.

27 June William James McNeven leaves for Paris to aid Edward Lewins's attempts to secure support from French revolutionaries for the United Irishmen.

9 July d. Edmund Burke (68), political philosopher, orator and author.

11 July Parliament dissolved.

12 July Several thousand Orangemen march in their first public procession in Belfast city; Gen. Lake reviews Orange Order marchers at Lisburn and at Lurgan; fighting between militia and soldiers (24th Dragoons) in Stewartstown results in seven militia-men dead and seven wounded.

25 July Robert Stewart, Lord Castlereagh, appointed acting C.S. in absence of Thomas Pelham (*see* 3 Nov. 1798).

28 Sept. Pub. first issue of *The Press*, organ of the United Irishmen, founded by Arthur O'Connor (suppressed on 6 Mar. 1798).

14 Oct. William Orr, first person to be tried under the Insurrection Act (defended by John Philpot Curran), hanged at Carrickfergus, Co. Antrim, for administering oath of the United Irishmen; popularly believed to be innocent, his death arouses widespread indignation.

22 Nov. Describing events in Ireland, Lord Moira tells the British House of

Lords that he has seen 'the most disgusting tyranny that any nation ever groaned under . . . creating universal discontent and hatred of the English name'.

Pub. *Essays in Practical Education* (2 vols) by Richard Lovell Edgeworth and Maria Edgeworth.

Pub. *General Collection of the Ancient Music of Ireland* by Edward Bunting, Vol. I (includes 66 airs not previously published); Vol II appears in 1809, and Vol. III in 1840.

1798

9 Jan. Parliament opens; John Foster re-elected Speaker of the House of Commons (leading opponent of the Union).

19 Feb. Leinster provincial executive of the United Irishmen resolves 'that they would not be diverted from their purpose by anything which could be done in parliament'; meeting is attended by Thomas Reynolds, who betrays the plans (*see* 12 Mar.).

22 Feb. Samuel Neilson released (imprisoned since 1796); rearrested on 23 May.

26 Feb. Sir Ralph Abercromby, C.-in-C., issues general order in which he describes his army as 'in a state of licentiousness which must render it formidable to everyone but the enemy' (*see* 25 Apr.).

8 Mar. Meeting of the Orange Order in Dublin organises the movement on a national basis, establishing the Grand Lodge of Ireland in Dublin (*see* 9 Apr.).

12 Mar. Leinster provincial executive of the United Irishmen, meeting at the home of Oliver Bond in Dublin, betrayed by Thomas Reynolds, arrested; only two leaders remain free (*see* 17–18 May).

30 Mar. L.L. proclaims the country in rebellion and directs the C.-in-C. to deal with it; free quarters for military; effective martial law.

9 Apr. First meeting of the Grand Lodge of Ireland at the home of Thomas Verner in Dublin.

25 Apr. Abercromby resigns and is replaced by Gen. Gerard Lake as C.-in-C. (*see* 20 June).

27 Apr. Co. Wexford proclaimed by magistrates meeting at Gorey.

17–18 May New National Directory of United Irishmen meets.

19 May Lord Edward FitzGerald, betrayed by Francis Magan, wounded during arrest (dies on 4 June).

21 May Arrest of the brothers John and Henry Sheares, betrayed by Capt. John Warneford Armstrong (*see* 14 July).

23 May Rising, as planned, breaks out in Leinster; insurgents repulsed at Naas and Clane, defeated at Rathangan, and massacre North Cork Militia at Prosperous.

d. John Scott, Earl of Clonmell, Chief Justice of the King's Bench since 1774.

Beauchamp Bagenal Harvey, John Colclough and Edward FitzGerald, Wexford landowners considered 'notorious for the violence of their political opinions', arrested and imprisoned in Wexford (*see* 30 May).

24 May Dublin: insurgents defeated at Lucan, Lusk, Rathfarnham and Tallaght.

Kildare: insurgents defeated at Kilcullen Bridge, Monasterevin and Naas, and claim victories at Old Kilcullen and Rathangan.

Kilkenny: insurgents successful at Barrettstown.

Meath: insurgents successful at Dunboyne, defeated at Slane.

Wicklow: insurgents defeated at Baltinglass.

Wicklow Militia (reportedly) shoot dead 34 prisoners at Dunlavin, Co. Wicklow; 28 prisoners are reported massacred at Carnew, Co. Wexford, by militia and yeomen on 25th.

Gen. Lake instructs Gen. Loftus to 'take no prisoners'.

Proclamation empowers general of-ficers to use the death penalty on all persons assisting in the rebellion.

26 May Insurgents defeated at Tara, Co. Meath, by Capt. Preston and Lord Fingall (ends resistance in Meath).

26–27 May Destruction of houses and parish church of Fr John Murphy by North Cork Militia at Boolavogue, Co. Wexford; militia's Lieut. Bookey killed.

27 May North Cork Militia and yeomen routed at Oulart Hill, Co. Wexford, by insurgents led by Fr John Murphy.

29 May Wexford insurgents encamp at Vinegar Hill, beside Enniscorthy.

350 insurgents who have agreed terms with Gen. Dundas are slaughtered by Sir James Duff at the Curragh, Co. Kildare.

30 May Wexford insurgents defeat yeomen at Three Rocks, capturing howitzers.

Insurgents occupy Wexford town (until 21 June) and release prisoners from Wexford jail, including Beauchamp Bagenal Harvey; Harvey unanimously appointed commander by the insurgents and reluctantly leads them until deposed after the battle of New Ross (*see* 5 June).

1 June Wexford insurgents defeated at Bunclody (Newtownbarry) and at Ballymenane Hill near Gorey.

2–3 June Insurgents defeated at Kilcock, Co. Kildare, by Major-Gen. Sir James Duff and the North Cork Militia.

4 June Fr Murphy defeats Col. Walpole (who is killed in action) at Ballymore Hill and moves on to Gorey.

5 June Insurgents led by Beauchamp Bagenal Harvey defeated at New Ross, Co. Wexford, by Major-Gen. Henry Johnson; Lord Mountjoy and John Kelly of Killann killed in action; Fr Philip Roche replaces Harvey as insurgent commander.

Massacre of between 100 and 200 Protestant prisoners (and some Catholics, mainly servants) in a barn at Scullabogue, Co. Wexford.

7 June Henry Joy McCracken leads insurgents in attack on Antrim town and after initial victory is defeated (McCracken executed in Belfast on 17 July); Lord O'Neill fatally wounded.

9 June Fr Murphy and insurgents defeated by Major-Gen. Francis Needham at Arklow, Co. Wicklow, despite insurgents' overwhelming odds; Fr Michael Murphy killed in action.

United Irishmen rise in Co. Down led by Henry Monro.

10 June William Aylmer, leading 500 insurgents, overcomes the garrison at Maynooth, Co. Kildare (*see* 18 June).

Insurgents repulsed at Portaferry, Co. Down.

11 June Insurgents led by Henry Monro take Ballynahinch, then leave it next day when it is reoccupied by government troops.

12 June Insurgents repulsed at Borris, Co. Carlow; town fired.

13 June Insurgents led by Henry Monro defeated at Ballynahinch by

KILKENNY COUNTY LIBRARY

Gen. Nugent (Monro executed at Lisburn on 15 June); Ballynahinch pillaged and looted by troops; end of the rising in Ulster.

16 June Luke Teeling, father of Bartholomew and Charles Hamilton Teeling, arrested (held without charge until 1802).

17 June Insurgents burn Tinahely, Co. Wicklow.

18 June William Aylmer's Kildare insurgent force routed by Gen. Dundas at Ovidstown, near Kilcock.

19 June Fr Philip Roche and insurgents forced to retreat from Lacken Hill to Three Rocks near Wexford.

20 June Charles, Marquis Cornwallis, succeeds Camden as L.L. and also holds office of C.-in-C.

Major-Gen. Sir John Moore defeats Fr Philip Roche and insurgents at Goff's Bridge (Foulke's Mill), Co. Wexford.

21 June Wexford town retaken by government forces; Enniscorthy retaken by Gen. Johnson, while Gen. Lake routs the insurgents at Vinegar Hill; some insurgents escape to Three Rocks.

22 June Fr John Murphy and Wexford insurgents leave Three Rocks for Kilkenny; they reach Castlecomer on 24th and then retrace for Wexford; retreating insurgents surprise party of yeomen and loyalists at Gorey, killing 37.

25–26 June Fr Philip Roche and Matthew Keogh and others hanged on Wexford Bridge.

Insurgents capture Hackettstown, Co. Carlow, and burn government and Protestant property.

26 June Fr Murphy and Wexford insurgents defeated at Kilcomney Hill by Sir Charles Asgill; Fr Murphy probably tortured and killed by yeomen on the same day.

2 July Insurgents scatter yeomen at Ballyraheen Hill.

5 July Wexford insurgents dislodged from their White Heap mountain base; rising in Wexford effectively over.

14 July John and Henry Sheares executed.

17 July Lord Castlereagh delivers King's message of mercy to the House of Commons (*see* 6 Oct.).

L.L. Cornwallis proclaims amnesty for non-leaders of the rising (terms of amnesty are ignored by Gen. Lake and the yeomanry).

Role of informer Thomas Reynolds publicly revealed at the trial of John McCann.

20 July Trials of William Michael Byrne and Oliver Bond for high treason on evidence of Thomas Reynolds (Byrne executed on 25 July; Bond reprieved and dies in prison).

4–16 Aug. Thomas Addis Emmet, Arthur O'Connor, William James McNeven, Samuel Neilson and Oliver Bond make detailed statements to the government on the history of the United Irishmen and are examined by secret committee of the House of Lords.

12 Aug. Rev. William Steel Dickson, arrested with others on 4 June, removed to prison ship (until 19 Mar. 1799).

22 Aug. French force led by Gen. Jean Humbert arrives at Kilcummin, Killala Bay, Co. Mayo.

25–26 Aug. Humbert's army, reinforced by Irish peasants, marches to Ballina, and from there by the foot of Nephin mountain to Castlebar.

26 Aug. Gen. Lake arrives to reinforce Gen. Francis Hutchinson at Castlebar.

27 Aug. Humbert's Franco-Irish army defeats government forces in 'Races of Castlebar'.

31 Aug. Humbert proclaims the Provisional Republic of Connaught under President John Moore.

L.L. Cornwallis issues general order calling on his officers 'to assist him in putting a stop to the licentious conduct of the troops, and in saving wretched inhabitants from being robbed, and in the most striking manner ill-treated by those to whom they had a right to look for safety and protection'.

3–4 Sept. Humbert evacuates Castlebar, which is then occupied by government forces; L.L. Cornwallis reaches Hollymount, c. 13 miles from Castlebar, on 4th.

4 Sept. Small French expeditionary force with James Napper Tandy aboard the *Anacreon* sails from Dunkirk for Ireland (*see* 16 Sept.).

4–6 Sept. United Irish rising in Longford–Westmeath crushed at Granard and Wilson's Hospital.

5 Sept. Humbert's Franco-Irish army diverted from Sligo by skirmish with Col. Charles Vereker's force of militia, which they defeat at Collooney, Co. Sligo.

7 Sept. Humbert crosses the Shannon into Co. Longford.

8 Sept. Humbert surrenders to L.L. Cornwallis and Gen. Lake at Ballinamuck, Co. Longford, where his Irish followers are massacred.

16 Sept. Napper Tandy comes ashore on Rutland Island, Co. Donegal, then re-embarks and returns to France (*see* 12 Sept. 1800).

20 Sept. French expedition, including Wolfe Tone, sails for Ireland from Brest with 3,000 troops.

23 Sept. Humbert's Irish supporters in the Killala region overwhelmed by Gen. Trench; end of rising in Connaught.

24 Sept. Bartholomew Teeling, Humbert's aide-de-camp, executed.

6 Oct. Act grants pardon to certain categories of persons engaged in the recent rebellion and subject to banishment.

Fugitives Act calls on insurgents to surrender or be attainted of high treason.

Henry Grattan's name struck off the list of Irish Privy Councillors on (groundless) charge that he was a 'sworn member of the United Irishmen'; his name also erased from roll of freemen of Dublin and Londonderry.

Parliament prorogued.

12–20 Oct. British ships intercept the French expedition and capture seven of the ten ships (20th); Tone arrested at Buncrana, Co. Donegal, and sent to Dublin (*see* 10 Nov.).

3 Nov. Robert Stewart, Viscount Castlereagh, appointed Chief Secretary (until 21 May 1801).

10 Nov. Tone tried and convicted by court martial; his plea to be shot as a soldier is ignored and he is sentenced to be hanged; cuts his throat on 12th and dies on 19th.

9 Dec. Meeting of lawyers called by William Saurin in Dublin resolves that a legislative union between Ireland and Great Britain would be 'highly dangerous and improper to propose at the present juncture' (carried by 166 votes to 32).

18 Dec. Meeting of Dublin bankers and merchants condemns legislative union while affirming loyalty to the Crown.

27 Dec. Pub. first issue of *Anti-Union* newspaper.

1799

5 Jan. Grand Orange Lodge of Ireland passes resolution forbidding members to take sides on the legislative union.

17–19 Jan. Catholic bishops unanimously agree that they will accept government veto on episcopal appointments (response to an offer from Lord Castlereagh) and that 'A provision through government for the Roman Catholic clergy of the kingdom, competent and secured, ought to be thankfully accepted.'

22 Jan. Parliamentary session opens; Speech from the Throne introduces proposal for a legislative union.

31 Jan. P.M. Pitt puts the case for legislative union to the British House of Commons.

12 Mar. William Sampson of the United Irishmen arrested on suspicion of having written *Arguments For and Against a Union Considered* (actually by Under-Secretary Edward Cooke).

19 Mar. Thomas Addis Emmet, Thomas Russell, Samuel Neilson, Rev. William Steel Dickson, Robert Simms and other leading United Irishmen removed in custody to Fort George, Scotland; arrive on 9 Apr. (released on 30 June 1802).

25 Mar. Indemnity Act condones transgressions of the law which have occurred since 6 Oct. 1798 provided they were for suppressing the rebellion and preserving the public peace and safety of the realm.

Act empowers L.L. to authorise courts martial to try persons involved in insurrection of 1798.

22 June George Ponsonby's resolution 'that the House would be ready to enter into any measure short of surrendering their free, resident, and independent legislature as established in 1782' passes by majority of two.

4 Aug. d. James Caulfield (71), 1st Earl of Charlemont, leader of the Irish Volunteers.

11 Aug. Gideon Ouseley, preaching in Irish at Riverstown, Co. Sligo, starts his mission for Methodism.

Cold and wet year; crop failure leads to famine.

1800

13 Jan. Daniel O'Connell makes his first public speech, in opposition to the Union.

15 Jan. Irish parliament opens for its last session; 39 writs for new elections (to facilitate Union proposals) issued in the first four days; amendment to the address to the Crown to expunge paragraph on the Union (138–96).

5–6 Feb. King's message to the Irish parliament recommending legislative Union carried in the largest division ever recorded in the Irish House of Commons (158–115).

15 Feb. Henry Grattan wounds Isaac Corry (Chancellor of the Exchequer) in duel over accusation that Grattan encouraged 1798 rebellion.

24 Feb. Ireland's contribution to U.K. Exchequer set at 2:15.

1 Mar. 31 Orange Lodges meeting at the Maze, Co. Down, resolve that 'We consider a legislative Union with Great Britain as the inevitable ruin to peace, prosperity and happiness in this kingdom.'

8 Mar. Grand Orange Lodge of Co. Antrim meeting in Belfast expresses regret at 'the appearance of division and discord' among Orangemen on the proposed Union and calls for adherence to the resolution issued by the Grand Lodge of Ireland that Orangemen should remain neutral on the question.

12 Mar. Meeting of 36 Orange lodges of Counties Armagh and Monaghan at the home of James McKean in Armagh adopts resolution protesting against the Union.

13 Mar. Sir John Parnell's motion seeking dissolution of parliament and advice of constituencies before commitment to legislative Union defeated (150–104).

28 Mar. Articles of Union agreed by Irish House of Commons; agreed by British parliament on 12 May.

1 May Lay college opens at St Patrick's College, Maynooth (until 1817).

21 May House of Commons votes to allow C.S. Castlereagh to introduce a bill for the Union (160–100).

26 May Grattan makes his last speech against the Union in the House of Commons; denounces C.S. Castlereagh; retires to Tinnehinch, Co. Wicklow.

6 June First ordination to the priesthood in St Patrick's College, Maynooth.

7 June Bill for Union passes Irish House of Commons by 65 votes; passes House of Lords by 69; parliament thereby enacts its own dissolution.

1 Aug. Act of Union receives royal assent.

First stone laid for King's Inns in Dublin; architects James Gandon and Henry Aaron Baker.

2 Aug. Last sitting of the Irish House of Commons.

12 Sept. Napper Tandy tried for high treason; charge fails, but he is rearrested for role in Rutland Island landing (*see* 16 Sept. 1798); under pressure from Napoleon, Lord Cornwallis decides to banish Tandy, who is later unconditionally released (arrives in Bordeaux on 14 Mar. 1802).

2 Nov. d. Thomas ('Buck' or 'Jerusalem') Whaley (34), adventurer (*see* 22 Sept. 1788).

28 Nov. d. Matthew Young (50), C.I. Bishop of Clonfert since Feb. 1799, scholar, painter and botanist.

20 Dec. John Toler appointed Chief Justice, Court of Common Pleas.

Irish national debt £28 million (doubles in one year since 1799); taxation increases to £2½ million to help Britain in the war against France.

Meteorological observations commence at the Botanic Gardens, Glasnevin, Dublin.

William Ritchie constructs Belfast's first graving dock.

Pub. *Castle Rackrent* by Maria Edgeworth.

1801

1 Jan. Act of Union comes into force; amalgamation of Irish and British parliaments.

14 Mar. P.M. William Pitt resigns, following conflict with the King over Catholic Emancipation; succeeded by Henry Addington (Tory) on 17th.

21 May C.S. Castlereagh resigns.

25 May Philip Yorke, Earl of Hardwicke, sworn in as L.L.; Charles Abbott appointed C.S.

5 Dec. d. Sir John Parnell (57), politician.

30 Dec. Rev. William Steel Dickson, Presbyterian and United Irishman, brought to Ireland from Fort George, Scotland (released on 13 Jan. 1802).

1802

8 Jan. d. Fr Arthur O'Leary (73), Capuchin priest, author, controversialist and noted preacher.

19 Jan. d. Francis Higgins (56) (the 'Sham Squire'), owner of the *Freeman's Journal* and informer on United Irishmen in 1798.

28 Jan. d. John Fitzgibbon (53), Earl of Clare, Lord Chancellor.

13 Feb. William Wickham appointed C.S.

15 Mar. John Freeman Mitford appointed Lord Chancellor of Ireland; opponent of Catholic Emancipation (dismissed in 1806).

31 Mar. d. Rev. Sinclare Kelburn (48), noted Presbyterian preacher and ardent Volunteer of the 1780s.

30 June Following Peace of Amiens (27 Mar.) United Irishmen are released from Fort George in Scotland on condition that they go into exile (Thomas Addis Emmet, Dr William James McNeven, Thomas Russell and Arthur O'Connor).

12–31 July General election; Henry Addington continues as P.M.

1803

18 May U.K. and France resume war.

9 June Mount Sion, Waterford, formally opened by Bishop Thomas Hussey; first school established by Edmund Ignatius Rice, founder of the Irish Christian Brothers (*see* 15 Aug. 1808).

8 July d. Frederick Augustus Hervey (73), 4th Earl of Bristol, eccentric and largely absentee C.I. Bishop of Derry since 1768.

11 July d. Thomas Hussey, R.C. Bishop of Waterford and Lismore since 1797, first President of St Patrick's College, Maynooth (1795).

16 July Explosion at munitions factory of Robert Emmet kills one and injures three.

23 July Robert Emmet's rising in Thomas Street, Dublin; he issues proclamation of the Provisional Government of the Irish Republic; his followers, disorganised and lacking leadership, murder Lord Kilwarden and his son-in-law, Rev. Richard Wolfe, in their carriage; rising quickly collapses; Emmet flees into hiding around Dublin. The only other action is at the Coombe, where Col. Browne of the 21st Scottish Fusiliers is killed, as are two members of the Liberty Rangers.

24 July Thomas Russell issues proclamation to 'the Men of Erin' as a 'member of the Provisional Government and General-in-Chief of the Northern District'.

29 July *Habeas corpus* suspended; bills read thrice and royal assent given on the same day; legislation also passed empowering L.L., advised by the Lord Chancellor, to try persons under martial law.

21 Aug. Proclamation by Lord Mayor of Dublin imposes curfew (9 p.m. to 6 a.m.) and obligatory posting of inhabitants' names on doorways.

24 Aug. d. James Napper Tandy (63), revolutionary, Volunteer and United Irishman.

25 Aug. Robert Emmet arrested in Harold's Cross at home of Mrs Palmer.

29 Aug. d. Samuel Neilson (42), co-founder of the United Irishmen (1791).

9 Sept. Having come south, Thomas Russell is arrested by Major Henry Sirr and held at Kilmainham jail; then transferred to Downpatrick for trial (executed on 21 Oct.).

10 Sept. John Killen executed for murder during Emmet's rebellion (23 July), although, according to witnesses, he played no part.

19 Sept. Robert Emmet tried at Green Street Court House; hanged and decapitated on 20th.

14 Dec. Michael Dwyer, in revolt in Wicklow since 1798, surrenders with Hugh Byrne, Martin Bourke, Arthur Devlin and John Mearn to Capt. Hume; all transported for life to New South Wales, Australia, on 28 Aug. 1805, where Dwyer eventually becomes High Constable of Sydney.

Bank of Ireland takes over the old Parliament House in College Green.

1804

6 Feb. Sir Evan Nepean appointed C.S.

10 May William Pitt again appointed P.M., following resignation of Henry Addington.

May Cork Street Fever Hospital, Dublin, opens.

11 Nov. Thomas Addis Emmet and family arrive in New York (Emmet has distinguished career at New York Bar, becoming Attorney-General for State of New York in Aug. 1812).

1805

23 Mar. Nicholas Vansittart appointed C.S.

25 Mar. Irish Catholic petition presented to parliament.

9 Apr. Pope Pius VII confirms rules of the community of the Presentation Sisters, founded by Nano Nagle (originally approved by Pope Pius VI in 1791), constituting the congregation an order of the Catholic Church.

27 July d. Brian Merriman (c. 65), poet, author of *Cúirt an Mheáin-Oíche*.

25 Sept. Sir John Newport appointed Chancellor of the Irish Exchequer.

27 Oct. d. Rev. Walter Blake Kirwan, C.I. Dean of Killala, formerly a Roman Catholic.

5 Nov. d. John Claudius Beresford (67), politician.

7 Nov. d. William George Digges La Touche, who extended the La Touche banking business in Dublin.

Agrarian unrest breaks out in the barony of Tyrawley, Co. Mayo; agitators known as 'Carders', 'Threshers' or 'Shakers' object to paying C.I. tithes and R.C. priests' dues; complaining of low wages for farm labourers, weavers and others involved in local industry, they threaten to use combs for carding wool to scrape flesh from bones of their opponents (*see* 2 Sept. 1806).

1806

23 Jan. d. P.M. William Pitt (47); succeeded by Lord Grenville on 11th ('Ministry of All the Talents', including Charles James Fox; *see* 24 Mar. 1807).

24 Feb. d. Edmund Sexton Pery (87), politician.

17 Mar. Foundation stone laid for the College of Surgeons, Dublin; architect Edward Parke.

28 Mar. John Russell, Duke of Bedford, sworn in as L.L.; William Elliot appointed C.S.

21 July L.L. empowered to appoint commissioners to inquire into the state of education in Ireland (reports presented between 1809 and 1813).

2 Sept. Some 30 Threshers (peasant movement) extort money from 10 houses in the district of Corton Watt or Windy Gap in Co. Sligo, a prelude to violent unrest in the Sligo region during the winter, spreading into Leitrim and Longford.

KILKENNY COUNTY LIBRARY

8 Sept. d. Patrick Cotter (*alias* O'Brien) (45), Irish giant (8 ft 1 in. or 246 cm. tall).

10 Nov. Hibernian Bible Society formed.

13 Nov. Granard Militia called out to combat around 500 Threshers, who are quickly dispersed.

5 Dec. Seven Threshers executed for murder of Thady Lavin, who had supplied information on their activities in Sligo.

1807

19 Jan. Inaugural meeting of the Gaelic Society, Dublin.

24 Mar. Lord Grenville's 'Ministry of All the Talents' falls in disagreement over bill to extend the right of Catholics to hold commissions in the army; Whig administration formed under the Duke of Portland on 31st.

Frost destroys 50 per cent of the potato crop.

19 Apr. Charles Lennox, Duke of Richmond, sworn in as L.L.; Sir Arthur Wellesley appointed C.S.

13 May – 6 June General election; Duke of Portland continues as P.M.

May 20 people killed at a faction fight involving Shanavests and Caravats at a fair in Golden, Co. Tipperary.

5 June d. Sir Boyle Roche (64), politician, noted for his 'Irish bulls'.

1 Aug. Insurrection Act empowers L.L. on request of seven local magistrates to proclaim a county or any part of a county as being in a disturbed condition for three years; trial by jury suspended; penalty for breaking curfew (sunset to sunrise) or for administering illegal oaths or possession of arms is transportation for seven years (re-enacted on 30 July 1814).

11 Aug. d. Sylvester O'Halloran (78), doctor and historian.

19–20 Nov. Country swept by severe blizzards; many people killed; two transport ships lost off the east coast.

Nov. Pub. first issue of the *Irish Magazine*, edited by Watty Cox; pro-Irish, pro-Catholic and anti-establishment (runs until 1815).

Pub. *Irish Melodies* by Thomas Moore, with music by Sir John Stevenson; continuations issued regularly until 1834.

1808

30 Jan. Work starts on Nelson's Pillar, sculpted by Thomas Kirk, R.H.A. (121 ft Doric column surmounted by 13 ft statue of Admiral Nelson) (*see* 8 Mar. 1966).

5 May d. Sarah Curran (26), Robert Emmet's beloved, subject of Thomas Moore's 'She Is Far From the Land', then wife of Capt. Henry Sturgeon.

25 May Henry Grattan's motion for a committee to take Catholic petition into consideration defeated (281–128).

George Ponsonby, who has been misinformed, announces during debate on Catholic petition that the Irish clergy are willing to accept royal veto on appointments to vacant bishoprics; start of the 'veto controversy'.

15 Aug. Irish Christian Brothers founded by Edmund Ignatius Rice in Waterford (*see* 5 Sept. 1820).

15 Sept. Catholic hierarchy rejects veto proposal.

1809

7 Mar. Belfast Harp Society inaugurated; Edward Bunting musical director; appoints Arthur O'Neill to supervise school to teach harping to the sightless (project abandoned in 1813).

13 Apr. Robert Dundas appointed C.S.

18 Apr. Henry Brooke Parnell fails to bring forward resolution in favour of assimilating the currencies of Ireland and Great Britain.

24 May Re-establishment of General Committee of the Catholics of Ireland to seek Catholic Emancipation.

30 May Henry Brooke Parnell loses motion for inquiry into manner in which tithes are collected (again fails on 13 Apr. 1810).

18 Oct. William Wellesley-Pole appointed C.S.

7 Nov. Sir Patrick Dun's Hospital opens, established under School of Physic Act (1 Aug. 1800).

1810

12 Apr. d. Joseph Cooper Walker (49), antiquary.

20 June Unlawful Oaths (Ireland) Act extends powers against oath-bound secret societies.

3 July Foundation stone laid for the Belfast Academical Institution (opens on 1 Feb. 1814; known as Royal Belfast Academical Institution from 1831).

10 July Grand Orange Lodge of Ireland adopts new rules which omit secret articles adopted in 1800.

18 Sept. Dublin freemen and freeholders resolve to prepare petition against the Union.

6 Oct. d. Donnchadh Ruadh Mac Con Mara (Denis MacNamara), poet, author of *Eachtra Ghiolla an Amarráin* ('The Adventures of a Luckless Fellow').

3 Nov. 22 killed and over 40 injured in explosion of stolen gunpowder stored in labourer's cottage at Brandy Lane, Cork.

1811

12 Feb. C.S. Wellesley-Pole issues circular to sheriffs and magistrates instructing them to proceed under the Convention Act of 1793 against Catholics involved in appointing delegates to the Catholic Committee.

30 July Proclamation declares illegal the appointment of local representatives to the Catholic Committee.

2 Dec. Society for Promoting the Education of the Poor in Ireland, better known as the Kildare Place Society, founded to organise non-denominational schools. (By 1830 the Society is instructing some 137,639 pupils in 1,621 schools and is in receipt of an annual state grant of £30,000.)

Dec. General meeting of the Catholic Committee in Dublin dispersed by a magistrate as illegal; they reconvene in a nearby tavern.

1812

21 Feb. John Magee (jun.) found guilty of publishing a libel on the Dublin police (*see* 27 July 1813).

Feb. Percy Bysshe Shelley visits Ireland for two months, issuing *An Address to the Irish People.*

11 May P.M. Spencer Perceval assassinated in the lobby of the House of Commons; succeeded by Lord Liverpool (Tory) on 8 June.

18 June Catholic Board (recently formed revival of the Catholic Committee) attributes change of attitude of the Prince of Wales to Catholic Emancipation as due to the malign influence of his mistress, Lady Hertford.

4 Aug. Robert Peel, M.P. for Cashel, appointed C.S. (arrives in Dublin on 1 Sept.).

10 Oct. – 10 Nov. General election; Lord Liverpool returns with increased parliamentary majority.

Agrarian unrest by 'Threshers' or 'Carders', secret societies of cottiers and labourers who resent the high prices demanded by farmers for their produce (in order to pay their own high rents).

Pub. *An Account of Ireland, Statistical and Political* (2 vols) by Edward Wakefield.

1813

Feb. 'Carders' active in Westmeath, Roscommon and King's County; movement spreads to Waterford, Kilkenny, Tipperary and Limerick.

24 May Henry Grattan's Emancipation Bill withdrawn when amendment excluding Catholics from sitting in parliament has been carried by the House of Commons (251–247).

2 July Arms Act limits possession of arms to 'responsible' persons who can demonstrate a need for them; permission for possession is to be granted by local magistrates.

10 July Act provides for Board of Commissioners of Education in Ireland.

27 July John Magee, defended by Daniel O'Connell, convicted of libel on the L.L., the Duke of Richmond; fined £500 and imprisoned for two years.

26 Aug. Charles, Viscount Whitworth, sworn in as L.L.

Economic depression causes rise in agrarian violence.

10 Sept. Fall of Ireland's largest recorded meteorite, the 65 lb 'Limerick Stone'.

22 Dec. d. David Richard Pigot, Chief Baron of the Irish Exchequer.

1814

Jan. Roads rendered impassable for several weeks by snowstorm, considered the worst on record.

1 Feb. Dr William Drennan delivers the inaugural address at the Belfast Academical Institution in College Square (prefix 'Royal' awarded in 1831).

16 Feb. Monsignor Quarantotti, Secretary of the Sacred Congregation for the Propagation of the Faith (Rome), issues rescript (published in Dublin on 5 May) to the effect that Catholic bishops should allow the King veto over episcopal appointments in Ireland, and also permit the government the right to inspect correspondence from Rome; opposition led by Daniel O'Connell leads to withdrawal of rescript (*see* 26 Apr. 1815).

3 June Catholic Board declared illegal.

14 July Clongowes Wood College, Jesuit secondary school, opens.

25 July C.S. Peel's Peace Preservation Act permits the L.L. to establish constabulary force (Peace Preservation Force) at the request of the local magistrary in disturbed areas, to be placed at the disposal of stipendiary magistrates. The policemen become popularly known as 'Peelers'.

30 July Insurrection Act renewed.

12 Aug. First stone laid for the G.P.O. in Sackville Street (now O'Connell Street), Dublin; first building in Ireland specifically designed as a post office.

14 Dec. Leinster House purchased by Dublin Society.

Baptist Irish Society founded in London; considered to be a proselytising agency for Protestantism in Ireland, it uses the Irish language, establishing 60 schools in Connaught.

Pub. *A Statistical Account or Parochial Survey of Ireland* (Vol. I) by William Shaw Mason (completed in 3 vols in 1819).

1815

19 Jan. Daniel O'Connell warns the Catholic authorities in Ireland and Rome that there will be a revolt if veto on episcopal appointments is accepted (*see* 26 Apr.).

1 Feb. Daniel O'Connell kills John D'Esterre, member of the Dublin Corporation, in a duel at Bishopscourt (20 miles from Dublin).

10 Feb. d. Francis Moylan, R.C. Bishop of Cork since 1787.

3 Mar. St Patrick's Catholic Church in Donegall Street, Belfast, consecrated, after which Belfast Catholics issue thanks to 'our much esteemed Protestant and Dissenting Brethren . . . for the disinterested generosity which they manifested'.

28 Mar. John Thomas Troy, R.C. Archbishop of Dublin, lays the foundation stone for St Mary's Metropolitan Chapel (better known as the Pro-Cathedral), in Marlborough Street, Dublin (opened by Archbishop Murray on 14 Nov. 1825); architect John Sweetman.

26 Apr. Cardinal Litta, Prefect of the Sacred Congregation for the Propagation of the Faith, in the 'Genoese Letter' informs the Irish Catholic hierarchy that Rome now rejects proposal to allow British inspection of Roman correspondence (*see* 16 Feb. 1814) but that the Pope does not object to a scheme for submitting names of episcopal candidates for vacant Irish dioceses to the Crown for approval; rejected by the bishops (*see* 24 Aug.).

30 May Henry Brooke Parnell loses motion for committee on laws affecting Catholics.

6 July Charles Bianconi starts a regular service between Clonmel and Cahir, Co. Tipperary (8 miles) (one-horse two-wheeled car ferries passengers, goods and mail; soon increases to two horses, carrying six passengers for approximately 6d).

15 Aug. Disgruntled weavers in Belfast set fire to the home of Francis Johnston, prominent Belfast employer (*see* 20 Jan. 1816).

19 Aug. Meagher, a tithe proctor, is killed when he and his party of eight assistants are attacked by members of an agrarian secret society protesting against collection of tithes in Tipperary.

24 Aug. R.C. bishops adopt anti-veto resolutions for transmission to Rome (*see* 1 Feb. 1816).

1 Sept. Mother Mary Aikenhead appointed superior-general of the Irish Sisters of Charity.

21 Nov. d. James Archibald Hamilton (68), first astronomer of Armagh Observatory.

Dan Donnelly, prize-fighter, beats the English champion Cooper in seven rounds at the Curragh, Co. Kildare (place known as 'Donnelly's Hollow').

Pub. *National Airs* by Thomas Moore.

Pub. *Fugitive Pieces* by William Drennan, containing 'Erin To Her Own Tune' in which he coined the expression 'Emerald Isle' for Ireland.

1816

20 Jan. Weavers again attack the home of Belfast employer Francis Johnston, for which three weavers are hanged in the last public executions in Belfast (*see* 15 Aug. 1815).

1 Feb. Pope, replying to the Irish bishops, reaffirms that he has no objection to the British government exercising veto over Irish episcopal appointments (*see* 26 Apr. 1815).

26 June Act facilitates landlords in recovery of possession of landholdings.

7 July d. Richard Brinsley Sheridan (65), dramatist and politician.

24 Aug. John Herrick and James Cullen hanged in Tipperary town for murder of magistrate William Baker.

Poor harvest, leading to a famine in 1817.

Outbreak of typhus which lasts until late 1819, killing around 50,000.

Nov. d. Arthur O'Neill (90), harper, who taught the instrument to blind children in Belfast.

Halfpenny Bridge, Dublin, built.

1817

5 Jan. Exchequers of Ireland and Great Britain united.

9 May Henry Grattan's motion for Catholic Emancipation defeated.

June First total abstinence society in Europe established in Skibbereen, Co. Cork, by Jeffrey Sedwards.

13 June d. Richard Lovell Edgeworth (73), educationist and inventor.

17 June Foundation stone laid for the Wellington Obelisk in Phoenix Park (completed in 1820); architect Robert Smirke.

8 July d. George Ponsonby (62), politician, former Lord Chancellor.

11 July Act provides 'for the establishment of asylums for the lunatic poor'.

22 July William Sadler makes the first balloon crossing of the Irish sea, from Portobello Barracks, Dublin, to Anglesey, Wales, in six hours.

9 Oct. Charles, Earl Talbot, sworn in as L.L.

14 Oct. d. John Philpot Curran (67), lawyer.

13 Nov. d. John Keogh (77), leading Emancipationist and leader of radical section of Catholic Committee in 1790s.

4 Dec. d. (by suicide, drowning in River Foyle, Derry) Rev. Robert Black (65), supporter of parliamentary reform and Catholic Emancipation; synod agent for the *regium donum* from 2 Dec. 1788.

Trustee Savings Bank established.

Pub. Report of select committee on *The Expediency of Making Further Provision for the Relief of the Lunatic Poor in Ireland.*

Pub. *Irish–English Dictionary* by Edward O'Reilly (reissued in 1821; new edition with supplement by John O'Donovan in 1864).

1818

6 Jan. G.P.O. in Sackville Street, Dublin, opens to the public.

28 Jan. Hiberno-Celtic Society founded.

10 Feb. d. Lady Eleanor Palmer, *née* Ambrose (c. 98), noted beauty.

9 June – 25 July General election; Lord Liverpool (Tory) retains power.

13–14 June First steam crossing between the Clyde and Belfast (in the *Rob Roy*, built by Ritchie & MacLaine, Belfast, with engine made at a Lagan foundry).

30 June Rev. Henry Montgomery elected Moderator of the General Synod of Ulster.

9 July Presbyterian Secession Synod formed (*see* 10 July 1840).

10 July First meeting of the Primitive Wesleyan Methodist Conference, at which Adam Averell is elected President (until 1841); Primitives reunited with Irish Wesleyan Conference in 1878.

3 Aug. Robert Peel replaced as C.S. by Charles Grant.

Pub. *History of the City of Dublin* (2 vols) by John Warburton and James Whitelaw (d. 4 Feb. 1813); completed by Robert Walsh.

1819

3 May Henry Grattan defeated (243–241) on petition in favour of Catholic relief and for a committee of inquiry into laws affecting Catholics. Two days later he speaks in the House of Commons for the last time.

13–14 July The 'Colleen Bawn' murder: Ellen Hanly murdered on the Shannon, providing basis of Gerald Griffin's *The Collegians* (1829); two men, Scanlan and Sullivan, hanged for the killing.

5 Nov. Co. Roscommon placed under Peace Preservation Act; three chief constables, 12 mounted police and 118 foot police under Major Wills assume authority for law and order.

15 Dec. Government asked to 'proclaim' four baronies in Galway in response to Ribbon activity, now found in 14 counties (*see* 26 Jan. 1820).

Pub. *Historical Memoirs of the City of Armagh for a period of 1,373 years* by James Stuart.

1820

19 Jan. Grand Orange Lodge of Ireland issues new set of rules which prohibit members from assisting at or sanctioning 'the making of any member in any other order purporting to be part of the Orange system, than the Orange and Purple'.

26 Jan. Two more baronies in Galway proclaimed for unrest through activities of the Ribbonmen (*see* 18 Feb.).

29 Jan. d. George III; the Regent, the Prince of Wales, succeeds as George IV.

5 Feb. d. William Drennan (66), poet (author of 'The Wake of William Orr') and United Irishman.

18 Feb. Seven more baronies in Galway proclaimed for peasant discontent (all but four western baronies are now under the jurisdiction of the Peace Preservation Force).

13 Mar. – 13 Apr. General election; Lord Liverpool retains power.

6 May Lord John George Beresford enthroned as C.I. Archbishop of Dublin (appointed Archbishop of Armagh and Primate on 17 June 1822).

20 May d. Rev. Paul O'Brien (57), Professor of Irish at Maynooth College from 1802 and author of *Practical Grammar of the Irish Language* (1809).

May Bank failures in Cork herald Munster banking crisis which spreads to Dublin.

4 June d. Henry Grattan (74), politician and orator.

29 June Dublin Society adopts prefix 'Royal' (R.D.S.).

5 Sept. Pope Pius VII issues brief *Ad pastoralis*, sanctioning the 'Religious Brothers of the Christian Schools (Ireland)' or Irish Christian Brothers founded by Edmund Ignatius Rice.

Bull Wall completed to the north of Dublin Bay; beginning of silting up of North Bull Island.

Pub. *A Dictionary of Irish Writers* by Edmund O'Reilly.

Pub. *History of the Town and County of Galway* by James Hardiman.

1821

18 Jan. Theatre Royal opens in Hawkins Street, Dublin.

2 Apr. Bill for Catholic relief including veto passes third reading in the House of Commons by 19 votes (loses by 39 votes in the House of Lords on 17th).

5 June Belfast Natural History Society formed by eight scholars meeting at the home of James Drummond.

2 July Bank of Ireland loses its monopoly when new act permits joint-stock banks outside of Dublin.

12 Aug. – 3 Sept. George IV visits Ireland; Dunleary renamed Kingstown in his honour (now Dún Laoghaire).

Potato failure, leading to famine in 1822.

14 Oct. Major Going, chief constable of the Peace Preservation Force in Limerick, murdered, a victim of Rockite peasant agitation which is now endemic in Munster.

19 Nov. 17 people at the Shea home in Tubber, near Slievenamon, Co. Tipperary, burnt to death, believed to be victims of Rockite agitators.

29 Dec. Richard, Marquis Wellesley, sworn in as L.L; Henry Goulburn appointed C.S.

1822

21 Jan. Lord Bantry and a party of soldiers and police attacked near Buttevant, Co. Cork, by 400 agrarian agitators.

11 Feb. New Insurrection Act becomes law and *habeas corpus* is suspended to combat new wave of peasant agitation (*see* 1 Aug.).

30 Apr. George Canning introduces Catholic Peers Bill to permit Catholic peers to sit in the House of Lords; passes in the House of Commons, but is defeated in the House of Lords by 42 votes (22 June).

6 May d. William Stuart (67), C.I. Archbishop of Armagh and Primate since 1800.

5 July Window and hearth taxes abolished.

22 July Richard ('Humanity Dick') Martin's act 'to prevent the cruel and improper treatment of cattle'.

1 Aug. Constabulary Act empowers L.L. to establish a constabulary in each county, organised on a baronial basis under a chief constable; requires magistrates to appoint constables and sub-constables up to a maximum of 16 per barony or half-barony; chief constables to report to C.S. every three months.

12 Aug. d. (suicide) Robert Stewart (53), 2nd Marquis of Londonderry, formerly Lord Castlereagh, C.S. 1798–1801.

24 Oct. William Magee, C.I. Archbishop of Dublin, inaugurates the 'Second Reformation' when he states in St Patrick's Cathedral that Catholics have a church without a religion, and the Dissenters a religion without a church; counter-attack issued by James Warren Doyle, R.C. Bishop of Kildare and Leighlin ('J.K.L.').

5 Nov. Loreto nuns begin educational work in Ireland at Loreto Abbey, Rathfarnham, Dublin.

14 Dec. 'Playhouse' or 'Bottle' riot at the Theatre Royal, Hawkins Street, Dublin, when a bottle is thrown at L.L. Wellesley by Orangemen who take exception to his support for Catholic Emancipation.

Rev. Henry Cooke, Presbyterian minister of Killyleagh, Co. Down, attacks what he holds to be the Arian views of the staff at the Belfast Academical Institution (Arians deny that Jesus shared fully in the divine nature of God) (*see* 18–20 Aug. 1829).

St George Steam Packet Co. (later City of Cork Steam Packet Co.) for cross-channel traffic founded.

1823

12 Jan. d. Rev. Andrew George Malcolm, Presbyterian, Moderator of the General Synod of Ulster.

11 Feb. Col. Henry White (backed by Daniel O'Connell) defeats the Orange candidate, Sir Compton Domville, to win Dublin County by-election (994–849).

21 Feb. d. Rev. Charles Wolfe (32), poet (author of 'The Burial of Sir John Moore at Corunna').

25 Apr. Daniel O'Connell and Richard Lalor Sheil preside at meeting of 20 Catholics in Dempsey's tavern, Sackville Street, Dublin, which resolves to form an organisation to agitate for Catholic Emancipation; they inaugurate the Catholic Association on 12 May at the same venue.

11 May d. John Thomas Troy (84), R.C. Archbishop of Dublin since 1786; succeeded by Daniel Murray.

12 June Rioting at a fair in Maghera, Co. Londonderry, between Orangemen and Catholics results in several killed and many wounded.

18 July Unlawful Oaths Act directed against all Irish secret societies, including the Orange Order (*see* 4 Aug.).

Act abolishes minimum charge on stills and encourages improvement in plant and product; standard liquor measures are prescribed for Ireland, England and Scotland in Sept. 1824 (*see* 5 Jan. 1826).

19 July Irish Tithe Composition Act permits C.I. clergymen and parishioners to appoint arbitrators to determine fixed money payments due from parish as a substitute for tithes.

4 Aug. Orange Order, in the wake of the Unlawful Oaths Act (*see* 18 July), changes rules: there is to be no oath on admission, but members must show that at some time they have taken an oath of allegiance or of supremacy or of abjuration before a magistrate.

5 Aug. Royal Hibernian Academy of Arts receives charter (new charter issued in 1861).

30 Aug. Belfast gas lighting system goes into operation; stated by American experts to be 'the best constructed and most complete which they had ever beheld'.

9 Sept. Protestants interrupt a Catholic funeral to object to Catholic prayers in the Protestant cemetery at St Kevin's Church, Dublin; Catholic Association committee decides to buy land for Catholic graveyards (Golden Bridge opened in 1829; Glasnevin opened in 1831).

Harp removed from Irish coinage (reappears in 1928).

1824

Feb. Catholic Association introduces the 'Catholic Rent' on proposal of Daniel O'Connell.

18 May Select committee of the House of Lords begins sitting (to 23 June) in investigation into faction-fighting in Ireland.

21 May Resolution of the Grand Orange Lodge of Ireland bans all demonstrations on 12 July.

14 June Commission of inquiry into education in Ireland (final report on 30 May 1825).

21 June Report of the committee of the House of Commons on 'general survey and valuation' of Ireland (Spring Rice Report); next day the Board of Ordnance orders Thomas Colby to undertake a cartographic survey of the country (*see* 9 May 1833).

10 July John Jebb, C.I. Bishop of Limerick, defends tithes in the House of Lords.

29 Oct. Pub. first issue of the Dublin *Morning Register,* founded by Michael Staunton.

16 Dec. Daniel O'Connell's 'Bolivar' speech leads to charges of uttering seditious language (20 Dec.) (*see* 3 Jan. 1825).

27 Dec. d. Rev. William Steel Dickson (80), Presbyterian United Irishman who fought for Catholic Emancipation.

Pub. *An Inquiry into the Principles of the Distribution of Wealth* by William Thompson.

Pub. *A Vindication of the Religious and Civil Principles of the Irish Catholics* by James Warren Doyle, Bishop of Kildare and Leighlin ('J.K.L.').

1825

3 Jan. Indictment against Daniel O'Connell rejected by Dublin Grand Jury (Protestant) (*see* 16 Dec. 1824).

Jan. Four Inspectors-General of the County Constabulary installed: George Warburton (Connaught); Thomas Powell (Leinster); Richard Willcock (Munster); Thomas D'Arcy (Ulster).

9 Mar. Unlawful Societies (Ireland) Act forbids 'political confederacies'; directed at the Catholic Association and the Orange Order (*see* 18 Mar.).

18 Mar. Final meeting of the Orange Order (*see* 9 Mar.); members are advised 'that any lodge meeting after this day commits a breach of the law'; Order replaced by the Loyal and Benevolent Orange Institution of Ireland, with the Earl of Aldborough as Grand Master.

Catholic Association dissolves (*see* 9 Mar. *and* 13 July).

21 Mar. Patrick Curtis, R.C. Archbishop of Armagh, argues case for Catholic Emancipation before the House of Lords.

25 Mar. Sir Francis Burdett moves for a committee of the House of Commons to consider laws affecting Catholics; his bill proposes two 'wings': disfranchisement of forty-shilling freeholders and payment of clergy (*see* 25 Apr. *and* 10 May).

25 Apr. Duke of York (the King's brother) strongly opposes Burdett's Catholic Relief Bill.

10 May Burdett's Catholic Relief Bill passed by the Commons, but is defeated in the House of Lords on 18th.

13 July Daniel O'Connell launches the 'new' Catholic Association (to circumvent Unlawful Societies Act).

23 Aug. d. Michael Dwyer (53), United Irishman, at Cabramatta, Liverpool, New South Wales, Australia, where he has been a police chief.

Northern, Hibernian and Provincial Banks founded.

James Murphy founds Midleton, Co. Cork, distillery.

Richard Lonergan's *Carrick's Morning Post* (founded in 1812) becomes the first Irish newspaper to have labour problems.

Pub. *The Fairy Legends and Traditions of the South of Ireland* by Thomas Crofton Croker.

1826

5 Jan. Separate Irish currency (a concept with no reality) abolished when Irish currency is assimilated with British; Irish gallon and bushel measures standardised to facilitate excise collection.

7 Mar. Sir Francis Burdett's second motion on Catholic relief defeated (276–272); the first pro-Catholic vote to be lost in the Commons since 1819.

13 Mar. Pope Leo XII's encyclical *Quo graviara* condemns secret societies.

26 May Act provides for uniform valuation of lands and tenements for local taxation; Richard Griffith later appointed commissioner of valuation.

12 June – 8 July General election; Lord Liverpool retains power.

1 July Richard Power (1,426 votes) and Henry Villiers Stuart (1,357 votes), Protestant pro-Emancipationist, supported by Daniel O'Connell, defeat Lord George Thomas Beresford (527) in Co. Waterford.

9 July Weavers from the Liberties of Dublin protest against unemployment.

9 Oct. d. Michael Kelly (62), actor, vocalist and composer.

Pub. *Christian Examiner* by Rev. Caesar Otway and J. H. Singer, the first Irish religious magazine associated with the Established Church.

1827

10 Apr. George Canning (Liberal Tory) succeeds Liverpool as P.M.; supports Catholic Emancipation; Sir Robert Peel resigns Home Office.

19–25 Apr. Debate on matters of religion between Rev. Richard T. P. Pope (representing Evangelical Protestantism) and Fr Thomas Maguire, jointly chaired by Admiral Oliver and Daniel O'Connell, at the Dublin Institution arouses great public interest.

29 Apr. William Lamb appointed C.S.

8 Aug. d. P.M. George Canning; succeeded by Viscount Goderich (Liberal Tory) (*see* 11 Dec.).

5 Nov. Sir Anthony Hart appointed Lord Chancellor of Ireland.

11 Dec. P.M. Goderich proffers resignation, then withdraws it (*see* 8 Jan. 1828).

Rev. Henry Cooke successfully presses for declaration of Trinitarian belief by the Presbyterian General Synod, leading to the withdrawal of Rev. Henry Montgomery and Arians (*see* 16 Oct. 1828 *and* 18–20 Aug. 1829).

Pub. *Personal Sketches of His Own Times* (Vols I–II) by Sir Jonah Barrington (completed in 3 vols in 1832).

1828

8 Jan. P.M. Goderich resigns; succeeded by the Duke of Wellington (Tory) (22nd), from whom the King extracts a promise that Catholic Emancipation will not be a cabinet question.

13 Jan. First of the simultaneous parish meetings organised by the Catholic Association (meetings are held in some 1,600 of the country's 2,500 parishes).

1 Feb. Daniel O'Connell issues 'Address of the Catholic Association to the Protestant Dissenters of England'.

1 Mar. William Henry Paget, Marquis of Anglesey, sworn in as L.L.

12 May Government defeat when Sir Francis Burdett's motion for settlement of the Catholic question is passed by the House of Commons (272–266); motion defeated in the House of Lords (9 July).

21 May C.S. Lamb resigns; succeeded by Lord Francis Leveson-Gower on 21 June.

24 June Catholic Association declares opposition to the new Wellington administration and to all Irish M.P.s who support it.

2 July L.L. Anglesey writes to C.S. recommending 'earnest consideration' of Catholic Emancipation.

5 July Following five days of polling, Daniel O'Connell (2,057 votes) defeats William Vesey-FitzGerald (982) in Clare by-election (*see* 15 May 1829).

7 July d. Rev. John Lanigan (70), ecclesiastical historian, author of *An Ecclesiastical History of Ireland* (4 vols, 1812).

26 July L.L. Anglesey points out that Ireland is on the verge of rebellion and urges concessions to Catholics.

29 July d. Charles O'Conor (64), librarian at Stowe and antiquary; author of *Rerum Hibernicarum Scriptores Veteres* (4 vols, 1814–28).

1 Aug. P.M. Wellington advises the King that Ireland is on the verge of rebellion and that the majority in the House of Commons believe that Catholic Emancipation is the only solution.

14 Aug. At a banquet hosted by the Duke of Brunswick, Thomas Langlois Lefroy founds the Brunswick Constitutional Club to preserve 'the integrity of the Protestant Constitution'.

23 Aug. d. John Foster (88), Baron Oriel, last Speaker of the Irish House of Commons.

4 Sept. Annaghdown boating tragedy on Lough Corrib, Co. Galway, when 19 are drowned; lament 'Anach Cuain' subsequently composed by Antoine Ó Reachtabhra.

15 Sept. Revival of the Orange Order is marked by the visit of the British Grand Secretary, Eustace Chetwoode, who gives the English signs and passwords to the Irish Orangemen.

Oct. – Nov. Unrest in Clare over the existence of a Brunswick Club in Mountshannon; spreads to Limerick and Tipperary.

16 Oct. Rev. Henry Montgomery (Arian leader) and supporters adopt the 'Remonstrance' in Belfast, in opposition to Rev. Henry Cooke (Trinitarian leader); proposals for separation and reorganisation within the Presbyterian Church arranged on 8 Sept. (*see* 18–20 Aug. 1829).

23 Dec. Augher, Co. Tyrone, almost destroyed in fighting between Catholics and Protestants after a fair.

28 Dec. L.L. Anglesey informed by Wellington that he is to be recalled.

Pub. *Personal Narrative of the Rebellion of 1798* by Charles Hamilton Teeling (*A Sequel* pub. in 1832).

1829

1 Jan. Publication of a letter from L.L. Anglesey to Patrick Curtis, R.C. Archbishop of Armagh, recommending that all constitutional means should be used to forward the cause of Catholic Emancipation; Anglesey recalled.

27 Jan. Rev. Henry Montgomery, leading Presbyterian, speaks in favour of Catholic Emancipation at a meeting in St Patrick's, Donegall Street, Belfast, presided over by William Crolly, R.C. Bishop of Down and Connor.

5 Feb. Parliamentary session opens; King's Speech announces proposal for Catholic Emancipation.

Coombe Hospital opens (founded in 1826 by Margaret Boyle); Richard Gregory first Master.

5 Mar. Sir Robert Peel introduces Catholic Relief Bill (*see* 13 Apr.).

'Act for the suppression of dangerous associations or assemblies in Ireland'; Catholic Association suppressed.

6 Mar. Hugh Percy, Duke of Northumberland, sworn in as L.L.

14 Mar. d. Francis Johnston (69), architect (G.P.O., Dublin).

13 Apr. 'Act for the relief of His Majesty's Roman Catholic subjects' receives royal assent, permitting Catholics to enter parliament by taking a new oath and allows them access to a variety of other state and military offices.

Irish parliamentary elections act raises property qualification for franchise from 40s to £10 freehold; reduces Irish electorate from 216,000 to 37,000.

15 May Daniel O'Connell presents himself before the bar of the House of Commons to claim his seat, but is refused on 18th on the grounds that the Catholic Relief Act is not retrospective.

30 July O'Connell again returned as M.P. for Clare, unopposed (*see* 4 Feb. 1830).

Poor harvest, leading to famine in 1830.

18–20 Aug. Rev. Henry Montgomery and his Arian followers secede from Presbyterian General Synod and establish their own Remonstrant Synod, which meets for the first time on 25 May 1830.

19 Sept. d. Jeremiah John Callanan (34), poet (author of 'Gougane Barra').

18 Oct. Mary Street Church opened in Belfast for the Rev. Henry Cooke, prominent Presbyterian preacher.

22 Oct. 'Doneraile Conspiracy' trial ends, a triumph for Daniel O'Connell, defending.

The Queen's Theatre, formerly the Adelphi, founded.

Pub. *The Collegians* (3 vols, anon.) by Gerald Griffin.

1830

4 Feb. Daniel O'Connell becomes the first Catholic in modern history to take seat in the House of Commons.

Famine widespread.

10 May Zoological Society of Dublin formed; Zoological Gardens, Dublin, third oldest in the world, open to the public on 1 Sept. (a wild boar the first animal housed).

26 June d. George IV (68); succeeded by William IV.

July Food riots in Limerick and Leitrim.

17 July Sir Henry Hardinge appointed C.S.

Aug. First Dublin Horse Show.

2–24 Aug. General election (*see* 16 Nov.).

17 Aug. The O'Gorman Mahon elected M.P. for Clare, but unseated on charges of bribery.

Oct. John O'Donovan appointed to the topographic department of the Irish Ordnance Survey, under George Petrie (survey discontinued in 1839 on grounds of expense).

25 Oct. d. Denys Scully (57), leading Catholic advocate and political writer.

16 Nov. Duke of Wellington's administration resigns; Earl Grey (Whig) forms government on 22nd.

29 Nov. Edward Stanley appointed C.S.

23 Dec. Marquis of Anglesey returns as L.L., this time in opposition to Daniel O'Connell's demand for Repeal.

Pub. *Traits and Stories of the Irish Peasantry,* first series (2 vols) by William Carleton.

1831

Jan. – June Agrarian unrest fomented by the Terry Alts breaks out in Clare and Limerick.

3 Mar. Confrontation over tithes at Graiguenamanagh, Co. Kilkenny; start of 'tithe war'.

KILKENNY COUNTY LIBRARY

R.C. Bishop James Doyle ('J.K.L.'), in pamphlet on the origin, nature and destination of church property, advocates policy of passive resistance to tithes.

4–21 May General election; Earl Grey returns with increased parliamentary majority.

31 May 17 killed during clash over tithes at Castlepollard, Co. Westmeath.

18 June Yeomen fire into a crowd at Newtownbarry, Co. Wexford, killing 17 and wounding 20.

12 July Appearance of yeomen in an Orange procession sparks off a riot at Belturbet, Co. Cavan.

27 July d. John Toler (86), 1st Earl of Norbury, judge whose wit sometimes compensated for his notoriously defective knowledge of the law. (Daniel O'Connell failed to have him dismissed from the Bench, but he was induced to retire in 1827 with a pension of £3,046).

18 Aug. d. William Magee, C.I. Archbishop of Dublin since 1822, noted supporter of the Evangelical or 'Second Reformation' movement.

9 Sept. C.S. Stanley secures £30,000 to provide for a system of 'national education' (*see* 31 Oct.).

15 Oct. Barrack Board or Board of Works reorganised by act.

Tumultuous Risings Act substitutes transportation for capital punishment for certain crimes.

23 Oct. Richard Whately consecrated C.I. Archbishop of Dublin (founds chair of Political Economy at T.C.D. in 1832).

31 Oct. 'Stanley Letter', in which C.S. Stanley outlines his scheme for a national system of non-denominational education to the Duke of Leinster (*see* 26 Nov.).

Nov. John Scott Vandeleur founds pioneering agricultural co-operative on his estate at Ralahine, Co. Clare, primarily to offset influence of secret societies in the area; venture collapses within two years, largely as a result of Vandeleur's gambling excesses.

1 Nov. Belfast Museum opens.

26 Nov. Commissioners of National Education appointed.

12 Dec. Sisters of Mercy established, with Catherine McAuley as superior (papal approval received on 24 Mar. 1835).

14 Dec. 40 policemen on 'tithe duty' clash with a mob of some 2,000 at Carrickshock, Co. Kilkenny; chief constable and 16 of his men killed and 7 seriously wounded.

Pub. *Irish Minstrelsy or Bardic Remains of Ireland* (2 vols) by James Hardiman.

1832

5 Jan. Pub. first issue of the *Dublin University Magazine,* co-founded by Isaac Butt (runs until 1877).

18 Jan. Daniel O'Connell's National Council meets for the first time.

Feb. Agrarian unrest fomented by the Whitefeet in the midlands.

15 Mar. First reports of cholera (Belfast); reported in Dublin on 25th and in Cork on 12 Apr.

9 May P.M. Grey resigns when the House of Lords rejects his third reform bill; reinstated as P.M. when Wellington fails to form a government.

30 June Pub. first issue of the *Dublin Penny Journal,* founded and edited by Rev. Caesar Otway with George Petrie.

24 July d. Patrick Curtis (92), R.C. Archbishop of Armagh and Primate since 1819.

7 Aug. Representation of the People (Ireland) Act (Irish Reform Act) increases Irish representation in the House of Commons from 100 to 105; £10 franchise in boroughs; electorate increases to 92,141 (1.2 per cent of the population, giving enfranchisement of 1 in 115 in Ireland compared with 1 in 24 in England).

16 Aug. Party Processions Act, designed to curb sectarian conflict.

Irish Tithe Composition Act provides for commutation.

Nov. College of Surgeons staff open the Royal City of Dublin Hospital in Upper Baggot Street with 52 beds and an out-patient department.

12 Dec. – 2 Jan. 1833 General election; Earl Grey continues as P.M.

22 Dec. Rioting in Belfast when mob attacks the mainly Catholic Hercules Street; four people killed by policemen.

Pub. *Abstract of a Course of Lectures on Electricity and Galvanism delivered in the Roman Catholic College, Maynooth* by Rev. Nicholas Callan.

1833

29 Jan. Opening of the first parliament to be held under the provisions of the Reform Act of 1832.

28 Mar. d. William Thompson (48), political economist and social reformer.

C.S. Stanley transferred to the colonial office.

29 Mar. Sir John Cam Hobhouse appointed C.S., but does not come over.

2 Apr. Coercion Act empowers L.L. to proclaim a disturbed area; declares it unlawful to hold meetings of any kind in such an area; provides for trial by courts martial; suspends *habeas corpus* for any prisoner for three months after arrest; L.L. Anglesey resigns in protest.

9 May 6-inch maps of Co. Londonderry presented to the King, the first results of the survey undertaken by Thomas Colby (*see* 21 June 1824).

17 May Edward John Littleton appointed C.S.

14 Aug. Church Temporalities (Ireland) Act abolishes church cess, paid by Protestants and Catholics alike for the upkeep of C.I. property; replaces it by tax on all clerical incomes of over £200 p.a.; 10 C.I. bishoprics abolished, reducing C.I. dioceses to 12.

25 Sept. Royal Commission of Inquiry into the Conditions of the Poorer Classes in Ireland established under chairmanship of Richard Whately, C.I. Archbishop of Dublin (first report in 1835).

26 Sept. Marquis Wellesley again sworn in as L.L.

25 Oct. d. John Walker (65), founder of the 'Church of God' or 'Separatists' or 'Walkerites' (c. 1804).

25 Dec. Rioting in Belfast at York Street, Millfield and Peter's Hill.

Pub. *The Rise and Fall of the Irish Nation* by Sir Jonah Barrington (Paris).

1834

6 Jan. d. Richard ('Humanity Dick') Martin (80), politician; founder of the Royal Society for the Prevention of Cruelty to Animals (1824).

23 Jan. St Vincent's Hospital, St Stephen's Green, Dublin, opens under the Sisters of Charity.

27 Jan. d. Roger O'Connor (71), United Irishman and author.

8 Apr. d. Sir Jonah Barrington (74), politician and historian.

4 June Royal Commission established to investigate 'the state of religious and other instruction in Ireland'; produces the first complete, systematic enumeration of religious affiliation.

15 June d. James Warren Doyle (48), R.C. Bishop of Kildare and Leighlin since 1819, noted controversialist (writing under pseudonym 'J.K.L.').

24 June Over 200 killed and several hundred injured when an estimated 3,000 participate in one of the bloodiest faction fights of the century, between the Cooleens and the Lawlor-Black Mulvihills at Ballyveigh Strand, Co. Kerry.

16 July William Lamb, Lord Melbourne (Liberal), appointed P.M.

31 July First train runs in Ireland, from Dublin to Kingstown, drawn by horses (*see* 17 Dec.).

2 Aug. John MacHale, R.C. Bishop of Killala, translated to Tuam.

1 Nov. d. Archibald Hamilton Rowan (83), United Irishman.

14 Nov. King effectively dismisses P.M. Melbourne; Sir Robert Peel (Conservative) forms a government on 10 Dec.

16 Dec. Sir Henry Hardinge again appointed C.S.

17 Dec. First train drawn by steam-power runs from Dublin to Kingstown (from Westland Row station, carrying directors and wives, followed by the first regular passenger train, the *Hibernia*); takes 19½ minutes; ships are diverted from the port of Dublin to Kingstown harbour to link up with the new service.

18 Dec. Attempt to collect tithes at Gortroe, Rathcormac, Co. Cork, leads to at least nine deaths in the last major confrontation of the 'tithe war'.

23 Dec. Evangelical Rev. Edward Nangle opens his first school at Slievemore on Achill Island, the start of his Achill mission (*see* 31 July 1837).

Last reported sighting of the Great Auk, off Waterford harbour.

Pub. *History of the Presbyterian Church in Ireland* (Vol. I) by James Seaton Reid (Vol. II, 1837).

1835

6 Jan. Thomas Hamilton, Earl of Haddington, sworn in as L.L.

14 Jan. d. Thomas Kelly, R.C. Archbishop of Armagh.

18 Feb. Daniel O'Connell meets with prominent Whigs and Radicals at Lichfield House, London, where a 'compact' is agreed: Radicals are committed to co-operation with Whigs and O'Connell.

27 Feb. O'Connell offers to help Whigs defeat P.M. Peel in return for amendment of the Irish Reform Act (7 Aug. 1832) to give equality of terms with England, Irish municipal reform and tithe reform (including principle of commutation).

28 Mar. Lord John Russell presides over a dinner attended by 264 members of the Whig, Radical and Irish parties.

30 Mar. Debate on the Irish Tithe Bill begins.

3–8 Apr. P.M. Sir Robert Peel suffers defeats on 3rd, 6th and 7th; resigns.

18 Apr. Lord Melbourne again appointed P.M. and announces his ministry.

22 Apr. George William Frederick Howard, Viscount Morpeth, appointed C.S.

8 May William Crolly, R.C. Bishop of Down and Connor, translated to Armagh.

11 May Constantine Phipps, Earl of Mulgrave, sworn in as L.L.

20 July House of Commons receives first and second reports of the select committee on Orangeism (two other reports presented on 6 Aug. and 7 Sept.).

25 July Thomas Drummond appointed Under-Secretary (d. in office on 15 Apr. 1840).

25 Dec. d. Antoine Ó Reachtabhra (Raftery) (c. 51), Gaelic poet.

William Jury opens his hotel in College Green, Dublin.

Potato failure in Ulster.

Royal Commission on poverty (*see* 25 Sept. 1833) reveals that 75 per cent of labourers in Ireland exist without regular employment.

Pub. *Ordnance Survey of the County of Londonderry* by Thomas Larcom.

1836

14 Apr. Orange Order dissolved.

20 May Constabulary (Ireland) Act amalgamates Peace Preservation Force and the County Constabulary, centralising executive authority under an Inspector-General, with two deputies, four inspectors for the provinces, 32 sub-inspectors and 18 chief constables per county (*see* 4 July).

3 June d. Barry O'Meara (47), Napoleon's doctor on St Helena.

2 July Daniel O'Connell forms the General Association of Ireland (National Association for Municipal Reform).

4 July Dublin Police Act establishes a constabulary force for the Dublin metropolitan area (Dublin Metropolitan Police).

9 Aug. Rev. Henry Cooke's expulsion of the Arian leaders from the Presbyterian Synod of Ulster is followed by the enactment of unqualified subscription to the Westminster Confession.

18 Aug. d. Thomas Reynolds (65), United Irishman and informer.

Widespread failure of the potato crop.

15 Nov. George Nicholls presents his first report on the Poor Law in Ireland (opposes any form of outdoor relief).

28 Dec. d. William Sampson (72), United Irishman, in New York.

Royal and Ulster Banks founded.

1837

11 Jan. d. John Field (55), composer, in Moscow.

20 June d. William IV (72); succeeded by Queen Victoria.

31 July – 17 Aug. General election; Lord Melbourne continues as P.M.

31 July Pub. first issue of *Achill Missionary Herald and Western Witness*, owned and published by Rev. Edward Nangle, Evangelical in Connaught, to 'bear a faithful and uncompromising testimony against the superstition and idolatry of the Church of Rome'.

Further failure of the potato crop.

24 Nov. d. Dr Bartholomew Lloyd (65), Provost of T.C.D. since 1831, pioneering mathematics teacher, also Regius Professor of Greek and lecturer in Divinity.

Pub. *A Topographical Dictionary of Ireland* (2 vols) by Samuel Lewis.

1838

4 Apr. *Sirius*, the first steamship to cross the Atlantic unaided by sail, leaves Cork, captained by Richard Roberts (b. Passage West, 1803); arrives in New York on 22 Apr., eight

KILKENNY COUNTY LIBRARY

hours before its rival, the *Great Western*.

10 Apr. With the words 'Here goes, in the name of God', Fr Theobald Mathew starts his temperance movement in a schoolroom in Cove Street, Cork, assisted by William Martin, a Quaker; 60 people take pledge to abstain from 'all intoxicating drinks, except used medicinally'.

11 July Stephen Woulfe becomes the first Catholic in modern times to be appointed Chief Baron of the Irish Exchequer (d. 2 July 1840).

31 July Poor Relief (Ireland) Act divides the country into 130 'unions', each of which is to have a workhouse to administer indoor relief only, under a Board of Guardians, consisting of representative ratepayers.

15 Aug. Tithe Rent-charge Act commutes the tithe into a rent-charge, reducing the amount payable.

1 Sept. George Nicholls takes up post of Poor Law Commissioner for Ireland (until Dec. 1842).

11 Sept. Four Assistant Commissioners of the Poor Law, all with experience of administration of Poor Law in England, meet in Dublin to organise administration for Ireland (present their report on 9 Oct.).

Report of the Wyse Committee on education.

1839

6–7 Jan. 'Night of the Big Wind' causes widespread devastation.

11 Jan. d. William Saurin (82), lawyer.

19 Feb. d. Rev. Robert Magill (51), Presbyterian orthodox preacher, poet and satirist.

3 Mar. d. Robert Perceval (83), physician and philanthropist, known as the 'Irish Howard' for his work on prison reform; first Professor of Chemistry at T.C.D. (1783).

25 Mar. d. Power Le Poer Trench (69), C.I. Archbishop of Tuam since 1819, leading Evangelical who promoted the 'Second Reformation' in Connaught.

3 Apr. Hugh Fortescue, Viscount Ebrington, sworn in as L.L.

8 Apr. The 130 Irish Poor Law unions come into existence (*see* 24 Apr. 1840).

13 May d. Gideon Ouseley (77), Methodist who preached among the native Irish-speakers, mainly in Ulster.

12 Aug. Opening of the Ulster Railway in Great Victoria Street, Belfast; the first railway in Ulster.

24 Aug. Unlawful Oaths Act, directed against societies making use of signs and passwords or formed to obtain arms.

4 Dec. d. Rev. James Armstrong (59), Unitarian minister, founder of the Association of Irish Non-Subscribing Presbyterians (1835).

Royal Institute of Architects founded.

Adelaide Hospital under Protestant management by Dr Albert Jasper Walsh at 43 Bride Street, Dublin.

Gosford Castle, Markethill, Co. Armagh, largest castle in Ulster, completed.

Pub. *Lives of Illustrious and Distinguished Irishmen* (Vol. I) by James Wills (Vol. II, 1840; completed in 1847; reissued as *The Irish Nation*).

Pub. *L'Irlande Sociale, Politique et Religieuse* (2 vols) by Gustave de Beaumont (Paris).

1840

17 Mar. Irish Archaeological Society founded by George Petrie, William Stokes and Lord Dunraven.

15 Apr. Daniel O'Connell forms the National Association of Ireland from the Precursor Society (*see* 13 July).

d. Thomas Drummond (43), whose handling of the 'tithe war' as Under-Secretary (1835–40) was generally acclaimed.

20 Apr. d. Standish O'Grady (74), 1st Viscount Guillamore, lawyer, Attorney-General (1803–5).

24 Apr. First union workhouse opened (South Dublin).

12 June d. Gerald Griffin (37), novelist and poet, author of *The Collegians* (1829).

10 July Union of the General Synod of Ulster and Secession Synod to form General Assembly of the Presbyterian Church in Ireland; first Moderator Rev. Samuel Hanna.

13 July National Association of Ireland renamed the Loyal National Repeal Association, led by Daniel O'Connell.

26 July First great meeting for repeal of the Act of Union held at Castlebar, Co. Mayo.

10 Aug. Irish Municipal Reform Act reorganises the local authorities: dissolves 58 municipal corporations and reconstitutes 10; towns with a valuation of less than £100 to be administered by the Poor Law Guardians.

1841

7 Jan. d. Major Henry Charles Sirr, police chief in Dublin (1798–1826), magistrate (1808); antiquary (his collection purchased by the R.I.A.); captor of Lord Edward FitzGerald and Robert Emmet.

17–19 Apr. Thomas Davis and John Blake Dillon join the Repeal Association.

5 June P.M. Melbourne defeated (312–311) on vote of confidence (*see* 30 Aug.).

6 June First reliable census of the population of Ireland conducted under the direction of Thomas Larcom; 8,175,124 (increase of 5.25 per cent since 1831; estimated increase of 172 per cent since 1779).

1–19 July General election (*see* 30 Aug.).

12 July d. Dr William McNeven (78), United Irishman and author, in New York.

30 Aug. Sir Robert Peel (Conservative) appointed P.M.

Pub. first issue of the *Cork Examiner*, founded by John Francis Maguire to support Daniel O'Connell.

1842

16 Mar. d. Rev. Caesar Otway (62), writer and Protestant controversialist.

8 June d. (suicide) Henry Brooke Parnell (66), politician and historian.

18 June Death penalty abolished for numerous offences under the Capital Punishment (Ireland) Act.

13 Aug. d. John Banim (44), novelist, playwright and poet.

21 Aug. d. William Maginn (49), poet and journalist, co-founder of *Fraser's Magazine* (1830).

6 Sept. Edward, Lord Eliot, appointed C.S.

15 Sept. Thomas, Earl de Grey, sworn in as L.L.

22 Sept. Johann Georg Kohl arrives in Ireland; his observations, *Travels in Ireland*, pub. 1844.

15 Oct. Pub. first issue of the *Nation*, founded by Charles Gavan Duffy, John Blake Dillon and Thomas Davis; sells out by noon; 6d per copy; organ of movement to be known as Young Ireland.

18 Oct. Fr John Hand opens All Hallows College to train students for missionary work.

Pub. 'Lament for the Death of Owen Roe O'Neill' in the *Nation* establishes Thomas Davis as a patriotic poet.

1 Nov. Daniel O'Connell elected Lord Mayor of Dublin.

10 Nov. Papal rescript permits each bishop to decide his attitude towards the Board of National Education.

d. Catherine McAuley (63), founder of the Irish Sisters of Mercy.

Passenger Act regulates general passenger conditions aboard ships.

It is estimated that £6 million p.a. leaves the country to absentee landlords.

1843

7 Jan. 'Munster War Song', first published contribution by Richard D'Alton Williams, appears in the *Nation*.

25–28 Feb. Dublin Corporation debates Daniel O'Connell's motion 'that a petition should be presented to parliament from the Corporation of Dublin for the repeal of the Union between Great Britain and Ireland'; carried by 45 votes to 15.

9 Mar. Repeal monster meeting held at Trim, Co. Meath.

31 Mar. Foundation stone laid for Conciliation Hall, O'Connell's headquarters (opens on 23 Oct.).

19 Apr. An estimated 120,000 attend Repeal meeting at Limerick.

23 Apr. 150,000 attend Repeal meeting at Kells, Co. Meath.

1 May Meeting of followers of Joshua Jacob ('White Quakers') in Dublin.

9 May P.M. Peel announces that he will not hesitate to ask parliament for powers to counter the Repeal agitation.

14 May Addressing a Repeal meeting at Mullingar, Co. Westmeath, William Higgins, R.C. Bishop of Ardagh and Clonmacnoise, announces: 'I know that every Catholic bishop in Ireland, without an exception, is an ardent Repealer' (this is rejected by the Archbishop of Dublin, Daniel Murray, on 23 May).

15 May Pub. *The Spirit of the Nation*; 2nd ed. on 10 Sept.; Part II on 11 Nov.; new ed. begins monthly publication on 1 July 1844; last ed. (59th) in 1934.

21 May 500,000 estimated at Repeal meeting at Cork; 300,000 reported at Cashel, Co. Tipperary.

11 June At a Repeal meeting at Mallow, Co. Cork, O'Connell issues his 'Mallow Defiance'.

15 Aug. O'Connell holds monster meeting at Tara, Co. Meath, where he is joined by John McLaughlin, R.C. Bishop of Derry, and John Cantwell, R.C. Bishop of Meath, in front of 750,000 people (the largest gathering held in Ireland until the Eucharistic Congress of 1932).

7 Oct. L.L. proclaims O'Connell's proposed meeting at Clontarf, scheduled for 8th; O'Connell cancels the meeting.

14 Oct. O'Connell arrested on charge of conspiracy.

16 Oct. Mathematician Sir William Rowan Hamilton, having suddenly discovered the formula for multiplication of quaternions, scratches it on bridge over the Royal Canal, Ballyboggan, Dublin (*see* 1853).

20 Oct. William Smith O'Brien joins the Repeal Association.

6 Nov. d. Charles Kendal Bushe (76), 'the Incorruptible', lawyer and Lord Chief Justice (1822–41).

20 Nov. Devon Commission appointed to examine the law and practice relating to occupation of land in Ireland (reports on 14 Feb. 1845).

1844

15 Jan. Daniel O'Connell, his son John, Charles Gavan Duffy, Thomas Steele, John Gray and Richard Barrett ('traversers') put on trial for conspiracy; found guilty in Feb.; Daniel O'Connell receives 12 months' imprisonment, £2,000 fine and security of £5,000; others receive nine months, £50 fines and securities of £1,000 (*see* 30 May).

29 Mar. Ireland's only 'atmospheric railway' opens, between Kingstown (Dún Laoghaire) and Dalkey, Co. Dublin (trains hauled to Dalkey by atmospheric power generated from a stationary engine, and make return journey under their own momentum; railway converted to steam working on 12 Apr. 1854).

9 May William Parsons, 3rd Earl of Rosse, explains construction of his telescope (the largest in the world) to the Royal Society; on 19 June reveals details of his observations through the telescope.

24 May Foundation stone of Amiens Street railway station, Dublin, laid by L.L. de Grey.

30 May Daniel O'Connell and leaders of the Repeal Association begin prison sentences; leadership of Repeal movement assumed by William Smith O'Brien (*see* 4 Sept.).

26 July William A'Court, Lord Heytesbury, sworn in as L.L.

6 Aug. Act of Incorporation allows for development of Dublin–Cork rail link, at 165 miles the (then) longest in the British Isles (completed on 29 Oct. 1849 to temporary station at Blackpool, Cork).

9 Aug. Charitable Donations and Bequests Act establishes board of eight Protestants and five Catholics to administer bequests.

29 Aug. d. Edmund Ignatius Rice (82), philanthropist; founder of the Irish Christian Brothers.

4 Sept. House of Lords considers sentences on Daniel O'Connell and Repeal leaders; overturns court sentence; they are released on 13 Sept.

Dec. St Vincent de Paul Society establishes a Conference in Dublin.

Cold and foggy winter.

Molly Maguires, agrarian movement, active in Leitrim, Longford and Roscommon.

Pub. *The Industrial Resources of Ireland* by Dr Robert Kane.

1845

1 Feb. Sir Thomas Francis Fremantle appointed C.S.

14 Feb. Report of the Devon Commission into the state of the law and practice in respect of the occupation of land in Ireland recommends compensation for improvement.

Eighty-Two Club, uniformed, established within the Repeal Association.

Spring chilly and wet.

13 Apr. d. Whitley Stokes (82), United Irishman.

9 May Academic Colleges Bill introduced, proposing establishment of three 'Queen's Colleges' at Cork, Galway or Limerick, Belfast or Derry, on non-denominational basis with no religious lectures or tests.

23 May 21 Catholic bishops adopt a resolution on the Academic Colleges Bill, withholding their approbation as they deem it dangerous to the faith and morals of Catholics; they note the conditions upon which they will be prepared to co-operate with the proposed colleges.

26 May William Smith O'Brien and Thomas Davis welcome proposed Queen's Colleges on the principle of mixed (non-denominational) education; Daniel and John O'Connell denounce the colleges.

30 June Despite some 470 petitions against it, Maynooth College Act provides annual grant of over £26,000 and a capital grant of £30,000 for the college.

mid-July Rainy, showers and high winds, low day temperatures.

31 July Colleges (Ireland) Act establishes Queen's Colleges of the Queen's University in Ireland at Belfast, Galway and Cork (*see* 18 Nov.).

Aug. First reports of potato failure in England; appears in Ireland during the third week of Aug.

9 Sept. *Dublin Evening Post* reports appearance of potato blight in Ireland; further report in *Gardiner's Chronicle* on 13th.

16 Sept. d. Thomas Davis (31), poet and journalist.

Oct. First velocipede, forerunner of the bicycle, in Ireland, owned by Harold Kingston, Rathmines, Dublin.

17 Oct. L.L. reports that the potato crop has failed almost everywhere in Ireland (*see* 15 Nov.).

24 Oct. Lord Monteagle, former Chancellor of the Exchequer, warns P.M. Peel of impending disaster due to potato failure.

31 Oct. Members of influential Mansion House Committee, including Daniel O'Connell and the Duke of Leinster, meet L.L., urging emergency measures to combat potato failure.

15 Nov. Report from Lyon Playfair and Professor John Lindley informs P.M. Peel that at least half the potato crop is useless; deducting seed potato, they estimate that three-eighths of the harvest will be available as food.

Acting on his own initiative and without Treasury sanction, P.M. Peel orders purchase of £100,000 worth of Indian corn (maize) from U.S.A. for shipment to Ireland.

17 Nov. Meeting in Philadelphia organised by John Binns, the first organised for Irish famine relief (New York follows suit on 26 Dec.).

18 Nov. Catholic bishops divide on approach to the Queen's Colleges: 19 are opposed and 9 are supportive, though with some reservations.

20 Nov. First meeting of the Relief Commission on Ireland, under former Under-Secretary Edward Lucas (*see* 9 Feb. 1846).

22 Nov. John Mitchel publishes 'Threats of Coercion' in the *Nation*, pointing out how sabotage of railways can be organised; protests from O'Connell and others.

26 Dec. First appearance in the *Nation* of a poem by 'Eva' (Mary Eva Kelly, later wife of Kevin Izod O'Doherty).

Museum of Economic Geology established in Dublin (known as Museum of Irish Industry from 1847).

Pub. *A Grammar of the Irish Language* by John O'Donovan.

Pub. *Ecclesiastical Architecture of Ireland* by George Petrie.

Pub. 'The Library of Ireland' series, established by Charles Gavan Duffy; starts with *History of the Volunteers of 1782* by Thomas McNevin; other works appear bi-monthly until 1847.

Pub. *Introduction to the Irish Language* by William Neilson, printed at the Mission Press, Achill, Co. Mayo.

1846

9 Feb. Resident Poor Law Commissioner Twistleton refuses assistance of his department to the Relief Commission on grounds that relief scheme is illegal in that relief is to be distributed *outside* the workhouse.

14 Feb. Henry Pelham-Clinton, Earl of Lincoln, appointed C.S.

19 Feb. Remodelled Relief Commission, with Sir Randolph Routh as chairman, now in daily session, but is subordinate to Charles Trevelyan, Permanent Secretary to the Treasury, in London.

25 Feb. Charter difficulties and escalating transport costs beset the efforts of the Relief Commission.

5 Mar. Act authorises county relief works to be administered by the Board of Works.

13 Mar. Some 300 tenants evicted from the Gerrard estate in Baltinglass, Co. Galway, so that the land can be used for grazing; despite widespread condemnation and a debate in the House of Lords, the evictions are not rescinded.

24 Mar. Temporary Fever Act authorises commissioners of health to encourage Poor Law Boards of Guardians to set up temporary hospitals (allowed to lapse on 31 Aug.).

3 Apr. d. Michael Moran (52), 'Zozimus', Dublin balladeer.

30 Apr. William Smith O'Brien confined on instructions of the House of Commons for refusing to sit on committee (released on 25 May).

15 May Depots open for the sale of Indian corn.

22 June d. Martha Maria Magee, widow of a Presbyterian clergyman (d. 9 July 1800); she leaves £20,000 in trust for erection and endowment of a college for the education of Presbyterian ministry (Magee College opens in Derry on 10 Oct. 1865).

26 June P.M. Peel carries repeal of the Corn Laws; resigns office on 29th following defeat on an Irish Coercion Bill; succeeded by Lord John Russell (Whig) on 30th; Charles Wood (later Viscount Halifax) becomes Chancellor of the Exchequer.

6 July Henry Labouchere appointed C.S.

9 July John O'Connell seeks repudiation of physical force from all members of the Repeal Association (*see* 27–28 July).

11 July John Ponsonby, Earl of Bessborough, sworn in as L.L.

Thomas Redington appointed Under-Secretary (first Catholic to hold the post).

13 July Debate in Repeal Association on special committee report which states that the Association is 'seeking amelioration of political institution by peaceable and legal means alone'; opposed by John Mitchel and Young Ireland extremists (*see* 27–28 July).

Congregation in Rome decides against Catholic involvement in the new Queen's Colleges on the grounds that they are harmful to religion; suggests that the Irish bishops should set up their own university.

14 July Sir Randolph Routh, chairman of the Relief Commission, advises Trevelyan that disease is appearing again on potato crop (total destruction confirmed on 3–7 Aug.).

27–28 July Young Ireland or *Nation* group within the Repeal Association secedes on the principle of physical force (*see* 15 Dec.); John Mitchel states: 'Nobody is the least afraid of physical force, but there are many of us mortally afraid of Whiggery'; Thomas Francis Meagher delivers his 'sword' speech: 'I look upon the sword as a sacred weapon.... There are times when arms alone will suffice.'

15 Aug. Food depots and majority of public works close down on Trevelyan's orders (*see* 6 Sept.).

17 Aug. P.M. Russell, in face of threat of merchant boycott of food imports into Ireland by government, stands by the principle of *laissez-faire* despite the Irish famine.

18 Aug. Irish railway gauge standardised at 5 ft 3 in.

28 Aug. Poor Employment (Ireland) Act empowers Board of Works to execute relief works by means of Treasury loans; moneys advanced to be repaid by districts in which spent. In a letter to P.M. Russell, Archbishop MacHale of Tuam is scornful of £50,000 advanced under scheme when compared with £20 million sent by England 'to emancipate negroes of the West Indies'.

30 Aug. Discovery of new species of fungus harboured by potato plant—potato blight—first described to the Paris meeting of the Société Philomatique by Dr Montagne.

31 Aug. As temporary Fever Act expires the Central Board of Health ceases its functions, but is re-established in Feb. 1847 (continues to Aug. 1850).

6 Sept. To alleviate widespread hardship L.L. Bessborough authorises restarting relief works uncompleted at 15 Aug.

29 Sept. Several people killed by military at Dungarvan, Co. Waterford, during a food riot while attempting to prevent export of 'rent' grain.

Sir Randolph Routh estimates amount of oats *alone* leaving the country (to pay rent) at £60,000.

14 Oct. Captain of an American packet docking at Liverpool announces that orders for new-season Indian corn are ten times greater than the amount available.

6 Nov. 110,000 employed on relief works; 200,000 on 19th; 300,000 on 23rd.

13 Nov. Meeting of Irish Quakers establishes Central Relief Committee of the Society of Friends, with a sister committee in London; William Forster and James Hack Tuke arrive on 30 Nov. on fact-finding mission.

15 Dec. Young Ireland delegates meet with Daniel O'Connell and arbitrators, but fail to reach compromise; O'Connell repudiates Young Ireland a week later (*see* 27–28 July).

28 Dec. Authorised opening of western food depots for sale of food at *market prices* (which people cannot afford).

winter 1846–47 One of the severest winters in living memory; snow in early Nov., with almost continuous frost, renders roads virtually impassable; famine situation is compounded by increased cost of transport and huge rise in cereal prices.

Joshua Bewley opens café at Sycamore Avenue, off Dame Street, Dublin.

Pub. *A Chorographical Description of West or h-Iar Connacht* by Roderic O'Flaherty (1629–1718), ed. James Hardiman.

1847

1 Jan. 'The British Association for the Relief of the Extreme Distress in the Remote Parts of Ireland and Scotland', formed at Rothschild's Bank in London; collects £470,000.

First operation carried out under anaesthesia in Ireland is performed at the Richmond Hospital by Dr John McDonnell when he amputates arm of Mary Kane from near Drogheda, using ether.

11 Jan. Pub. James Fintan Lalor's first letter to the *Nation*, asserting that the land question is of greater importance than Repeal.

13 Jan. Young Ireland secessionists from the Repeal Association form the Irish Confederation, under the leadership of William Smith O'Brien.

14 Jan. Lord Sligo forms an 'Irish party', organisation of landlords.

18 Jan. Outbreak of typhus and 'relapsing fever'.

25 Jan. P.M. Russell proposes to substitute soup kitchens for public works and that local rates should finance outdoor relief.

26 Jan. Duties on corn imports suspended until 1 Sept.

2 Feb. Major-Gen. Sir John Burgoyne replaces Sir Randolph Routh as chairman of the Relief Commission.

8 Feb. Ailing Daniel O'Connell appears in the House of Commons for the last time, his voice barely audible.

9 Feb. Washington committee, whose members include Vice-President George M. Dallas, Daniel Webster, Sam Houston and Andrew Johnson, meets to discuss famine aid for Ireland.

American battleship *Jamestown* arrives in Cork with food for famine victims.

25 Feb. Fr Denis Collins, P.P., Mallow, and his curate, Fr Justin McCarthy, meet P.M. Russell to plead for aid for starving parishioners.

26 Feb. Destitute Poor (Ireland) Act, better known as the 'Soup Kitchen Act', provides for direct relief through provision of government-sponsored soup kitchens (lapses on 30 Sept.; superseded by Irish Poor Relief Extension Act).

Feb. – Mar. U.S.A. Congress passes two stringent Passenger Acts which effectively reduce ships' passenger capacity by one-third, forcing huge increases in fares and heralding the arrival of 'coffin-ships'.

5 Apr. Chef Alexis Soyer opens model soup kitchen in Dublin (Royal Barracks Esplanade) where he offers his 'celebrated' recipe of 100 gallons of soup for less than £1, including fuel allowance.

10 Apr. Fever epidemic peaks, with 2,613 deaths *officially* reported from workhouses in previous week.

13 Apr. James Fintan Lalor co-opted onto the council of the Irish Confederation.

27 Apr. Irish Fever Act 'to make temporary provision for the relief of destitute poor persons afflicted with fever' (until Aug. 1850).

4 May William Smith O'Brien leads Irish Confederation delegates in talks with John O'Connell and Repeal Association; talks break down when Confederation seeks dissolution of the Repeal Association.

7 May d. John Francis O'Donnell (37), poet.

15 May d. Daniel O'Connell (72) at Genoa, *en route* to Rome; buried in Glasnevin cemetery, Dublin, on 5 Aug.

May Speculators cause wheat prices to soar to £5 15s per quarter, but over-production in America and promising potato market at home brings market stability (price almost £2 9s 6d per quarter by Sept.).

16 May d. L.L. Bessborough (66); succeeded by George Villiers, Earl of Clarendon (sworn in on 26 May).

26 May Ulster Tenant Right Association formed in Derry.

8 June Poor Relief (Ireland) Act empowers Boards of Guardians to grant outdoor relief to certain categories of destitute persons, but 'quarter–acre clause' excludes those with more than that amount of a holding (*see* 7 Aug. 1862).

16 June William Sharman Crawford's bill to legalise 'Ulster custom' refused a second reading (112–25).

4 July 681,794 persons in receipt of outdoor relief.

Potato harvest small but healthy.

22 July Sir William Meredyth Somerville appointed C.S.

Act creates separate Poor Law Commission for Ireland.

29 July Treasurer of New York Irish Relief Committee advises Society of Friends of ending famine relief effort (over $1 million in cash alone has been raised, excluding clothing and money sent separately by Irish immigrants; *see* 1 July 1848).

31 July – 18 Aug. General election; Russell continues as P.M.

Aug. Indian corn now available at £7 10s per ton, compared to Feb. price of £19; remains unsold as people are destitute owing to closure of public works.

10 Sept. Charles Wood, Chancellor of the Exchequer, informs Poor Law inspectors that from 1 Oct. no fresh moneys will be available from Exchequer for relief, which must henceforth be met from local funds (rates).

1 Oct. All soup kitchens close; Trevelyan visits Dublin for talks with Burgoyne on overhaul of public works.

3 Oct. Archbishop MacHale lays foundation stone for a Franciscan monastery on land donated by George Henry Moore on the banks of Lough Mask, Co. Mayo.

Oct. Speculation in gold brings sterling crisis, further inhibiting Exchequer aid for famine relief works.

20 Dec. Crime and Outrage (Ireland) Act to combat upsurge in agrarian crime as landlords press penniless tenants for rents. 15,000 extra troops drafted (5,000 each deployed to Arklow, Clonmel and Limerick).

Pub. *Ecclesiastical Antiquities of Down, Connor and Dromore* by Rev. William Reeves.

Pub. *A Visit to Connaught in 1847*, a pamphlet by James Hack Tuke, Quaker philanthropist (*see* 13 Nov. 1846).

Pub. *A Voice for Ireland: The Famine in the Land* by Isaac Butt.

1848

3 Jan. Pius IX publishes rescript to Irish bishops urging them to forbid clerical political activity.

5 Feb. John Mitchel and followers withdraw from the Irish Confederation.

12 Feb. Pub. first issue of the *United Irishman* by John Mitchel, inspired by Wolfe Tone; despite its relative expense (2s), 5,000 copies sold on the day of issue.

22–24 Feb. Revolution in France; abdication of King Louis-Philippe.

15 Mar. Irish Confederation passes resolution of congratulations to the citizens of the French Republic; William Smith O'Brien, Thomas Francis Meagher and Edward Hollywood sent to present resolution to the French Provisional Government (presented to Alphonse de Lamartine on 3 Apr.).

16 Mar. d. Rev. John Paul (71), Presbyterian controversialist.

O'Brien, Meagher and Mitchel arrested; O'Brien and Meagher released on bail (*see* 22 May).

27 Mar. d. John Burke (61), genealogist, author of *Burke's Peerage*.

15 Apr. Thomas Francis Meagher presents the green, white and orange tricolour flag, brought from France to the Irish Confederation.

22 Apr. Treason-Felony Act gives Irish executive special powers to deal with Young Ireland revolutionaries.

29 Apr. William Smith O'Brien stoned and injured in Limerick by a crowd protesting at John Mitchel's attack on Daniel O'Connell in the *United Irishman*.

9 May Limerick–Tipperary railway line open.

First meeting of the Protestant Repeal Association.

16 May William Smith O'Brien acquitted on sedition charges.

22 May John Mitchel tried for treason-felony; 'packed' jury finds him guilty on 26th, and he is sentenced to 14 years' transportation (*see* 27 May).

27 May John Mitchel begins his *Jail Journal* (concludes it on 29 Nov. 1853; begins serialisation in the *Citizen* on 14 Jan. 1854 and appears in book form the same year in New York).

1 June John Mitchel transported to Australia on board H.M.S. *Scourge*.

15 June d. Thomas ('Honest Tom') Steele (60), lieutenant to Daniel O'Connell.

21 June Council of the Irish Confederation decides to dissolve.

24 June Pub. first issue of the *Irish Felon,* ed. John Martin, intended as successor to Mitchel's *United Irishman;* James Fintan Lalor a major contributor; last issue (no. 5) appears on 22 July; Martin arrested on 8 July.

1 July 833,889 persons in receipt of outdoor relief (the highest number for one day).

Funds of British Famine Relief Association exhausted, having administered in excess of £500,000; its admin-istrator, Count Strzelecki, leaves Ireland on 12 Sept., refusing any payment, as do Baring Brothers, who had organised American purchases of Indian corn.

8–9 July Charles Gavan Duffy, John Martin, and Richard D'Alton Williams arrested; following three trials, Duffy is released after nine months' imprisonment.

10 July Kevin Izod O'Doherty arrested; found guilty after three trials and sentenced to 10 years' transportation in Van Diemen's Land (Tasmania).

21 July Irish Confederation 'war directory' appointed: John Blake Dillon, Thomas Francis Meagher, Thomas Devin Reilly, Richard O'Gorman and Fr John Kenyon.

Potato crop fails again; incessant rain devastates wheat and corn crops.

25 July *Habeas corpus* suspended (until 1 Mar. 1849); all stages rushed through the House of Commons in less than 24 hours and through the House of Lords in similar fashion three days later.

27 July James Fintan Lalor arrested and held under Habeas Corpus Suspension Act.

28 July *Nation* newspaper suppressed (revived by Charles Gavan Duffy on 1 Sept. 1849).

29 July William Smith O'Brien and followers encounter police seeking to arrest O'Brien at Ballingarry, Co.

Tipperary; police occupy the home of the Widow McCormack, which O'Brien does not storm because Mrs McCormack's children are inside; rising quickly collapses, and O'Brien is captured on 5 Aug. (*see* 28 Sept.).

13 Aug. Thomas Francis Meagher arrested; sentenced to be hanged, drawn and quartered on 23 Oct. (commuted to transportation).

14 Aug. Encumbered Estates Act facilitates sale of mortgaged estates.

19 Aug. John Martin sentenced to 10 years' transportation.

31 Aug. Unlawful Oaths Act.

16 Sept. Maximum rate reduced from 5s to 3s.

28 Sept. Trial of William Smith O'Brien for high treason starts in Clonmel, Co. Tipperary; sentenced to be hanged, drawn and quartered on 9 Oct. (commuted to transportation; *see* 29 July 1849).

8 Oct. Number of known evictions rises to 16,686 as tenants unable to pay rents are evicted by landlords trying to avoid rates on holdings.

10 Oct. Terence Bellew McManus tried for high treason at Clonmel, Co. Tipperary; sentenced to transportation.

Nov. Cholera outbreak.

2 Nov. d. Richard Mant, C.I. Bishop of Down and Connor since 1823; scholar and historian, author of hymns, poetry and theology.

3 Nov. Kevin Izod O'Doherty sentenced to 10 years' transportation for treason-felony (released in 1854).

Passenger Act amends regulations governing passenger vessels, increasing by 20 per cent individual passenger spacings and allowing for surgeon and cook in vessels of 100-passenger capacity.

Royal Academy of Music founded.

Pub. *Annals of the Four Masters*, Vol. I of the translation from the Irish by John O'Donovan (completed in 7 vols in 1851).

Pub. *The Irish Crisis* by Charles Edward Trevelyan, defending export of food from Ireland.

1849

18 Mar. d. Mrs Matilda Wilson, formerly widow of Wolfe Tone, in Georgetown, U.S.A.

29 Mar. Evangelical Rev. Alexander R. C. Dallas founds the Society for Irish Church Missions to the Roman Catholics.

6 Apr. d. William Crolly, R.C. Archbishop of Armagh since 1835, from cholera (*see* 24 Feb. 1850).

22 May d. Maria Edgeworth (82), novelist.

24 May Despite opposition and resignation of Edward Twistleton, Chief Commissioner of the Irish Poor Law, Trevelyan announces rate-in-aid scheme (to 31 Dec. 1850) whereby the more prosperous unions are rated an additional 6d to support distressed unions; government advances £100,000 (half the proposed fund) immediately.

Potato fails again; cholera epidemic.

4 June d. Marguerite, Countess of Blessington (60), novelist.

20 June d. James Clarence Mangan (40), poet (author of 'My Dark Rosaleen').

26 June Passenger Act prohibits berthing together of single men and women.

2 July Fr Theobald Mathew arrives in New York; remains in U.S.A. for over two years, administering 500,000 abstinence pledges.

10 July William Pirrie opens the Victoria Channel, Belfast, built by William Dargan.

12 July Ribbonmen and supporters routed by Orangemen at Dolly's Brae, near Castlewellan, Co. Down.

28 July Encumbered Estates Act establishes a special body of three Encumbered Estates Commissioners sitting as a 'court' (first sitting on 24 Oct.).

29 July William Smith O'Brien, Thomas Francis Meagher, Terence Bellew McManus and Patrick O'Donoghue transported aboard the brig *Swift* for Van Diemen's Land.

3–12 Aug. Queen Victoria and Prince Albert in Ireland; visit Cork, Dublin and Belfast.

Oct. Queen's Colleges open to students.

14 Oct. Tenant Protection Society founded at Callan, Co. Kilkenny, by Fr Matthew Keeffe and Fr Thomas O'Shea; example followed in Tipperary.

27 Dec. d. James Fintan Lalor (42), agitator for agrarian reform.

Catholic Young Men's Society (C.Y.M.S.) founded by Dean Richard O'Brien in Limerick.

Pub. *Natural History of Ireland,* (Vol. I) by William Thompson (completed in 4 vols in 1856).

Pub. *The Felon's Track* by Michael Doheny.

1850

5 Jan. Pub. the *Tablet* in Dublin (moved from London by its owner and publisher, Frederick Lucas).

24 Feb. Paul Cullen consecrated R.C. Archbishop of Armagh and Primate of All Ireland (in Rome).

12 Mar. Party Processions (Ireland) Act empowers confiscation of arms and emblems (*see* 27 June 1872).

8 June Opening of Cork–Passage railway, first in the city of Cork.

d. Edward Walsh (45), poet and schoolmaster, author of *Reliques of Irish Jacobite Poetry* (1844) and *Irish Popular Songs* (1847).

10 Aug. Tenant League founded by Charles Gavan Duffy, Frederick Lucas, Sir John Gray and John Francis Maguire.

14 Aug. Representation of the People (Ireland) Act enfranchises ratepayers holding £12 Poor Law valuation in counties and £8 rated occupations in boroughs, trebling county electorate and reducing by one-quarter the borough electorate; overall increases the electorate to over 163,000.

22 Aug. – 19 Sept. Synod of Catholic bishops at Thurles, Co. Tipperary; declares opposition to Catholics attending the Queen's Colleges (decrees promulgated on 1 Jan. 1852).

3 Sept. Queen's University in Ireland established by charter (Queen's Colleges in Belfast, Cork and Galway).

29 Sept. Papal brief issued by Pope Pius IX re-establishes the Catholic hierarchy in Great Britain and Ireland; denounced in Britain as 'papal aggression' and leads to the Ecclesiastical Titles Act (*see* 7 Feb. 1851).

29 Dec. d. William Hamilton Maxwell, novelist, author of *History of the Great Rebellion in 1798* (1845).

Pub. first issue of *Transactions of the Kilkenny Archaeological Society* (retitled *Journal of the Royal Society of Antiquaries of Ireland* in 1892).

1851

7 Feb. House of Commons begins debate on proposed Ecclesiastical Titles Bill (*see* 29 Sept. 1850); becomes law on 1 Aug., prohibiting assumption of ecclesiastical titles by R.C. archbishops, bishops and deans in U.K.

1 Mar. Frederick Lucas's *Tablet* dubs the Irish M.P.s opposing the Ecclesiastical Titles Bill the 'Irish Brigade' (they subsequently also become known as 'the Pope's Brass Band').

26 Mar. d. James Seaton Reid (53), historian of the Presbyterian Church in Ireland (*see* 1834).

25 May d. Richard Lalor Sheil (60), lawyer, co-founder of the Catholic Association.

5 June Terence Bellew McManus escapes from Van Diemen's Land (to U.S.A.).

7 Aug. Medical Charities Act (Poor Relief (Ireland) Act) establishes dispensary system, dividing the country into 723 dispensary districts by May 1852.

19 Aug. Meeting of U.K. Catholics in Rotunda, Dublin, forms opposition to the Ecclesiastical Titles Act and leads to establishment of the Catholic Defence Association by George Henry Moore, M.P., William Keogh, M.P., and John Sadleir, M.P.

18 Sept. d. (of impoverishment) Anne Devlin (c. 73), former housekeeper to Robert Emmet.

Census shows population of 6,552,385 (decrease of 19.85 per cent since 1841).

1852

3 Jan. Thomas Francis Meagher in Van Diemen's Land gives notice to his jailers that he is withdrawing his parole not to escape; subsequently escapes.

21 Feb. P.M. Russell and ministry resign; Lord Derby (Conservative) appointed P.M. on 23rd.

25 Feb. d. Thomas Moore (73), poet.

26 Feb. d. Daniel Murray (84), R.C. Archbishop of Dublin since 1823 (*see* 3 May).

27 Feb. d. Rev. William Henry Krause, noted Evangelical.

1 Mar. Richard Southwell Bourke, Lord Naas, appointed C.S.

5 Mar. Custody of state papers vested in Master of the Rolls as keeper of the public records; State Paper Office forms a branch of the Record Department.

10 Mar. Archibald Montgomerie, Earl of Eglinton, sworn in as L.L.

21 Mar. d. John Frazer (c. 48), Young Ireland poet.

23 Apr. d. Rev. Samuel Hanna (80), first Moderator of the General Assembly of the Presbyterian Church in Ireland (1840–41).

25 Apr. d. Arthur O'Connor (89), United Irishman, in France (of which he became a naturalised citizen on 11 Apr. 1818).

3 May Paul Cullen, R.C. Archbishop of Armagh, translated to Dublin (enthroned on 29 June).

10 May – 7 June John Henry Newman delivers the first five lectures on university education (pub. as *Discourses on the Scope and Nature of University Education*, later *The Idea of a University Defined and Illustrated*).

1 June Submarine telegraph cable between Holyhead and Howth links Britain and Ireland for the first time.

30 June Act provides for valuation ('Griffith's Valuation') of rateable property for the whole country on the basis of tenements.

9–29 July General election; P.M. Derby continues in power (*see* 17 Dec.).

July – Aug. Potato crop again affected by blight.

8–9 Sept. National conference of the Tenant League resolves that 'M.P.s who have been returned on Tenant Right principles should hold themselves perfectly independent of, and in opposition to, all governments which do not make it a part of their policy . . . to give the tenants of Ireland a full measure fully embodying the principles of Sharman Crawford's bill' (*see* 17 Dec.).

14 Sept. d. the Duke of Wellington (83).

21 Nov. Joseph Dixon consecrated R.C. Archbishop of Armagh and Primate.

17 Dec. Having been defeated on the budget, P.M. Derby resigns; Lord Aberdeen forms a Peelite government on 19th; inclusion of William Keogh and John Sadleir deals a fatal blow to the Tenant League principle of independent opposition (*see* 8–9 Sept.); further desertions to Liberals reduce strength of the Irish party to 26.

1853

6 Jan. Edward Eliot, Earl of St Germans, sworn in as L.L.; Sir John Young appointed C.S.

14 Feb. *Queen Victoria* sinks in snowstorm off Howth Head with loss of 55 lives.

17 Mar. Ossianic Society founded to promote study and publication of early Irish literature.

20 Mar. d. Robert James Graves (57), physician, discoverer of Graves's Disease (toxic goitre).

12 May – 31 Oct. Irish Industrial Exhibition organised by William Dargan, who loses £20,000 on the venture.

9 June John Mitchel in Van Diemen's Land withdraws his parole; escapes on 19 July and arrives in San Francisco in Oct.

15 June Opening of three-quarter-mile Omagh–Fintona railway line, destined to be the last line in the British Isles to carry horse-drawn carriages.

23 June d. William Eliot Hudson (57), bibliophile.

28 June Income tax extended to Ireland, effective from 5 Apr.

20 Aug. Act to Substitute in Certain Cases Other Punishments in Lieu of Transportation (amended by an act of 26 June 1857).

29 Aug. – 4 Sept. Queen Victoria visits Ireland to attend the Irish Industrial Exhibition (visits William Dargan, who turns down a baronetcy).

1 Nov. First meeting of the Irish Institution in Charlemont House, Dublin, with the object of promoting art in Ireland by forming a permanent exhibition in Dublin and eventually forming an Irish National Gallery (*see* 4 Jan. 1854).

Pub. *Aural Surgery* by Dr William Wilde; first scientific work on surgery of the ear.

Pub. *Lectures on Quaternions* by Sir William Rowan Hamilton.

1854

4 Jan. First annual exhibition of Irish art, organised by the Irish Institution at the Royal Hibernian Academy, Abbey Street, Dublin.

d. William Conyngham Plunket, 1st Baron Plunket, lawyer and politician; anti-Union and advocate of Catholic relief; Lord Chancellor (1830–41).

7 Jan. Pub. first issue of the *Citizen*, founded by John Mitchel in New York.

26 Feb. William Smith O'Brien receives pardon; returns to Ireland on 8 July 1856.

KILKENNY COUNTY LIBRARY

6 Mar. d. Thomas Devin Reilly (30), Young Ireland journalist.

16 Mar. 'The Great Clare Find': large hoard of gold objects discovered near Quin, Co. Clare, during construction of the Limerick–Ennis railway.

4 June John Henry Newman installed as Rector of the Catholic University (*see* 3 Nov.).

21 June Irishman David Lucas, mate on H.M.S. *Hecla,* hurls an unexploded shell from the deck during a bombardment, earning the first award of the Victoria Cross.

8 Aug. d. Thomas Crofton Croker (56), antiquary, author of *Fairy Tales and Legends of the South of Ireland* (1825).

21–26 Aug. Donnybrook Fair, Dublin, established by charter in 1204, held for the last time (suppressed in 1855).

3 Nov. Catholic University of Ireland opens (without power to grant degrees).

Dec. Edward Harland arrives in Belfast to become manager of Robert Hickson's shipyard at Queen's Island.

Pub. *History of the City of Dublin* (Vol. I) by John Thomas Gilbert (completed in 3 vols in 1859).

Pub. *Jail Journal* by John Mitchel (New York).

1855

29 Jan. Lord Aberdeen's government defeated on Crimean War issue; resigns on 1 Feb.; Viscount Palmerston (Liberal) appointed P.M. on 6 Feb.

Feb. Emmet Monument Association established in New York by Michael Doheny and John O'Donovan, to seek Irish independence (*see* Apr. 1859).

1 Mar. Edward Horsman appointed C.S.

3 Mar. U.S. Passenger Act increases passenger comforts, increasing food/water allowance, with master of the ship liable to $1,000 fine on default; masters also required to pay $10 fine for every passenger over eight years of age who dies on voyage.

13 Mar. George Howard, Earl of Carlisle, sworn in as L.L.

5 Apr. Dublin–Belfast railway line completed.

16 Aug. Charles Gavan Duffy makes valedictory address to electors of New Ross; leaves for Australia on 6 Nov., having transferred the *Nation* to A. M. Sullivan and Michael Clery.

11 Sept. Ireland's first cricket international; Ireland defeats England by 107 runs at the Phoenix Cricket Club, Dublin.

22 Oct. d. Frederick Lucas (43), founder of the *Tablet* (16 May 1840) and co-founder of the Irish Tenant League.

Cork's Penrose Quay railway station opens; its 1,355-yard approach tunnel is one of Ireland's longest.

Pub. *The Ancient Music of Ireland,* ed. George Petrie, sponsored by the Society for the Preservation and Publication of the Melodies of Ireland.

1856

17 Feb. d. (suicide) John Sadleir (42), politician and swindler, whose Tipperary Joint-Stock Bank, established in 1827, collapsed on 13 Feb.

9 Apr. Pub. first issue of *Irish News* by Thomas Francis Meagher, John Savage and James Roche in New York (runs until 1860).

1 May Catholic University Church, St Stephen's Green, Dublin, opens.

20 June Peace Preservation Act continues main provisions of Treason-Felony Act (1848) but reduces term of imprisonment to one year.

8 Dec. d. Fr Theobald Mathew (66), founder of temperance crusade (said to have administered 7 million pledges).

Jeremiah O'Donovan (later known as O'Donovan Rossa) establishes the Phoenix National and Literary Society at Skibbereen, Co. Cork (*see* May 1858).

1857
4 Feb. d. Michael Slattery (75), R.C. Archbishop of Cashel since 1834, theologian; leading opponent of Queen's Colleges.

28 Feb. d. Philip Gray, Young Irelander.

3 Mar. Lord Palmerston's government defeated by combination of Peelites, Liberals and Irish.

20 Mar. – 16 Apr. General election; P.M. Palmerston returns with increased majority.

27 May d. Michael Joseph Brenan (28), Young Ireland poet and journalist.

Henry Arthur Herbert appointed C.S.

12 July Address by Rev. Thomas Drew to members of the Orange Order sparks off 10 days of continuous rioting in Belfast (*see* 6 Sept.).

27 July d. Rev. Laurence Renehan (60), President of Maynooth College since 1845.

Aug. Pub. first issue of *The Celt*, journal of national literature, founded by Dr Robert Kane of Kilkenny; supported by Charles J. Kickham, Robert Dwyer Joyce and William Kennedy.

6 Sept. Rioting in Belfast city centre provoked by Rev. 'Roaring' Hugh Hanna.

20 Nov. Commission on Belfast rioting (*see* 12 July *and* 6 Sept.) criticises Orange festival for leading 'to violence, outrage, religious animosities, hatred between classes, and, too often, bloodshed and loss of life'.

17 Dec. d. Sir Francis Beaufort (83), hydrographer who originated the Beaufort Scale.

Pub. *History of Ireland*, translation of Geoffrey Keating's *Foras Feasa ar Éirinn* by John O'Mahony (New York).

1858
26 Feb. Lord Derby (Conservative) appointed P.M. (minority government), following resignation of Lord Palmerston.

28 Feb. 28 Irish-Americans calling themselves 'the Irish Revolutionary Committee' appoint James Stephens chief executive of the Irish revolutionary movement; they dispatch this commission and money to Ireland with Joseph Denieffe (*see* 17 Mar.).

4 Mar. Lord Naas again appointed C.S.

12 Mar. Earl of Eglinton again sworn in as L.L.

17 Mar. James Stephens founds the Irish Revolutionary Brotherhood (later known as Irish Republican Brotherhood) (I.R.B.) in Dublin, a secret, oath-bound organisation dedicated to establishment of an Irish republic through physical force; John O'Mahony establishes Fenians (by which title the whole movement is often known) in New York in Apr. 1859.

27 Mar. d. John Hogan (58), sculptor.

May O'Donovan Rossa's Phoenix National and Literary Society in Skibbereen, Co. Cork, incorporated into James Stephens's I.R.B.

17 July Pub. first issue of the *Irishman*, founded and edited in Belfast by Denis Holland (published in Dublin from 23 Apr. 1859); Richard Pigott in charge of printing (*see* June 1865).

22 July d. Mother Mary Aikenhead (71), founder of the Irish Sisters of Charity and St Vincent's Hospital, Dublin (first Irish hospital to be served by nuns).

29 July d. Thomas Ledwich (35), anatomist.

2 Aug. Landed Estates (Ireland) Act rationalises Encumbered Estates Acts and substitutes 'Landed Estates Court, Ireland' for the 1849 courts.

10 Aug. Society for Promotion and Cultivation of the Irish Language commences operations in rooms in Middle Abbey Street.

11 Aug. d. Catherine Hayes (36), internationally famed soprano.

16 Aug. First official message on transatlantic cable between Valentia Island and Newfoundland: 'Europe and America are united by electric Telegraph. Glory to God in the highest, on earth peace, and good will towards men'.

17 Aug. d. Dr Robert Kane (51), Repealer and Young Irelander.

23 Aug. – 17 Sept. England's Cardinal Wiseman visits Ireland, the first cardinal in Ireland for 200 years.

12 Nov. John Henry Newman leaves the Rectorship of the Catholic University.

8–15 Dec. Government swoops on Cork members of the Phoenix Society (now part of the I.R.B.); only one convicted.

9 Dec. James Stephens in New York is granted 'supreme control and absolute authority' over the revolutionary movement 'at home and abroad' (Thomas Francis Meagher withdraws his agreement to this commission on 26 Jan. 1859).

Edward Harland, backed by G. C. Schwabe of Liverpool (uncle of Gustav Wolff), buys Queen's Island shipyard in Belfast from Robert Hickson for £5,000.

Pub. *Catalogue of the Contents of the Museum of the Royal Irish Academy* (Vol. I) by Sir William Wilde (completed in 3 vols in 1862).

1859

29 Mar. Pub. first issue of the *Irish Times* (price 1d), founded by Major Laurence Knox.

31 Mar. Lord Derby's ministry defeated.

Apr. John O'Mahony reconstitutes the Emmet Monument Association in New York as the Fenian Brotherhood (*see* 17 Mar. 1858).

14 Apr. d. Sydney, Lady Morgan (76), novelist and poet.

30 Apr. – 20 May General election; Viscount Palmerston (Liberal) again appointed P.M. on 12 June.

d. Rev. Mortimer O'Sullivan (68), Protestant apologist.

24 June Edward Cardwell appointed C.S.

13 July Earl of Carlisle again sworn in as L.L.

2–5 Aug. Meeting of Catholic hierarchy, called by Archbishop Paul Cullen to discuss educational matters; they forward memorial to L.L., seeking separate schools for the religious denominations.

15 Oct. The *Nation* promotes the idea of physical support for the Pope against the Italian nationalists; Battalion of St Patrick is raised for action (*see* 25 Feb. *and* 16 May 1860).

12 Dec. Carlisle Pier, Dublin, opened.

Queenstown (modern Cóbh), Co. Cork, becomes port of call for Atlantic liners.

Belfast High School for Girls founded.

Pub. *Places of 5,345 Stars Observed at Armagh from 1828 to 1854* by Thomas Romney Robinson.

1860
Poor weather leads to agricultural depression.

25 Feb. £11,000 collected at church doors in Dublin for papal fight against Italian nationalists; £80,000 collected nationwide (*see* 16 May *and* 11 Sept.).

8 May The O'Donoghue brings petition for plebiscite on self-determination to London, with 423,026 signatures.

15 May Land Improvement (Ireland) Act authorises loans for erection of labourers' dwellings.

16 May To counter recruitment in Ireland for the Irish papal brigade, L.L. issues proclamation pointing out the penalties under the Foreign Enlistment Act; Battalion of St Patrick eventually reaches 1,000.

3 June Archbishop Cullen issues letter condemning emigration and mixed education; he warns against 'the scandalous practice of kidnapping or buying Catholic children for the purpose of educating them into a religion different from that of their parents'.

28 Aug. Richard Deasy's Landlord and Tenant Law Amendment (Ireland) Act states that relationship between landlord and tenant is 'deemed to be founded on the express or implied contract of the parties and not upon tenure or service'; strengthens the landlord's hand by allowing him to dictate terms.

Party Processions (Ireland) Act places more rigorous controls on conduct of processions (*see* 27 June 1872).

11 Sept. Papal states in Italy invaded by troops from Piedmont–Sardinia; Irish battalion fails to defend Spoleto on 17th.

3 Nov. Irish papal battalion returns, landing at Queenstown.

21–23 Nov. Partry evictions: Thomas Plunket, C.I. Bishop of Tuam, evicts 68 families from his estate at Partry, Co. Mayo.

First use of external electric light in Dublin, arc lamp outside the offices of the *Freeman's Journal*.

Pub. *The History of Ireland, Ancient and Modern* by Martin Haverty.

Pub. *The Last Conquest of Ireland (Perhaps)* by John Mitchel.

1861
15 Jan. d. Terence Bellew McManus (59) in San Francisco (*see* 4 Nov.).

22 Feb. Select committee of the House of Commons appointed 'to inquire into the administration of the relief of the poor in Ireland' (presents report on 5 July).

18 Mar. Foundation of the National Brotherhood of St Patrick, republican organisation chaired by Thomas Neilson Underwood (condemned by the Catholic bishops in Aug. 1863).

8–10 Apr. Derryveagh evictions in Co. Donegal: John George Adair evicts 47 tenants and destroys their dwellings.

12 Apr. Confederates attack Fort Sumter, Charleston; start of the American Civil War (*see* 21 July).

21 July First battle of Bull Run in American Civil War; Thomas Francis Meagher forms Irish Brigade in New York during Sept.–Oct. (*see* 3 Feb. 1862).

29 July Sir Robert Peel (jun.) appointed C.S.

12 Aug. d. Arthur Blennerhassett Rowan, antiquary.

21–30 Aug. Queen Victoria in Ireland.

2 Sept. Dungannon–Omagh railway line opens (linking Belfast with Enniskillen).

24 Sept. Opening of the first part of the Mater Misericordiae Hospital in Dublin, built by the Sisters of Mercy at a cost of £27,000; designed by John Bourke.

18 Oct. d. William Sharman Crawford (80), politician.

4 Nov. Remains of Terence Bellew McManus lie in state at the Mechanics' Institute, Dublin, until funeral to Glasnevin cemetery (10th), where Fr Patrick Lavelle of Partry, in defiance of Archbishop Cullen, delivers panegyric.

9 Dec. d. John O'Donovan (52), scholar; edited the *Annals of the Four Masters* in 7 vols (1848–51).

Census shows population of 5,798,967 (decrease of 11.5 per cent since 1851); first to inquire into religious denominations in the country (shows that Establishej Church has adherence of 11.9 per cent).

Fenian John Devoy joins the French Foreign Legion to study infantry warfare (deserts in 1863).

Post Office Savings Bank established.

d. Mrs Mary Dwyer (93), widow of United Irishman Michael Dwyer, in Sydney, Australia.

Pub. *Construction of Specula of Six-Feet Aperture and a Selection from the Observations of Nebulae Made with Them* by 3rd Earl of Rosse.

Pub. *Ballads, Romances and Songs* by Robert Dwyer Joyce.

Pub. (anon.) *Leaders of Public Opinion in Ireland* by W. E. H. Lecky.

1862

1 Jan. Edward Harland and G. W. Wolff enter partnership to form Harland & Wolff shipbuilding company in Belfast.

24 Jan. d. Miles Byrne (82), United Irishman and Chevalier of the French Legion of Honour.

3 Feb. Thomas Francis Meagher becomes Brigadier-General of the Irish Brigade in the American Civil War (sees action at Antietum (17 Sept.), the second battle of Bull Run (29–30 Aug.) and Fredericksburg (13 Dec.); regiment annihilated at Chancellorsville (2–4 May 1863) and Meagher resigns commission).

16 Apr. d. Sir Thomas Wyse (71), politician and Catholic Emancipationist.

16 May Francis FitzGerald, landlord, shot dead near Kilmallock, Co. Limerick (for which three men are hanged).

5 July Lord Palmerston rejects request from Catholic University for a charter, informing them that the government believes 'that the best system of education . . . is a mixed system'.

d. Richard D'Alton Williams (40), Young Ireland journalist, in U.S.A.

18 July d. Lord John George Beresford (89), C.I. Archbishop of Armagh and Primate since 1822.

20 July Foundation stone laid for the new buildings of the Catholic University in Dublin.

30 July d. Eugene O'Curry (66), scholar.

7 Aug. Relief of the Destitute Poor in Ireland Amendment Act (Poor Relief (Ireland) Act) abolishes 'quarter-acre clause' (*see* 8 June 1847).

Pub. *The Leadbeater Papers* by Mary Leadbeater (d. 27 June 1826).

1863

1 Apr. d. Michael Doheny (58), Young Irelander, author of *The Felon's Track.*

20 Apr. Registration of Births and Deaths (Ireland) Act (*see* 28 July).

28 Apr. Foundation stone laid for the Synge Street Christian Brothers' School (opens on 11 Apr. 1864).

18 July Opening of Avoca–Arklow railway line, Co. Wicklow, considered one of the country's most picturesque routes.

28 July Registration of Marriages (Ireland) Act (*see* 20 Apr.).

8 Oct. d. Richard Whately (76), C.I. Archbishop of Dublin since 1831.

13 Nov. St Stephen's Green, Dublin, opens to the public.

28 Nov. Pub. first issue of the *Irish People,* Fenian organ established by Thomas Clarke Luby with Jeremiah O'Donovan Rossa, John O'Mahony and Charles J. Kickham (*see* 15 Sept. 1865).

Report of the select committee on the Royal Dublin Society and Scientific Institutions.

Pub. *Memoirs* (3 vols) by Miles Byrne (Paris).

1864

1 Jan. Scheme for compulsory vaccination of babies in Ireland introduced under act.

Richard Chenevix Trench consecrated C.I. Archbishop of Dublin; poet and scholar (d. 28 Mar. 1886).

14 Jan. d. Fr Nicholas Callan (65), pioneer electrical scientist at Maynooth College.

21 Jan. John Martin founds the Irish National League for 'the restoration of a separate and independent Irish legislature'.

30 Jan. National Gallery of Ireland formally opened by L.L. Carlisle; George Mulvany first director.

17 Mar. Archbishop Cullen denounces Fenianism in pastoral letter.

15 Apr. First Dublin Horse Show, organised by the Royal Agricultural Society.

18 June d. William Smith O'Brien (61), politician and Young Ireland leader, in Wales.

5 July First meeting of the Royal College of Physicians in Kildare Street, Dr Dominic Corrigan presiding.

8 Aug. Catholics and Protestants, Archbishop Cullen and several bishops march through the streets of Dublin for the laying of the foundation stone of the O'Connell Monument in Sackville Street, attended by an estimated 500,000; triggers off sectarian warfare in Belfast for more than a week when a Protestant crowd from Sandy Row burn effigy of O'Connell at the Boyne Bridge; by 18 Aug. 12 are reported killed and over 130 injured.

13 Oct. d. William Pembroke Mulchinock (44), poet, author of 'The Rose of Tralee'.

8 Nov. John, Lord Wodehouse, sworn in as L.L.

8 Dec. Pope Pius IX issues 'Syllabus of Errors', which includes socialism, liberalism and freemasonry as principal evils of the modern age.

10 Dec. d. 'Honest' Louis John Perrin (82), judge.

29 Dec. National Association of Ireland established with the support of Archbishop Cullen, to secure compensation for tenants' improvements, disestablishment of the Church of Ireland, and state finance for church-controlled education.

Irish telegraphic network begins operating.

Pub. *An Appeal on Behalf of the Idiotic and Imbecile Children of Ireland* by George Hugh Kidd.

Pub. first issue of the *Irish Ecclesiastical Record*, founded by Archbishop Cullen; ed. Rev. Patrick Moran and Rev. George Conroy.

1865

31 Jan. d. Quain Jones, author of the *Elements of Anatomy*.

1 Apr. Last major battle of the American Civil War: victory for Gen. Philip Sheridan at Five Forks (Sheridan b. Killinkere, Co. Cavan, on 6 Mar. 1831); war ends on 26 Apr.

June Patrick James Smyth sells the *Irishman* to Richard Pigott.

12–24 July General election; Lord Palmerston (Liberal) retains power (*see* 18 Oct.).

2 Sept. d. Sir William Rowan Hamilton (60), mathematician and astronomer.

15 Sept. Series of raids on Fenian centres closes the *Irish People* (last issue on 16th) and leads to arrest of John O'Leary, Thomas Clarke Luby and Jeremiah O'Donovan Rossa (*see* 11 Nov.).

10 Oct. Magee College, Derry, opens (*see* 22 June 1846).

12 Oct. d. William Vincent Wallace (53), composer of *Maritana*.

18 Oct. d. P.M. Palmerston (8 1); succeeded by Lord John Russell (Liberal).

20 Oct. d. John Fisher Murray (54), Young Ireland poet and humorist.

11 Nov. Further arrests of leading Fenians, including Charles J. Kickham, James Stephens, Edmund Duffy and Hugh Brophy (*see* 24–25 Nov.).

24–25 Nov. James Stephens, aided from within by J. J. Breslin, escapes from Richmond Prison, Dublin (escapes to France in Mar. 1886).

27 Nov. Thomas Clarke Luby, defended by Isaac Butt, sentenced to 20 years' imprisonment.

2 Dec. Fenian Brotherhood splits when John O'Mahony is deposed as Head Centre (*see* 3 Jan. 1866).

5–6 Dec. Irish independent M.P.s meet in Dublin to consider their attitude towards government policy, bringing about apparent reunification of Independent Irish Party (*see* 27 Apr. 1866).

6 Dec. John O'Leary sentenced to 20 years' imprisonment.

7 Dec. Chichester Fortescue appointed C.S.

16 Dec. Jeremiah O'Donovan Rossa sentenced to 20 years' imprisonment.

18 Dec. d. Rev. Henry Montgomery (77), leading Presbyterian and noted Arian.

21 Dec. Charles Underwood O'Connell, Fenian, sentenced to 10 years' imprisonment.

Pub. *Lays and Legends of Thomond* by Michael Hogan ('The Bard of Thomond').

Pub. *Lays of the Western Gael* by Sir Samuel Ferguson.

Pub. *Ancient Laws of Ireland,* Vol. I (completed in 6 vols in 1901), under sponsorship of Brehon Law Commissioners.

Pub. *The Cromwellian Settlement of Ireland* by John Patrick Prendergast.

1866

3 Jan. John O'Mahony and followers hold convention in New York and restore O'Mahony as Head Centre of the Irish-American revolutionary movement; the Senate wing of the movement now led by William R. Roberts.

5 Jan. Trial of Charles J. Kickham starts; sentenced to 14 years' transportation.

17 Jan. d. George Petrie (76), antiquary, musician and artist.

7 Feb. d. Thomas Spring Rice, 1st Baron Monteagle and Brandon, politician.

17 Feb. *Habeas corpus* suspended (*see* 31 May 1867).

18 Feb. John Boyle O'Reilly arrested in Dublin; recruiting for the Fenians while serving in the British army, he is sentenced to be shot (9 July), but sentence is commuted to 20 years' transportation to Australia; escapes in Apr. 1869 and makes his way to U.S.A. (d. 10 Aug. 1890).

19 Apr. American authorities foil Fenian plan to attack Campo Bello, New Brunswick, Canada (*see* 31 May – 2 June).

27 Apr. Independent Irish opposition M.P.s split on the Reform Bill; majority, led by John Blake Dillon, support the government.

29 Apr. d. Joseph Dixon (60), R.C. Archbishop of Armagh and Primate.

15 May James Stephens, now leading the former O'Mahony wing of the Fenian movement in New York, promises New York crowd that the war in Ireland will be prosecuted before the end of the year.

18 May d. Rev. Francis Sylvester Mahony ('Fr Prout') (62), poet (author of 'The Bells of Shandon').

31 May – 2 June Fenian Col. John O'Neill leads force of 800 across Canadian border and captures Fort Erie; following battle with Canadian authorities at Lime Ridgeway, Fenians retreat, having flown their flag emblazoned with 'I.R.A.' and gold harp of Ireland.

9 June James Stephens confers with U.S. Secretary of State Seward.

22 June Archbishop Paul Cullen becomes Ireland's first cardinal.

28 June Lord Derby (Conservative) again appointed P.M.

10 July Lord Naas again appointed C.S. (succeeds as 6th Earl of Mayo on 12 Aug. 1867).

20 July James Hamilton, Marquis of Abercorn, sworn in as L.L.

27 July Submarine cable completed between Valentia, Co. Kerry, and Newfoundland.

24 Aug. d. Andrew Mulholland, leading cotton and linen manufacturer in Belfast.

15 Sept. d. John Blake Dillon (50), Young Irelander, co-founder of the *Nation*.

11 Oct. Alexandra College opens in Dublin to provide education for young ladies.

17–29 Dec. James Stephens attempts to secure American agreement to another postponement of war in Ireland; he is attacked by New York Fenians for his failure to organise rising in Ireland and is replaced as Head Centre by Col. Thomas J. Kelly.

Pub. *Land Tenure in Ireland: A Plea for the Celtic Race* by Isaac Butt.

1867

4 Feb. James Stephens arrives in Brest, France, from New York.

7 Feb. d. William Dargan (68), engineer and railway-builder.

10 Feb. John J. Corydon betrays plans for Capt. John McCafferty's attack on the arsenal at Chester Castle for the 11th to the Liverpool police; Fenians disperse, and over 60 are arrested upon arrival at the North Wall, Dublin (*see* 23 Feb.).

11–12 Feb. Original date set for Fenian rising, which is postponed to 5 Mar.; Fenians in Kerry under Col. J. J. O'Connor, unaware of the postponement, rise and attack Kells and then disperse.

17 Feb. David Moriarty, R.C. Bishop of Kerry, denounces the Fenians, stating that 'eternity is not long enough nor hell hot enough to punish such miscreants'.

23 Feb. Fenian Capt. John McCafferty arrested in Dublin; sentence of death commuted to life imprisonment on 18 May.

26 Feb. Irish Fenians informed that 5 Mar. is the date set for the rising; J. J. Corydon informs police.

4 Mar. Godfrey Massey arrested at Limerick Junction, Co. Tipperary, by Inspector John Mallon, to whom he divulges Fenian plans for a rising the next day.

5 Mar. Fenian rising fails, although outbreaks occur in Counties Dublin, Louth, Wicklow, Tipperary, Cork, Limerick and Clare; in one successful engagement Capt. John McClure captures Knockadoon coastguard station.

6 Mar. Fenian Thomas F. Burke captured at Ballyhurst Fort, Co. Tipperary; sentence of death on 24 Apr. commuted to life imprisonment.

31 Mar. Capt. John McClure and Edward Kelly captured at Kilcloney Wood (on the Limerick–Cork border, near Kildorrery, Co. Cork), where their companion Peter O'Neill Crowley is mortally wounded (dies in Mitchelstown, Co. Cork).

12 Apr. The *Jackmel*, commanded by Fenians, leaves Sandy Hook, U.S.A., for Ireland, carrying arms; renamed *Erin's Hope* during the crossing (*see* 20 May *and* 1 June).

13 May Government commission starts its investigation into treatment of Fenian prisoners.

20 May *Erin's Hope* arrives in Sligo Bay, but leaves a few days later.

31 May Suspension of *habeas corpus* continued until 1 Mar. 1868.

1 June 28 Irish-American Fenians put off the *Erin's Hope* at Cunigar, near Dungarvan, Co. Waterford, are arrested shortly afterwards.

13 June d. Lady Dufferin, poet and novelist (author of 'Lament of the Irish Emigrant').

20 June Clan na Gael or the United Brotherhood, Fenian organisation, founded in New York by Jerome J. Collins.

1 July Thomas Francis Meagher (44), temporary governor of Montana, disappears from the *G. A. Thompson* on the Missouri, presumed drowned.

12 Aug. Public Records (Ireland) Act establishes Public Record Office

(P.R.O.) at the Four Courts and regulates the State Paper Office (S.P.O.) at Dublin Castle.

17 Aug. Col. Thomas J. Kelly appointed Head Centre of the I.R.B. (Fenians) at a convention in Manchester.

11 Sept. Col. Thomas J. Kelly, Head Centre of the Fenians, and Capt. Timothy Deasy arrested in Manchester.

12 Sept. Police force granted the prefix 'Royal'—Royal Irish Constabulary (R.I.C.)—in recognition of its services in suppressing the Fenian rising of 5 Mar.

18 Sept. Ricard O'Sullivan Burke organises the rescue of Kelly and Deasy by Fenians from prison van; Police Sergeant Charles Brett killed when the lock is shot off the prison van (*see* 28 Oct.).

Oct. Royal College of Science formed from the Museum of Irish Industry (taken over by the Department of Agriculture and Technical Instruction in 1899 and incorporated into the Department of Science at U.C.D. in 1926).

2 Oct. The Abercorn Basin (a floating dock) and the Hamilton Dock opened in Belfast.

28 Oct. William Philip Allen, Michael Larkin and Michael O'Brien and others are tried for the murder of Sergeant Charles Brett during rescue of Kelly and Deasy (*see* 18 Sept.); all the accused sentenced to death on 1 Nov.

30 Oct. Protestant demonstration at Hillsborough, Co. Down, addressed by leading Presbyterian, Rev. Henry Cooke, defending the Established Church.

31 Oct. d. William Parsons (67), 3rd Earl of Rosse, astronomer.

21 Nov. Following representations, conviction of Thomas Maguire for murder of Sergeant Brett (*see* 18 Sept.) is cancelled; sentence of Edward Meagher Condon is commuted.

23 Nov. William Philip Allen, Michael Larkin and Michael O'Brien executed at Salford jail, Manchester (the 'Manchester Martyrs').

28 Nov. Fenian William Mackey Lomasney (known as Capt. Mackey) steals 120 revolvers and five rifles from Richardsons, gunsmiths, Patrick Street, Cork.

7 Dec. Pub. (in the *Nation*) 'Song' by T. D. Sullivan (soon known as 'God Save Ireland'), which becomes the anthem of Irish nationalists until 1916.

8 Dec. An estimated 60,000 attend a 'public funeral procession' in honour of the 'Manchester Martyrs' (*see* 23 Nov.) in Dublin, addressed by John Martin among others.

12 Dec. L.L. bans future processions 'to take place in honour of certain men lately executed in Manchester for the crime of murder'.

13 Dec. 12 killed and over 50 injured when Fenians, Capt. John Murphy and Jeremiah Sullivan, cause an explosion in an unsuccessful attempt to rescue Ricard O'Sullivan Burke from Clerkenwell Detention Centre in London.

16–28 Dec. Prominent nationalists, including John Martin and A. M. Sullivan, summoned for taking part in 'illegal processions' and 'a seditious assembly' in Dublin (discharged when juries fail to agree in Feb. 1868).

26–27 Dec. William Mackey Lomasney attacks Martello tower, Fohty (Fota), Cork, disarms the guards and steals arms and ammunition.

Ernest Dowden (24) becomes first Professor of English at T.C.D. (first chair of English in the world).

1868

c. 1 Jan. Having raided Allport's Cork gun shop on 30 Dec., William Mackey Lomasney raids powder magazine at Ballincollig, Co. Cork.

14 Jan. Powis Commission established to inquire into primary education (reports on 21 May 1870).

7 Feb. William Mackey Lomasney arrested in Cronin's grocery and spirit shop in Market Street, Cork; a constable mortally wounded in the struggle (*see* 20–21 Mar.).

27 Feb. Benjamin Disraeli (Conservative) succeeds the retired Earl of Derby as P.M. ('I have climbed to the top of the greasy pole').

29 Feb. William Johnston of Ballykilbeg imprisoned for one month for defying Party Processions Act (*see* 21 Nov.).

5 Mar. Inaugural meeting of the Ulster Protestant Defence Association (to resist disestablishment of the Church of Ireland).

10 Mar. C.S. the Earl of Mayo announces that the government has decided to grant a charter to the Catholic University.

20–21 Mar. William Mackey Lomasney tried for high treason; sentenced to 12 years' imprisonment.

23 Mar. W. E. Gladstone proposes an end to the establishment of the Church of Ireland.

7 Apr. Thomas D'Arcy McGee, former Young Irelander, Minister for Agriculture in Canada, who has denounced a threatened Fenian invasion of Canada, shot dead in Ottawa.

15 Apr. Howard Featherstonehaugh, J.P., a landlord, shot dead at Killucan, Co. Westmeath; one of a series of six murders linked to agrarian unrest (the last occurs on 29 Dec. 1870 outside Mullingar) which provokes a parliamentary inquiry and suspension of *habeas corpus* (*see* 16 June 1871).

26 May Michael Barrett executed for the Clerkenwell explosion (*see* 13 Dec. 1867); last public execution in British Isles (public executions abolished under the Capital Punishment Amendment Act of 29 May).

6 July d. Samuel Lover (71), novelist, poet and painter.

13 July Representation of the People (Ireland) Act reduces rated occupier franchise in boroughs from £8 to £4 and introduces franchise for lodgers.

31 July Promissory Oaths Act reduces the number of persons required to take oaths in Ireland to a few (including L.L., Lord Chancellor and Commander-in-Chief of the armed forces).

14 Aug. Vincent Scully, a landlord, wounded in the process of evicting tenants at Ballycohey, Co. Tipperary; bailiff and a policeman killed and others wounded.

15 Aug. Teachers' conference in Dublin leads to foundation of the Irish National Teachers' Organisation (I.N.T.O.).

29 Sept. John Wilson-Patten appointed C.S.

5 Nov. John McCorry initiates organisation to work for the release of political prisoners; at first called Irish Liberation Society (*see* 28 June 1869).

17 Nov. – 2 Dec. General election; Disraeli defeated; William Ewart Gladstone (Liberal) forms his first administration on 3 Dec.

21 Nov. William Johnston of Ballykilbeg (Conservative) elected M.P. for Belfast; the first Irishman to be elected to parliament as a direct result of serving a jail sentence (*see* 29 Feb.).

13 Dec. d. Rev. Henry Cooke (80), Presbyterian leader.

18 Dec. Thomas O'Hagan becomes the first Catholic Lord Chancellor of Ireland since the reign of James II (enters House of Lords on 21 June 1870; d. 1 Feb. 1885).

23 Dec. John, Earl Spencer, sworn in as L.L.; Chichester Fortescue again appointed C.S.

Pub. *Life and Labours in Art and Archaeology of George Petrie* by William Stokes.

1869
30 Jan. d. William Carleton (75), writer.

22 Feb. C.S. Fortescue announces the names of 49 imprisoned Fenians to be released (15 in English jails, the rest in Australia).

6 Mar. Publication starts in Richard Pigott's *Irishman* of a series of articles claiming ill-treatment of imprisoned Fenians.

21 Mar. d. Fr John Kenyon (57), Young Irelander.

28 June Isaac Butt elected President of the new Amnesty Association founded at the Rotunda, Dublin, seeking release of imprisoned Fenians; secretary John 'Amnesty' Nolan; committee includes Fr Patrick Lavelle, John Martin, A. M. Sullivan and Richard Pigott.

d. Rev. James Henthorn Todd (64), scholar.

26 July Irish Church Act provides for disestablishment and partial disendowment of the Church of Ireland; substitutes capital sums for *regium donum* of the Presbyterian Church and for Maynooth Grant; tenants to be permitted to purchase church land; effective from 1 Jan. 1871.

18 Aug. New Supreme Council of the I.R.B. adopts the first known 'Constitution of the Irish Republic', vesting all authority in the 11-man Supreme Council.

Sept. Friedrich Engels in Ireland with his wife Lydia (*née* Burns) and Eleanor Marx; visits Dublin, Wicklow, Killarney and Cork; collects material for a *History of Ireland* (unfinished, appears in Russian in 1948).

28 Sept. Irish Tenant League inaugurated in Tipperary town, led by Isaac Butt.

27 Nov. Jeremiah O'Donovan Rossa, imprisoned Fenian, returned as M.P. in Co. Tipperary by-election (1,131 votes), defeating Denis Caulfield Heron (Liberal, 1,028), but is disqualified as a convicted felon (*see* 28 Feb. 1870).

29 Nov. In a letter to Karl Marx, Friedrich Engels discusses the significance of the Tipperary by-election (*see* 27 Nov.).

Stewart Institution for Idiotic and Imbecile Children established at Palmerstown, Co. Dublin (later Stewart's Hospital).

Pub. *Origin and History of Irish Names of Places* (Vol. I) by P. W. Joyce (completed in 3 vols in 1870).

1870
12 Jan. Holy Office authorised by the Pope to condemn the Fenians.

2–3 Feb. Land Conference in Dublin.

3 Feb. Henry Munster (Liberal, 91 votes) defeats Major Laurence Knox (Conservative; proprietor of the *Irish Times*; 83 votes) in Mallow by-election. Munster is unseated, and Knox, running as a Home Ruler, again defeated on 10 May by George

Waters, Q.C. (Liberal) (93 votes to 85).

28 Feb. Denis Caulfield Heron (Liberal, 1,668 votes) narrowly defeats Charles J. Kickham (Independent Nationalist, (1,664) in Co. Tipperary by-election.

12 Mar. Serialisation of *Knocknagow* by Charles J. Kickham in the *Emerald* in New York; in Dublin serialised in the *Shamrock* from 19 Mar. (*see* 1873).

20 Mar. d. Robert Jocelyn (82), 3rd Earl of Roden, noted Evangelical and leader of the Orange Order.

4 Apr. Peace Preservation (Ireland) Act.

19 Apr. d. George Henry Moore, politician and landlord.

25 Apr. d. Daniel Maclise (64), painter.

19 May Home Government Association founded at the Bilton Hotel, Dublin, by Isaac Butt and John Martin; first public meeting at the Rotunda on 1 Sept. (*see* 18–21 Nov. 1873).

29 July Michael Davitt sentenced to 15 years' imprisonment with hard labour at the Old Bailey, London (released on 19 Dec. 1877).

1 Aug. Gladstone's Landlord and Tenant (Ireland) Act, his first Land Act, tries unsuccessfully to provide all Irish tenants with the benefits of the 'Ulster custom'; 'Bright clause' provides for tenant purchase (*see* 1 May 1877).

10 Aug. Glebe Loans (Ireland) Act authorises Commissioners of Public Works to grant loans for two-thirds of the cost of purchase of glebes.

27 Aug. *Oceanic* launched, built by Harland & Wolff, Belfast, for the White Star Line, the first modern liner.

1 Sept. Pub. first issue of the *Belfast Evening Telegraph*, Ireland's first halfpenny newspaper.

Pub. first issue of *Irish World* by Patrick Ford in New York (runs until his death on 23 Sept. 1913).

3 Oct. d. Richard Barter (68), physician who introduced the first Turkish baths in the British Isles at the Hydropathic Institute, St Ann's, Blarney, Co. Cork (1842).

7–8 Oct. Over 200 Irish volunteers forming an ambulance corps sail for Le Havre to assist France, at war with Prussia.

20 Oct. d. Michael William Balfe (62), composer (*The Bohemian Girl*, 1843, his best-known opera).

26 Dec. Statue in memory of William Smith O'Brien unveiled in Dublin; sculptor Thomas Farrell.

Pub. *Lives of the Lord Chancellors of Ireland* (2 vols) by James Roderick O'Flanagan.

Pub. *The Irish Landlords since the Revolution* by Fr Patrick Lavelle.

Pub. *Home Government for Ireland: Irish Federalism, Its Meaning, Its Objects and Its Hopes* by Isaac Butt.

1871

1 Jan. Church of Ireland becomes a voluntary body under the terms of Disestablishment.

12 Jan. Spencer Compton Cavendish, Marquis of Hartington, appointed C.S.

Jan. 33 Fenians released, including Jeremiah O'Donovan Rossa, John Devoy, John O'Leary, Thomas Clarke Luby and William Mackey Lomasney; O'Donovan Rossa, Devoy, Charles Underwood O'Connell, Henry S. Mulleda and John McClure leave for the U.S.A. on board S.S. *Cuba* (the '*Cuba* Five').

17 Jan. John Martin (Ind. Nat.) wins Home Government Association's first seat when he defeats the Hon. G. J. Plunkett (Conservative) (1,140 votes to 684) in Meath by-election.

16 June Protection of Life and Property in Certain Parts of Ireland Act ('Westmeath Act') empowers L.L. to suspend *habeas corpus* and imprison anyone suspected of membership of a Ribbon society (*see* 15 Apr. 1868).

1 July d. John Edward Pigot (69), Young Ireland poet.

4 July d. James Duffy (62), publisher to Young Ireland.

2 Oct. d. Sir Thomas Deane (79), builder and architect.

5 Oct. Fenian John O'Neill again launches attack on Canada, and holds custom house at Pembina, Manitoba, briefly, before retreating.

6 Oct. d. Edwin Richard Windham Wyndham-Quin (59), 3rd Earl of Dunraven, scholar, co-founder of the Irish Archaeological Society (1840) and the Celtic Society (1845).

27 Nov. Gaiety Theatre, Dublin, custom built by John and Michael Gunn, opens with Goldsmith's *She Stoops to Conquer*.

30 Nov. St Fin Barre's Cathedral (C.I.) in Cork consecrated; architect William Burges.

Census of population: 5,412,377 (decrease of 6.67 per cent since 1861).

Pub. *History of the Land Tenures and Land Classes of Ireland* by George Sigerson.

Pub. *The Annals of Loch Cé* (2 vols), ed. William Maunsell Hennessy.

1872

1 Feb. First Dublin trams from the city to Rathmines (fare 3d).

12 Feb. R. P. Blennerhassett (Protestant Home Ruler, 2,237 votes) defeats J. A. Dease (Liberal, 1,398) in Kerry by-election.

14 Feb. d. Robert Patterson (70), naturalist.

16 Feb. d. Robert Daly (89), C.I. Bishop of Cashel and Waterford since 1843, noted Evangelical.

1–27 May Trial before Judge William Nicholas Keogh arising out of Galway by-election; J. P. Nolan unseated on grounds of undue influence used by R.C. clergy; Keogh's comments about Catholic hierarchy and clergy, when delivering his judgment on 27 May, much resented

20 May d. Stephen Catterson Smith, portraitist, president of R.H.A. (1859–64).

1 June d. Charles Lever (66), author.

3 June Select committee of the House of Lords appointed to inquire into working of Gladstone's Land Act of 1870.

27 June Party Processions Acts of 1850 and 1860 repealed.

18 July Secret Ballot Act enables tenants to vote for candidates of their choice.

10 Aug. Act establishes Local Government Board for Ireland, absorbing the functions of the Poor Law Commission.

d. William Steuart Trench (64), land agent; author of *Realities of Irish Life* (1868).

28 Aug. First tramcars, drawn by horses, in Belfast.

1 Nov. d. John Francis Maguire (57), founder of the *Cork Examiner* (1841).

26 Nov. Lord Granard launches Catholic Union of Ireland in Dublin to oppose persecution of religious orders throughout the world, to oppose interference with the authority of the Catholic Church in educational matters, and to promote the restoration of the Pope's temporalities.

Pub. *Ballads of Irish Chivalry* by Robert Dwyer Joyce.

Pub. *The English in Ireland in the Eighteenth Century* (Vol. I) by James Anthony Froude (completed in 3 vols in 1874).

1873

7 Feb. d. Joseph Sheridan Le Fanu (59), novelist.

Feb. Home Rule Confederation of Great Britain founded in Manchester; Isaac Butt president.

12 Mar. Gladstone's Irish University Bill defeated by three votes (287–284); 35 Irish Catholic M.P.s vote against it, under pressure from Catholic hierarchy.

17 Mar. I.R.B. adopts new constitution (recognising Supreme Council as provisional government of the Irish Republic 'virtually established').

26 May Act abolishes all religious tests for Trinity College, Dublin, except for the Divinity faculty.

July Pub. first issue of *Irish Monthly*, periodical founded by Fr Tom Finlay and Fr Matthew Russell; becomes the *Lyceum* in 1887, then *All Ireland Review* (1894–1911), and later superseded by *Studies*.

5 Aug. d. Rev. John Magan, Presbyterian writer and co-founder of the Ulster Temperance Society (1829).

15 Aug. Irish section of the National Agricultural Labourers' Union formed in Kanturk, Co. Cork.

7 Sept. Start of climactic campaign by Amnesty Association: 250,000 addressed by Isaac Butt at Clontarf; runs for nine Sundays until 23 Nov., when 300,000 assemble at Glasnevin, Dublin.

18–21 Nov. Home Government Association holds conference at the Rotunda, Dublin; renamed the Irish Home Rule League 'to obtain . . . self-government'.

Pub. (posthumously) *On the Manners and Customs of the Ancient Irish* (3 vols) by Eugene O'Curry, ed. W. K. Sullivan.

Pub. (in book form) *Knocknagow, or The Homes of Tipperary* by Charles J. Kickham.

1874

31 Jan. – 12 Feb. General election; Gladstone (Liberal) succeeded as P.M. by Disraeli (Conservative).

27 Feb. Sir Michael Hicks Beach appointed C.S.

3 Mar. Isaac Butt's Home Rule Party (59 M.P.s) pledges to 'individually and collectively hold ourselves aloof from, and independent of, all party combinations'.

18 Mar. Charles Stewart Parnell (Home Rule, 1,235 votes) defeated by T. E. Taylor (Conservative, 2,183) in Co. Dublin by-election.

30 June – 2 July Isaac Butt's motion that the House of Commons go into committee 'to consider the present parliamentary relations between Great Britain and Ireland' rejected (458–61).

1 July William James Pirrie becomes a partner in Harland & Wolff.

30 July Extremists in the Home Rule Party led by Joseph Biggar adopt policy of 'obstruction'; repudiated by Butt.

27 Aug. d. John Henry Foley (56), sculptor (works include statues of Burke and Goldsmith, T.C.D.).

30 Aug. d. Michael Banim (78), novelist.

21 Sept. d. Arthur Jacob (84), oculist, discoverer of 'membrana Jacobi'.

12 Dec. d. James Thomas O'Brien (82), C.I. Bishop of Ossory, Ferns and Leighlin since 1842, noted Evangelical.

14 Dec. Irish Football Union formed in Dublin (*see* 5 Feb. 1880).

d. Biddy Early (c. 75), white witch in Clare.

Pub. *Prison Life: Six Years in Six English Prisons* by Jeremiah O'Donovan Rossa (republished as *Irish Rebels in English Prisons*, 1882).

1875

17 Feb. John Mitchel arrives in Ireland from U.S.A., having been returned unopposed as M.P. for Co. Tipperary on the previous day; result declared void on 18 Feb.; successfully contests new by-election on 11 Mar., but d. 20 Mar. (aged 60).

29 Mar. d. John Martin (63), Young Irelander, M.P. for Meath; his seat is won by Charles Stewart Parnell (Home Rule) on 17 Apr.

9 Apr. d. Sir John Gray (59), owner of the *Freeman's Journal*.

22 Apr. Charles Stewart Parnell enters parliament as M.P. for Meath; joins Home Rule obstructionists.

28 May Peace Preservation (Ireland) Act (new Coercion Act).

Sept. d. Charles Bianconi (89), businessman, promoter of Irish road-car services.

24 Oct. d. Rev. William Hickey (88), philanthropist and prolific writer on horticultural and agricultural matters.

1876

Mar. Jeremiah O'Donovan Rossa establishes 'Skirmishing Fund' in U.S.A. for terrorist activities directed against Britain.

17–18 Apr. American Fenians (Clan na Gael) rescue six Fenian prisoners from Fremantle, Western Australia, on board the *Catalpa* (the '*Catalpa* Six') (arrive in New York on 19 Aug.).

19 Apr. d. Sir William Wilde (61), physician and scholar.

30 June C. S. Parnell causes furore in House of Commons by defending the 'Manchester Martyrs' who have been referred to by C.S. Sir Michael Hicks Beach as 'Manchester murderers'.

30 June – 1 July Debate on Isaac Butt's motion on Home Rule (defeated by 291 votes to 61).

20 Aug. I.R.B. Supreme Council withdraws support for Home Rule; calls on republican M.P.s to leave Westminster (5 Mar. 1878) and expels those who refuse (Joseph Biggar and John O'Connor Power).

15 Nov. A. M. Sullivan transfers the *Nation* to his brother T. D. Sullivan.

12 Dec. John Winston Spencer Churchill, Duke of Marlborough, sworn in as L.L.

29 Dec. Society for the Preservation of the Irish Language formed in Dublin.

Pub. *A Cabinet of Irish Literature* (Vol. I), ed. Charles Anderson Read (completed in 4 vols in 1878; Vol. IV ed. T. P. O'Connor)

1877

2 Jan. d. Thaddeus O'Malley (81), political writer and controversialist.

2 Feb. O'Donovan Rossa succeeds John O'Mahony as Head Centre of the Fenian Brotherhood in New York.

7 Feb. d. John O'Mahony (61), founder of the Fenians, in U.S.A.; remains brought to Dublin on 26 Feb. for burial in Glasnevin.

13 Feb. Re-enactment of the 12.30 a.m. closure rule in the House of Commons stimulates the Irish obstructionists.

1 May Commission under G. J. Shaw-Lefevre appointed by House of Commons to inquire into the failure of the land purchase provisions of the 1870 Land Act (*see* 27 June 1878).

27 July – 6 Aug. Isaac Butt fails in his attempts to prevent obstructionist tactics within his party; during 31 July – 1 Aug. Home Rule obstructionists filibuster for 21 hours of a 45-hour session in the House of Commons.

14 Aug. Supreme Court of Judicature (Ireland) Act establishes Supreme Court with two permanent divisions, High Court of Justice and Court of Appeal (effective from 1 Jan. 1878).

27–28 Aug. Home Rule Confederation of Great Britain holds annual convention in Liverpool; C. S. Parnell replaces Isaac Butt as president.

Failure of potato crop in Connaught produces fear of famine.

15 Sept. d. Joshua Jacob (72), founder of the 'White Quakers' (1843).

1 Oct. d. David Moriarty (63), R.C. Bishop of Kerry since 1856.

9 Oct. General Prisons Board of Ireland in operation.

7 Nov. W. E. Gladstone receives freedom of the city of Dublin (during visit from 17 Oct. to 12 Nov.).

Dec. – 5 Jan. 1878 Pub. (in *Freeman's Journal*) 'Christmas in the Galtees' by William O'Brien; draws national attention to living conditions of tenants on the Buckley estate on the Galtee hillsides; published as a pamphlet in Mar. 1878.

Fitzwilliam Lawn Tennis Club, Dublin, founded.

Pub. *A History of the Town of Belfast from the Earliest Times to the Close of the Eighteenth Century* (Vol. I) by George Benn (Vol. II, 1880).

1878

10 Jan. d. William Stokes (74), physician to Queen Victoria, author and founder of the Pathological Society (1838).

13 Jan. Michael Davitt and other released Fenians receive public reception upon arrival at Kingstown (Dún Laoghaire); Parnell and leading M.P.s present.

14–15 Jan. Home Rule conference fails to heal rift over tactics in the House of Commons.

20 Jan. Huge funeral procession for Charles Heapy McCarthy, ex-prisoner, who died on 15 Jan. while breakfasting with Parnell and Davitt.

23 Jan. d. Charles Anderson Read (37), author and editor.

26 Jan. Michael Davitt arrives in Mayo to a huge reception, organised by James Daly, editor of the *Connaught Telegraph*.

15 Feb. James Lowther appointed C.S.

2 Apr. William Sydney Clements, 3rd Earl of Leitrim, landlord, together with his clerk and his car-driver, murdered on the shores of

Mulroy Bay, near Milford, Co. Donegal; killers (Neil Shiels and Michael McElwee) never apprehended.

26 May d. John Gregg (80), C.I. Bishop of Cork, Cloyne and Ross since 1862; noted Evangelical; commissioned building of St Fin Barre's Cathedral, Cork.

27 June Shaw-Lefevre Commission (*see* 1 May 1877) reports, recommending that tenants should be afforded greater facilities for buying their holdings.

8 Aug. Public Health (Ireland) Act governs water supply, sewage disposal and public hygiene and introduces legislation to deal with sales of diseased food.

16 Aug. Intermediate Education (Ireland) Act establishes board for intermediate (secondary) education.

16 Sept. Davitt starts his American lecture tour at the Concert Hall, Philadelphia; finishes in Boston on 8 Dec.

22 Sept. d. Sir Richard Griffith (94), geologist and engineer.

30 Sept. d. (suicide) Judge William Nicholas Keogh (61), one-time member of the Independent Irish Party (1850–52).

13 Oct. Michael Davitt, speaking at the New Park Theatre, Brooklyn, on a platform with John Devoy, calls for participation in constitutional politics by Fenians and a combination of parliamentary action and agrarian agitation.

24 Oct. John Devoy sends telegram from New York to James O'Connor to show to Charles J. Kickham, seeking abandonment of Butt's federal demand and its replacement by a general declaration in favour of self-government and agitation for peasant proprietorship; rejected by Kickham (published in New York on 25 Oct. and in Dublin on 11 Nov.; start of manoeuvres leading to the 'New Departure'; *see* 27 Oct.)

d. Paul, Cardinal Cullen (75), R.C. Archbishop of Dublin since 1852; first Irish cardinal (1866).

26 Oct. Mayo Tenants' Defence Association founded by J. J. Louden and James Daly: 'the land of Ireland for the people of Ireland' (John O'Connor Power).

27 Oct. New York *Herald* heads a news article 'An Irish New Departure' (written by John Devoy), heralding policy of co-operation between the republican movement, the constitutionalists and the agrarian movement, which has approval of leaders of Clan na Gael.

3 Nov. Parnell addresses a meeting of the Ballinasloe Tenants' Defence Association; his first visit to Connaught.

10 Nov. d. Rev. Edward Joseph O'Reilly (67), S.J., theologian.

4 Dec. d. Rev. Richard Smyth (52), Presbyterian minister and politician.

12 Dec. Davitt leaves New York for Ireland (arrives at Queenstown on 23rd).

Pub. *History of England in the Eighteenth Century* (Vols I–II) by W. E. H. Lecky (completed in 8 vols in 1890; includes material published separately in 1892 as *History of Ireland in the Eighteenth Century*).

Pub. *History of Ireland: Heroic Period* (Vol. I) by Standish James O'Grady (completed in 3 vols in 1881).

1879

19–26 Jan. Supreme Council of the I.R.B., meeting in Paris under the chairmanship of its President, Charles J. Kickham, rejects 'New Departure' proposals presented by Davitt and Devoy.

4 Feb. Isaac Butt, in his last attendance at a Home Rule meeting, is subjected to a withering attack from John Dillon.

Feb. – Mar. Disturbances in west Galway over the activities of the proselytising Irish Church Missions to Roman Catholics.

Mar. Pub. *Progress and Poverty* by Henry George (said to have sold 2 million copies by 1900).

7–9 Mar. Parnell, Devoy and John O'Leary discuss the proposed 'New Departure' at Boulogne.

20 Mar. d. Michael Henry Gill (85), publisher (co-founder of McGlashan & Gill, now Gill & Macmillan).

Mar. – Sept. Wettest year on record; during this period it rains on 125 out of 183 days; the harvest is the worst since the famine of the 1840s; Connaught particularly adversely affected.

20 Apr. Tenant Right Association led by James Daly of the *Connaught Telegraph* and P. W. Nally, with the support of Michael Davitt, organises a meeting of tenants at Irishtown, Co. Mayo, attracting around 10,000 to protest at rent charges and successfully seeking rent abatements (*see* 16 Aug.).

5 May d. Isaac Butt (66), founder of the Home Rule movement.

May Rural distress greatly worsens in Connaught.

1 June Parnell, Devoy and Davitt meet to consider 'New Departure'.

15 June d. Sir Thomas Larcom (78), official who drew up the census of 1841 using classifications subsequently adopted in England.

21 July Irish Convention Act of 1793 repealed.

26 July James Lysaght Finigan, Parnell's candidate, wins Ennis by-election (83 votes), defeating William O'Brien, Q.C. (moderate Home Ruler, 77 votes), who has local clerical support.

14 Aug. Commission under the Duke of Richmond appointed to inquire into the condition of agriculture in the U.K. (reports on 14 Jan. 1880).

15 Aug. James Daly, speaking at Gurteen, Co. Sligo, advises tenants that it is their duty to reinstate any of their number who are evicted.

University Education (Ireland) Act provides for dissolution of the Queen's University in Ireland, to be replaced by a new examining body with university status (Royal University, established by charter on 27 Apr. 1880).

16 Aug. National Land League of Mayo founded in Castlebar by Davitt, James Daly and J. J. Louden (*see* 21 Oct.).

21 Aug. Reported apparition of the Virgin Mary at Knock, Co. Mayo.

31 Aug. – 19 Oct. Tenants' meetings held throughout the country as a result of the worsening land crisis.

29 Sept. Parnell and Davitt issue 'Appeal to the Irish Race' to establish a committee to appeal to the Irish abroad to aid the new land agitation seeking the ownership of the soil by the occupiers.

21 Oct. Irish National Land League founded in Dublin by Davitt, Parnell, Thomas Brennan and Patrick Egan.

22 Nov. 100 police withdraw from attempt to evict Anthony Dempsey, Balla, Co. Mayo, when Parnell heads a crowd of 8,000 demonstrators.

18 Dec. Duchess of Marlborough, wife of the L.L., establishes fund for the relief of the distressed tenantry, now in the grip of famine (raises over £130,000 within a year).

Dec. Dan Lowrey opens Dublin's first regular music hall, the Star of Erin, Palace of Varieties, later called the Empire and subsequently the Olympia (*see* 13 Nov. 1898).

Pub. *History of Our Own Times* by Justin McCarthy.

Pub. *Early Bardic Literature of Ireland* by Standish James O'Grady.

1880

2 Jan. Mansion House Fund for the relief of distressed tenantry inaugurated by the Lord Mayor, Edmund Dwyer Gray of the *Freeman's Journal*.

Parnell and Dillon arrive in New York to raise funds for the Land League and for the relief of distress in Ireland; later joined by T. M. Healy (leave for Ireland on 11 Mar.).

2 Feb. Parnell addresses the U.S. House of Representatives.

5 Feb. Irish Rugby Football Union founded from the Irish Football Union.

20 Feb. Speaking in Cincinnati, Parnell is reported as saying: 'None of us, whether we be in America or in Ireland, or wherever we may be, will be satisfied until we have destroyed the last link which keeps Ireland bound to England.'

1 Mar. Seed Supply (Ireland) Act authorises Boards of Guardians to supply tenants with seed potatoes.

11 Mar. Parnell initiates a new body called the 'Irish National Land and Industrial League of the United States' in New York (American Land League; *see* 18 May).

15 Mar. Relief of Distress (Ireland) Act permits temporary outdoor relief in the form of food and fuel to be given to able-bodied men and their families in areas of exceptional distress, financed by £1½ million from Church Disestablishment Fund (*see* 2 Aug.).

21 Mar. Parnell, Dillon and Healy return from the U.S.A., having raised £70,000, mostly for famine relief.

31 Mar. – 13 Apr. General election; Gladstone (Liberal) forms his second administration on 23 Apr.

18 Apr. Thomas Nulty, R.C. Bishop of Meath, authorises church-door collection for Parnell.

29 Apr. 250 delegates, including 18 M.P.s, attend Land League conference chaired by John Ferguson at the Rotunda, Dublin; Fenians disrupt the proceedings and at one stage push Davitt off platform.

30 Apr. William Edward Forster appointed C.S.

4 May Salvation Army begins mission in Ireland; first unit in Belfast.

5 May Francis, Earl Cowper, sworn in as L.L.

6 May Carlisle Bridge, Dublin, reopened under the name O'Connell Bridge (originally built in 1794, designed by James Gandon).

17 May Parnell elected Chairman of the Home Rule Party (23 votes to 18 for William Shaw).

18 May American Land League holds first convention, at which Davitt is appointed secretary for duration of his visit.

24 May Thomas Maguire becomes the first R.C. Fellow of T.C.D. (d. 26 Feb. 1889).

30 May Thomas William Croke, R.C. Archbishop of Cashel, gives his support to the Land League: 'It is neither sin nor treason to say that where a man labours he has a right to be fed.'

KILKENNY COUNTY LIBRARY

1 June Peace Preservation Act expires.

28–30 June Jeremiah O'Donovan Rossa establishes the United Irishmen of America, a revolutionary organisation in opposition to Clan na Gael, in Philadelphia.

5 July d. Rev. John Scott Porter (79), Presbyterian lecturer and scholar.

27 July St Stephen's Green, Dublin, opened to the public.

29 July Parliamentary commission under the Earl of Bessborough appointed to inquire into the working of the 1870 Land Act.

2 Aug. Relief of Distress (Ireland) Amendment Act indemnifies local authorities that have extended their powers in advancing money, and authorises grants for public works and outdoor relief.

13–18 Sept. Trades Union Congress meets for the first time in Ireland.

19 Sept. Parnell, speaking at Ennis, Co. Clare, calls for a 'moral Coventry' to be imposed on those who act contrary to the desires of the Land League, launching the campaign of 'boycotting' (first used against Capt. Charles Cunningham Boycott of Lough Mask House, Co. Mayo, on 24 Sept.; *see* 11–26 Nov.).

25 Sept. Viscount Mountmorres, landlord, murdered in Co. Galway.

14 Oct. Speaking in Galway, Parnell says: 'I would not have taken off my coat and gone to this work [land reform] if I had not known that we were laying the foundation in this movement for the regeneration of our legislative independence.'

24 Oct. First meeting of the Ladies' Land League, founded by Fanny Parnell, Jane Byrne and Ellen Ford in New York (*see* 26 Jan. 1881).

2 Nov. Parnell and 13 others charged with criminal conspiracy (hearing on 28 Dec.; jury disagrees on 25 Jan. 1881).

11–26 Nov. 50 Orange labourers under heavy escort work Lord Erne's Mayo estate at Lough Mask, where Erne's agent is Capt. Boycott (harvesting the crop is estimated to cost £10,000) (*see* 19 Sept.).

21 Dec. d. Henry O'Neill (80), archaeologist.

Dec. Irish landlords form the Property Defence Association 'to uphold the rights of property against organised combination to defraud'.

First manual telephone exchange, Dame Street, Dublin, has five subscribers.

Pub. *Irish Distress and Its Remedies* by James Hack Tuke (*see* 13 Nov. 1846 *and* 1847).

Pub. *The Irish Question* by the 4th Earl of Dunraven.

1881

3 Jan. Pope Leo XIII issues manifesto to Edward McCabe, R.C. Archbishop of Dublin, advising that Catholics in Ireland should not 'seem to have cast aside the obedience due to their lawful rulers'.

4 Jan. Bessborough Commission reports, recommending the legalisation of the 'Three Fs' (fair rent, free sale and fixity of tenure).

14 Jan. Minority report of the Richmond Commission, signed by Lord Carlingford, recommends the 'Three Fs'.

Fenian dynamiters set off explosions at Salford military barracks in Lancashire, killing a child and damaging property.

16–17 Jan. William Shaw and his 'Whig' followers secede from the Parnellite Home Rule Party in protest at the policy of peasant proprietorship.

17 Jan. d. Dr Humphrey Lloyd (81), Provost of T.C.D. since 1867, a noted scientist.

21 Jan. Memorial signed by over 20,000 Ulster Protestant farmers demands the 'Three Fs'.

26 Jan. Land League executive, over Parnell's objections, sanctions formation of a Ladies' Land League in Ireland to be led by Anna Parnell.

31 Jan. – 2 Feb. Home Rule Party forces the House of Commons into a 41-hour sitting when Irish members obstruct the Protection of Person and Property (Ireland) Bill (*see* 2 Mar.); sitting ends when Speaker assumes powers of closure.

3 Feb. Davitt arrested and imprisoned (released on 6 May 1882).

13 Feb. First public meeting of the Ladies' Land League, in Claremorris, Co. Mayo; League condemned in pastoral letter by Archbishop McCabe of Dublin on 13 Mar.

2 Mar. Protection of Person and Property (Ireland) Act empowers Irish executive to arrest and imprison without trial (until no later than 30 Sept. 1882) any person reasonably suspected of treasonable practices or agrarian offences.

21 Mar. Peace Preservation (Ireland) Act (new Coercion Act).

2 May John Dillon arrested (released on 8 Aug.).

20 May Fr Eugene Sheehy becomes first priest arrested during the Land War when the committee of the Kilmallock, Co. Limerick, branch of which he is president, is arrested.

24 May Committee of the Kilfinane, Co. Limerick, branch of the Land League arrested.

2 Aug. Richard Pigott sells his newspapers, the *Irishman*, the *Flag of Ireland* and the *Shamrock*, to Parnell's Irish National Publishing Company.

13 Aug. Pub. first issue of Parnellite organ, *United Ireland*, edited by William O'Brien (official organ of the Land League, runs until 1898).

22 Aug. Land Law (Ireland) Act, Gladstone's second Land Act, establishes the principle of dual ownership, legalises the 'Three Fs', establishes a Land Commission and Land Court; the 'Healy clause' ensures that tenant improvements do not result in rent increases.

15–17 Sept. Parnell advises the Land League convention in Dublin to 'test the [Land] Act'.

7 Oct. Gladstone, speaking in Liverpool, attacks Parnell for opposing the Land Act: 'Mr Parnell desires to arrest the operation of the Land Act, to stand, not as Moses stood, to arrest, but to extend the plague.'

9 Oct. Parnell, speaking in Wexford, describes Gladstone as 'this masquerading knight-errant'.

13 Oct. Parnell arrested and held at Kilmainham jail.

14 Oct. Thomas Sexton and P. J. Quinn arrested and held at Kilmainham jail.

15 Oct. William O'Brien, John Dillon, Joseph G. Biggar, T. D. Sullivan and others arrested and held at Kilmainham jail.

18 Oct. Imprisoned Land League leaders issue the 'No-Rent Manifesto'.

20 Oct. Land League outlawed by proclamation which describes it as 'an unlawful and criminal association'.

Land Commission court established under the Land Law (Ireland) Act opens.

21 Oct. Archbishop Croke's protest against the 'No-Rent Manifesto' appears in the *Freeman's Journal*.

5 Nov. d. Robert Mallet (71), engineer, whose Victorian foundry eventually took over all the bigger engineering works in Ireland; inventor of the buckled plate (patented in 1852).

7 Nov. d. John MacHale (90), R.C. Archbishop of Tuam since 1834.

16 Dec. 'Special Resident Magistrates' appointed to direct the Resident Magistrates, police and military in the attack on agrarian crime.

Census of population: 5,174, 836 (decrease of 4.39 per cent since 1871).

1882
3 Feb. Queen's University dissolved.

28 Feb. d. Rev. Thomas Romney Robinson (89), director of the Armagh Observatory since 1823.

27 Mar. Edward McCabe, R.C. Archbishop of Dublin, created cardinal.

31 Mar. 'Tuke Committee' formed at the home of the Duke of Bedford to administer funds raised by James Hack Tuke; assists some 9,500 persons to emigrate in 'family emigration', spending an estimated £70,000.

7 Apr. d. Denis Florence McCarthy (65), poet.

10–24 Apr. Parnell, released on parole, moves towards a negotiated settlement with Gladstone (the so-called 'Kilmainham Treaty'), using Mrs Katharine O'Shea and Capt. W. H. O'Shea as intermediaries (*see* 2 May); terms conveyed to Justin McCarthy on 25 Apr. include withdrawal of 'No-Rent Manifesto' and an attempt to stop agrarian outrages in return for settlement of the arrears question and extension of the benefits of the Land Act to leaseholders.

28 Apr. L.L Cowper resigns.

2 May Parnell and other imprisoned Land League leaders released under the 'Kilmainham Treaty'; C.S. Forster resigns in protest.

6 May Earl Spencer again sworn in as L.L.

Michael Davitt released from Portland jail.

Newly arrived C.S. Lord Frederick Cavendish and his Under-Secretary T. H. Burke murdered by the Invincibles in Phoenix Park, Dublin (*see* 13 Jan. 1883).

9 May George Otto Trevelyan appointed C.S.

30 June – 1 July Home Rule Party forces the House of Commons into 28-hour sitting.

12 July Prevention of Crime (Ireland) Act (additional Coercion Act).

20 July d. Frances ('Fanny') Parnell (33), sister of Charles Stewart Parnell.

8 Aug. Maamtrasna murders in Co. Galway: father, mother and three children murdered, for which three people are hanged and another five imprisoned (one of those hanged, Miles Joyce, is widely believed to be innocent).

16 Aug. Parnell receives freedom of the city of Dublin.

15 Aug. Centenary commemorations held for the Volunteers of the 1780s.

Exhibition of Irish Arts and Manufactures held at the Rotunda Hospital gardens in Dublin.

18 Aug. Arrears of Rent (Ireland) Act and Labourers' Cottages and Allotments (Ireland) Act.

Charles Dawson, Lord Mayor of Dublin, chairs Mansion House Committee for the Relief of Evicted Tenants.

21 Aug. Irish Labour and Industrial Union established in Dublin to promote and harmonise the interests of agricultural labourers and industrial workers; organised by Parnell and Davitt.

22 Aug. d. Charles J. Kickham (54), President of the Supreme Council of the I.R.B., poet and novelist.

23 Sept. d. Rev. William Baillie, noted Presbyterian preacher.

4 Oct. d. Dr Michael Roberts (65), Professor of Mathematics, T.C.D. (1862–79).

17 Oct. National conference called by Parnell forms the Irish National League, constituency organisation of the Home Rule Party.

Nov. Pub. first issue of *Irisleabhar na Gaeilge: the Gaelic Journal.*

Pub. *Reminiscences of an Irish National Journalist* by Richard Pigott.

1883

13 Jan. 17 members of the Invincibles arrested (*see* 6 May 1882).

31 Jan. d. Michael Joseph McCann (59), Young Ireland poet, author of 'O'Donnell Abu' (originally known as 'The Clanconnell War Song').

4 Feb. – 4 June Davitt imprisoned in the Richmond Bridewell, Dublin, for a speech he made at Navan, Co. Meath.

3 Mar. Parnell National Tribute collection raises around £38,000 by 11 Dec., despite condemnation from Rome (11 May), which is deeply resented by Irish nationalists.

13 Apr. d. Joseph O'Kelly (51), geologist; involved in Geological Survey of Ireland (1854).

14 Apr. d. James Talbot, 1st Baron Talbot de Malahide, scholar.

24 Apr. d. John Cornelius O'Callaghan (78), historian (author of *History of the Irish Brigades in the Service of France,* 1870); contributor to the *Nation.*

14 May – 9 June Joseph Brady, Daniel Curley, Timothy Kelly, Michael Fagan and Thomas Caffrey, members of the Invincibles, executed for the Phoenix Park murders (6 May 1882) (*see* 29 July).

11–14 June Trial of Henry Wilson (i.e. Thomas J. Clarke) and others for dynamiting conspiracy; sentenced to life imprisonment (Clarke released on 29 Sept. 1898).

30 June T. M. Healy (Home Rule, 2,376 votes) defeats John Monroe, Q.C. (Conservative, 2,011) in Co. Monaghan by-election.

2 July d. Fr Thomas Nicholas Burke (53), Dominican preacher.

17 July William Redmond (Home Rule, 307 votes) defeats The O'Conor Don (Liberal, 126) in Wexford town by-election.

29 July James Carey, informer on the Invincibles for the Phoenix Park murders (*see* 6 May 1882), shot dead on board the *Melrose Castle* off Capetown by Patrick O'Donnell (who is executed on 17 Nov.).

16 Aug. d. Rev. Robert Knox (68), noted Presbyterian preacher; co-founder of the Sabbath School Society for Ireland.

25 Aug. Labourers (Ireland) Act empowers local authorities to build dwellings for agricultural labourers on security of rates.

24 Oct. d. Robert Dwyer Joyce (53), poet.

26 Oct. University College (formerly the Catholic University of Ireland, renamed on 3 Oct. 1882) transferred to the Society of Jesus.

First electric tram in Ireland, Portrush to Giant's Causeway, Co. Antrim, is also the first in the world to use hydro-electricity.

Tramways and Light Railways (Ireland) Act provides for construction of light railways to serve outlying or sparsely populated areas.

1884

1 Aug. John Daly of Limerick, Fenian, sentenced to life imprisonment for treason-felony (released on 20 Aug. 1896).

1 Oct. Resolution of the Catholic hierarchy places Irish educational interests in the hands of Parnell's Home Rule Party.

17 Oct. d. Alexander Martin Sullivan (54), politician (Nationalist) and owner and editor of the *Nation* (1858–77); author of the *Story of Ireland* (1870).

22 Oct. Royal University confers degrees on the first women to graduate in Ireland.

23 Oct. Henry Campbell-Bannerman appointed C.S.

25 Oct. d. Richard Townsend (63), mathematician and Professor of Natural Philosophy, T.C.D., since 25 June 1870.

1 Nov. Gaelic Athletic Association founded in Hayes's Commercial Hotel, Thurles, Co. Tipperary, by Michael Cusack, Maurice Davin, John Wyse Power, John McKay, John K. Bracken, Thomas St George McCarthy, P. J. O'Ryan and F. R. Moloney.

6 Dec. Representation of the People Act creates a uniform householder and lodger franchise for the whole of the U.K., giving the right to vote to all householders in counties and boroughs and to lodgers in counties; increases Irish electorate from 224,018 to 737,965.

13 Dec. William Mackey Lomasney and two other Fenians killed in explosion under London Bridge.

18 Dec. T. W. Croke, R.C. Archbishop of Cashel, accepts invitation to become a patron of the Gaelic Athletic Association in a letter which becomes known as the 'charter of the G.A.A.'.

Crawford Institute, Cork, founded.

1885

12 Jan. d. Patrick James Smyth (59), Young Irelander who aided John Mitchel's escape from Tasmania.

21 Jan. Speaking in Cork, Parnell says: 'No man has the right to fix the boundary to the march of a nation' (these words inscribed on his monument in Dublin).

24 Jan. Fenian dynamiting campaign (begun in 1883) culminates in simultaneous explosions in the Tower of London, Westminster Hall and the House of Commons.

27 Jan. Parnell turns the first sod for the West Clare Railway at Miltown Malbay, where he is greeted by one of the largest crowds ever assembled in Clare; he is presented with a silver spade and wheelbarrow made of bog-oak (*see* 2 July 1887 *and* 31 Jan. 1961).

11 Feb. d. Edward, Cardinal McCabe, R.C. Archbishop of Dublin since 1879; succeeded by William Joseph Walsh on 23 June.

21 Feb. Irish Amateur Athletic Association established in opposition to the G.A.A.

10 Apr. Foundation stone for the Science and Art Museum and the

National Library of Ireland laid by the Prince and Princess of Wales.

1 May Irish Loyal and Patriotic Union founded to resist Home Rule, led by Lord Castletown, Lord de Vesci, Lord Meath, Col. A. L. Tottenham, Arthur Patton and Rev. J. H. Jellett; fields 55 candidates in forthcoming general election, with only one success (Dublin University).

9 June Gladstone's government defeated on the budget by a combination of Conservatives and Home Rulers; Lord Salisbury (Conservative) forms a 'caretaker' government on 23rd.

25 June Sir William Hart Dyke appointed C.S.

Redistribution of Seats Act disfranchises 22 boroughs and changes Belfast's boundaries; all counties (except for Antrim and Down) retain old boundaries, and all (except for Carlow) are divided into parliamentary divisions; Belfast and Dublin boroughs are divided, and Dublin extended; each constituency elects one M.P., except for Cork City and Dublin University, which have two each.

30 June Henry Herbert, Earl of Carnarvon, sworn in as L.L.

14 July Munster Bank suspends payments; fails, and is succeeded by the Munster and Leinster Bank in 1886.

14 Aug. Purchase of Land (Ireland) Act (the Ashbourne Act) provides entire loan required for tenant purchase (£5 million at first, over 49 years at 4 per cent, supplemented by another £5 million); 942,600 acres purchased.

2 Nov. Archbishop Croke of Cashel states in a letter to the *Freeman's Journal* that it was never any part of his design in supporting the G.A.A. 'absolutely to discourage, and even denounce, all sports and pastimes that are not national'.

10 Nov. Parnell, speaking in Liverpool, seeks a Liberal declaration on Home Rule which Gladstone refuses.

24 Nov. – 9 Dec. General election: Liberals, 335; Conservatives, 249; Home Rule, 86. P.M. Salisbury (Conservative) remains in power with support of Home Rulers (until 28 Jan. 1886).

17 Dec. 'Hawarden Kite', announcing Gladstone's conversion to Home Rule, appears in the *Leeds Mercury* and the London *Standard*.

22 Dec. Grand Orange Lodge of Ireland meets in Dublin and resolves to work with all opposed to the Home Rule cause; Earl of Enniskillen, Orange Grand Master, sends memo to all Orange lodges calling for demonstrations against Home Rule.

Pub. *Leaves from a Prison Diary; or Lectures to a Solitary Audience* (2 vols) by Michael Davitt.

Pub. first lyrics by W. B. Yeats (in *Dublin University Review*).

1886

1 Jan. Salisbury's government rejects Gladstone's proposal for a bipartisan solution to the Irish demand for Home Rule.

9 Jan. Northwest Loyal Registration and Electoral Association founded at a meeting in Omagh presided over by the Duke of Abercorn.

8 Jan. Demonstration organised against Home Rule by the Belfast Conservative Association; decides to call itself the Ulster Loyalist Anti-Repeal Union.

12 Jan. Parliament opens.

L.L. Carnarvon resigns.

23 Jan. William Henry Smith appointed C.S.

25 Jan. Irish Unionist Party founded under leadership of Col. Edward J. Saunderson.

26 Jan. Government resolves to announce return to coercion; defeated (329–250) when the Irish Party unites with the Liberals on the address, through an amendment on agricultural policy, on 27th.

1 Feb. Gladstone (Liberal) appointed P.M. and forms his third administration.

1–10 Feb. Parnell imposes Capt. W. H. O'Shea, husband of Katharine, on the Irish Party in the Galway by-election; O'Shea (942 votes) defeats Michael Lynch, also a Nationalist (54 votes).

5 Feb. d. Richard Robert Madden (88), doctor and historian (author of *The United Irishmen, their Lives and Times*, 7 vols, 1843–46).

6 Feb. John Morley appointed C.S.

10 Feb. John Gordon, Earl of Aberdeen, sworn in as L.L.

16 Feb. d. Rev. William Fleming Stevenson (54), first Presbyterian minister appointed chaplain to the L.L. (Earl of Aberdeen).

22 Feb. Lord Randolph Churchill addresses 10,000 Unionists at the Ulster Hall in Belfast: 'Ulster will fight; Ulster will be right.'

Catholic hierarchy's support for Home Rule reported in the *Freeman's Journal*.

27 Mar. Joseph Chamberlain resigns from cabinet.

5 Apr. Parnell meets with P.M. Gladstone and C.S. Morley to discuss financial and fiscal aspects of Home Rule.

8 Apr. Gladstone introduces the Government of Ireland Bill (First Home Rule Bill).

13 Apr. Liberal Unionists and Conservatives protest against Home Rule Bill in the Ulster Hall, Belfast.

22 May Inaugural meeting of the Irish Protestant Home Rule Association in Belfast; formed by a group which wishes to counter the idea that Irish Protestants unanimously reject Home Rule.

1 June Meeting in Dublin to establish national organisation of the Irish Protestant Home Rule Association.

3–4 June Rioting on Belfast docks; spreads through the city and continues until Sept.; worst rioting of the century (*see* 8–10 June).

4 June Ulster Liberal Unionist Committee formed.

8 June Second reading of the Home Rule Bill; defeated (341 – 311) in the House of Commons.

8–10 June Protestant mob seizes control of sections of the city around Shankill Road and Sandy Row, Belfast; seven killed by police and army called in.

26 June Parliament dissolved.

1–17 July General election fought on the issue of Home Rule for Ireland; Conservatives return under Lord Salisbury on 25th.

4 July Michael Cusack dismissed from secretaryship of the G.A.A. for 'neglecting administrative work, not answering letters or acknowledging affiliation fees'.

July – Sept. 32 killed and 377 injured in Belfast during rioting; 31 pubs wrecked and 442 arrests made.

5 Aug. Charles Vane-Tempest-Stewart, Marquis of Londonderry, sworn in as L.L.; Sir Michael Edward Hicks Beach appointed C.S.

9 Aug. d. Sir Samuel Ferguson (76), poet and antiquary.

20–27 Aug. 'Siege of Saunders' Fort': 20 defenders at the home of Thomas Saunders at Woodford, Co. Galway, hold off over 700 police, two companies of soldiers and 40 'emergency men' carrying out evictions on behalf of the Marquis of Clanricard.

21 Oct. d. Rev. Thomas Young Killen (60), Moderator of the Presbyterian General Assembly (1882–83).

29 Sept. Commission under Earl Cowper established to inquire into the operation of the Land Acts of 1881 and 1885 (reports on 21 Feb. 1887).

23 Oct. *United Ireland* publishes 'A Plan of Campaign' by Timothy Harrington, outlining strategy for renewal of assault on landlordism in new agricultural crisis (*see* 18 Nov.).

30 Oct. Irish and English Catholics meet with P.M. Salisbury to discuss diplomatic relations between Great Britain and the Vatican and Catholic higher education.

18 Nov. John Dillon and William O'Brien support tenants on the Clanricard estate at Portumna, Co. Galway, who offer the land agent rents due less 40 per cent (on condition that evicted tenants are reinstated); this becomes the model for the Plan of Campaign.

2 Dec. In an interview with W. T. Stead of the *Pall Mall Gazette* Archbishop Walsh endorses the Plan of Campaign.

16 Dec. John Dillon, Matthew Harris, William O'Brien and David Sheehy arrested at Loughrea collecting rents for the Plan of Campaign; charged with criminal conspiracy (jury disagrees on 24 Feb. 1887).

18 Dec. British government denounces the Plan of Campaign as 'an unlawful and criminal conspiracy'.

Pub. *The League of North and South* by George Gavan Duffy.

1887

7 Mar. Arthur James Balfour appointed C.S.

London *Times* begins publication of series on 'Parnellism and Crime' which runs until Dec., alleging complicity of Home Rulers in acts of terrorism during the Land War (1879–82) (*see* 18 Apr.).

15 Apr. William O'Brien arrested.

17 Apr. John Dillon arrested.

18 Apr. London *Times* publishes article 'Parnellism and Crime: Mr Parnell and the Phoenix Park Murders', including a letter allegedly written by Parnell, dated 15 May 1882, condoning the murder of T. H. Burke in Phoenix Park (*see* 6 May 1882); Parnell denounces the letter as a 'felonious and bare-faced forgery'.

2–15 June 28 families evicted off his Bodyke, Co. Clare, estate by Col. John O'Callaghan of Maryfort, Tulla, Co. Clare; witnessed by over 5,000 people.

2 July West Clare Railway (Ennis–Miltown Malbay section) opens.

7 July Arrival of two envoys from the Vatican, Monsignor Ignazio Persico and Monsignor Enrico Gualdi (*see* 20 Apr. 1888).

19 July Criminal Law and Procedure (Ireland) Act (Crimes Act) enables L.L. to declare the National League a dangerous association 'which . . . provokes and incites to acts of violence and intimidation'.

20 July 80 Liberals and 50 Home Rule M.P.s attend banquet at the National Liberal Club where Parnell extols the achievements of Gladstone.

24 July Resident Magistrates given increased powers under the Crimes Act (19 July) to prosecute in courts of

KILKENNY COUNTY LIBRARY

summary jurisdiction in cases of intimidation and boycotting.

23 Aug. Land Law (Ireland) Act enables leaseholders to avail of the terms of the 1881 Land Act and provides for revision of rents judicially fixed during 1881–85.

9 Sept. Three killed and two wounded at Mitchelstown, Co. Cork, when police open fire on Plan of Campaign supporters being addressed by John Dillon ('Mitchelstown massacre'); Inspector Brownrigg of the R.I.C. resigns.

15 Oct. Sir Joseph West Ridgeway appointed Under-Secretary.

9 Nov. I.R.B. candidate E. M. Bennett ousts Maurice Davin from the presidency of the G.A.A. (Davin reinstated in Jan. 1888).

c. 11 Nov. Archbishop Croke breaks with the G.A.A.: 'It [a G.A.A. meeting] was packed to the throat with Fenian leaders. . . . The chairman is a notorious propagandist.'

Pub. *Ancient Legends of Ireland* by Lady Wilde.

Pub. *Ogham Inscriptions in Ireland, Wales and Scotland* by Sir Samuel Ferguson, edited by his widow.

1888

8 Feb. d. Stephen Joseph Meany (63), Young Ireland journalist.

19 Feb. d. Rev. John Hewitt Jellett (71), mathematician, Provost of T.C.D. since 1881.

28 Feb. Pneumatic cycle tyres first used (on tricycle belonging to Johnny, son of Belfast inventor, John Boyd Dunlop).

29 Feb. Lartigue Railway, 9¼-mile monorail from Listowel to Ballybunion, Co. Kerry, opens; total cost, including rolling stock, is £630,000 (*see* 14 Oct. 1924).

1 Apr. First All-Ireland Hurling Championship Final, at Birr, King's County (Co. Offaly): Tipperary (Thurles) defeat Galway (Meelick), 1 goal 2 pts to nil.

20 Apr. Papal rescript issued by the Vatican condemning the Plan of Campaign and boycotting, a result of the Persico mission (*see* 7 July 1887); condemned by John Dillon on 7 May and by Lord Mayor and Dublin Corporation on 24 May.

29 Apr. First All-Ireland Football Championship Final, at Clonskeagh, Dublin: Limerick (Commercials) defeat Dundalk (Young Irelands), 1 goals 4 pts to 3 pts.

5 May Pub. first issue of the *Irish Catholic*, founded by T. D. Sullivan.

8 May Parnell, addressing the Liberal Eighty Club, dissociates himself from the Plan of Campaign.

20 May Monster meeting in Phoenix Park, Dublin, organised by Dillon, O'Brien, Thomas Sexton and John Redmond rejects the papal rescript on the Plan of Campaign.

26 May Edward T. O'Dwyer, R.C. Bishop of Limerick, in a letter to the *Irish Catholic* upbraids those who reject the papal rescript and is himself attacked by Home Rule leaders and Michael Davitt.

2 June Catholic hierarchy announce their resolutions on the papal rescript, stating that it is 'intended to affect the domain of morals alone, and in no way to interfere with politics, as such, in the country'.

5 June F. H. O'Donnell, former Home Rule M.P., loses his case against the London *Times* in connection with the series 'Parnellism and Crime' (*see* 17 Sept. – 22 Nov. 1889).

11 June Bishop O'Dwyer of Limerick in a letter read at all churches in his diocese states that 'Boycotting and the Plan of Campaign . . . stand condemned as violations of the moral law of charity and justice.'

20 June Dillon sentenced to six months' imprisonment in Dundalk jail (released in Sept. on grounds of ill-health).

24 June Pope Leo XIII in a letter to the Catholic hierarchy in Ireland (received on 30 June) repeats that Sacred Congregation 'has decreed that those methods of warfare known as boycotting and the Plan of Campaign . . . may not lawfully be used'.

17 Sept. – 22 Nov. 1889 Special Commission to inquire into allegations made against Parnell by the *Times* (*see* 7 Mar. *and* 18 Apr. 1887), consisting of three judges, established under an act of 13 Aug., holds 129 sittings (*see* 13 Feb. 1890).

9 Oct. d. John Savage (60), Young Ireland poet and journalist.

1889

3 Feb. District Inspector William Martin murdered when attempting to arrest Fr James McFadden, Gweedore, Co. Donegal.

5 Feb. Henri Le Caron appears as witness before Special Commission, revealing himself as a spy for the British government since the 1860s.

20–22 Feb. Richard Pigott appears as witness before Special Commission and is cross-examined by Sir Charles Russell (acting for Parnell); Pigott exposed as a forger by his misspelling, indicating his authorship of the letters which appeared in the *Times* series (*see* 18 Apr. 1887).

1 Mar. Richard Pigott, confronted by police at the Hotel Embajadores, Madrid, shoots himself.

Parnell, entering the House of Commons, receives a standing ovation (the first in seventy years).

6 Mar. – 20 Apr. John Dillon in Australia to raise money for the Plan of Campaign.

22 Apr. d. James McKeown (75), Ulster humorist-poet.

30 Apr. – 8 May Parnell gives evidence before Special Commission.

4 May Irish Federated Trade and Labour Union holds its first conference, in Dublin.

June Total Abstinence League of the Sacred Heart founded by Fr James A. Cullen; later known as Pioneer League.

12 June Armagh railway disaster: 80 killed and 400 injured.

14 June Irish Society for the Prevention of Cruelty to Children founded as an interdenominational organisation.

30 Aug. Technical Instruction Act.

14 Sept. First successful parachute descent from balloon by Mr Spencer over Clonturk Park, Drumcondra, Dublin.

5 Oct. Lawrence Dundas, Earl of Zetland, sworn in as L.L.

16 Oct. d. Ellen O'Leary (58), poet, sister of John O'Leary.

21 Oct. d. John Ball (71), politician, first president of the Alpine Club (1857).

25 Oct. Tenants' Defence Association launched at the Mansion House, Dublin, supported by Parnell.

18 Nov. d. William Allingham (65), poet (author of 'The Faeries').

2 Dec. 152 tenants evicted by A. H. Smith-Barry in Tipperary town (*see* 12 Apr. 1890).

24 Dec. Capt. W. H. O'Shea files for divorce, citing Parnell as co-respondent (*see* 17 Nov 1890).

25 Dec. d. Arthur MacMurrough Kavanagh (58), M.P.; born with only rudimentary limbs, he became an expert horseman, angler, huntsman, shooter and painter.

Pub. *The Wanderings of Oisin and other poems* and *Crossways* first collections of poetry by W. B. Yeats.

1890

14 Jan. Royal Society of Antiquaries of Ireland formed from the Kilkenny Archaeological Society (founded in Feb. 1849).

13 Feb. Report of Special Commission finds the letters published by the *Times* to be forgeries; exonerates Parnell of all serious charges.

19 Feb. d. Joseph Gillis Biggar (62), M.P. (Home Rule); originated obstructionist tactics in the House of Commons; once forced the Prince of Wales to leave the House ('I spy a stranger').

14 Mar. d. Rev. Charles Patrick Meehan (78), poet and historian.

12 Apr. 'New Tipperary' opened by leaders of the Plan of Campaign.

11 July John Dillon in the House of Commons attacks R.C. Bishop of Limerick, Edward T. O'Dwyer, who is accused of having 'written a most violent and dastardly letter'.

14 July Bishop O'Dwyer's letter appears in the *Freeman's Journal*, describing John Dillon as 'dishonest, a coward and disrespectful to the people'.

29 Aug. Science and Art Museum and National Library of Ireland opened.

18 Sept. John Dillon and William O'Brien arrested on charge of criminal activities in connection with Plan of Campaign (break bail and flee to France on 9 Oct.) (*see* 12 Feb. 1891).

d. Dion Lardner Boucicault (70), actor-manager and dramatist (author of *The Colleen Bawn*, 1860).

21 Sept. Pub. first issue of *Labour World*, ed. Michael Davitt.

13 Oct. Top stone of statue of Fr Theobald Mathew laid in Sackville Street (O'Connell Street), Dublin; sculpted by Mary Redmond.

12 Nov. d. John O'Hagan (68), lawyer, judge and poet.

17 Nov. *O'Shea v. O'Shea* divorce action, suit undefended; verdict finds that Mrs Katharine O'Shea had committed adultery with Parnell and awards Capt. O'Shea custody of the children.

20 Nov. Meeting of Irish Nationalists and Liberals at Leinster Hall, Dublin, pledges support for Parnell.

24 Nov. Gladstone informs Justin McCarthy that Liberal support for Home Rule is no longer possible if Parnell remains leader of the Home Rule Party (Irish Parliamentary Party).

25 Nov. Parnell unanimously reelected chairman of the Irish Parliamentary Party; M.P.s not yet aware of Gladstone's position.

26 Nov. Letter from Gladstone to John Morley outlining the Liberal position in relation to Parnell published.

28 Nov. Parnell's 'Manifesto to the Irish People' attacks Gladstone; published in press on 29th.

30 Nov. Dillon, O'Brien, T. P. O'Connor, T. P. Gill and T. D. Sullivan repudiate Parnell's leadership of the Irish Parliamentary Party.

1–6 Dec. The Irish Parliamentary Party meets in Committee Room 15 of the House of Commons to discuss the problem of Parnell's leadership; Archbishop Walsh calls on them to act 'manfully', and the standing committee of the Catholic hierarchy calls on the people to reject Parnell (3rd); the party splits when 44 M.P.s led by Justin McCarthy walk out, leaving Parnell with 28 followers (6th).

6 Dec. Matthew Bodkin, acting editor of *United Ireland*, supports Anti-Parnellites.

10 Dec. Parnell forcibly takes possession of *United Ireland*.

13 Dec. Matthew Bodkin publishes Anti-Parnellite *'Suppressed' United Ireland;* also appears on 15 and 16 Dec.; Parnell serves injunction against use of 'United Ireland' in the title and Bodkin publishes *Insuppressible* (until 24 Jan. 1891).

22 Dec. Sir John Pope-Hennessy (Anti-Parnellite, 2,527 votes) defeats Vincent Scully (Parnellite, 1,362) in Kilkenny North by-election.

30–31 Dec. Parnell meets with William O'Brien at Boulogne (talks break down on 11 Feb. 1891).

Pub. *Beside the Fire*, first collection of tales by Douglas Hyde.

1891

21 Jan. Davitt founds the Irish Democratic and Trade and Labour Federation in Cork.

12 Feb. John Dillon and William O'Brien rearrested and imprisoned (*see* 18 Sept. 1890).

7 Mar. Anti-Parnellites launch the *National Press*.

10 Mar. Anti-Parnellites launch the Irish National Federation, a constituency organisation, led by Justin McCarthy, William O'Brien, John Dillon and T. M. Healy.

2 Apr. Bernard Collery (Anti-Parnellite, 3,261 votes) defeats V. B. Dillon (Parnellite, 2,493) in Sligo North by-election.

6 Apr. Irish Loyal and Patriotic Union becomes the Irish Unionist Alliance.

1 May City of Dublin railway junction opens, with 'loop line' connecting Westland Row (making it a through station) with the Great Northern at Amiens Street and the Midland Great Western.

15 June d. Charles James Mahon (91), The O'Gorman Mahon, M.P. (Nationalist) and adventurer.

25 June Parnell and Katharine O'Shea marry in registry office at Steyning, Sussex.

8 July John Hammond (Anti-Parnellite, 3,755 votes) defeats A. J. Kettle (Parnellite 1,539) in Carlow by-election.

30 July Dillon and O'Brien, upon release from jail, make moderate speeches but clearly reject Parnell's leadership of the Home Rule Party.

31 July Edmund Dwyer Gray repudiates Parnell's leadership; his paper, the *Freeman's Journal*, follows suit on 21 Sept.

5 Aug. Purchase of Land (Ireland) Act (Balfour's Act) provides £33 million for land purchase, of which only just over £13 million is taken up owing to complexity of purchase clauses; establishes Congested Districts Board.

25 Sept. James Stephens, founder of the I.R.B., in exile since 1866, returns to Ireland.

6 Oct. d. Charles Stewart Parnell (45) at Brighton.

11 Oct. 100,000 attend the funeral of Parnell from Dublin City Hall to Glasnevin cemetery.

9 Nov. d. P. W. Nally (34), Fenian and athlete, inspirational in formation of the G.A.A.

William L. Jackson appointed C.S.

18 Dec. Pub. first issue of the *Irish Daily Independent,* Parnellite organ (becomes *Irish Independent* in 1905).

23 Dec. John Redmond (Parnellite, 1,775 votes) defeats Michael Davitt (Anti-Parnellite, 1,229) in Waterford City by-election.

28 Dec. Irish Literary Society founded in London by W. B. Yeats, T. W. Rolleston, Charles Gavan Duffy and Douglas Hyde.

Census of population: 4,704,750 (decrease of 9.08 per cent since 1881).

1892

12 Jan. d. William Reeves (77), C.I. Bishop of Down, Connor and Dromore since 1886, scholar.

23 Jan. Amnesty Association of Great Britain and Ireland founded in London by Dr Mark Ryan.

20 Feb. d. George Augustine Chichester May, jurist; edited the first volumes of the Irish *Law Reports* (1867).

8 Mar. d. Rev. Thomas McNamara (84) of the Congregation of the Mission (Vincentian order), co-founder of the Castleknock College, Co. Dublin, of which he was superior (1864), and Rector of the Irish College, Paris (1868–89); founded Institute for the Deaf and Dumb, Cabra, Dublin (1846).

17 June Ulster Unionist Convention, bringing together Conservatives and Liberal Unionists, held in the Botanic Gardens, Belfast, attended by 12,000 delegates of all Unionist organisations, who dedicate themselves to opposing Home Rule.

23 June Southern Unionists hold convention.

27 June Irish Education Act makes primary schooling compulsory up to 14; abolishes fees in primary schools.

4–18 July General election; Gladstone forms his fourth and last administration on 15 Aug., dedicated to bringing in Irish Home Rule.

16 Aug. National Literary Society founded in Dublin by W. B. Yeats and Douglas Hyde.

22 Aug. Robert Milnes, Baron Houghton, sworn in as L.L.; John Morley again appointed C.S.

23 Sept. Dublin Corporation electricity station in Fleet Street goes into operation under Dublin Electric Lighting Order (1892).

29 Sept. Belfast Labour Party formed; first socialist party in Ireland.

9 Dec. *Widowers' Houses,* first play by George Bernard Shaw, opens at the Royalty Theatre, Dean Street, Soho, London.

Pub. first issue of the *Journal of the Cork Historical and Archaeological Society.*

1893

6 Feb. d. John Patrick Prendergast (85), historian (author of *The Cromwellian Settlement of Ireland,* 1865).

13 Feb. Gladstone introduces Second Home Rule Bill; passes Commons (301–267) on 2 Sept.; defeated in the House of Lords (419–41) on 9 Sept.

2 Mar. William Johnston of Ballykilbeg carries resolution in favour of passive resistance to Home Rule at Orange demonstration in the Ulster Hall, Belfast.

4 Apr. 100,000 Loyalists march through Belfast in an anti-Home Rule demonstration organised by the Ulster Defence Union.

31 July Conradh na Gaeilge, the Gaelic League, inaugurated by Douglas Hyde, Eoin Mac Néill and Fr Eugene O'Growney, with Hyde as first President.

'New Irish Library' series, ed. Charles Gavan Duffy, begins publication (13 volumes published in all).

First cross-channel telephone connection between Donaghadee, Co. Down, and Portmore, Scotland.

Pub. *Abhráin Grádh Chúige Connacht or Love Songs of Connacht* (bilingual) by Douglas Hyde.

Pub. *The Bog of Stars* by Standish James O'Grady.

1894

3 Mar. Gladstone retires after 61 years as M.P.; succeeded as P.M. on 5th by Lord Rosebery (Liberal), who heads a divided cabinet until 23 June 1895.

17 Mar. National Maternity Hospital in Holles Street reopens (closed in 1893).

18 Apr. Irish Agricultural Organisation Society founded by Horace (later Sir Horace) Plunkett, who becomes its first president.

27–28 Apr. Irish Trade Union Congress (I.T.U.C.) meets for the first time.

26 May Commission under H. C. E. Childers appointed to examine financial relations between Ireland and Great Britain (reports on 28 Mar. 1895 and on 5 Sept. 1896).

29 June d. William Joseph O'Neill Daunt (87), Repealer and Home Ruler (secretary of Home Government Association); diaries published as *A Life Spent for Ireland* in 1896.

12 July T. M. Healy, speaking at Liverpool, inveighs against unification of the anti-Parnellite majority in the Irish Parliamentary Party with the Parnellites (led by John Redmond).

7 Nov. Reunification of the Northern Presbytery with the Antrim Presbytery (separated since 21 Feb. 1862).

Pub. *Simple Lessons in Irish* (Part 1) by Fr Eugene O'Growney.

Pub. *The Real Charlotte* by E. Œ. Somerville and 'Martin Ross' (Violet Martin).

1895

1 Mar. d. Richard O'Gorman (69), Young Irelander; judge of the New York Supreme Court.

9 Mar. Pub. first issue of the *Irish Homestead*, organ of the Irish Agricultural Organisation Society, ed. George Russell ('AE').

25 May Oscar Wilde sentenced to two years' imprisonment with hard labour for homosexual offences (*see* 30 Nov. 1900).

23 June Lord Rosebery (Liberal) resigns as P.M. (resigns leadership of Liberal Party on 6 Oct. 1896); succeeded by Lord Salisbury (Conservative) on 25th.

4 July Gerald Balfour appointed C.S.

8 July George, Earl of Cadogan, sworn in as L.L.

12–26 July General election; P.M. Lord Salisbury retains power.

19 Sept. d. William Shaw, provisional leader of the Home Rule Party (1879–80).

11 Oct. – 27 Jan. 1896 Engineers on strike at the Harland & Wolff shipyard, Belfast.

12 Oct. d. Mrs Cecil Frances Alexander (77), hymn-writer.

7 Nov. T. M. Healy expelled from the Irish National League of Great Britain; replaced by Michael Davitt.

13 Nov. T. M. Healy and others expelled from the executive of the Irish National Federation.

29 Nov. d. Denny Lane (77), Young Irelander, Home Ruler and poet (author of 'Carrig Dhoun').

21–24 Dec. Violent storm; 15 members of the Kingstown (now Dún Laoghaire) lifeboat drowned (24th).

Pub. *The Story of Early Gaelic Literature* by Douglas Hyde.

1896

13 Jan. d. James Hack Tuke (77), Quaker philanthropist, active in Ireland in 1847 and 1881–82.

2 Feb. Justin McCarthy announces his resignation from the leadership of the anti-Parnellite section of Home Rulers (*see* 18 Feb.).

d. Lady Wilde (70), 'Speranza' of the *Nation,* widow of Sir William Wilde, mother of Oscar.

Feb. Discovery of the Limavady or Broighter gold hoard.

18 Feb. John Dillon elected leader of the anti-Parnellite Home Rulers (38 votes to 21).

16 Mar. R. Bolton McCausland makes first recorded use of X-ray in Ireland, at Dr Steevens' Hospital, Dublin.

31 Mar. Poor Law Guardians (Ireland) Act empowers election of women to Boards of Guardians.

20 Apr. First screening of a cinema film in Ireland, using the Lumière process, at Dan Lowrey's Star of Erin Palace of Varieties, Dublin (later the Olympia Theatre) (*see* 29 Oct.).

29 May Irish Socialist Republican Party founded by James Connolly.

26–27 July Belfast shipyards damaged by fire.

Poor potato crop in the west of Ireland, leading to severe shortage in early 1897.

1 Aug. 'Recess Committee' presents report to C.S. on need for state promotion of agriculture and industry.

14 Aug. Land Law (Ireland) Act (Gerald Balfour's Land Act) removes many restrictions of the 1891 act and empowers the Land Court to sell 1,500 bankrupt estates to tenants.

Locomotives on Highways Act permits practical use of motor-cars by removing restrictions.

1–3 Sept. Irish Race Convention held in Dublin, R.C. Bishop Patrick O'-Donnell of Raphoe presiding.

29 Oct. – 14 Nov. First regular cinema screenings in Ireland, at Dan Lowrey's Star of Erin Palace of Varieties, using the Lumière process; 7,000 attend during first week (*see* 20 Apr.).

Pub. *Recollections of Fenians and Fenianism* (2 vols) by John O'Leary, dedicated to Thomas Clarke Luby.

1897

12 Jan. First meeting of subscribers to the People's Rights Fund leads to formation of People's Rights Association by T. M. Healy.

Mar. Foundation stone of St Brendan's Cathedral, Loughrea, Co. Galway, laid.

17 May Oireachtas (Irish Literary Festival, loosely based on Welsh Eisteddfod) held for the first time.

5 June *Nation* ceases publication; succeeded by the *Weekly Nation.*

14 Aug. d. William Archer (67), naturalist; first Librarian of the National Library (1877–95).

12 Oct. *Cymric* launched, built by Harland & Wolff for the White Star Line; 23,000 tons displacement, 6,800 h.p. from quadruple expansion engines; the largest and most powerful ship afloat (*see also* 14 Jan. 1899).

13 Nov. Dan Lowrey reopens his Star of Erin Palace of Varieties as the Empire Palace (*see* 29 Oct. 1896).

Pub. *Dracula* by Bram Stoker.

Pub. *Bards of the Gael and Gall* by George Sigerson.

Pub. *The Outlook for Ireland: The Case for Devolution and Conciliation* by the 4th Earl of Dunraven.

Pub. *Erin's Hope* by James Connolly.

1898

8 Jan. Pub. *Fáinne an Lae* ('Dawn'), Gaelic League newspaper; first newspaper to carry domestic and foreign news in the Irish language (incorporated into *An Claidheamh Soluis* from 4 Aug. 1900).

23 Jan. United Irish League launched by William O'Brien at Westport, Co. Mayo, prompted by famine conditions in the west of Ireland, with the slogan 'The Land for the People'.

20 Mar. First *feis* under Gaelic League auspices held at Macroom, Co. Cork.

29 Mar. Registration (Ireland) Act confers local government franchise on women and peers.

Countrywide celebrations for the centenary of the rising of the United Irishmen; also celebrated in U.S.A., Australia and South Africa.

12 Aug. Local Government (Ireland) Act replaces the Grand Juries (dominated by Protestant landlord class) with a new local government structure: county councils, borough corporations, urban district councils and rural district councils (*see* 22 Dec.).

13 Aug. Pub. first issue of the *Workers' Republic,* founded and edited by James Connolly.

29 Sept. Fenian Thomas J. Clarke released from jail in England and returns to Ireland before emigrating to the U.S.A.

22 Dec. Order of L.L. issued under the Local Government (Ireland) Act qualifies women to sit on district councils and town commissioners (though not on county or borough councils; *see* 16 Dec. 1911).

Pub. *The Ballad of Reading Gaol* by Oscar Wilde.

Pub. *Life of Wolfe Tone* by Alice Milligan.

1899

Jan. First local government elections for urban councils held; elections to county councils held in Apr.

14 Jan. *Oceanic II* launched, built by Harland & Wolff for the White Star Line; 17,274 gross tons, 685.7 ft long, 68.3 ft beam, two screws powered by four-cylinder triple expansion engines, 28,000 h.p. with a top speed of 21 knots; the first ship to exceed Isambard Kingdom Brunel's *Great Eastern* in length.

16 Jan. W. B. Yeats and Edward Martyn urge foundation of an Irish Literary Theatre at a meeting of the Irish National Literary Society (*see* 8–9 May).

7 Feb. John Dillon resigns leadership of the anti-Parnellite Home Rulers (*see* 30 Jan. 1900).

4 Mar. Pub. first issue of the *United Irishman,* founded and edited by Arthur Griffith (runs until 1906, when replaced by *Sinn Féin*).

18 Mar. Pub. first issue of *An Claidheamh Soluis* ('The Sword of Light'), organ of the Gaelic League, edited first by Eoin Mac Néill, later by Patrick Pearse (runs until 1916).

4 Apr. Conference of nationalists considers reunification of the Home Rule Party (*see* 30 Jan. 1900).

8–9 May *The Countess Cathleen* by W. B. Yeats first performed at the Antient Concert Rooms in Great Brunswick Street, Dublin; *The*

KILKENNY COUNTY LIBRARY

Heather Field by Edward Martyn performed there the following night.

20 June Catholic Truth Society of Ireland founded.

9 Aug. Agricultural and Technical Instruction (Ireland) Act establishes Department of Agriculture and Technical Instruction.

Aug. Report of the Commission on Intermediate Education.

11 Oct. Boer War starts (Davitt withdraws from the House of Commons on 25th as a protest against the war).

18 Oct. d. Fr Eugene O'Growney (36), co-founder of the Gaelic League (1893).

30 Oct. Hugh Carberry, Armagh nationalist, dies fighting on the side of the Boers and is hailed as a hero in nationalist Ireland.

8. Nov. d. Sir Thomas Newenham Deane (71), architect of the National Library and the National Museum, Kildare Street, Dublin.

Irish Texts Society founded by Eleanor Hull.

Rathmines and Rathgar Musical Society ('R. & R.') founded; oldest surviving musical society in Ireland.

Pub. *A Literary History of Ireland* by Douglas Hyde.

Pub. *Some Experiences of an Irish R.M.* by E. Œ. Somerville and 'Martin Ross' (Violet Martin).

1900

30 Jan. Reunification of the Home Rule Party (Irish Parliamentary Party) (*see* 6 Feb.).

6 Feb. John Redmond elected chairman of the Home Rule Party (*see* 19–20 June).

16 Mar. d. Sir William Burton (84), portraitist who executed death-mask of James Clarence Mangan.

3–26 Apr. Queen Victoria in Ireland; issues orders for a new regiment (Irish Guards) on 5 Apr. The visit is recorded on film, oldest known taken in Ireland (copy in Irish Film Society's archives).

20 Apr. 'New Richmond' Hospital opens in Dublin.

19–20 June Home Rule convention recognises United Irish League as the constituency organisation of the Home Rule Party (*see* 4 Dec. 1901).

6 Aug. Act extends Dublin city area by 4,125 acres and population by 26,000.

Intermediate Education (Ireland) Act substitutes capitation for 'payment by results'.

1 Sept. Pub. first issue of the *Leader*, founded and edited by D. P. Moran.

Sept. Revised Programme for National Schools, based on the report of the Commission on Practical and Manual Instruction (Belmore Commission, established in Jan. 1897).

20 Sept. T. W. Russell, founder of North Antrim Land Association and a member of the government, calls for the British Treasury to provide £120 million to resolve the land question and to include a measure of compulsion and bonuses as compensation for compulsion.

29 Sept. – 12 Oct. General election; P.M. Lord Salisbury (Conservative) retains power; Nationalists (Home Rulers) secure 81 seats.

30 Sept. Cumann na nGaedheal (political pressure group) formed by Arthur Griffith (*see* 21 Apr. 1907).

9 Nov. George Wyndham appointed C.S.

30 Nov. d. Oscar Wilde (46), poet and dramatist.

11 Dec. T. M. Healy expelled from Irish Parliamentary Party.

1901

21 Jan. d. Aubrey de Vere (88), poet.

22 Jan. d. Queen Victoria (81); succeeded by Edward VII.

29 Apr. d. James Stephens, founder of the I.R.B. (1858).

6 May d. William Rooney (29), poet, co-founder of the *United Irishman* with Arthur Griffith.

5 June T. W. Russell forms the Ulster Farmers' and Labourers' Union and Compulsory Purchase Association.

21 Oct. Irish Literary Theatre produces Douglas Hyde's *Casadh an tSúgáin* ('The Twisting of the Rope'), first play in Irish performed on a professional stage, and *Diarmuid and Grania* by W. B. Yeats and George Moore at the Gaiety Theatre, Dublin.

1 Dec. d. Thomas Clarke Luby (79), Fenian.

4 Dec. United Irish League of America formed in New York.

21 Dec. d. Vere Foster (81), philanthropist; designed copy-books to teach handwriting to primary schoolchildren.

Census of population: 4,458,775 (decrease of 5.23 per cent since 1891).

1902

14 Feb. Lord Rosebery effectively repudiates the Liberal Party commitment to Home Rule when, speaking at Liverpool, he refers to 'the somewhat mouldy programmes which have crushed the Liberal Party in the past'.

2 Apr. Irish National Theatre Society produces *Deirdre* by George Russell ('AE') and W. B. Yeats's *Cathleen Ni Houlihan* at St Teresa's Hall, Clarendon Street, Dublin.

31 May Treaty of Vereeniging ends Boer War.

11 July P.M. Lord Salisbury (Conservative) resigns on grounds of old age; succeeded by Arthur James Balfour (Conservative) on 12th.

22 July d. Thomas William Croke (78), R.C. Archbishop of Cashel since 1875; first patron of the G.A.A.

16 Aug. William Ward, Earl of Dudley, sworn in as L.L.

18 Aug. T. H. Sloan of the Belfast Protestant Association (Independent Unionist, 3,795 votes) defeats C. W. Dunbar-Buller (Unionist, 2,969) in Belfast South by-election.

3 Sept. Publication in the *Times* of letter by Capt. John Shawe-Taylor, calling for a land conference between landlord and tenant representatives (*see* 20 Dec.).

Nov. Palestrina Choir established at Pro-Cathedral, Dublin, brainchild of Edward Martyn, supported by Archbishop Walsh; John McCormack is an early member; choir trained by Vincent O'Brien.

8 Nov. Sir Antony MacDonnell appointed Under-Secretary to C.S. Wyndham.

20 Dec. Land Conference meets: tenants' representatives John Redmond, William O'Brien, Timothy Harrington and T. W. Russell meet with landlords represented by Lord Dunraven, the Earl of Mayo, Col. William Hutcheson-Poë and Col. Nugent Everard (*see* 3 Jan. 1903).

Pub. *History of the County of Dublin* (Vol. I) by F. Elrington Ball (completed in 4 vols in 1906).

1903

3 Jan. Report of the Land Conference (*see* 20 Dec. 1902) recommends Treasury loans to enable tenants to buy out landlords (*see* 14 Aug.).

11 Jan. d. Helen Blackburn (60), pioneer of female suffrage.

9 Feb. d. Sir Charles Gavan Duffy (87), co-founder of the *Nation* and a leader of Young Ireland.

2 Mar. Patrick Pearse assumes editorship of Gaelic League paper, *An Claidheamh Soluis* (until 1909).

27 Mar. Bank Holiday (Ireland) Act declares 17 Mar. (St Patrick's Day) a bank holiday.

24 Apr. d. Walter Osborne (44), painter.

6 June National Council meets, founded by Arthur Griffith to protest against forthcoming royal visit; remains in existence with a platform seeking abolition of slums and police tax and restriction of monopolies (*see* 5 Sept. 1907).

11 June T. H. Sloan, M.P., founds the Independent Orange Order (*see* 13 July 1905).

21 July – 1 Aug. Edward VII in Ireland.

14 Aug. Wyndham's Land Act follows recommendations of the Land Conference report (*see* 3 Jan.).

18 Sept. James Connolly emigrates to U.S.A. (returns on 26 July 1910).

9 Oct. David Sheehy (Redmondite Nationalist, 2,245 votes) defeats John Howard Parnell (Independent Nationalist, 1,031) in Meath South by-election.

22 Oct. d. William Edward Hartpole Lecky (65), historian.

6 Nov. William O'Brien announces his resignation from the Home Rule Party (*see* 17 Jan. 1908).

Kuno Meyer and Richard Irvine Best found the School of Irish Learning in Dublin.

Speed limit of 20 m.p.h. for motor vehicles replaces red flag.

Report of the Robertson Commission, set up on 1 July 1901 to examine university education outside of T.C.D., recommends restructuring Royal University.

1904

2 Jan. Arthur Griffith begins publication of series 'The Resurrection of Hungary' in the *United Irishman* (published as a pamphlet in Nov.).

Jan. Pogrom directed against Jews in Limerick provoked by sermon by Fr John Creagh, Redemptorist priest.

25 Jan. Winston Churchill, M.P., lecturing the Institute of Bankers on 'Ireland and the Fiscal Question' declares: 'You will find the pedigree in the stud-book—Rule Britannia by Free Trade out of An Island.'

26 Apr. – 5 May Edward VII in Ireland.

16 June 'Bloomsday'; James Joyce meets his future wife Nora Barnacle and later makes it the date of the action of *Ulysses* (1922).

4 July Coláiste na Mumhan, Ballingeary, Co. Cork, opens; first college to train teachers of Irish.

25 Aug. Land Conference dissolves; William O'Brien and Lord Dunraven form the Irish Reform Association on 26th with the support of Sir Antony MacDonnell, Under-Secretary.

26 Sept. Irish Reform Association outlines a proposal for devolved government for Ireland.

27 Sept. Letter from C.S. George Wyndham in the *Times* condemns devolution proposal; start of a concerted attack on Under-Secretary MacDonnell.

2 Dec. Unionist conference in Belfast calls for 'consistent and continuous political action' to resist devolution and resolves 'That an Ulster Council be formed . . . to form an Ulster Union for bringing into line all local

Unionist associations in the province of Ulster' (*see* 3 Mar. 1905).

27 Dec. Abbey Theatre, Dublin (formerly the Mechanics' Institute in Abbey Street, bought for the Irish Literary Theatre Society by Anne Horniman and designed by Joseph Holloway) opens with *Spreading the News* by Lady Gregory and *On Baile's Strand* by W. B. Yeats.

Life on the Great Southern and Western Railway by Louis Le Clerq, first Irish film documentary.

Pub. *The Fall of Feudalism in Ireland* by Michael Davitt.

Pub. *Foclóir Gaedhilge agus Bearla: An Irish–English Dictionary* by Fr Patrick S. Dinneen (many subsequent editions, revised and enlarged).

Pub. *English–Irish Dictionary* by Timothy O'Neill Lane (enlarged ed., 1922).

Pub. first issue of *Éiru: the Journal of the School of Irish Learning*, ed. Kuno Meyer and John Strachan.

1905

3 Mar. Ulster Unionist Council holds first meeting, in the Ulster Minor Hall, Belfast.

6 Mar. C.S. George Wyndham resigns, driven from office by Unionist hostility.

8 Mar. Dungannon Clubs founded in Belfast by Bulmer Hobson (*see* 21 Apr. 1907).

12 Mar. Walter Long appointed C.S. (replaced on 14 Dec. after government falls).

22 Apr. d. Capt. William Henry O'Shea (65), politician, adventurer, former husband of Katharine O'Shea Parnell.

13 July Independent Orange Order issues 'Magheramore Manifesto', the work of Robert Lindsay Crawford, calling on all Irishmen to 'hold out the right hand of friendship to those who, while worshipping at other shrines, are yet our countrymen'.

15 July d. Kevin Izod O'Doherty (82), Young Irelander; co-founder of the *Irish Tribune*, husband of 'Eva' of the *Nation*.

11 Nov. Dr Douglas Hyde embarks on lecture tour of the U.S.A., netting $64,000 for the Gaelic League.

28 Nov. At annual convention of National Council Máire Butler names Arthur Griffith's new policy 'Sinn Féin' ('Ourselves'); adopts the resolution 'That the people of Ireland are a free people, and that no law made without their authority or consent is, or can ever be, binding on their conscience'; Arthur Griffith proposes Council of Three Hundred to function as an unofficial Irish parliament (*see* 21 Apr. 1907).

4 Dec. P.M. Balfour (Conservative) resigns; Sir Henry Campbell-Bannerman (Liberal) forms administration on 5th.

5 Dec. Belfast electric tramway system opens.

14 Dec. Earl of Aberdeen again sworn in as L.L.; James Bryce appointed C.S.

Pub. *The History of Irish Music* by William Henry Grattan Flood.

Pub. *The Philosophy of Irish Ireland* by D. P. Moran.

1906

13–27 Jan. General election; P.M. Campbell–Bannerman (Liberal) retains power.

5 May Pub. first issue of *Sinn Féin*, founded and edited by Arthur Griffith.

31 May d. Michael Davitt (60), former Fenian, co-founder of the Land

League (1879), labour organiser and journalist.

31 July Rosslare harbour opens for direct cross-channel services.

1 Aug. Belfast City Hall opens; designed by Alfred Brumwell-Thomas.

4 Aug. Labourers (Ireland) Act provides extra finance for labourers' cottages.

14 Oct. Laurence Ginnell, M.P., denounces the grazing system at Downs, Co. Westmeath, advocating a policy of 'cattle-driving' which becomes known as the 'Downs policy'—taking cattle off the land and driving them to wander the countryside.

21 Oct. d. Col. E. J. Saunderson (69), leader of the Unionists since 1886.

1 Nov. Walter Hume Long elected leader of the Unionist Parliamentary Party; establishes Union Defence League in Jan. 1907.

27 Nov. d. Michael Cusack (59), co-founder and general secretary of the G.A.A.; original of the 'Citizen' in James Joyce's *Ulysses*.

1907

Jan. James ('Big Jim') Larkin arrives in Belfast as organiser for the National Union of Dock Labourers (N.U.D.L.) (*see* 11 Aug.).

c. 20 Jan. John Beirne, grazier at Tonlagee, Co. Roscommon, intimidated by 'cattle-driving' (*see* 14 Oct. 1906) surrenders his farm publicly to John Dillon at Ballinasloe, Co. Galway.

26 Jan. *The Playboy of the Western World* by J. M. Synge opens at the Abbey; rioting occurs in the theatre on 28–30 Jan.

29 Jan. Augustine Birrell appointed C.S.

16 Mar. d. John O'Leary (77), Fenian.

21 Apr. Sinn Féin League formed from the Dungannon Clubs (*see* 8 Mar. 1905) and Cumann na nGaedheal (*see* 30 Sept. 1900).

1 May d. John Kells Ingram (84), scholar and poet (author of 'The Memory of the Dead' and 'Who Fears to Speak of '98?')

6 May Dock strike in Belfast; Larkin assumes leadership, and it turns into a lock-out (striking ends in Sept.).

7 May C.S. Birrell introduces Irish Council Bill in House of Commons.

3 June P.M. Campbell-Bannerman announces the dropping of Birrell's Irish Council Bill.

June C.S. Birrell confirms that 327 grazing farms are receiving police protection.

21 June d. Edward Hallaran Bennett (70), surgeon; first to describe fracture at base of metacarpal bone ('Bennett's fracture').

6 July Irish State Jewels, valued at £50,000, missing from Dublin Castle; never recovered.

24 July R.I.C. in Belfast on strike; 7,000 troops brought in to assume police duties during the strike and lock-out.

2 Aug. Pope Pius X issues *Ne temere* decree: marriages between Catholics and Protestants are null and void unless performed in a Catholic church; children of such marriages are to be reared as Catholics.

11 Aug. James Larkin forms branch of the N.U.D.L. in Dublin (*see* Jan.).

28 Aug. Evicted Tenants (Ireland) Act allows for reinstatement of displaced tenants and empowers Land Commissioners to purchase land compulsorily for evicted tenants.

5 Sept. Arthur Griffith's National Council subsumed into the Sinn Féin League (*see* 21 Apr.).

13 Sept. Central Fire Station in Tara Street, Dublin, opens.

19 Sept. 64 cattle driven off the Perceval farm at Newtownforbes, Co. Longford.

17 Oct. Marconi transatlantic wireless telegraphy service starts between Clifden, Co. Galway, and Cape Breton, Canada.

17 Dec. d. William, Lord Kelvin (83), scientist, inventor and writer.

19 Dec. Joint Committee of Unionist Associations of Ireland founded.

Irish Wives and English Husbands by Arthur Melbourne-Cooper, probably the first fiction film made in Ireland.

Pub. *Chamber Music*, poems by James Joyce.

1908

Jan. William and Frank Fay resign from the Abbey Theatre, supported by Edward Martyn, on artistic policy (they wish to broaden the scope and style of the theatre).

17 Jan. William O'Brien rejoins the Home Rule Party (*see* 6 Nov. 1903).

20 Jan. Dublin Municipal Art Gallery, first gallery for modern art in British Isles, opens to public.

10 Feb. Hugh Lane receives the freedom of the city of Dublin (knighted in 1909 for his services to Irish art).

21 Feb. Leitrim North by-election; first ever contested by a Sinn Féin candidate (C. J. Dolan).

3 Apr. P.M. Campbell-Bannerman (Liberal) resigns; succeeded by Henry Herbert Asquith (Liberal) on 8 Apr.

17 Apr. d. Gustave W. Wolff, partner in Harland & Wolff, Belfast.

July Sir Antony MacDonnell resigns as Under-Secretary; succeeded by Sir James Brown Dougherty on 14th.

1 Aug. Irish Universities Act abolishes the Royal University and leads to establishment of the National University of Ireland (N.U.I., with colleges in Dublin, Cork and Galway) and the Queen's University, Belfast.

Old Age Pensions Act, which within two years costs Exchequer £2,400,000 for Ireland.

8 Sept. Patrick Pearse establishes **St Enda's school for boys (Scoil Éanna)** at Cullenswood House, Rathmines (moves to The Hermitage, Rathfarnham, in 1910).

30 Sept. 44 'cattle-drivers' at Ennistymon, Co. Clare, imprisoned.

11 Nov. Irish Women's Franchise League founded by Hanna Sheehy-Skeffington and Margaret Cousins.

21 Dec. Housing of the Working Classes (Ireland) Act empowers local authorities to build houses; sets up housing fund to finance house construction.

31 Dec. Martin J. Sheridan from Bohola, Co. Mayo, wins two gold medals (free discus and Greek discus) at the London Olympic Games.

Tuberculosis Prevention (Ireland) Act establishes T.B. hospitals.

A Cattle-Drive in Galway, film by Robert Paul about the Irish Land War.

Pub. *The Making of Ireland and Its Undoing* by Alice Stopford Green.

1909

4 Jan. James Larkin, formerly of the N.U.D.L., forms the Irish Transport and General Workers' Union (originally proposed at a meeting of N.U.D.L. members on 28 Dec. 1908).

KILKENNY COUNTY LIBRARY

24 Mar. d. John Millington Synge (37), dramatist and poet.

16 Aug. Fianna Éireann formed by Constance, Countess Markievicz, and Bulmer Hobson; recruiting agency for I.R.B.

30 Nov. House of Lords rejects Lloyd George's 'People's Budget'; first money bill rejected by Lords in 200 years (*see* 30 Aug. 1911).

3 Dec. Irish Land Act (Birrell's Act) gives Congested Districts Board powers of compulsory purchase; increases finance available for tenant purchase.

20 Dec. Volta Cinema, first custom-built cinema in Ireland, opens in Mary Street, Dublin; manager James Joyce.

31 Dec. Harry Ferguson records first flight by plane built entirely in Ireland when he pilots it for some 130 yd at 12 ft from the ground at Hillsborough, Co. Down (*see* 8 Aug. 1910).

1910

15–28 Jan. General election; P.M. Asquith retains power.

21 Feb. Sir Edward Carson assumes leadership of the Unionist Party.

12 Mar. d. Timothy Harrington (59), politician (Home Rule).

31 Mar. William O'Brien founds All-for-Ireland League in the Cork City Hall.

6 May d. Edward VII (69); succeeded by George V.

7 May Miss Anne Horniman withdraws financial support from the Abbey Theatre, which did not close in mourning for the King.

21 May d. Mary Anne Kelly (84), wife of Kevin Izod O'Doherty; 'Eva' of the *Nation*.

June – Nov. Conference fails to resolve constitutional crisis over House of Lords' rejection of 1909 budget.

23 June N.U.I. Senate decrees that Irish is essential for matriculation (from 1913).

8 Aug. Harry Ferguson makes first air flight of significant distance (3 miles) at Dundrum Bay, near Newcastle, Co. Down, winning £100 (*see* 31 Dec. 1909).

20 Oct. *Olympic* launched, built by Harland & Wolff, Belfast, for the White Star Line; two-cylinder triple-expansion engines, 46,000 h.p., 45,324 gross tons, the biggest ship ever launched; sister ship of the *Titanic* (*see* 1 Apr. 1911).

Nov. Pub. first issue of *Irish Freedom*, I.R.B. organ co-founded and managed by Seán Mac Diarmada, published by Thomas J. Clarke; editors inclu-e Bulmer Hobson and Patrick McCartan (*see* 2–4 Dec. 1914).

3 Dec. – 13 Jan. 1911 General election; P.M. Asquith retains power.

Sidney Olcott makes *The Lad from Old Ireland,* filmed in Killarney, believed to be the first American film made on location outside the U.S.A.

Pub. *A History of the Irish Parliamentary Party* (2 vols) by Frank Hugh O'Donnell.

Pub. *Labour in Irish History* and *Labour, Nationality and Religion* by James Connolly.

Pub. *Onomasticon Goedelicum* (index of Gaelic names of places and tribes) by Edmund Hogan.

1911

23 Jan. Ulster Women's Unionist Council founded for 'the maintenance of the legislative Union between Great Britain and Ireland'.

1 Apr. *Titanic* launched, built by Harland & Wolff, Belfast, for the White

Star Line; sister ship of the *Olympic* but 1,000 gross tons heavier (46,324 gross tons) (*see* 14 Apr. 1912).

27 May Pub. first issue of the *Irish Worker*, organ of the I.T.G.W.U., ed. James Larkin; sales average 20,000 per issue; suppressed in Dec. 1914, revived 1930–32, ed. James Larkin (jun.).

30 June Dublin Employers' Federation founded under the influence of William Martin Murphy, its first president (*see* 26 Aug. 1913).

7–12 July George V in Ireland.

21 Aug. Irish Women's Suffrage Federation founded (comprising Belfast Women's Suffrage Society, Irishwomen's Reform League and Munster Women's Franchise Association).

26 Aug. Wexford foundrymen locked out for attempting to join the I.T.G.W.U. (until 12 Feb. 1912).

30 Aug. Parliament Act removes veto from the House of Lords, deprives it of all power over money bills and leaves it with suspensory veto of two years; duration of parliament reduced to five years (from seven) (*see* 30 Nov. 1909).

5 Sept. Irish Women Workers' Union formed by Delia Larkin as an affiliate of the I.T.G.W.U.

20 Sept. d. Anna Catherine Parnell (59), sister of Charles Stewart Parnell; founder of the Ladies' Land League.

23 Sept. Sir Edward Carson addresses 50,000 members of the Orange Order and Unionist Clubs at Craigavon House: 'We must be prepared . . . the morning Home Rule passes, ourselves to become responsible for the government of the Protestant province of Ulster.'

1 Oct. Parnell Monument (88 ft; foundation stone laid in Oct. 1899) unveiled by John Redmond in Sackville Street, Dublin; sculptor Augustus Saint-Gaudens, who receives £5,000 for the commission.

13 Nov. Andrew Bonar Law replaces A. J. Balfour as leader of the Conservative and Unionist Party.

16 Dec. Local Authorities (Ireland) (Qualification of Women) Act allows women to become members of county and borough councils.

Census of population: 4,390,219 (decease of 1.54 per cent since 1901).

Pub. *The Framework of Home Rule* by Robert Erskine Childers.

Pub. *The Circle and the Sword*, poetry by Joseph Mary Plunkett.

1912

5 Jan. Grand Orange Lodge of Ulster secretary, Col. Robert H. Wallace, applies to Belfast magistrates for authorisation of drilling.

8 Feb. Winston Churchill in Belfast; shares platform at Celtic Park with John Redmond.

31 Mar. Demonstration in favour of Home Rule in Dublin, addressed by Patrick Pearse among others.

11 Apr. P.M. Asquith introduces Third Home Rule Bill in the House of Commons.

14 Apr. *Titanic* on her maiden voyage strikes an iceberg at 11.40 p.m., sustaining 300-foot gash in her hull; sinks at 2.20 a.m. on 15th, with 711 of her 2,201 passengers and crew saved.

20 Apr. d. Abraham ('Bram') Stoker (65), novelist (author of *Dracula*, 1897).

24 Apr. d. Justin McCarthy (82), politician (Home Rule), historian and novelist; leader of anti-Parnellites (1891–96).

2 May T. C. Agar-Roberts, M.P. (Liberal), proposes exclusion of four Ulster counties (Antrim, Armagh, Down and Londonderry) from Home Rule; his amendment to this effect introduced on 11 June is defeated on 18 June.

28 June Irish Labour Party founded at Clonmel, Co. Tipperary, when the Irish Trade Union Congress (I.T.U.C.) constitutes itself the 'Irish Trade Union Congress and Labour Party'.

18–20 July P.M. Asquith in Ireland; English suffragettes protest in Dublin.

12 Sept. d. Fr Matthew Russell (78), founder-editor of *Catholic Ireland* (later *Irish Monthly*) from 1873.

14 Sept. Riot at Celtic Park, Belfast, football match, between Celtic (Catholic) and Linfield (Protestant) supporters.

28 Sept. 'Ulster Day': 237,368 men sign Ulster's Solemn League and Covenant, led by Sir Edward Carson; 234,046 women sign a parallel declaration.

Pub. 'Amhrán na bhFiann' ('The Soldiers' Song'), words by Peadar Kearney, music by Patrick Heeney, later adopted as National Anthem.

Pub. *The Crock of Gold* by James Stephens.

1913

1 Jan. Sir Edward Carson's amendment to exclude Ulster from the Third Home Rule Bill defeated.

16 Jan. Home Rule Bill carried (367–257) in the House of Commons; defeated (326–69) in Lords on 30 Jan. (*see* 7 July).

31 Jan. Ulster Volunteer Force (U.V.F.) formed in Belfast; commanded by Gen. Sir George Richardson and Capt. Wilfrid Spender; H.Q. at the Old Town Hall, Victoria Street.

27 Mar. British League for the Support of Ulster and the Union announced.

7 July Home Rule Bill again carried (352–243) in the House of Commons; again defeated (302–64) in the Lords on 15 July.

18 Aug. William Martin Murphy dismisses 40 men who refuse to resign from the I.T.G.W.U.

26 Aug. James Larkin calls general strike of I.T.G.W.U. workers; starts with tram-car drivers and conductors, bringing transport to a halt in Dublin; Dublin employers led by W. M. Murphy lock out their workers.

28 Aug. Larkin and four other I.T.G.W.U. workers arrested and charged with 'seditious conspiracy' (released on bail).

29 Aug. James Connolly arrives in Dublin from Belfast for labour demonstration in Beresford Square, where Larkin burns proclamation banning his demonstration for the 31st.

30 Aug. Connolly sentenced to three months' imprisonment (warrant issued for Larkin); fights break out at night between police and workers; James Nolan clubbed to death by police, James Byrne fatally injured.

31 Aug. Larkin addresses crowd in Sackville Street (now O'Connell Street) from the balcony of the Imperial Hotel (owned by William Martin Murphy); Larkin's arrest followed by rioting, and the crowd is baton-charged by the D.M.P., resulting in several hundred injured (Larkin released on bail on 12 Sept.).

2 Sept. Two tenement houses collapse, killing seven people, in Church Street, Dublin.

3 Sept. Majority of the Dublin Employers' Federation demand workers' pledges not to join the I.T.G.W.U.

7 Sept. James Connolly starts hunger-strike (released on 14th).

8 Sept. Dublin City Council rejects (23 votes to 21) proposal to build a gallery over the Liffey to house Hugh Lane collection of modern art.

24 Sept. 500 delegates to the Ulster Unionist Council approve the establishment of a 'Provisional Government' of Ulster to be chaired by Sir Edward Carson (*see* 10 July 1914).

Sept. 25,000 workers now locked out for refusing to sign non-union pledge directed against the I.T.G.W.U.

27 Sept. The *Hare*, first foodship carrying supplies raised by British trade unionists for Dublin workers, sent by James Larkin from England, arrives in Dublin; another foodship, the *Fraternity*, arrives on 4 Oct.

5 Oct. d. Canon Patrick Augustine Sheehan (61), novelist, whose *Glenanaar* (1905) contains a graphic account of the 'Doneraile Conspiracy' (1829).

6 Oct. Report of the court of inquiry into the lock-out (at which T. M. Healy represented employers and Harry Gosling the workers) suggests that workers should be reinstated without having to give a pledge not to join the I.T.G.W.U., but that they should promise not to strike for two years unless employers reject conciliation; employers refuse these recommendations.

15 Oct. James Connolly leads 4,000 workers through the streets of Dublin.

19 Oct. d. Emily Lawless (68), novelist and poet.

21 Oct. Letter from Archbishop Walsh of Dublin denounces Larkin's plans for sending hungry children of locked-out workers to the homes of English trade unionists for the duration of the struggle.

1 Nov. Pub. 'The North Began' by Eoin Mac Néill in *An Claidheamh Soluis*; calls for a southern counterpart to the U.V.F.

11 Nov. Meeting at Wynn's Hotel, Dublin, where Eoin Mac Néill, Bulmer Hobson, Seán Mac Diarmada and Patrick Pearse, among others, consider formation of a southern organisation on the lines of the U.V.F. (*see* 25 Nov.).

12 Nov. Civic League at T.C.D. formed to aid Dublin workers; Capt. Jack White proposes formation of Citizen Army from among the workers to bring discipline 'into the distracted ranks of labour'.

18 Nov. Larkin and Connolly and delegates of the Dublin Trades Council meet with Parliamentary Committee of the British Trades Union Congress (*see* 9 Dec.).

19 Nov. Irish Citizen Army formed by the Civic League.

23 Nov. Capt. Jack White admits the first two companies of the Irish Citizen Army at Croydon Park, Dublin, to defend workers from the police, raise worker morale and provide a workers' force to oppose employers.

25 Nov. Irish Volunteers formed at a meeting in Rotunda Rink, Dublin, under chairmanship of Eoin Mac Néill.

4 Dec. I.T.G.W.U. conference agrees to relinquish sympathetic strike but seeks in return reinstatement of workers locked out since 26 Aug.

Ban announced on the importation of arms into Ireland.

9 Dec. Special meeting of British T.U.C. rejects Larkin's proposal for a boycott of Dublin goods.

Pub. *Irish Minstrels and Musicians* by Francis O'Neill (Chicago).

1914

7 Jan. d. P. W. Joyce (87), historian and musicologist.

18 Jan. Closed session of the I.T.G.W.U. adopts James Connolly's proposal that workers return to work if not obliged to take a pledge.

31 Jan. Builders' Labourers' Union (3,000 strong) promises employers that members will not join or support the I.T.G.W.U.

First photographs of the Irish Citizen Army appear in *An Claidheamh Soluis*.

7 Feb. Pub. first issue of the *Irish Volunteer*.

11 Feb. British T.U.C. winds up its Dublin Relief Fund.

26 Feb. *Britannic* launched, built by Harland & Wolff for the White Star Line; sister ship of the *Olympic* (*see* 20 Oct. 1910) and the *Titanic* (*see* 1 Apr. 1911); largest ship built in the U.K. (destroyed in the Aegean Sea in 1914).

2 Mar. During fund-raising tour of the U.S.A. Patrick Pearse states: 'I can only speak for myself when I say that before this generation has passed the Volunteers will draw the sword for Ireland. . . . I do not know how nationhood is achieved except by armed men.'

4 Mar. British Anti-Home Rule Covenant launched.

20 Mar. 'Curragh Incident' (also known as the 'Curragh Mutiny'): 57 out of 70 officers at the Curragh, under the leadership of Major–Gen. Sir Hubert Gough, decide that they will resign their commissions before they will be used to enforce Home Rule against the wishes of the Ulster Unionists; officers are informed on 22nd that the affair has been due to a misunderstanding, and the orders are never issued.

22 Mar. Seán O'Casey's constitution for the Irish Citizen Army ratified; it affirms that 'The ownership of Ireland, moral and material, is vested of right in the people of Ireland.'

31 Mar. d. T. D. Sullivan, editor (the *Nation*), politician (Home Rule), author ('God Save Ireland'); founded *Irish Catholic* (1888).

2 Apr. Cumann na mBan founded as women's auxiliary to the Irish Volunteers.

24–25 Apr. *Clydevalley* lands 35,000 rifles and 2½ million rounds of ammunition at Larne, Donaghadee and Bangor for the U.V.F. under the direction of Gen. Sir William Adair and Capt. Wilfrid Spender.

25 May Home Rule Bill carried in the House of Commons for the third and last time (*see* 18 Sept.).

10 June John Redmond suggests, in a letter to the *Freeman's Journal*, that 25 nominees of his Home Rule Party should have seats on the provisional committee of the Irish Volunteers; suggestion accepted on 16 June.

21 June I.T.G.W.U. general meeting refuses to accept James Larkin's resignation.

23 June Government of Ireland (Amendment) Bill introduced in the House of Lords, seeking temporary exclusion by county option of parts of Ulster from Home Rule.

8 July Amendment Bill amended in the House of Lords to permit the permanent exclusion of Ulster from Home Rule (indefinitely postponed on 30 July).

10 July Provisional Government of Ulster meets.

21–24 July Buckingham Palace Conference brings Unionist and Nationalist representatives together in an attempt to break the *impasse* over Home Rule; fails.

26 July *Asgard*, navigated by Erskine Childers, lands 1,500 guns for the Irish Volunteers at Howth, Co. Dublin.

4 killed and 37 wounded when troops, returning to Phoenix Park, having failed to impound the imported weapons from the Volunteers, open fire on a crowd at Bachelor's Walk, Dublin.

1 Aug. *Kelpie* lands guns for the Irish Volunteers at Kilcoole, Co. Wicklow.

3 Aug. Germany declares war on France.

John Redmond in the House of Commons pledges Ireland's support for Britain, should she enter the war, stating that 'With our brethren in the North, we will ourselves defend the coasts of our country' (*see* 20 Sept.).

4 Aug. Britain declares war on Germany.

Defence of the Realm Act (D.O.R.A.).

12 Aug. d. John Philip Holland (79), inventor of submarine.

15 Aug. Press censorship introduced (until 1921).

9 Sept. Supreme Council of the I.R.B., presided over by Thomas J. Clarke with Patrick Pearse, Joseph Plunkett, Eamonn Ceannt, Thomas MacDonagh, Seán Mac Diarmada and James Connolly present, resolves to recruit greater numbers into the militant nationalist movements (Irish Volunteers, Citizen Army and Cumann na mBan) and to plan a rising before the end of the war.

18 Sept. Home Rule Act suspended for the duration of the war.

20 Sept. John Redmond, speaking at Woodenbridge, Co. Wicklow, calls on the Irish Volunteers to fight for Britain in the war; causes split in the Volunteer movement; Redmond's followers become the National Volunteers.

24 Sept. Eoin Mac Néill and executive of the Irish Volunteers repudiate John Redmond and his nominees on the committee; they retain title 'Irish Volunteers' and determine 'to resist any attempt to force the men of Ireland into military service under any government, until a free national government of Ireland is empowered by the Irish people to deal with it'.

25–26 Sept. P.M. Asquith in Dublin; shares platform with John Redmond at recruiting meeting in the Mansion House.

28 Sept. Irish Neutrality League established under presidency of James Connolly.

12 Oct. Sir Matthew Nathan appointed Under-Secretary.

17 Oct. Speaking at Kilkenny, John Redmond states: 'The Union of 1800 is dead. . . . A new era has arisen for our country. We have won at last a free constitution.'

24 Oct. James Larkin leaves for U.S.A.; succeeded as 'acting general secretary' of I.T.G.W.U. by James Connolly (*see* 30 Apr. 1923).

25 Oct. Irish Volunteers refuse Connolly's proposal that the Citizen Army affiliate to them.

20 Nov. German government gives Roger Casement a formal declaration of support for Irish nationalist aspirations.

2–4 Dec. Newspapers *Sinn Féin, Irish Freedom* and *Irish Volunteer* suppressed.

5 Dec. James Connolly's *Irish Worker* appears with leader-page blank in protest at government censorship (leading article appears as a leaflet on 9 Dec., published 'while the censor wasn't looking').

Intermediate Education (Ireland) Act provides first direct Treasury grant for intermediate education and establishes a registration council (comes into force on 31 July 1918).

Pub. *Report into the Housing of the Dublin Working Classes* indicating that 87,000 of Dublin's 300,000 population live in slums (with 26,000 families living in 5,000 tenements).

Pub. *Dubliners* by James Joyce.

1915
3 Feb. Sir Hugh Lane, in unsigned codicil to his will, bequeathes the city of Dublin 39 French Impressionist paintings (*see* 7 May).

18 Feb. Ivor Churchill Guest, Baron Wimborne, sworn in as L.L.

13 Mar. The seven commandants of the Irish Volunteers (Pearse, Plunkett, Bulmer Hobson, Edward Daly, Thomas MacDonagh, Eamonn Ceannt and Eamon de Valera) discuss possibility of a rising in Sept.

4 Apr. Easter Sunday: Patrick Pearse organises a mock battle outside Dublin.

7 May *Lusitania* torpedoed, off the Old Head of Kinsale; Sir Hugh Lane a.ong the 1,198 drowned (*see* 3 Feb.) (several hundred victims buried at Queenstown (Cóbh), Co. Cork).

25 May Coalition government formed under P.M. Asquith.

29 May Pub. first issue of the *Workers' Republic* (replacing the *Irish Worker*), edited by James Connolly at Liberty Hall.

John Redmond declines office in new administration, which includes eight Unionists as well as Sir Edward Carson, who, as Attorney-General, has seat in cabinet.

May Secret Military Council set up within the I.R.B.; first members are Patrick Pearse, Joseph Plunkett and Eamonn Ceannt.

19 June Pub. first issue of *Nationality*, ed. Arthur Griffith.

21 June Belfast railway workers on strike, supported by James Connolly and I.T.G.W.U. (employers concede increase of 2s per week on 14 Aug.).

18 July Connolly leads anti-conscription meeting at Liberty Hall.

29 July Militant nationalists, led by Patrick Pearse, take control of the Gaelic League at Dundalk conference, leading to Douglas Hyde's resignation from presidency; replaced by Eoin Mac Néill.

1 Aug. Funeral of Jeremiah O'Donovan Rossa (d. 30 June in New York); Patrick Pearse's oration delivered at Glasnevin: 'They have left us our Fenian dead, and while Ireland holds these graves, Ireland unfree shall never be at peace.'

Dec. Military Council within the I.R.B. expanded to include Thomas J. Clarke and Seán Mac Diarmada; James Connolly joins in Jan. 1916 and Thomas MacDonagh in Apr.

21 Dec. d. Violet Martin (53), the 'Martin Ross' of the Somerville and Ross literary partnership.

Pub. *Mo Scéal Féin*, autobiography of An tAthair Peadar Ó Laoghaire.

1916
19–22 Jan. Patrick Pearse, Joseph Plunkett and Seán Mac Diarmada of the I.R.B. secret Military Council in secret meeting with James Connolly; he is co-opted onto the Council, and they agree to organise a rising no later than Easter.

5 Feb. Clan na Gael in New York is informed that there will be a rising in Dublin on Easter Sunday, 23 Apr.

12 Feb. Joseph McGarrity of Clan na Gael in New York is informed by Pearse that guns will be required between Good Friday and Easter Sunday (*see* 9 Mar.).

4 Mar. 2,300 delegates attend the Irish Race Convention at New York's Astor Hotel, chaired by Judge Goff, with representatives from Clan na Gael, Ancient Order of Hibernians and all active Irish organisations in U.S.A.; Convention creates 'Friends of Irish Freedom' organisation to lobby for Irish independence when war ends and establishes fund for this purpose.

9 Mar. Clan na Gael informs Pearse and Clarke that guns will arrive (from Germany) during 23–25 Apr.

17 Mar. Eoin Mac Néill takes salute from reviewing stand at Irish Volunteer rally at College Green, Dublin.

28 Mar. Executive of Irish Volunteers publishes warning that any attempt to deprive Volunteers of arms will be resisted by force.

3 Apr. Patrick Pearse issues 'general orders' for Volunteer manoeuvres starting on 23 Apr. and lasting three days.

5 Apr. Thomas MacDonagh co-opted onto the Military Council of the I.R.B.

6 Apr. Joseph Plunkett communicates Easter Sunday as date for the rising to Roger Casement in Germany, seeking landing of German arms in Tralee Bay on the Saturday morning, together with German officers and submarines in Dublin harbour; Casement's veto on officers and submarines not forwarded from Germany.

8 Apr. Patrick Pearse in the *Irish Volunteer* calls for general manoeuvres throughout the country on Easter Sunday, approved by Eoin Mac Néill (*see* 23 Apr.).

9 Apr. German ship, the *Aud*, leaves Lübeck for Ireland with 20,000 rifles and ammunition for the Irish Volunteers, to arrive off Kerry coast on 20 Apr.

12 Apr. Roger Casement, Robert Monteith and Sergeant Julian Bailey leave Germany in a U-boat to rendezvous with the *Aud* on 20 Apr.

18 Apr. U.S. authorities raid the New York offices of a German agent, Wolf von Igel, and discover details of German and Irish-American collusion in an imminent rising in Ireland.

19 Apr. 'Castle Document', a forgery by Joseph Plunkett intended to secure support of Eoin Mac Néill for military action, provides a detailed plan for a British military occupation of Dublin and the disarming of nationalist organisations.

20 Apr. Eoin Mac Néill invests Bulmer Hobson with authority over all Dublin city Volunteers and Commdt J. J. O'Connell with supreme authority in the south, and cancels all orders not endorsed personally or by Hobson.

20–21 Apr. The *Aud*, carrying arms for the Volunteers, sails into Tralee Bay; local Volunteers expect it three days later and fail to make rendezvous; when British naval patrol, the *Bluebell*, arrests her the German captain, Karl Spindler, scuttles the ship in Cork harbour; government orders a news blackout on fate of the *Aud*.

Bulmer Hobson learns of the proposed rising; he informs Mac Néill, who confronts Pearse, MacDonagh and Mac Diarmada, who admit to the plans; Mac Néill, assured of the arrival of the German arms ship, agrees to allow the plans to proceed, countermanding his order of 20th.

21 Apr. Casement, Monteith and Bailey put ashore from a submarine at Banna Strand, near Fenit, Co. Kerry; Casement captured there, Bailey captured later, but Monteith escapes to Cork; three Dublin Volunteers, Con Keating, Charlie Monaghan and Donald Sheehan, *en route* to rendezvous with the *Aud*, drown when their car plunges off Ballykissane pier, Co. Kerry.

22 Apr. Military Council of the I.R.B. receives message from Monteith confirming arrests of Casement and Austin Stack (Commdt, Kerry Brigade, Irish Volunteers) and advising against rising if it is contingent on German aid.

Casement transferred to Dublin, where he is identified.

Eoin Mac Néill learns that the 'Castle Document' is a forgery and that the *Aud* with its arms shipment is destroyed and moves to cancel the rising planned for the following day.

23 Apr. Eoin Mac Néill's cancellation of Volunteer manoeuvres appears in the *Sunday Independent*, causing confusion among Volunteers throughout the country; I.R.B. Military Council, joined from a nursing home by the dying Joseph Plunkett, meets in Liberty Hall and decides to start the rising at noon the next day; Pearse, to avoid isolated incidents, sends out orders confirming Mac Néill's.

24 Apr. Easter Rising: G.P.O. occupied without a shot fired; key buildings in Dublin captured; proclamation entitled *The Provisional Government of the Irish Republic to the People of Ireland* issued by Pearse from the steps of the G.P.O.

25 Apr. Brig.-Gen. Lowe takes command in Dublin and proclaims martial law throughout Dublin city and county; British reinforcements arrive with artillery back-up; Citizen Army is forced to vacate the College of Surgeons; route from the North Wall to Kingsbridge (now Heuston Station) is cordoned off, effectively splitting the republican forces; *Irish War News* appears with Pearse's first communiqué announcing the setting up of the Provisional Government.

26 Apr. From noon until 8 p.m. 17 men deployed by Eamon de Valera (Boland's Mills) hold off a battalion of Sherwood Foresters at Mount Street Bridge; British suffer 230 killed and wounded.

Gunboat *Helga* sails up the Liffey and shells the centre of Dublin, demolishing Liberty Hall and the upper storey of the G.P.O.

Francis Sheehy-Skeffington, pacifist, and two journalists, Thomas Dickson and Patrick McIntyre, having been taken into military custody, are killed by Capt. J. C. Bowen-Colthurst (subsequently found guilty of murder but insane; released from Broadmoor asylum on 26 Jan. 1918).

27 Apr. 12,000 British troops now in Dublin; city centre cordoned off.

C.S. Birrell arrives in Ireland with Gen. Sir John Maxwell, C.-in-C. (until 4 Nov.).

The O'Rahilly killed in Dublin.

Thomas Ashe leads successful ambush on R.I.C. at Ashbourne, Co. Meath.

29 Apr. Pearse makes an unconditional surrender to Gen. Lowe; end of Easter Rising. (Casualties: nationalist insurgents: 64 killed, 120 wounded; British forces and police: 132 killed, 397 wounded; civilians: 300 killed, 2,000 wounded.)

1 May First Irish internees arrive in Britain.

3 May Pearse, Clarke and MacDonagh executed.

Redmond in the House of Commons expresses his revulsion at the rising, but appeals for clemency in dealing with the prisoners.

C.S. Birrell resigns; functions performed by Home Secretary Herbert Samuel until 3 Aug.

4 May Plunkett (who married Grace Gifford a few hours previously), Edward Daly, Michael O'Hanrahan and William Pearse executed.

5 May Major John MacBride, husband of Maud Gonne, father of Seán MacBride, executed.

8 May Con Colbert, Eamonn Ceannt, Seán Heuston and Michael Mallin executed.

Redmond warns the House of Commons of the dangers of continuing a stringent executions policy.

9 May Thomas Kent executed (in Cork).

10 May P.M. Asquith announces appointment of commission under Lord Hardinge to inquire into the events of Easter (opens on 18 May; reports on 3 July); responding to questions, Asquith announces that 13 executions have taken place, 73 sentenced to penal servitude, and six to imprisonment with hard labour, while 1,706 were deported.

11 May During House of Commons debate on the events in Ireland John Dillon urges an end to the executions.

12 May Connolly and Seán Mac Diarmada executed.

12–18 May P.M. Asquith in Ireland.

17 May R.C. Bishop Edward O'Dwyer of Limerick refuses Gen. Maxwell's request that he discipline two of his priests for their republican sentiments: 'You took good care that no plea for mercy should interpose on behalf of the poor young fellows who surrendered to you in Dublin. . . . Personally, I regard your action with horror, and I believe that it has outraged the conscience of the country.'

25 May P.M. Asquith advises the House of Commons that the old system of government in Ireland has broken down and the time is opportune for a new approach.

29 May Lloyd George shows draft proposals for an Irish settlement to Sir Edward Carson and Lord Midleton; Carson, pledged to secrecy, accepts Lloyd George's proposal of Home Rule with permanent exclusion of Ulster; Lloyd George then secures Redmond's acceptance of Home Rule with temporary exclusion of Ulster until after the war.

1 June Executive committee of the Irish Unionist Alliance resolves against a settlement which concedes Home Rule (repeats this on 9, 21 and 27 June).

At meeting of cabinet committee on Ireland Lord Lansdowne and Walter Long object to scheme offering self-government to Ireland.

1–9 June Lloyd George holds meetings with Southern Unionists, seeking agreement to an Irish settlement (which they reject).

12 June Ulster Unionist Council accepts Lloyd George's proposal for Home Rule, but with exclusion of six counties.

23 June John Redmond informs Ulster nationalist convention in Belfast of exclusion from Home Rule of six counties of Antrim, Armagh, Down, Fermanagh, Tyrone and Londonderry, and that he, John Dillon and Joseph Devlin will resign their positions if the meeting rejects proposal; convention accepts it.

26–27 June Irish Unionist Alliance visits London, meets Unionist cabinet ministers and protests to P.M. Asquith and Lloyd George over proposed settlement.

26–29 June Trial of Roger Casement for high treason; prosecution led by F. E. Smith (later Lord Birkenhead), defence led by Serjeant A. M. Sullivan; Casement sentenced to death (*see* 3 Aug.).

1 July Battle of the Somme begins; 36th (Ulster) Division (U.V.F.) sustains heavy casualties in the worst single day of the war (provokes total work stoppage in Belfast on 12th).

13 July Lord Midleton confirms Redmond's view that Lloyd George's scheme is provisional; Redmond is adamant that the Irish Party will totally oppose Home Rule with permanent exclusion of Ulster; Lloyd George shelves proposal.

3 Aug. Roger Casement executed at Pentonville prison (his remains reinterred in Glasnevin cemetery, Dublin, on 1 Mar. 1965).

Henry Edward Duke appointed C.S.

25 Oct. d. John Todhunter (77), physician, poet and playwright, influential in Irish Literary Society in London.

4 Nov. Lt-Gen. Sir Bryan Mahon appointed C.-in-C.

19 Nov. d. Fr Michael O'Hickey (55), Professor of Irish at Maynooth College (1896 – 1909).

7 Dec. David Lloyd George replaces Asquith as P.M. (of coalition government).

22–23 Dec. 600 untried Irish internees released from Frongoch (Wales) and Lewes jails and are greeted by torchlight procession and bonfires on return to Ireland; convicted prisoners remain imprisoned.

Pub. *A Portrait of the Artist as a Young Man* by James Joyce.

Pub. *Songs of the Fields* by Francis Ledwidge.

Pub. (posthumously) *Poetical Works* and *Literature in Ireland* by Thomas MacDonagh.

Pub. *Insurrection in Dublin* by James Stephens.

1917

Jan. Compulsory tillage policy introduced, obliging farmers with more than 10 statute acres to bring an extra 10 per cent of their land under the plough, and a further 10 per cent in 1918 (continues to 1920).

3 Feb. Count Plunkett (endorsed by Sinn Féin, 3,022 votes) defeats T. J. Devine (Home Rule, 1,708) in Roscommon North by-election; does not take seat at Westminster.

17 Feb. Arthur Griffith's *Nationality* resumes publication.

7 Mar. Redmond and Home Rulers withdraw from the House of Commons when Lloyd George states that 'In the north-eastern portion of Ireland you have a population as hostile to Irish rule as the rest of Ireland is to British rule.'

15 Mar. Tsar Nicholas II of Russia abdicates; Russia ruled by provisional government led by Prince Lvov; soviets established throughout Russia.

6 Apr. U.S.A. enters the war.

17 Apr. d. Jane Barlow (60), writer (author of *Irish Idylls*).

19 Apr. Sinn Féin National Council established to deny 'the right of any foreign parliament to make laws for Ireland'.

8 May 16 R.C. and three Protestant bishops join laymen in declaration against partition of Ireland.

9 May Joseph McGuinness (Sinn Féin, 1,493 votes), prisoner in Lewes jail, defeats Patrick McKenna (Home Rule, 1,461) in Longford South by-election; first use by Sinn Féin of the slogan 'Put him in to get him out.'

16 May Redmond accepts Lloyd George's proposal of an Irish Convention for the purpose of enabling representative Irishmen 'to endeavour to find a settlement for themselves' which would be acceptable to all shades of political opinion on the island.

18 May Sinn Féin refuses to participate in the proposed Irish Convention.

7 June d. Major William Redmond (56), politician (Home Rule) (in action on the Western Front) .

16 June Remaining 120 Irish political prisoners released (including Eoin Mac Néill, Eamon de Valera and Countess Markievicz).

10 July Eamon de Valera (Sinn Féin, 5,010 votes) defeats Patrick Lynch, K.C. (Home Rule, 2,035) in Clare East by-election.

12 July De Valera says: 'If Ulster stands in the way of the attainment of Irish freedom, Ulster should be coerced.'

25 July Irish Convention meets for the first time at the Regent's House, T.C.D., under chairmanship of Sir Horace Plunkett.

31 July d. Francis Ledwidge (30), poet (in action near Ypres).

10 Aug. Alderman W. T. Cosgrave (Sinn Féin, 772 votes) defeats John Magennis (Home Rule, 392) in Kilkenny City by-election.

Sept. Agricultural Wages Board established to set minimum pay and conditions.

25 Sept. Thomas Ashe dies in Mountjoy Jail on hunger-strike (after being forcibly fed); funeral on 30th is a huge nationalist demonstration.

14 Oct. d. Nathaniel Hone (86), artist; his widow presents 500 of his oils and some 900 water-colours to the National Gallery.

25–26 Oct. Sinn Féin Ard-Fheis at the Mansion House, Dublin; de Valera elected President; adopts policy of seeking recognition for the Irish Republic and planning form of government best suited to the Irish situation.

27 Oct. De Valera elected President of the Irish Volunteers.

25 Nov. Southern Unionists produce compromise to Convention deadlock.

1918

15 Jan. Nationalists split over fiscal autonomy in the Irish Convention.

2 Feb. Patrick Donnelly (Home Rule, 2,324 votes) defeats Dr Patrick McCartan (Sinn Féin, 1,305) and T. W. Richardson (Independent Unionist, 40) in Armagh South by-election.

6 Feb. Representation of the People Act enfranchises all men over 21 and most women over 30; Redistribution of Seats Act provides for constituency electorates of approximately equal size.

20 Feb. Southern Unionist Committee formed in the Shelbourne Hotel, Dublin.

23 Feb. Sir Bryan Mahon, C.-in-C., issues order prohibiting carrying of arms by unauthorised persons throughout Ireland and prohibiting possession of arms in Clare, Galway and Tipperary.

27 Feb. Clare proclaimed a military area; the county is heavily garrisoned and authorities assume censorship

KILKENNY COUNTY LIBRARY

powers on post and telegrams; the *Clare Champion*, initially subject to strict censorship, is suppressed within month.

6 Mar. d. John Redmond (62), politician, leader of the Home Rule Party since 1900; his Waterford City seat is held by his son, Capt. W. A. Redmond (Home Rule, 1,242 votes), who defeats Dr V. J. White (Sinn Féin, 745) on 22nd.

12 Mar. John Dillon assumes leadership of the Irish Parliamentary Party (Home Rule Party).

15 Mar. Proposal to exclude Ulster from Home Rule defeated (52–19) in House of Commons.

3 Apr. Thomas J. S. Harbison (Home Rule, 1,802 votes) defeats Seán Milroy (Sinn Féin, 1,222) in Tyrone East by-election.

5 Apr. Report of the Irish Convention carried (44–19) (signed by less than half of the members on 8 Apr.); report proposes peripheral Home Rule with subservient Irish parliament; a minority report recommends a form of Dominion Home Rule; committee of three Unionists and two Nationalists advises against extending conscription to Ireland.

9 Apr. P.M. Lloyd George introduces Military Service Bill to apply conscription to Ireland (passes House of Commons in seven days, 301–103; becomes law on 18 Apr.); John Dillon withdraws the Home Rule Party from the House in protest at the proposed extension of conscription to Ireland.

Catholic hierarchy protests at conscription proposal.

18 Apr. Mansion House Conference called by Lord Mayor of Dublin, Laurence O'Neill, to discuss British government's conscription proposals for Ireland; the meeting, which represents all shades of nationalist opinion, issues an anti-conscription pledge drafted by Eamon de Valera.

19 Apr. Dr Patrick McCartan (Sinn Féin) returned unopposed in King's County by-election when the Home Rule Party withdraws its candidate in protest at proposal to extend conscription to Ireland.

21 Apr. Nationalists of all shades of opinion sign anti-conscription pledge.

22 Apr. First public screening of film version of *Knocknagow*, directed by Fred O'Donovan, at the Empire Palace, Dublin.

23 Apr. Nationalist one-day strike in protest at conscription, successful (except in Ulster).

4 May Edward Shortt appointed C.S.

11 May John, Viscount French, sworn in as L.L.

17–18 May About 100 Sinn Féin and Volunteer leaders rounded up in effort to discredit Sinn Féin—the so-called 'German Plot' arrests (there was no such 'plot').

June Ulster Unionist Labour Association founded (officers elected on 3 July).

3 June L.L. French calls for '50,000 Irish recruits before October to replenish the Irish divisions in the field, and after that date to raise 2,000 to 3,000 recruits per month in order to maintain these divisions'.

15 June L.L. French imposes martial law throughout most of the south and west of the country.

18 June Limerick and Tipperary declared 'special military areas' by the government.

20 June Conscription and Home Rule plans dropped.

Arthur Griffith (Sinn Féin, 3,795 votes) defeats J. F. O'Hanlon (Home

Rule, 2,581) in Cavan East by-election.

3 July Majority of nationalist organisations declared banned, including Irish Volunteers and Sinn Féin.

5 July Order proscribing 'the holding or taking part in any meeting, assemblies or processions in public places within the whole of Ireland'; secretly extended to include sports meetings, athletic meetings, *aeridheachta* and *feiseanna*, while hurling and Gaelic football matches are subjected to regular interruption by Crown forces.

15 Aug. Pub. first issue of *An tÓglach*, published by the Irish Volunteers.

Sept. *An Claidheamh Soluis* proscribed.

10 Oct. Dublin steam packet R.M.S. *Leinster* torpedoed by German submarine one hour out of Kingstown (Dún Laoghaire); 501 of the 771 on board die.

1 Nov. To ensure nationalist unity, Labour Party withdraws from the forthcoming general election.

2 Nov. Lloyd George claims the right to solve the Irish question by partition, effectively giving control of the six north-eastern counties to the Unionists.

New constitution of Irish Labour Party and Trades Union Congress.

11 Nov. Armistice brings the war to an end (11 a.m.). (49,000 Irish citizens died in action in the British forces.)

14 Nov. d. Séamus O'Kelly (43), playwright, novelist and journalist, from cerebral haemorrhage, following incursion into his office by rowdy anti-Sinn Féin celebrators of the armistice of 11 Nov.

21 Nov. Parliament (Qualification of Women) Act enables women to sit in the House of Commons (Countess Markievicz of Sinn Féin first woman elected (general election in Dec.), but does not take her seat at Westminster).

4 Dec. d. Richard Bagwell (78), historian (author of *Ireland under the Tudors*, 3 vols, 1885–90, and *Ireland under the Stuarts*, 3 vols, 1909–10).

14–28 Dec. General election; P.M. Lloyd George returns at head of coalition; Sinn Féin, standing on abstentionist platform, secures 73 of Ireland's 105 seats; Unionists, 25; Home Rule Party, 6; Independent Unionist, 1.

Pub. *The Valley of the Squinting Windows* by Brinsley Macnamara.

Pub. *Economic History of Ireland in the Eighteenth Century* by George O'Brien (companion volumes covering seventeenth and early nineteenth centuries published in 1919 and 1921).

1919

3 Jan. U.S. President Wilson receives the freedom of the city of Dublin.

7 Jan. 26 Sinn Féin M.P.s meet to appoint a committee for the first session of an Irish parliamentary assembly and invite 'all persons elected by the existing Irish constituencies to attend'.

13 Jan. James Ian Macpherson appointed C.S.

15 Jan. P.R. (single transferable vote) used for the first time in the Sligo municipal elections (*see* 15 Jan. 1920 *and* 24 May 1921).

21 Jan. Sinn Féin members returned in Dec. 1918 general election form Dáil Éireann ('Parliament of Ireland'); they issue a Declaration of Independence, adopt a constitution for the Dáil and a 'Democratic Programme' and issue a 'Message to the

Free Nations of the World'; Cathal Brugha elected acting President on 22 Jan. (*see* 1 Apr.).

Delegates appointed to represent the newly declared Republic at the Paris Peace Conference.

Local I.R.A. unit led by Séamus Robinson, Dan Breen and Seán Treacy ambushes and kills two policemen (R.I.C. constables MacDonnell and O'Connell) at Soloheadbeg, Co. Tipperary (later viewed as the start of the War of Independence).

24 Jan. Irish Unionist Alliance splits; Unionist Anti-Partition League formed.

25 Jan. Shipyard, gas, electricity and transport workers, involving 44 businesses, go on strike in Belfast for 44-hour working week (*see* 20 Feb.).

31 Jan. *An tÓglach* states that Volunteers are entitled 'morally and legally to slay British police and soldiers'.

3 Feb. De Valera escapes from Lincoln prison (*see* 6–10 Mar.).

7 Feb. Thomas Johnson and Cathal O'Shannon represent the Irish Labour Party at the International Labour and Socialist Conference at Berne, Switzerland, and are admitted as delegation separate from the British.

14 Feb. Troops take over the gasworks and electricity stations in Belfast.

20 Feb. Belfast strike ends when workers are granted 47-hour working week.

22 Feb. Over 5,000 delegates attending Irish Race Convention at Philadelphia draft resolution to President Wilson urging his support for full international recognition for Ireland at the Paris Peace Conference.

4 Mar. Over President Wilson's objections U.S. House of Representatives votes (216–45) that the Paris Peace Conference should favourably consider Ireland's claim to self-determination; Senate passes similar motion on 6 June, but recognition not forthcoming.

6–10 Mar. Remaining Sinn Féin prisoners released.

20 Mar. Countrywide Irish Volunteer arms raid culminates in seizure of arms at Collinstown (Baldonnell) Airport.

25 Mar. Turnstiles removed from the Halfpenny Bridge, Dublin (a toll bridge since 1816).

29 Mar. Resident Magistrate J. C. Milling shot at Westport, Co. Mayo (dies shortly afterwards).

1 Apr. Second session of Dáil Éireann opens; Eamon de Valera elected Príomh-Aire (President) of Dáil Éireann; Seán T. O'Kelly elected Ceann Comhairle (Speaker).

4 Apr. Michael Collins, Minister for Finance, seeks to raise loan through issue of 'republican bonds' to the value of £250,000 in sums of £1 to £1,000; all papers carrying the advertisement are immediately suppressed.

6 Apr. Robert Byrne, republican hunger-striker in St Camillus' Hospital, Limerick, killed, as is a guard, during attempted rescue; Limerick proclaimed a military area and general strike ensues.

8 Apr. At Sinn Féin Ard-Fheis de Valera re-elected President of Sinn Féin on proposal of Arthur Griffith.

14–25 Apr. Limerick Soviet: general strike organised by Limerick United Trades and Labour Council brings out some 15,000 workers and leads to establishment of 'soviet' in protest against martial law within the city.

30 Apr. d. Professor J. P. Mahaffy (80), scholar; Provost of T.C.D. since 1914.

3 May Frank P. Walsh, Edward F. Dunne and Michael J. Ryan arrive in Ireland as delegates from the Friends of Irish Freedom; they submit their report on conditions in Ireland to the Paris Peace Conference on 3 June.

13 May Two policemen killed during rescue of Seán Hogan by Dan Breen and Seán Treacy, who are wounded, at Knocklong railway station, Co. Limerick.

29 May Act provides for medical care for children receiving elementary education.

3 June Local Government (Ireland) Act: boroughs to be divided into wards containing at least six councillors, to be elected by P.R. (*see* 15 Jan. 1920).

11 June President Wilson informs delegates of the Friends of Irish Freedom of British veto on discussion of Ireland's claim to nationhood.

De Valera arrives in New York.

15 June John W. Alcock and Arthur Whitten Brown in Vickers Vimy biplane complete the first non-stop transatlantic flight from Newfoundland, landing near Clifden, Co. Galway, in 15 hours and 57 minutes at average speed of 115 m.p.h.

18 June Dáil Éireann establishes 'arbitration courts' to deal with land disputes (clergymen become *ex-officio* justices in the courts under Dáil resolution of 19 Aug.).

19 June Dáil approves National Loan prospectus and appoints three trustees (de Valera, James O'Mara and Bishop Fogarty of Killaloe).

23 June R.I.C. District Inspector Hunt shot dead by the I.R.A. in Market Square, Thurles, Co. Tipperary.

At U.S. press conference de Valera declares: 'From today I am in America as the official head of the Republic established by the will of the Irish people in accordance with the principles of self-determination.'

25 June d. William Martin Murphy (75), founder of Independent Newspapers, leader of the Employers' Federation during the lock-out of 1913–14.

31 July Detective Patrick Smith of G Division of the D.M.P. shot dead by I.R.A. squad in Dublin.

19 Aug. Widespread I.R.A. activity in Clare as patrols are ambushed and barracks attacked in I.R.A. effort to procure arms.

Fifth session of Dáil Éireann; debates plans for 'republican courts'; Robert Barton, Minister for Agriculture, submits a land-bond scheme of £250,000 whereby applicants are enabled to borrow three-quarters of price.

20 Aug. Dáil Éireann resolves on motion proposed by Cathal Brugha that all its members and officials and the Irish Volunteers must swear allegiance to the Dáil and the Irish Republic; the Volunteers thereby become the standing army of the Irish Republic (I.R.A.).

1 Sept. Castlecomer, Co. Kilkenny, railway opens under D.O.R.A. for shipment of high-quality anthracite; the last substantial standard-gauge branch and also the steepest standard-gauge railway in Ireland.

5 Sept. Roscommon man John O'Shehan sentenced to two years' imprisonment for singing 'The Felons of Our Land'.

7 Sept. North Cork Brigade of the I.R.A. under Liam Lynch attacks troops of the Shropshire Light Infantry in Fermoy, Co. Cork, killing one and wounding four; soldiers wreck shops that evening (first time such retaliation or reprisal used).

12 Sept. Dáil Éireann declared a dangerous association.

13 Sept. Detective John Hoey, who identified Seán Mac Diarmada for the military in 1916, shot dead outside police H.Q. in Brunswick Street, Dublin.

20 Sept. All republican newspapers suppressed.

26 Sept. North Cork T.D. Patrick O'Keeffe sentenced to two years' imprisonment for seditious speech.

30 Sept. Number of reported police and military raids on private houses for past nine months reaches 5,588 (number of reported raids by Crown forces during 1917, 1918 and 1919 estimated at 12,589).

15 Oct. Proclamation outlaws Sinn Féin, the Irish Republican Army, etc.; Sinn Féin, despite its proclamation, holds Ard-Fheis (from midnight to 3 a.m.).

10 Nov. Patrick Street, Cork, sacked and looted by Crown forces.

11 Nov. Pub. first issue of the *Irish Bulletin*, Sinn Féin and Dáil newssheet.

18 Dec. Winston Churchill in House of Commons places the number of troops currently in Ireland at 43,000, costing the British taxpayer £860,000 per month.

19 Dec. I.R.A. Lt Martin Savage killed during attempt to assassinate L.L. French.

21 Dec. I.R.A. raid offices of the *Irish Independent* and destroy plant in revenge for paper's description of Martin Savage as a 'would-be assassin' (*see* 19 Dec.).

22 Dec. C.S. Macpherson's Education Bill withdrawn following objection of Catholic hierarchy.

Pub. *Phases of Irish History* by Eoin Mac Néill.

1920

2 Jan. Former British army troops recruited as reinforcements to the R.I.C. under the command of Major-Gen. H. H. Tudor (later dubbed 'Black and Tans', they arrive in Ireland on 25 Mar.).

15 Jan. Using P.R. for the first time, local government elections give Sinn Féin, other nationalists and Labour control of 172 out of 206 borough and urban district councils (*see* 12 June).

27 Jan. In effort to seize money subscribed to the Dáil National Loan, troops raid Sinn Féin H.Q. (*see* 4 Apr. *and* 19 June 1919); only £1,000 is seized, as the bulk of the money is deposited in banks in the names of private individuals.

14 Feb. I.R.A. unit under Ernie O'Malley captures R.I.C. barracks at Shantonagh, Ballytrain, Co. Monaghan, the first such barracks taken in Ulster by the I.R.A.

23 Feb. Curfew (midnight to 5 a.m.), imposed on 20th, becomes effective in Dublin Metropolitan District.

25 Feb. Government of Ireland Bill introduced in House of Commons.

10 Mar. Ulster Unionist Council majority (2 to 1) accepts Government of Ireland Bill, offering a six-county state.

Six republican prisoners executed in Dublin, four of whom were convicted of high treason for levying war.

20 Mar. Tomás MacCurtain, Sinn Féin Lord Mayor of Cork and commandant of 1st Cork Brigade of I.R.A., shot dead at his home; coroner's jury finds that 'murder was organised and carried out by the Royal Irish Constabulary officially directed by the British government.'

21 Mar. d. An tAthair Peadar Ó Laoghaire (81), scholar (author of *Séadna,* 1894, and *Mo Scéal Féin,* 1915).

26 Mar. Magistrate Alan Bell, investigating funding of the republican movement, shot dead by Michael Collins's 'squad'.

12 Apr. Sir Hamar Greenwood appointed C.S.

Big cattle-drive on the property of Col. J. D. Featherstonehaugh, Rockview, Co. Westmeath; start of a policy of cattle-driving and enforced land redistribution.

19 Apr. Première of *Willy Reilly and his Colleen Bawn,* film directed by John MacDonagh, at the Bohemian Cinema, Dublin.

27 Apr. I.R.A. attack police barracks at Ballylanders, Co. Limerick; Black and Tans terrorise Limerick city the next day.

1 May Maurice Headlam leaves office of Treasury Remembrancer (since 1 Apr. 1912), the last person to hold it.

2 May d. Rev. Professor Walter McDonald (66), theologian at Maynooth College, prefect of the Dunboyne Establishment since 1888, author of *Reminiscences of a Maynooth Professor* (1925), ed. Denis Gwynn.

8 May De Valera repudiates the right of the British Ambassador to Washington to represent Ireland.

16–19 May 'Soviet' established at Knocklong creamery, Co. Limerick.

23 May Railwaymen on 'munitions strike' at Kingstown, Co. Dublin, joining dockers; soon spreads throughout the country and includes transporting armed troops (ends on 21 Dec.).

28 May I.R.A. attack on police barracks at Kilmallock, Co. Limerick.

12 June Elections to county councils, rural district councils and boards of Poor Law Guardians throughout Ireland under P.R. result in overwhelming Sinn Féin success; in Ulster Sinn Féin gains control of 36 of the 55 rural district councils.

14 June Mount Shannon, largest house in Co. Limerick, burnt out by the I.R.A.

16 June R.I.C. at Listowel, Co. Kerry, 'mutiny' in protest at activities of military forces; Constable Jeremiah Mee and some of his colleagues resign on 6 July.

24 June Decision made to revive the U.V.F.

26 June I.R.A. capture Gen. Lucas and two colonels while fishing near Fermoy, Co. Cork; one colonel wounded in attempted escape, and I.R.A. leave his colleague to attend him; Lucas escapes less than a month later.

28 June 'B' and 'C' Companies of the Connaught Rangers mutiny in the Punjab on hearing of British atrocities in Ireland; Private James Daly court-martialled and executed, and other mutineers sentenced to penal servitude (*see* 31 Oct. 1970).

29 June Dáil assembles for the first time since Oct. 1919; meeting in secret session on 11 July, it votes $1 million to the Department of Defence and establishes courts of justice and equity.

12 July Sir Edward Carson, speaking at Orange rally at Finaghy 'field', warns Britain: 'If . . . you are yourselves unable to protect us from the machinations of Sinn Féin . . . we tell you that we will take the matter into our own hands. We will reorganise.'

17 July Dáil Minister for Finance Michael Collins announces that the £250,000 internal National Loan issue has been over-subscribed by some £40,000.

19 July Sectarian violence erupts in Derry (which has a newly elected nationalist majority on council and a nationalist mayor); 19 killed and over 50 wounded in four days of continuous violence.

21 July 'Protestant and Unionist' workers at Workman & Clark's shipyard in Belfast, incited by Unionist politicians, resolve to drive out 'disloyal workers' (Sinn Féin and socialists); in three days of violence seven Catholics and six Protestants killed.

27 July British army ex-officers formed into the Auxiliary Division of the R.I.C. ('Auxiliaries').

6 Aug. Dáil sanctions boycott of goods emanating from Belfast.

8 Aug. Daniel Mannix, R.C. Archbishop of Melbourne, arrested at sea off Queenstown (Cóbh), Co. Cork, to prevent him speaking for nationalist cause; Dublin Corporation confers freedom of the city on him.

9 Aug. Restoration of Order in Ireland Act empowers authorities to impose curfews, restrict movement of traffic, establish military courts of inquiry to replace coroners' inquests, and provides for trial of civilians by court martial and imprisonment of Sinn Féiners on suspicion.

13 Aug. Anti-Partition League calls for settlement on Dominion basis.

22 Aug. Assassination in Lisburn, Co. Antrim, of District Inspector Swanzy, cited by Cork jury as being implicated in the murder by Crown forces of Tomás MacCurtain (*see* 20 Mar.); sparks off violence directed against nationalists in Lisburn and Belfast.

R.I.C. destroy creamery owned by Southern Unionist, Sir Thomas Cleeve, at Knocklong, Co. Limerick, which employed 50.

23 Aug. Six constables shot in ambush at Macroom, Co. Cork.

24 Aug. St Matthew's Church in the Short Strand and the Marrowbone, a Catholic area in north Belfast, attacked by Protestants. (By the end of the month there have been 180 fires, damage of around £1 million, 400 Catholic families have been driven from their homes, and 22 civilians are dead).

30 Aug. Army orders a curfew in Belfast (enforced until 1924).

2 Sept. British government concedes to Sir James Craig's demand for a force of full-time constabulary for the six-county state to be established under the Government of Ireland Act (recruitment begins on 1 Nov.).

9 Sept. Coroners' inquests abolished in 10 counties; replaced by secret military courts of inquiry.

20 Sept. Black and Tans raid Balbriggan, Co. Dublin.

Sept. 23 people killed in Belfast.

28 Sept. Liam Lynch and Ernie O'Malley lead I.R.A. capture of military barracks in Mallow, Co. Cork (the only military barracks captured by the I.R.A., during the War of Independence); leads to sack of the town by Crown forces in reprisal.

30 Sept. R.I.C. barracks captured and destroyed by the I.R.A. at Trim, Co. Meath; leads to sack of the town by Crown forces in reprisal.

14 Oct. Seán Treacy of the 3rd Tipperary Brigade, I.R.A., killed in gunbattle in Talbot Street, Dublin, in which Auxiliaries Lt Price and Sergeant Christian are also killed.

20 Oct. Summary by British Foreign Secretary to the House of Commons on I.R.A. activity from 1 Jan. 1919 to

18 Oct. 1920: courthouses destroyed, 64; vacated R.I.C. barracks destroyed, 492; vacated barracks damaged, 114; R.I.C.-occupied barracks destroyed, 21; R.I.C.-occupied barracks damaged, 48; raids on mails, 741; raids on coastguard stations and lighthouses, 40; policemen killed, 117; policemen wounded, 185; military killed, 23; military wounded, 71; civilians killed, 32; civilians wounded, 83; private residences of loyal citizens destroyed, 148.

24 Oct. Patrick McCartan, Dáil envoy in Washington, sends formal protest to the U.S. State Department, detailing British atrocities in Ireland.

25 Oct. Terence MacSwiney (41), Lord Mayor of Cork, arrested on 12 Aug., dies following 74 days of hunger-strike, at Brixton prison, London.

29 Oct. U.V.F. apprised of British government's intention to raise a force of special constabulary.

1 Nov. Kevin Barry (18), of Dublin I.R.A., executed for murder of an even younger soldier during I.R.A. raid in Dublin on 20 Sept.

Ulster Special Constabulary enrolled: 'A', full-time temporary constables; 'B', part-time, serving locally; 'C', emergency reserves.

2 Nov. Crown forces raid U.C.D. campus.

2–9 Nov. 'Battle of Ballinalee': I.R.A. unit under Gen. Seán Mac Eoin, having engaged R.I.C. in act of burning a priest's house, holds the town for some days; town burnt in reprisal when I.R.A. evacuate it.

14–15 Nov. Fr Michael Griffin, of Barna, Co. Galway, taken from his home to Crown military H.Q.; his body discovered next day near Barna with gunshot wounds.

16 Nov. American Association for the Recognition of the Irish Republic launched in the U.S.A. by de Valera; membership rises to 800,000 within the first year.

21 Nov. 'Bloody Sunday': I.R.A. 'squad' organised by Michael Collins kills 14 British secret service agents; Auxiliaries later kill prisoners at Dublin Castle (Dick McKee, Commdt of Dublin Brigade of the I.R.A., Peadar Clancy, Vice-Commdt, and Conor Clune); Black and Tans kill 12 during football match at Croke Park, including a player, Michael Hogan of Tipperary.

Three republican prisoners, Ernie O'Malley, Simon Donnelly and Frank Teeling, escape from Kilmainham jail, Dublin.

28 Nov. Gen. Tom Barry's Cork No. 3 (West Cork) Brigade wipes out 18–man Auxiliary patrol at Kilmichael (on Macroom-Dunmanway road, Co. Cork) with loss of two Volunteers.

5 Dec. d. Thomas William Rolleston (63), editor of *Dublin University Review* (1885–86), journalist and organiser at the Department of Agriculture and Technical Instruction.

10 Dec. Martial law proclaimed in Counties Cork, Kerry, Limerick and Tipperary.

11 Dec. I.R.A. ambush R.I.C. near Victoria Barracks, Cork city; rampaging Auxiliaries and Black and Tans later set fire to parts of the city (government claims that the arson was inflicted by citizens of Cork, but later pays £3 million compensation).

15 Dec. Septuagenarian Canon Magner, P.P. of Dunmanway, Co. Cork, and young parishioner, Timothy Crowley, shot dead by Auxiliary officer.

23 Dec. Act for the Better Government of Ireland creates states of Northern Ireland (six counties) and

Southern Ireland (26 counties) and a Council of Ireland; removes the restriction on Catholics holding office of L.L.; boycotted by Sinn Féin, which regards it as the 'partition act'.

De Valera arrives secretly in Dublin from the U.S.A., having spent 19 months away from Ireland on his American mission.

26 Dec. R.I.C. shoot five dead and injure 17 at dance at Bruff, Co. Limerick.

Pub. *The Hounds of Banba* by Daniel Corkery.

1921

1 Jan. Destruction of seven houses at Midleton, Co. Cork, by order of military signals beginning of government support for reprisals.

3 Jan. Cork's military governor, Gen. Strickland, commands the people 'under pain of death' to refuse succour to the I.R.A.

6 Jan. I.N.T.O. conference meets 'to frame a programme, or series of programmes, in accordance with Irish ideals and conditions – due regard being given to local needs and views'; report, signed on 28 Jan. 1922, becomes operational in the Free State on 1 Apr. 1922.

1 Feb. White Cross organisation founded by Sinn Féin to assist distribution of U.S.-based White Cross Fund.

4 Feb. Sir James Craig succeeds Sir Edward Carson as leader of the Ulster Unionists; appointed first Prime Minister of Northern Ireland on 7 June.

5 Feb. d. Katharine O'Shea Parnell (76), mistress of C. S. Parnell, whom she married on 25 June 1891.

Six republican prisoners executed in Cork; six British soldiers killed in Cork city.

19 Feb. Brig.-Gen. Frank Crozier, commandant of Auxiliaries, unable to curb the excesses of his command, resigns.

7 Mar. Unionist Anti-Partition League tries to bring Sinn Féin and British government together to discuss a more broadly based settlement.

George Clancy, Sinn Féin Mayor of Limerick, and Michael O'Callaghan, former Mayor, and Joseph O'Donoghue shot dead at their homes.

14 Mar. Six republican prisoners executed in Dublin.

1 Apr. As awards to seven Irish counties in respect of burnings, lootings and shootings reach £4,300,000, rates are drastically increased; in Co. Waterford alone an average increase of 35 per cent is levied.

9 Apr. d. William Walsh (80), R.C. Archbishop of Dublin since 1885.

13 Apr. Cabinet informed that cost of military campaign in Ireland is £20 million p.a. since 1919.

21 Apr. Lord Derby has secret meeting with Eamon de Valera in Dublin.

27 Apr. Pope Benedict XV donates £5,000 to help alleviate distress in Ireland.

2 May Viscount FitzAlan, first Catholic to hold the post since reign of James II, sworn in as L.L.

5 May Unproductive meeting in Dublin between P.M. Craig of Northern Ireland and de Valera.

13 May Nominations close for general elections to parliaments of Northern Ireland and Southern Ireland; 128 candidates nominated for 128 seats in Southern Ireland (124 Sinn Féin; 4 Independents (Unionists) representing Dublin University), all of whom are deemed to be elected.

24 May General election to the parliament of Northern Ireland (*see* 7 June); first in United Kingdom held under P.R.: Unionists 40; Sinn Féin, 6; Nationalists, 6.

25 May Custom House, Dublin, occupied by the Local Government Board, burnt by the I.R.A. (burns for five days); great destruction of local government records.

7 June Parliament of Northern Ireland meets; attended by Unionists only.

22 June George V during the opening of the parliament of Northern Ireland in the City Hall, Belfast, calls for reconciliation between the communities.

De Valera, arrested in Blackrock, Co. Dublin, is released on the intervention of the Assistant Under-Secretary, A. W. Cope.

28 June Parliament of Southern Ireland meets; attended by only 15 Senators (out of 64) and the 4 Dublin University M.P.s (out of 128 returned to the Commons); the 124 Sinn Féin members abstain; parliament adjourned *sine die* after fifteen minutes (*see* 16 Aug.).

4–8 July Meeting between de Valera, Arthur Griffith and Lord Midleton (representing Southern Unionists) at the Mansion House, Dublin; leads to Midleton acting as intermediary with Lloyd George, which leads to truce of 11 July.

9–15 July Reaction to the published draft terms of the truce causes rioting in east Belfast, resulting in 16 deaths, 68 serious injuries and destruction of Catholic-owned property.

11 July Truce in the Anglo-Irish war comes into effect.

14–21 July Three exploratory meetings in London between de Valera and Lloyd George; Lloyd George refuses to recognise the Irish Republic, and de Valera, with cabinet approval, rejects Dominion Home Rule.

13 Aug. Lloyd George in written reply to republican rejection of terms of settlement states that 'the British government could not acknowledge the right of Ireland to secede from allegiance to her King'.

16 Aug. Sinn Féin members returned in election to the parliament of Southern Ireland constitute themselves the Second Dáil Éireann and unanimously support cabinet rejection (on 10 Aug.) of terms of settlement.

29 Aug. Cardinal Logue, Archbishop of Armagh, rejects invitation from the Northern Ireland Minister of Education, Lord Londonderry, to nominate members of the proposed Commission on Education.

7 Sept. Frank Duff founds the Association of Our Lady of Mercy (renamed Legion of Mary on 15 Nov. 1925).

14 Sept. Dáil Éireann sanctions appointment of republican delegates to meet British representatives in London (Arthur Griffith, Michael Collins, George Gavan Duffy, Robert Barton and Eamonn Duggan).

23 Sept. U.S. Catholic hierarchy anticipating Anglo-Irish conference cables Cardinal Logue with expressions of sympathy with Ireland and good wishes for success at the conference.

29 Sept. Lloyd George offers de Valera the 'Gairloch Formula' for British and Irish representatives to meet 'with a view to ascertaining how the association of nations known as the British Empire may best be reconciled with Irish national aspirations'; accepted on 30th.

7 Oct. Treaty delegates conferred with credentials by Dáil cabinet, which also approves text of draft treaty 'A' as a discussion document.

9 Oct. Treaty delegates met by large crowd at London's Euston Station.

11 Oct. – 6 Dec. Anglo-Irish conference in London.

Nov. Communist Party of Ireland formed from the Socialist Party of Ireland, from which Roderick Connolly and Liam O'Flaherty expelled 'reformist' elements on 18 Oct.

5–10 Nov. Meetings between Lloyd George and Sir James Craig, during which Boundary Commission is mooted.

10 Nov. In a letter to P.M. Craig P.M. Lloyd George urges Northern Ireland to transfer legislative subordination from Westminster to a 'Dublin all-Ireland parliament'; rejected by Craig and the Unionist Party.

13 Nov. Arthur Griffith signs document for Lloyd George agreeing that Northern Ireland could stay outside a united Ireland if she agreed to a Boundary Commission (Lloyd George confronts him with this on 5 Dec.).

15–16 Nov. Southern Unionist representatives (Lord Midleton, J. H. Bernard and Andrew Jameson) consulted first by British government and then by Arthur Griffith in London.

17–18 Nov. National Unionist Association conference in Liverpool approves negotiations.

19–25 Nov. Rioting in Belfast leads to 27 deaths.

22 Nov. Northern Ireland government takes over imperial control of the R.I.C. and responsibility for law and order (under Minister of Home Affairs, Richard Dawson Bates).

5 Dec. P.M. Craig announces expansion of Northern Ireland Special Constabulary to bring 'A' Specials to 4,200, 'B' Specials to 8,500, and 'C' Specials to 22,000.

6 Dec. 18 Articles of Agreement and Annexe for a Treaty between Great Britain and Ireland (Anglo-Irish Treaty) signed in London at 2.10 a.m. under threat from P.M. Lloyd George of 'war within three days'.

8 Dec. De Valera denounces the Anglo-Irish Treaty as being 'in violent conflict with the wishes of the majority of this nation as expressed in successive elections during the past three years'.

9 Dec. British release interned I.R.A. members.

12 Dec. Dublin Committee of the Anti-Partition League accepts the Treaty.

14 Dec. Sir Edward Carson attacks the Treaty in the House of Lords.

Sir James Craig rejects the Boundary Commission clause in the Treaty and refuses to accept Sinn Féin's right to speak for all Ireland.

Dáil Éireann meets to debate the Treaty.

Local Government (Emergency Powers) Act empowers Northern Ireland government to dissolve any local council withholding recognition and co-operation (Fermanagh County Council dissolved on 21 Dec.).

14–16 Dec. U.K. parliament ratifies Treaty (Commons by majority of 343, Lords by majority of 119).

15 Dec. De Valera produces an alternative to the Articles of Agreement (Treaty) in a private session of Dáil Éireann; it becomes known as Document No. 2 (which he withdraws from consideration on 19 Dec.).

19 Dec. Arthur Griffith introduces motion, seconded by Seán Mac Eoin: 'That Dáil Éireann approves the Treaty between Great Britain and Ireland signed in London on December 6th, 1921' (*see* 7 Jan. 1922).

22 Dec. Dáil adjourns for Christmas (resumes on 3 Jan. 1922).

Pub. *Celtic Ireland* by Eoin Mac Néill.

Pub. *Michael Robartes and the Dancer* by W. B. Yeats.

1922

5 Jan. Pub. first issue of journal *The Republic of Ireland*, ed. Erskine Childers, stating the anti-Treaty case.

7 Jan. Dáil Éireann approves the Treaty (64–57).

9 Jan. De Valera resigns presidency of Dáil Éireann.

10 Jan. De Valera loses (60–58) on motion for his re-election as President of the Dáil; Arthur Griffith elected new President after de Valera and followers walk out before vote.

14 Jan. Meeting of members elected to sit in the House of Commons of Southern Ireland; attended by 60 pro-Treaty T.D.s and four (Unionist) M.P.s for Dublin University; boycotted by anti-Treaty T.D.s; resolutions are passed approving the Treaty and setting up a Provisional Government under chairmanship of Michael Collins (while the government of Dáil Éireann remains in existence under presidency of Arthur Griffith).

16 Jan. Michael Collins as Chairman of the Provisional Government takes formal control of Dublin Castle from L.L. FitzAlan.

Evacuation of British troops proceeds, as does disbanding of R.I.C.

19 Jan. Southern Unionists, meeting in the Engineers' Hall, Dawson Street, Dublin, resolve unanimously to recognise the Provisional Government and the Free State.

21 Jan. Craig-Collins agreement: Collins agrees to end the 'Belfast Boycott' (*see* 6 Aug. 1920); Craig undertakes to stop the attacks on Ulster Catholics and to protect Catholic workers in the Belfast shipyards; they also agree to accept findings of the Boundary Commission, but alter their positions later.

24 Jan. Provisional Government officially ends the 'Belfast Boycott' (remains unofficially in existence for another while).

30 Jan. First meeting of the committee to draft a constitution, under chairmanship of Michael Collins.

31 Jan. Free State army takes possession of its H.Q. at Beggars' Bush Barracks, Dublin.

2 Feb. Pub. *Ulysses* by James Joyce (Paris).

d. John Butler Yeats (83), artist, in New York; father of William Butler Yeats and Jack B. Yeats.

5 Feb. Cumann na mBan rejects the Treaty (419–63).

11 Feb. At Clones railway station, Co. Monaghan, four Special Constables and Commdt Fitzpatrick of the I.R.A. shot dead, leading to temporary suspension of evacuation of British troops.

12–15 Feb. 27 killed and 68 wounded in violence in Belfast.

21 Feb. Enlistment begins into police force of the Provisional Government; at first known as Civic Guard (*see* 8 Aug. 1923); the first member of the force is Patrick Joseph Kerrigan of Co. Mayo.

2 Mar. Anti-Treaty I.R.A. secure German arms landed at Helvic Head, Co. Waterford.

11 Mar. Following intervention of Oscar Traynor and Liam Lynch, anti-Treaty forces cede control of Limerick to pro-Treaty troops.

13–14 Mar. Lord Midleton discusses the problems of Unionists in the South of Ireland with Ministers of the Provisional Government.

14 Mar. T. K. Bewley, on loan to the Provisional Government from the British Treasury, takes up residence in Dublin (until 27 Jan. 1923), helping to organise the Irish Ministry of Finance.

15 Mar. Anti-Treaty minority form Cumann na Poblachta (League of the Republic) under the leadership of de Valera.

26–27 Mar. At Army Convention, held at the Mansion House and attended by 220 delegates representing 49 brigades of the I.R.A., anti-Treaty I.R.A. forms Executive Council under Oscar Traynor.

28 Mar. Rory O'Connor, on behalf of the 'Irregulars' (anti-Treaty I.R.A.), repudiates the authority of Dáil Éireann (*see* 13–14 Apr.).

29 Mar. Uniformed men, said to be 'B' Specials, shoot Catholic politician Owen McMahon and four members of his family dead at their home in Austin Road, Belfast.

Anti-Treaty supporters destroy machinery of the *Freeman's Journal*, which they allege has published misleading information on the Army Convention of 26–27 Mar.

Large quantity of explosives, guns and ammunition awaiting shipment to England captured by anti-Treaty forces at Cóbh, Co. Cork.

30 Mar. Craig-Collins Pact agreed in London: Craig agrees to recruit Catholics into the Special Constabulary and to reinstate Catholics in their jobs in the shipyards; Collins agrees to act against the I.R.A. units operating against the North from the South (neither side delivers on its undertakings).

Mar. 61 people die in outbreaks of violence in Northern Ireland.

1 Apr. Transfer of power from Britain to the Free State authority is officially signed by Churchill and Collins.

7 Apr. Civil Authorities (Special Powers) Act (N.I.) gives the Minister of Home Affairs power to detain suspects and set up courts of summary jurisdiction.

9 Apr. Anti-Treaty I.R.A. Executive appoints seven-man Army Council; Liam Lynch appointed Chief of Staff.

13–14 Apr. Rory O'Connor leads anti-Treaty I.R.A. in takeover of the Four Courts, Dublin, refusing to recognise the authority of the Provisional Government.

14 Apr. Anti-Treaty forces occupy Kilmainham jail, Dublin.

17 Apr. Rioting in Catholic Marrowbone area in north Belfast results in a Catholic and Protestant killed; some 50 homes in Antiqua and Saunderson Street burnt out.

23 Apr. Woman killed when a bomb is thrown at St Matthew's Church, Short Strand, Belfast.

24 Apr. General strike in protest against militarism takes place in Free State area, organised by the Labour Party.

25 Apr. Commdt O'Neill, 3rd Cork Brigade, I.R.A., shot dead at home of Protestant family (Hornibrooks) in Bandon, Co. Cork, leading to deaths by shooting of 10 Protestants in a series of reprisals.

26 Apr. Catholic hierarchy announces: 'We think that the best and wisest course for Ireland is to accept the Treaty and make the most of the freedom it undoubtedly brings us.'

27 Apr. Michael Collins protests to Sir James Craig against 'the abominations that have taken place in Belfast since signing of our pact'.

28 Apr. Lord Midleton discusses proposed Free State Constitution with ministers of the Provisional Government.

Apr. 36 die in outbreaks of violence in Northern Ireland.

1 May Commdt Tom Hales, 3rd Cork Brigade, I.R.A., publishes notice in national and local press promising 'all citizens in this area irrespective of creed or class every protection within my powers'.

Over £750,000 taken by anti-Treaty forces in raids on branches of the Bank of Ireland.

20 May Collins – de Valera Pact provides for Sinn Féin panel of candidates in the June general election to be drawn from pro- and anti-Treaty candidates in proportion to their existing Dáil strength; British government denounces the pact and summons Griffith and Collins to London (pact repudiated by Collins on 14 June).

20–22 May 14 killed in sectarian violence in Belfast; W. J. Twaddell, M.P. for West Belfast, shot dead in central Belfast (only M.P. in Northern Ireland to be killed until Rev. Robert Bradford in 1981).

27 May Draft Constitution of the Free State presented to the British government; rejected; compromise reached on 9 June.

31 May Shooting of two policemen in Belfast provokes indiscriminate reprisals; eight Catholics killed and over 80 Catholic families burnt out.

June – July Sectarian fighting in Belfast leads to death toll of 453 (257 Catholics, 157 Protestants, 2 of unknown affiliation, and 37 members of security forces); between 8,700 and 11,000 Catholics lose jobs, 23,000 forced from their homes, and 500 Catholic-owned businesses destroyed.

8 June Last meeting of the Second Dáil Éireann.

12–14 June British government and Provisional Government discuss proposed Free State Constitution; Provisional Government representatives also meet with Southern Unionist leaders.

15 June Draft Constitution of the Free State issued to the press for publication the next morning.

16 June General election in Free State area: Pro-Treaty, 58; Anti-Treaty, 36; Labour, 17; Farmers, 7; Independents, 6; University of Dublin (T.C.D.), 4 (*see* 9 Sept.).

18 June I.R.A. Convention meeting at the Mansion House, Dublin, splits on the issue of immediate resumption of I.R.A. offensive against British troops; the defeated minority, including three-quarters of the Executive, retire to the Four Courts.

22 June Gen. Sir Henry Wilson, military adviser to the government of Northern Ireland, shot dead in London; two Irishmen, Reginald Dunne and Joseph O'Sullivan, hanged for the crime on 10 Aug.

27–28 June Lt-Gen. J. J. ('Ginger') O'Connell captured by members of the Republican garrison in the Four Courts in reprisal for capture of Republican officer, Leo Henderson; Collins issues ultimatum, and bombardment of the Four Courts by the Provisional Government starts the Civil War (4 a.m. on 28th); first use of artillery by the Free State army.

30 June Four Courts abandoned by Republican garrison of 200, who blow up Public Record Office before surrender, when 1,000 prisoners are taken; street fighting continues until 5 July.

5 July Cathal Brugha, refusing order of his C.O. to surrender, is mortally wounded at the Hammam Hotel as he charges into the street with blazing guns (dies on 7th); Dublin now in the hands of the Provisional Government.

12 July War Council appointed by the Provisional Government; Michael Collins appointed C.-in-C.

20 July Limerick and Waterford fall to the Provisional Government.

Government revokes its stated intention to establish courts of law and equity and criminal jurisdiction; Gavan Duffy, Minister for Foreign Affairs and a distinguished lawyer, resigns in protest.

10 Aug. Free State troops enter Cork.

11 Aug. Anti-Treaty forces evacuate Fermoy, Co. Cork, last town under their control.

12 Aug. Arthur Griffith (51) dies in hospital (cerebral haemorrhage).

22 Aug. Michael Collins (31) shot dead during ambush at Béal na mBláth, Co. Cork, by Denis (Sonny) O'Neill (d. 1950).

25 Aug. William Thomas Cosgrave succeeds Collins as Chairman of the Provisional Government.

28 Aug. Huge crowds attend the funeral of Michael Collins in Dublin.

6 Sept. De Valera and Richard Mulcahy fail to agree a formula to enable anti-Treaty T.D.s to attend forthcoming Dáil session.

9 Sept. Third Dáil assembles (until 9 Aug. 1923); W. T. Cosgrave elected President; anti-Treaty deputies implement policy of abstentionism.

10 Sept. d. Wilfrid Scawen Blunt (82), Englishman active in Irish land agitation of the 1880s.

11 Sept. Local Government Act (N.I.) abolishes P.R. for local elections and requires declaration of allegiance from persons elected to or working for local authorities.

15 Sept. Appeal for writ of *habeas corpus* heard by the Lord Chief Justice at the King's Inns fails 'as state of war and rebellion exists' which justifies the application of martial law by the government.

18 Sept. Constitution Bill introduced by W. T. Cosgrave 'to enact a Constitution for Saorstát Éireann for implementing the Treaty between Great Britain and Ireland signed at London on the sixth day of December, 1921'.

28 Sept. Army Emergency Powers resolution approved by the Dáil (*see* 15 Oct.).

10 Oct. Catholic hierarchy issues joint pastoral condemning Republican resistance to the Free State: 'A republic without popular recognition behind it is a contradiction in terms.'

15 Oct. Army Emergency Powers becomes effective, empowering military courts to impose death penalty; 77 Republicans are executed in the Free State between 17 Nov. 1922 and 2 May 1923.

19 Oct. P.M. Lloyd George resigns; succeeded by Andrew Bonar Law (Conservative) on 23 Oct. (until 19 May 1923).

25 Oct. Constitution of the Irish Free State enacted by the Dáil; comes into force on 6 Dec.

De Valera declared 'President of the Irish Republic' by 'secret session' of 'alternative Dáil' composed of his followers.

27 Oct. District and parish courts established outside Dublin city.

31 Oct. John Leech, K.C., appointed by Northern Ireland government as commissioner to determine the new county council and rural district council areas.

2 Nov. Local Authorities (Election and Constitution) Act (N.I.) postpones local government elections until electoral areas have been examined.

15 Nov. General election in U.K.; Northern Ireland nationalists generally ignore the election, except in the two-seat constituency of Fermanagh and Tyrone, where Thomas J. S. Harbison and Cahir Healy (both Nationalist) top the polls; result: Unionists, 11; Nationalists, 2.

16 Nov. Irish peers in the House of Lords, meeting at Lord Oranmore's London home, decide not to oppose the Irish Free State Constitution Bill.

17 Nov. First executions of the Civil War: 'Irregulars' James Fisher, Peter Cassidy, John F. Gaffney and Richard Twohig at Kilmainham jail, Dublin.

24 Nov. Erskine Childers (arrested on 11th, found in possession of revolver, a present from Michael Collins) executed while awaiting appeal.

5 Dec. Irish Free State Constitution Act and the Consequential Provisions Act receive the royal assent; the King approves T. M. Healy as Governor-General designate of the Free State.

6 Dec. Saorstát Éireann (Irish Free State) comes into existence.

First issue of native postage stamp, value 2d, bearing white map of Ireland on green background.

7 Dec. Seán Hales, T.D., shot dead in Dublin and Pádraic Ó Máille, Leas Ceann Comhairle (Deputy Speaker) of the Dáil, wounded; in retaliation, the government the next morning executes the imprisoned Rory O'Connor, Liam Mellows, Joseph McKelvey and Richard Barrett (all imprisoned since fall of the Four Courts on 30 June).

Northern Ireland exercises its right to opt out of the Free State by petition to the King.

Anti-Partition League winds up its affairs; end of Irish Unionist Alliance activities in the South of Ireland.

10 Dec. Deliberate fire at the home of Seán McGarry, T.D., leads to the death of his son; inquest verdict of wilful murder.

11 Dec. First meeting of the Free State Senate; Lord Glenavy elected Chairman.

12 Dec. Duke of Abercorn sworn in as first Governor-General of Northern Ireland.

19 Dec. Meeting of the Oireachtas passes vote of thanks to the King for his address, read by the Governor-General.

Seven Republicans executed.

28 Dec. Commission on Agriculture established in Free State, chaired by James MacNeill (reports in Apr. 1924).

1923

1 Jan. De Valera announces plans for reorganising Sinn Féin.

8 Jan. Five Free State soldiers executed for 'treachery'.

12 Jan. Senator Oliver St John Gogarty escapes death at the hands of the anti-Treaty I.R.A. by swimming the Liffey.

13 Jan. Home of W. T. Cosgrave, President of the Executive Council, burnt down.

20 Jan. 11 Republicans executed; number of executed Republicans now 55 in 75 days.

23 Jan. Eight Protestant churches represented at the first meeting of the United Council of Christian Churches and Religious Communities in Ireland.

Jan. – Mar. Anti-Treaty I.R.A. campaign against political opponents includes the destruction of the homes of Senators: the Earl of Mayo and Sir Horace Plunkett (29 – 30 Jan.); Col. Maurice Moore and Thomas Linehan (1 Feb.); Dr William O'Sullivan (4 Feb.); Sir Bryan Mahon (16 Feb.); Sir John Kane (19 Feb.); Oliver St John Gogarty (23 Feb.); Sir Thomas Esmonde (9 Mar.).

8 Feb. Government offers amnesty to all who surrender with arms on or before 18 Feb.

11 Feb. Dr T. F. O'Higgins, father of Kevin O'Higgins (Minister for Home Affairs), shot dead at his home at Stradbally, Queen's County (Laois).

12 Feb. Anglo-Irish financial agreement signed by W. T. Cosgrave and Major John W. Hills under which Free State agrees to collect land annuities for transfer to London (worth some £3 million p.a.); details of agreement not published until 1932.

20 Feb. British government announces that approximately £1 million in respect of guns, ammunition, aeroplanes and motor vehicles has been received from the Free State government during the current financial year.

22 Feb. William O'Brien becomes first Chairman of the Free State Revenue Commissioners.

6 Mar. Report of the Blythe Commission on administrative reform in Free State (approved by Executive Council on 20 Mar.; leads to Ministers and Secretaries Act, 1924).

7 Mar. In one of the worst atrocities of the Civil War eight Republicans at Ballyseedy, Co. Kerry, are killed when, while they are tied to a log, Free State soldiers throw a mine amongst them; one survives and escapes.

8 Mar. Executive Council approves appointment of Joseph Brennan to position of Secretary of the Department of Finance (until Sept. 1927).

17 Mar. Clare-born Mike McTigue defeats Battling Siki in Dublin to win the World Light-Heavyweight Boxing Championship.

28 Mar. Local Government (Temporary Provisions) Act abolishes workhouse system in the Free State, providing alternatives through local authorities.

31 Mar. – 1 Apr. Separation of Free State fiscal system from U.K.; customs and excise barriers effective between Free State and U.K.

10 Apr. Liam Lynch (33), Chief of Staff of the anti-Treaty I.R.A., shot and mortally wounded by Free State troops in the Knockmealdown mountains, Co. Waterford; dies at Mitchelstown, Co. Cork.

12 Apr. *The Shadow of a Gunman* by Seán O'Casey, opens at the Abbey.

14 Apr. Austin Stack captured by Free State troops.

17 Apr. Dan Breen captured by Free State troops.

27 Apr. De Valera offers terms for negotiation to end the war which are rejected by the Free State.

30 Apr. James Larkin returns to Ireland from U.S.A. (*see* 3 June).

8 May First Free State Civil Service Commission appointed; chairman

Michael Hayes, with James O'Neill and C. J. Gregg.

19 May P.M. Andrew Bonar Law (Conservative) resigns; succeeded by Stanley Baldwin (Conservative) on 22 May.

24 May De Valera issues proclamation: 'Soldiers of the Republic, Legion of the Rearguard . . . Military victory must be allowed to rest for the moment with those who have destroyed the Republic'; Frank Aiken, new Chief of Staff, calls for a dumping of arms; fighting in the Civil War ends.

3 June Rift between James Larkin and William O'Brien of the I.T.G.W.U. leads to split in the labour movement (*see* 15 June).

8 June Board of Commissioners of Intermediate Education in Free State dissolved; replaced by two commissioners (Seosamh Ó Néill and Proinnsias Ó Dubhthaigh) (*see* 1 June 1924).

15 June James Larkin and his brother Peter form the Workers' Union of Ireland (W.U.I.).

22 June Education Act (N.I.) restructures primary and secondary education; provides for religious education as a voluntary appendage to a secular system.

Public Record Office of Northern Ireland (P.R.O.N.I.) established.

1 July Number of military prisoners in Free State officially estimated at 11,316.

16 July Censorship of Films Act (I.F.S.).

20 July Eoin Mac Néill announced as Free State representative on the Boundary Commission.

24 July Land Law (Commission) Act (I.F.S.) dissolves the Congested Districts Board and transfers its functions to the Land Commission.

31 July Appellate Court orders release of Mrs Nora Connolly O'Brien on the grounds that the state of war is over, but the Free State government detains her under an order of the Public Safety Act of 1 Aug.

1 Aug. Public Safety (Emergency Powers) Act permits Free State government to detain internees.

Pub. first issue of *Dublin Magazine*, published by Séamus O'Sullivan (James Sullivan Starkey); appears until Apr./June issue 1958.

3 Aug. Free State government passes Indemnity Bill to protect government forces from the consequences of actions taken by them against Republicans.

8 Aug. Civic Guard (*see* 21 Feb. 1922) reconstituted and renamed the Garda Síochána under act.

9 Aug. Hogan's Land Act (I.F.S.) makes compulsory the sale of all land not yet dealt with; first act to empower the state to acquire land through compulsory purchase.

Dáil dissolved (*see* 19 Sept.).

15 Aug. De Valera arrested in Ennis during election rally where his opponent is Eoin Mac Néill (released on 16 July 1924).

27 Aug. General election in Free State; Cumann na nGaedheal, 63; Sinn Féin, 44 (abstentionists); Labour, 14; Farmers, 15; Independents, 16; Independent Labour, 1; all government ministers are returned; in Clare constituency de Valera receives twice as many votes as Mac Néill.

10 Sept. Free State admitted to the League of Nations.

19 Sept. Fourth Dáil assembles (until 23 May 1927); W. T. Cosgrave (Cumann na nGaedheal) elected President of the Executive Council.

14 Oct. – 23 Nov. Several hundred Republican prisoners on hunger-strike in Free State; two die before strike is called off.

9 Nov. Seven Free State army officers at the Curragh refuse to accept demobilisation papers and are arrested and court-martialled; leads to involvement of nearly 60 officers in all (*see* 6–12 Mar. 1924).

14 Nov. W. B. Yeats becomes first Irishman to win the Nobel Prize for Literature (presented in Stockholm on 10 Dec.).

Dec. Free State Fiscal Inquiry Committee (appointed in June), chaired by T. A. Smiddy, issues report.

5 Dec. d. Edward Martyn (64), playwright and music-lover; established Palestrina Choir (1899).

7 Dec. Close of the first Free State National Loan (over-subscribed by £200,000); at first dealings on 7 Jan. 1924 on Dublin Stock Exchange it rises 4 points to 99.

1924

16 Jan. Renewal of Public Safety Act (I.F.S.) allows imprisonment without trial.

22 Jan. Free State cabinet approves the draft Old Age Pensions Bill which, on the recommendation of the Minister for Finance, Ernest Blythe, provides for an 'immediate all-round reduction . . . by 1s per week' (Old Age Pensions Act, 5 June).

James Ramsay MacDonald becomes first Labour P.M. (minority government) (*see* 4 Nov.).

18 Feb. Executive Council proposes to cut numbers in army by almost half, from 60,000 to 35,000 (*see* 6–12 Mar.).

6–12 Mar. Army Mutiny: Free State army officers issue ultimatum to the Executive Council, demanding removal of the Army Council, an end to demobilisation, and a declaration of the Free State government's intention to achieve an Irish Republic; leaders arrested.

7 Mar. Joseph McGrath, Minister for Industry and Commerce, resigns in protest at Executive Council's handling of the Army Mutiny; succeeded by Patrick McGilligan.

10 Mar. Gen. Eoin O'Duffy, Commissioner of the Garda Síochána, seconded to command of the Free State army.

12 Mar. Army Mutiny ends: committee of inquiry established to look into administration of the army; personnel requirements to be reviewed; no victimisation of those officers and men who returned to their posts; guarantee of army service pension.

19 Mar. In face of Executive Council criticism of attempts to arrest Army Mutiny leaders, Gen. Richard Mulcahy, Minister for Defence, resigns (post held by W. T. Cosgrave until Peter Hayes appointed on 21 Nov.).

21 Mar. Machine-gun attack on British soldiers vacating Spike Island at Cóbh; one soldier dead, 18 soldiers and five civilians wounded.

12 Apr. Free State judiciary reorganised.

21 Apr. Ministers and Secretaries Act regulates Free State government departments.

26 Apr. Following two inconclusive meetings between W. T. Cosgrave and Sir James Craig, the Free State government informs the British government of the impossibility of amicable agreement on territorial division between the Free State and Northern Ireland, and requests that in conformity with the Treaty (Article 12) a Boundary Commission be set up.

10 May P.M. Craig formally refuses to nominate Northern Ireland representative to the Boundary Commission (Westminster appoints J. R. Fisher on 24 Oct.).

20 May Executive Council dissolves the Dublin Corporation; municipality of Dublin administered by three commissioners (until 13 Oct. 1930).

1 June Free State Department of Education assumes centralised educational control; Intermediate Education (Amendment) Act establishes the Intermediate and Leaving Certificate Examinations; Irish declared compulsory for Intermediate in 1928 and for the Leaving in 1934 (compulsion abolished in 1973).

5 June Mr Justice Richard Feetham, Judge of the Supreme Court of South Africa, appointed chairman of the Boundary Commission.

1 July Free State Air Corps formed under Major-Gen. McSweeney.

11 July Free State registers Anglo-Irish Treaty with the League of Nations.

23 July Railway Act amalgamates the companies operating in the Free State into the Great Southern Railway Company.

2–17 Aug. Tailteann Games held at Croke Park, Dublin.

5 Aug. Military Pensions Act (I.F.S.) provides pensions for those who served in government forces from 1922 to 1923 and in the Irish Volunteers and I.R.A. from 1916 to 1921.

12 Aug. Anglo-Irish agreement: Britain to pay £900,000 to the Free State 'in full and final discharge of all liabilities of or claims against the British government in respect of compensation for damage to property in Ireland prior to the truce'.

14 Aug. Free State government receives Leinster House from the R.D.S. (becomes home of the Dáil and the Senate).

7 Oct. Sir James Craig states at the opening of the parliament of Northern Ireland that if the decision of the Boundary Commission is unacceptable to the parliament of Northern Ireland and if no honourable alternative can be found, he will resign to lead defence of any territory deemed unfairly transferred.

14 Oct. Civil War damage to rolling stock forces the closure of the Listowel–Ballybunion Lartigue Railway (monorail) in Kerry (*see* 29 Feb. 1888).

1 Nov. De Valera, arrested while speaking in support of a Sinn Féin candidate in Derry on 26 Oct., receives one month's imprisonment.

4 Nov. Stanley Baldwin (Conservative) appointed P.M.

Sinn Féin Ard-Fheis re-elects de Valera President.

6 Nov. First meeting of the Boundary Commission, in London (*see* 7 Nov. 1925).

8 Nov. Free State government declares amnesty for offences committed between 6 Dec. 1921 and 12 May 1923.

18 Nov. Free State government wins three of five by-elections; Sinn Féin wins the other two, showing a total gain of 29,000 votes since the general election of 1923.

19 Nov. d. Michael, Cardinal Logue (84), R.C. Archbishop of Armagh and Primate since 1887.

Fr Michael O'Flanagan commences the monumental task of editing John O'Donovan's archaeological survey (the fifty volumes completed in 1932).

end Nov. 14 vacancies in Dáil Éireann, 9 of them created by resignations of Joseph McGrath and his followers (*see* 7 Mar.).

19 Dec. Pub. last issue of the *Freeman's Journal* (started in 1763).

1925

27 Jan. Coimisiún na Gaeltachta established to inquire into the preservation of Irish-speaking areas in the Free State.

17 Feb. d. George Sigerson (89), scholar.

2 Apr. Act amalgamates Dublin Metropolitan Police with the Garda Síochána.

3 Apr. General election in N.I.: Unionists, 32; Independent Unionists, 4; Nationalists, 10; Republicans, 2; Labour, 3; Independent, 1 (*see* 28 Apr.).

14 Apr. First competitive examinations for entry to the Free State civil service held.

28 Apr. Joseph Devlin and T. S. MacAllister become first Nationalists to take their seats in the parliament of Northern Ireland.

28 May Unpurchased tenanted land in Northern Ireland vested in the Land Purchase Commission.

7 June d. Matt Talbot (69); cause for beatification now (1989) under consideration.

9 June d. Sir Antony MacDonnell (81), Baron MacDonnell of Swinford, Under-Secretary (1902–8).

4 July Shannon Electricity Act authorises the Shannon hydro-electric scheme at Ardnacrusha, Co. Clare.

7 Nov. *Morning Post* publishes 'leak' on the findings of the Boundary Commission, indicating that there will be no major change.

14 Nov. I.R.A. Convention; I.R.A. withdraws its allegiance from the de Valera 'Republican government' and establishes its own supreme authority, the Army Council.

20 Nov. Eoin Mac Néill resigns from the Boundary Commission; resigns as Minister for Education on 24th.

50 Republicans recently released from internment rearrested in the Catholic quarter of Belfast.

24 Nov. Kevin O'Higgins represents Free State at conference in London to discuss implications of Boundary Commission report (*see* 3 Dec.).

3 Dec. Tripartite agreement signed by Craig, Cosgrave and Baldwin shelving the Boundary Commission report and recognising the existing border between Northern Ireland and the Free State; powers of Council of Ireland in relation to Northern Ireland transferred to Northern Ireland government; Free State released from liability to portion of the British public debt and accepts liability for malicious damage since 21 Jan. 1919.

5 Dec. Irish Labour Party publishes manifesto denouncing agreement of 3 Dec. as an 'unmitigated betrayal'.

10 Dec. P.M. Craig announces that the 'A' Special Constabulary will be disbanded; 'A' Specials force conditions on the government before they disband.

Pub. *The Informer* by Liam O'Flaherty.

Pub. *Storm* by Peadar O'Donnell.

Pub. *The Hidden Ireland* by Daniel Corkery.

1926

1 Jan. Radio 2RN, the national broadcasting station of the Free State, opened by Dr Douglas Hyde (later known as Radio Éireann).

8 Feb. *The Plough and the Stars* by Séan O'Casey opens at the Abbey; rioting, organised by outraged nationalists, breaks out three days later.

5 Mar. Report of the conference on education in the Free State signed (I.N.T.O. seeks limitation of the compulsory subjects, Irish, English and Arithmetic).

8 Mar. Free State Banking Commission appointed under chairmanship of Professor Henry Parker-Willis (final report on 31 Jan. 1927); leads to Currency Act, 1927.

9–11 Mar. Sinn Féin Ard-Fheis; de Valera resigns presidency (*see* 16 May).

19 Mar. Ernest Blythe, Free State Minister for Finance, and Winston Churchill, British Secretary of State for the Colonies, sign Ultimate Financial Agreement: British Treasury waives some claims against Free State, which in turn agrees to honour payments of land annuities and undertakes payments of pensions to former members of the R.I.C.

16 May De Valera inaugurates Fianna Fáil party at La Scala Theatre, Dublin.

29 May Enforcement of Court Order Act (I.F.S.).

14 June d. Windham Thomas Wyndham-Quin (85), 4th Earl of Dunraven and Mount Earl, land reformer.

28 July Local Appointments Commission established to fill positions in local government in the Free State.

4 Aug. R.D.S. hosts its first international horse-jumping competition.

12 Aug. d. Sir William Ridgeway (73), scholar.

Sept. Capt. William Redmond launches the National League party.

5 Sept. 49 burnt to death at a cinema in Drumcollogher, Co. Limerick, during a showing of *The Ten Commandments*.

5 Oct. First meeting of the Technical Education Commission (Ingram Commission) 'to inquire into and advise upon the system of technical education in Saorstát Éireann in relation to the requirements of Trade and Industry' (reports on 5 Oct. 1927).

11 Nov. George Bernard Shaw awarded the Nobel Prize for Literature.

14 Nov. I.R.A. attacks on several garda barracks lead to deaths of two gardaí.

19 Nov. Public Safety (Emergency Powers) Act empowers the Free State government to declare a state of national emergency to deal with problem posed by I.R.A. violence.

Imperial Conference, attended by Free State, leads to definition of British Dominions as 'autonomous within the British Empire, equal in status, in no way subordinate one to another' (*see* 11 Dec. 1931).

24 Nov. First Fianna Fáil Ard-Fheis.

2 Dec. Tariff Commission appointed to examine applications for economic protection in the Free State.

Census of population: Free State: 2,971,992 (decrease of 5.34 per cent since 1911); Northern Ireland: 1,256,561 (increase of 0.5 per cent since 1911).

1927

1 Jan. Compulsory attendance at school for children between 6 and 14 becomes operative in the Free State (limit raised to 15 on 1 July 1972).

20 Jan. P.M. Sir James Craig created Viscount Craigavon of Stormont.

6 Apr. Dan Breen, Republican T.D., who had entered the Dáil despite the scruples of de Valera about the oath of allegiance, proposes the abolition of the oath.

19 Apr. First greyhound track in Ireland opens at Celtic Park, Belfast.

21 Apr. Ernest Blythe announces the establishment of the Economy Committee 'to bring about the economies which are requisite within the next couple of years'; first meets on 30 May (reports on 30 Nov. 1931).

23 May Dáil dissolved.

28 May Agricultural Credit Act (I.F.S.) authorises establishment of the Agricultural Credit Corporation.

Electricity (Supply) Act (I.F.S.) provides for the establishment of the Electricity Supply Board (E.S.B.) (established on 11 Aug.).

9 June General election in Free State: Cumann na nGaedheal, 47; Fianna Fáil, 44; Labour, 22; Farmers, 11; National League, 8; Sinn Féin, 5; Independents, 14; Independent Republicans, 2.

22 June Fifth Dáil assembles; Cosgrave re-elected President of the Executive Council; Fianna Fáil refuse to take the oath.

10 July Kevin O'Higgins, Minister for Justice, assassinated by Republicans (Timothy Gaughan, Archie Doyle and Bill Gannon, whose identities became known only in Oct. 1985).

15 July d. Countess Markievicz (59), Minister for Labour (1919–21).

20 July Free State government introduces emergency legislation: Public Safety Bill (*see* 11 Aug.) and Electoral (Amendment No. 2) Bill (*see* 9 Nov.).

28 July Ireland's first automatic telephone exchange, catering for 700 customers, opens at Ship Street, Dublin.

4 Aug. d. John Dillon (76), politician (Home Rule); last leader of party from Mar. 1918.

11 Aug. Public Safety Act empowers Free State government to declare unlawful any organisation which seeks the overthrow of the state.

De Valera, having described the oath as 'merely an empty political formula', leads 42 followers into the Dáil, having subscribed to the necessary form of the oath; they take their seats the next day.

16 Aug. Thomas Johnson, leader of the Labour Party, moves 'That the Executive Council has ceased to retain the support of a majority in Dáil Éireann'; absence of John Jinks results in tie (71–71), resolved by Ceann Comhairle's casting his vote for the Executive Council.

20 Aug. Currency Act establishes separate currency for the Free State (*see* 12 Dec. 1928).

25 Aug. Dáil dissolved.

15 Sept. General election in Free State: Cumann na nGaedheal, 62; Fianna Fail, 57; Labour, 13; Farmers, 6; National League, 2; Independents, 12; Independent Labour, 1.

21 Sept. J. J. McElligott succeeds Joseph Brennan as Secretary of the Department of Finance.

11 Oct. Sixth Dáil assembles; Cosgrave re-elected President of the Executive Council.

22 Oct. d. Patrick, Cardinal O'Donnell (71), R.C. Archbishop of Armagh and Primate since 1924.

28 Oct. Cleggan Disaster: 16 fishermen drowned off the coast of Galway, nine of them from Inishbofin.

9 Nov. Electoral (Amendment No. 2) Act (I.F.S.) requires that candidates before nomination must declare their intention of taking the prescribed oath if elected.

Pub. *Report of the Commission on the Relief of the Sick and Destitute Poor, including the Insane Poor* (I.F.S.).

Pub. *The Archaeology of Ireland* by Robert A. S. Macalister.

1928

7 Jan. d. Francis Elrington Ball (65), historian (author of *The Judges of Ireland,* 1926).

25 Jan. d. James Brown Armour (87) ('Armour of Ballymoney'), dissident Presbyterian minister.

25 Feb. d. William O'Brien (76), politician (Home Rule), founder of United Irish League (1898), journalist (editor of *United Ireland* in 1880s) and author.

21 Mar. Seán Lemass describes Fianna Fáil as 'a slightly constitutional party' in the Dáil, adding: 'Our object is to establish a republican government in Ireland. If that can be done by the present methods we have, we will be very pleased, but, if not, we would not confine ourselves to them.'

12–13 Apr. *Bremen,* monoplane, crewed by Col. James Fitzmaurice, Capt. Hermann Köhl and Baron Günther von Hünefeld, flies from Baldonnell Airport, Co. Dublin, to Greenly Island, Labrador; first east–west transatlantic flight, at an average speed of 59 m.p.h., in 36½ hours; carries two copies of the *Irish Times,* first European newspaper to cross the Atlantic by air.

May Joseph Devlin forms the National League of the North.

3–7 May De Valera fails in his attempt to present to the Dáil a petition (96,000 signatures) seeking a referendum on an amendment to abolish the oath (*see* 12 July).

18 May d. Standish James O'Grady (82), historian and novelist.

12 July Act abolishes the right to referendum under the Free State Constitution.

30 July Irish tricolour raised for the first time at the Olympic Games as Dr Pat O'Callaghan becomes first citizen of an independent Ireland to win a gold medal at an Olympic Games (Amsterdam; hammer-throw).

27 Aug. Taibhdhearc na Gaillimhe (Galway Gaelic Theatre) opens with *Diarmaid agus Gráinne* by Mícheál Mac Liammóir (co-founder of the theatre).

29 Sept. d. John Devoy (86), Fenian.

6 Oct. d. Pádraic Ó Conaire (46), writer and story-teller in Irish.

10 Oct. Irish Manuscripts Commission established; chairman Eoin Mac Néill (until 1945).

14 Oct. Dublin Gate Theatre Studio, founded by Mícheál Mac Liammóir and Hilton Edwards, opens at the Peacock Theatre with *Peer Gynt* (company moves to its own premises in 1930).

5 Dec. First meeting of the all-party Dáil Economic Committee 'to inquire into the general economic situation in Saorstát Éireann'.

12 Dec. Issue of new Free State currency, designed by Percy Metcalfe.

New Free State Senate meets; T. W. Westropp Bennett elected Chairman.

Pub. *Islanders* by Peadar O'Donnell.

1929

23 Feb. Managerial system of local government piloted in Cork (Cork City Management Act).

KILKENNY COUNTY LIBRARY

27 Feb. Formal order for closure of Kilmainham jail, Dublin (which had housed Republican prisoners during the Civil War).

16 Apr. P.R. abolished in Northern Ireland.

6 May First issue of new Free State banknotes.

22 May General election in N.I.: Unionists, 37; National League, 11; Independent Unionists, 3; Labour, 1. Craigavon continues as P.M.

28 May d. Senator Mrs Alice Stopford Green (82), historian (author of *The Making of Ireland and Its Undoing*, 1908).

June Primary Certificate, examination to be taken at the end of sixth class in Free State primary schools, introduced as an option; made compulsory in Irish, English and Arithmetic in 1943; abolished in 1967).

5 June James Ramsay MacDonald (Labour) again appointed P.M. (minority government).

16 June Start of countrywide week-long festivities to mark the centenary of Catholic Emancipation.

1 July First screening, at the Capitol Cinema, Dublin, of Ireland's first sound film, documentary on the Catholic Emancipation centenary ceremonies.

16 July Censorship of Publications Act (I.F.S.).

29 July Official opening of Ardnacrusha Hydro-electric Station in Co. Clare; begins commercial operations on 21 Oct.

14 Sept. Free State signs Article 36 (Optional Clause) of the Permanent Court of International Justice at Geneva, without reservation (recognising as compulsory the jurisdiction of the court in justiciable disputes between signatories) (approved by Dáil on 26 Feb. 1930 and by Senate on 7 May 1930).

23 Oct. Security prices crumble in a wave of panic selling on Wall Street, New York; crisis temporarily averted by J. P. Morgan & Co.

29 Oct. 'Black Tuesday': 16,410,030 shares of stock sold as Wall Street crashes; followed by economic depression which affects the world's economies.

18 Nov. d. Thomas Power (T. P.) O'Connor (81), politician (Home Rule) and journalist; first official film censor (from 1917).

29 Nov. Savoy Cinema in Dublin opened by W. T. Cosgrave; première of *Ireland*, documentary produced by the government.

20 Dec. Act authorises grants and loans for housing in Gaeltacht areas of Free State.

25 Dec. Celebrated 'missing postman' case: postman Larry Griffin left his Kilmacthomas, Co. Waterford, home and was never seen again.

Pub. *Recollections of an Irish Rebel* by John Devoy.

Pub. *An tOileánach* by Tomás Ó Criomthain (English translation by Robin Flower in 1934).

1930

17 Feb. Mícheál Mac Liammóir and Hilton Edwards open the Gate Theatre with Goethe's *Faust*.

26 Feb. National Monuments Act (I.F.S.).

Mar. Pub. first issue of *Analecta Hibernica*, published by the Irish Manuscripts Commission.

1 Apr. Irish Trade Union Congress and Labour Party splits into two separate organisations (I.T.U.C.; Labour Party).

17 June Education Act (N.I.) grants representation on local authority school committees to nominees of former managers, empowers minister to pay half cost of building and equipping new voluntary schools, and requires local authority schools to provide undenominational Bible instruction if requested by 10 parents (children whose parents disapprove are not required to attend).

17 July Local Government (Dublin) Act extends administrative area of the city; 35-member council and a city manager.

21 July Vocational Education Act (I.F.S.) establishes 38 vocational education committees, funded by state and local authorities from the rates, to cater for general and technical education at second level.

17 Sept. Free State elected to the Council of the League of Nations.

Nov. Free State imposes duty on imported butter.

17 Nov. In first Irish Sweepstakes draw (inaugurated on 4 June by Joseph McGrath) three Belfastmen share £208,792 first prize.

31 Dec. Mayo County Council dissolved by ministerial order for refusing to appoint Miss Letitia Dunbar-Harrison, a Protestant, recommended candidate of the Local Appointments Commission for position of County Librarian.

Release of *Song O' My Heart*, starring John McCormack; first attempt to break with Hollywood stage-Irish conventions (McCormack received £100,000 for the 11 songs in the film).

1931

30 Jan. Patrick J. Carroll, police agent in the I.R.A., shot dead in Dublin.

22 Mar. d. James Henry Mussen Campbell (80), 1st Baron Glenavy, lawyer, first Chairman of the Free State Senate (1922–28).

26 Mar. d. Timothy Michael Healy, politician (Home Rule) and first Governor-General of the Free State (1922–28).

30 Mar. Garda Superintendent Seán Curtin shot dead near his home in Tipperary by I.R.A. after he had taken action to prevent illegal drilling in the area.

2 Apr. d. Katharine Tynan (Hinkson) (70), poet and novelist.

7 May An Óige, Irish hostelling movement, founded by T. Trench to provide hostel accommodation for hikers and cyclists.

17 May Muintir na Tíre founded by Canon John Hayes.

24 Aug. Ramsay MacDonald's Labour government resigns; he forms national coalition government.

5 Sept. Pub. first issue of the *Irish Press*, founded by Eamon de Valera.

21 Sept. Britain abandons the gold standard.

29 Sept. d. Sir William Orpen (52), painter; official war artist, 1914–18.

17 Oct. Constitution (Amendment No. 17) Act (I.F.S.), a new Public Safety Act, establishes a five-member military tribunal to deal with political crime (*see* 18 Mar. 1932).

18 Oct. Joint pastoral of the Catholic bishops read out in every Catholic church, condemning the I.R.A. and denouncing Saor Éire as a 'frankly communistic organisation'.

20 Oct. Constitution (Declaration of Unlawful Associations) Order outlaws the I.R.A., Saor Éire and 10 other organisations in Free State (*see* 18 Mar. 1932).

30 Oct. Supplementary budget in Free State: petrol to rise 4d per gallon and income tax by 6d in the £ sterling.

6 Nov. Custom Duties (Provisional Imposition) Act allows imposition or variation of duties to prevent dumping of goods in the Free State (first duties imposed on 20 Nov.).

11 Dec. Statute of Westminster empowers any Dominion parliament to repeal or amend any act of the U.K. parliament which is part of Dominion law (opposed by Winston Churchill).

Pub. *Guests of the Nation*, first collection of short stories by Frank O'Connor.

Pub. *Mise agus an Conradh* by Douglas Hyde.

1932

17 Jan. d. Louis Brennan (80), inventor (dirigible torpedo and gyrostat monorail).

29 Jan. Dáil dissolved.

9 Feb. Army Comrades' Association formed by Commdt Edward Cronin, as a benevolent society for ex-members of the Free State army (*see* 11 Aug.).

Fianna Fáil election manifesto states that the party was seeking a mandate to retain the land annuities in the Free State treasury; 'The British government is neither legally nor justly entitled to receive them' (*see* 11 July).

16 Feb. General election in Free State: Fianna Fáil, 72; Cumann na nGaedheal, 57; Labour, 7 Farmers, 3; Independents, 14; Independent Labour, 14.

29 Feb. U.K. Import Duties Act introduces general tarrifs.

9 Mar. Seventh Dáil assembles; de Valera forms first Fianna Fáil government.

10 Mar. De Valera's government releases political prisoners.

18 Mar. Order suspends military tribunal, and order declaring the I.R.A. illegal lapses (*see* 17 *and* 20 Oct. 1931).

26 Mar. d. Sir Horace Plunkett (78), founder of the Irish co-operative movement.

27 Apr. Dáil debate on the oath of allegiance (*see* 19 May).

5 May Seán T. O'Kelly heads cabinet committee to recommend how to effect 'the reductions necessary in the remuneration of the civil service, Civic Guards, teachers and the army'; cuts of from 2 per cent to 20 per cent approved two days later (*see* 20 Sept.).

19 May Constitution (Removal of Oath) Bill passes the Dáil (*see* 3 May 1933); returned to Dáil with amendment by the Senate on 28 June.

20 May First transatlantic solo flight by a woman pilot, Amelia Earhart, from Harbour Grace, Newfoundland, ends in Culmore, Co. Londonderry – 2,206 miles in 13 hours.

22 May d. Augusta, Lady Gregory (80), co-founder of the Abbey Theatre (1904); playwright.

19 June 15,000 parade in military formation to Bodenstown, Co. Kildare, inspected by Moss Twomey, Chief of Staff of the I.R.A.

22–26 June 31st Eucharistic Congress, held in Dublin, formally opened by Cardinal Legate, Lorenzo Lauri; includes commemoration of the 1,500th anniversary of St Patrick's arrival in Ireland.

First appearance of 'Blue Huzzars' or mounted escort (duties taken over by cavalry motor-cycle escort in 1948).

30 June Government states that it is withholding payment of land annuities (worth £1½ million) due to the British Treasury, prompting an 'Economic War' between Free State and Britain (until 25 Apr. 1938).

11 July Irish Free State (Special Duties) Act permits the British government to collect sums due from the Free State by means of 20 per cent duties on butter, eggs, poultry, cream, game and live animals from the Free State; effective from 15 July (*see* 23 July).

11–12 July Publication, against de Valera's wishes, of correspondence between himself and the Governor-General, James MacNeill, covering MacNeill's complaints of 'calculated' discourtesy to the Governor-General by ministers.

15 July Unproductive meeting in London to discuss the land annuities dispute between de Valera and P.M. MacDonald.

21 July – 20 Aug. Seán T. O'Kelly heads Free State delegation at the Imperial Trade Conference, Ottawa, where it enters into trade agreements with the other Dominions, but not with Britain.

23 July Emergency Imposition of Duties Act empowers Free State government to retaliate against customs duties imposed by U.K.

1 Aug. Dr Pat O'Callaghan wins his second Olympic gold medal at Los Angeles in hammer event (*see* 22 Aug. 1937); Bob Tisdal wins gold in the 400 metres hurdles.

11 Aug. Dr T. F. O'Higgins elected president of the Army Comrades' Association, whose support he pledges 'to the lawfully constituted government of the state' and total opposition to communism; extends its membership to those who seek to uphold freedom of speech.

15 Sept. Farmers' organisation formed by Patrick Belton and Frank McDermot; becomes the National Farmers' and Ratepayers' League on 6 Oct.; later, with James Dillon, becomes the National Centre Party.

20 Sept. 'Cuts' committee established, chaired by Philip O'Connell, to advise on implementation of reductions in the pay of public and civil servants (report presented on 26 Oct., but only signed by three of the five members).

26 Sept. De Valera, Minister for External Affairs, makes inaugural speech as Chairman of the League of Nations assembly, Geneva.

30 Sept. Last sitting in the Belfast City Hall of the Northern Ireland parliament, marked by Jack Beattie, M.P. for Pottinger, throwing the mace on the floor as he complains about parliament's complacency in the face of widespread unemployment.

3 Oct. 600 outdoor relief workers in Belfast, organised by Tommy Geehan and Betty Sinclair of the Belfast Trades Council, strike for higher payments; later that evening 60,000 workers march from Frederick Street Labour Exchange to a rally at the Custom House.

Announcement that the King, on the advice of de Valera, 'has approved of Mr James MacNeill relinquishing the office of Governor-General of the Irish Free State' (*see* 26 Nov.).

9 Oct. Cumann na nGaedheal meeting at Kilmallock, Co. Limerick, attacked by some 200 Republicans, who are beaten off by 50 members of the Army Comrades' Association (Blueshirts).

11 Oct. Following a week of rioting in Belfast, the N.I. government bans marches under the Special Powers Act; violent conflict again between unemployed workers and the police in the Albert Street area of the Falls Road; Protestant workers from the Shankill Road area support Catholics; police baton-charge at Templenore Avenue; curfew imposed that night.

13 Oct. Belfast Board of Guardians summoned to meet the Northern Ireland cabinet.

14 Oct. Increases in outdoor relief in Northern Ireland sanctioned.

15 Oct. Protestants and Catholics march in the funeral of Samuel Baxter, trade unionist, led by Tom Mann, the British trade union leader.

29 Oct. Control of Manufactures Act (I.F.S.) empowers Minister for Industry and Commerce to license and lay down conditions governing manufacturing businesses in which the majority of shareholders are not nationals.

1 Nov. d. Thomas Sexton (84), politician (Home Rule), manager of the *Freeman's Journal* (1882–1912).

10 Nov. Frank Ryan of the I.R.A. states that 'While we have fists, hands and boots to use, and guns if necessary, we will not allow free speech to traitors.'

16 Nov. Prince of Wales opens Stormont, new home of the parliament of Northern Ireland; architect for parliament building Arnold Thornby.

26 Nov. Domhnall Ua Buachalla appointed to the office of Governor-General (entitled Seanascal by Irish government).

Dec. Federation of Irish Industry succeeded by the Confederation of Irish Industry.

Pub. *As I Was Going Down Sackville Street* by Oliver St John Gogarty (causes celebrated libel action).

1933

2 Jan. Dáil dissolved.

21 Jan. d. George Moore, novelist (author of *Esther Waters*, 1894).

24 Jan. General election in Free State: Fianna Fáil, 77; Cumann na nGaedheal, 48; National Centre Party, 11; Labour, 8; Independent, 8; Independent Labour, 1.

8 Feb. Eighth Dáil assembles; de Valera forms Fianna Fáil government.

22 Feb. Gen. Eoin O'Duffy removed from the commissionership of the Garda Síochána; rejects de Valera's offer of another post.

14 Mar. Dáil passes Wearing of Uniform (Restriction) Bill, but Senate rejects it (21 Mar. 1934).

30 Mar. Land (Purchase Annuity Fund) Act empowers the Free State to use the land annuities and other withheld payments for 'normal exchequer requirements'.

8 Apr. Army Comrades' Association parades in blue shirt and black beret (adopted on 24 Mar.); members become known as 'Blueshirts'.

3 May Constitution (Removal of Oath) Act (I.F.S.) removes the oath of allegiance from the Constitution.

4 May Agricultural Produce (Cereals) Act (I.F.S.) encourages wheat cultivation.

9 May Civil Authorities (Special Powers) Act (N.I.) gives permanent application to the 1922 act.

11 June Communist Party of Ireland re-established by the Revolutionary Workers' Group and the Workers' Party of Ireland.

20 July Eoin O'Duffy elected leader of the Army Comrades' Association (known as Blueshirts); changes name to the National Guard.

29–30 July Gardaí collect guns from private houses under a revocation order which cancels all firearms certificates.

31 July Industrial Credit Act (I.F.S.) sets up the Industrial Credit Company.

12 Aug. Government establishes a military tribunal and bans a proposed parade by the Blueshirts on 13th; O'Duffy cancels parade.

22 Aug. O'Duffy's National Guard proclaimed an unlawful association.

8 Sept. Union of Cumann na nGaedheal, National Centre Party and Blueshirts to form United Ireland Party, led by Gen. Eoin O'Duffy (party later known as Fine Gael).

13 Sept. O'Duffy's National Guard renamed the Young Ireland Association (*see* 8 Dec.).

15 Sept. Military tribunal closes offices of the Young Ireland Association for six months.

13 Oct. Free State government reduces land annuity payments by half.

23 Oct. Col. Charles Lindbergh, American aviator, makes a survey flight over Ireland in *Tingmissartog* to examine possible sites for proposed seaplane base in the Free State; lands in Galway harbour after flying across Cork, Kerry and Galway.

2 Nov. Constitution (Amendment No. 20) Act transfers from the Governor-General to the Executive Council the power of recommending the appropriation of money.

Constitution (Amendment No. 21) Act abolishes the Governor-General's power to withhold the King's assent to bills or to reserve bills for the King's pleasure (*see* 16 Nov.).

16 Nov. Constitution (Amendment No. 22) Act (I.F.S.) abolishes the right of appeal to the Judicial Committee of the Privy Council.

Unemployment Assistance Act (I.F.S.).

30 Nov. General election in N.I.: Unionists, 36; Independent Unionists, 3; Nationalists, 9; Labour, 2; Republican, 1; Independent, 1. Craigavon continues as P.M.

8 Dec. Government order declares O'Duffy's Young Ireland Association an unlawful organisation; O'Duffy dissolves it and sets up the League of Youth on 14 Dec.

Pub. *Fiche Bliain ag Fás* ('Twenty Years A-Growing') by Muiris Ó Súilleabháin.

1934

18 Jan. d. Joseph Devlin (63), leader of the Nationalist Party at Stormont; succeeded by T. J. Campbell.

8 Mar. d. Stephen McKenna (62), translator and journalist.

21 Mar. Free State Senate rejects the Wearing of Uniform (Restrictions) Bill.

7–8 Apr. Peadar O'Donnell, George Gilmore and Charlie Donnelly form the Republican Congress following Republican meeting in Athlone.

24 Apr. P.M. Craigavon describes Stormont as 'a Protestant parliament for a Protestant people'.

5 May Pub. first issue of *Republican Congress*.

6 May Première of *Man of Aran*, a film by Robert Flaherty, held in the presence of de Valera and members of the government.

1 June Free State Senate rejects bill for the abolition of the Senate.

1 Aug. Military Service Pensions Bill introduced in Dáil, to provide pensions for those who had fought on the Republican side in the Civil War, on same terms as those who had joined the Free State army (passes into law on 13 Sept.).

13 Aug. Members of armed 'S' Division of the Garda Síochána ('Broy Harriers') open fire in Marsh's saleyard in Cork city when a lorryload of men crash a barrier; a boy killed and seven wounded; High Court judgment of 5 Apr. 1937 condemns the shooting by the 'S' Division and finds a *prima facie* case of manslaughter (no further action taken).

18–19 Aug. First annual conference of the League of Youth resolves to call on farmers to refuse to pay land annuities into the exchequer and for labourers not to pay rates if the government will neither suspend the demand for payment nor refer the issue to an independent tribunal.

31 Aug. Announcement that Professor James Hogan has resigned from the United Ireland Party in protest at 'generally destructive and hysterical leadership' of Eoin O'Duffy.

21 Sept. Eoin O'Duffy resigns from the presidency of the United Ireland Party (Fine Gael).

29 Sept. d. An tAthar Pádraig Ó Duinnín (Fr Patrick S. Dinneen), scholar and lexicographer.

1 Oct. 'Revised Programme of Primary Education' implemented in Free State; issued by Minister for Education, Thomas Derrig, who desires greater progress in use of the Irish language, history and fosterage of a more patriotic Gaelic outlook.

12 Dec. Free State Senate reassembles following election; T. W. Westropp Bennett re-elected Chairman.

Closure of Workman & Clark shipyard in Belfast.

1935

3 Jan. Anglo-Irish Coal–Cattle Pact announced: British government agrees to increase imports of cattle from the Free State by one-third, and Free State agrees to buy its coal ($1\frac{1}{4}$ million tons p.a.) from Britain (*see* 17 Feb. 1936).

9 Feb. Roderick More O'Ferrall fatally wounded by the I.R.A. at his home outside Edgeworthstown, Co. Longford (*see* 24 Mar. 1936).

28 Feb. Criminal Law Amendment Act (I.F.S.) forbids importation of contraceptives and raises age of consent to 17 (from 16).

3 Mar. – 17 May Tram and omnibus strike starts in Dublin; army provides public transport from 20 Mar.

21 Mar. W. T. Cosgrave unanimously elected chairman of the United Ireland Party (Fine Gael).

10 Apr. Irish Nationality and Citizenship Act (I.F.S.) provides that persons born in Northern Ireland after 6 Dec. 1922 are to be citizens of the Free State up to age of 21, when they cease to be so unless they declare for retention of citizenship.

Aliens Act (I.F.S.) defines as aliens all other than Free State citizens, but Executive Council is empowered to exempt subjects of any country from the provisions of the act (British subjects are exempted).

12 May d. William Robinson (47), horticulturalist.

7 June P.M. Ramsay MacDonald (Labour) resigns; succeeded by Stanley Baldwin (Conservative) (*see* 28 May 1937).

8 June Eoin O'Duffy's League of Youth renamed the National Corporative Party.

20 June Pigs and Bacon Act (I.F.S.) establishes marketing boards (functions assumed by Pigs and Bacon Commission on 1 Jan. 1940).

12–21 July Worst rioting of the decade spreads from Lancaster Steet, Belfast, during Orange parade; nine killed, 514 Catholics driven from the York Street area.

15 July Aerial survey of Rineanna area (Co. Clare, shores of the River Shannon at the junction with the River Fergus) as site for transatlantic airport.

17 July d. George William Russell ('AE') (68), journalist, poet, mystic, philosopher and painter.

2 Aug. Widows' and Orphans' Pensions Act (I.F.S.).

22 Oct. d. Edward Carson (81), Baron Carson of Duncairn, Unionist leader (1910–21).

22 Nov. Malcolm MacDonald appointed British Secretary of State for the Dominions.

1936

20 Jan. d. George V (71); succeeded by Edward VIII (*see* 10 Dec.).

17 Feb. Anglo-Irish Coal–Cattle Pact renewed for a year (renewed again in Feb. 1937).

24 Feb. Ulster Society for Irish Historical Studies founded at Queen's University, Belfast (*see* 3 Nov.).

23 Mar. Seán Lemass opens pier at Foynes harbour, Co. Limerick, built by the 3rd Lord Monteagle to accommodate large vessels, in preparation for flying-boats (*see* 25 Feb. 1937).

24 Mar. Vice-Admiral Henry Boyle Somerville shot dead at his home at Castletownshend, Co. Cork, by I.R.A.

26 Apr. John Egan shot dead by the I.R.A. at Mitchell Street, Dungarvan, Co. Waterford.

19 May Final sitting of the Senate of the Free State; abolished on 29 May.

27 May Aer Lingus inaugural flight, from Baldonnell Military Airport, Dublin, to Bristol, a five-seater de Haviland Dragon, *Iolar* ('Eagle'), piloted by Capt. O. E. Armstrong.

6 June d. Eamonn Duggan (62), signatory to the Treaty.

18 June Free State government declares the I.R.A. an illegal organisation under the Special Powers Act.

19 June Meeting due to be held at Wolfe Tone's grave at Bodenstown, Co. Kildare, on 21 June banned by the government.

July Patrick Belton's Irish Christian Front formed.

14 July d. Patrick Hogan (45) (car accident); Minister for Agriculture (1922–32).

14 Aug. Air Navigation and Transport Act (I.F.S.) regulates air transport; Aer Lingus to be the national airline.

Aug. Dublin release of *The Dawn*, a film by Tom Cooper, the first full-length Irish sound feature film.

30 Sept. Seán Lester, Free State representative to the League of Nations, appointed Deputy Secretary-General (serves as the League's last Secretary-General, 1940–47).

9 Oct. Standing committee of United Ireland Party (Fine Gael) terminates existence of the League of Youth (Blueshirts) within the party; Edward Cronin leaves, taking some of the League of Youth with him.

3 Nov. Irish Historical Society established.

20 Nov. Gen. Eoin O'Duffy leads Blueshirt followers to Spain as an Irish Brigade to support Franco and the nationalist rebels in the Spanish Civil War (*see* 16 Dec.).

Foynes, Co. Limerick, is approved as a transatlantic seaplane base by a visiting Pan-Am party which includes Col. Charles Lindbergh.

27 Nov. Dáil adjourns (to 3 Feb. 1937).

10 Dec. Edward VIII abdicates; succeeded by George VI; de Valera summons Dáil for the next day.

11 Dec. Free State government introduces Constitution (Amendment No. 27) Bill 'to effect certain amendments to the Constitution in relation to the executive authority and power and in relation to the performance of certain executive functions'; removes the King from the Constitution and abolishes representation of the Crown (Governor-General); passes that same day.

12 Dec. Executive Authority (External Relations) Act leaves only one remaining link between the Free State and the Crown; the King can act 'for the purposes of the appointment of diplomatic and consular representatives and the conclusion of international agreements' on the advice of the Executive Council (*see* 21 Dec. 1948).

16 Dec. Frank Ryan leads Republican followers to Spain to fight in the International Brigade in support of the Republican government (*see* 20 Nov.).

Census of population in Free State: 2,968,420 (decrease of 0.12 per cent since 1926).

Pub. *On Another Man's Wound* by Ernie O'Malley.

Pub. *Peig,* dictated by Peig Sayers to her son and edited by Máire Ní Chinnéide (translated in 1973 by Bryan MacMahon).

Pub. *A History of Ireland* by Edmund Curtis.

1937

24 Feb. Spanish Civil War (Non-Intervention) Act forbids Free State citizens to involve themselves in the civil war in Spain.

25 Feb. Imperial Airways' *Cambria* becomes the first flying-boat to land on the River Shannon at Foynes, Co. Limerick; crew of two, including Capt. G. J. Powell, and four passengers (*see* 4 July).

27 Feb. d. Charlie Donnelly (27), poet, killed fighting in Spain in the Irish Republican column of the International Brigade.

10 Mar. Draft of new Constitution introduced in the Dáil (*see* 14 June).

1 Apr. Free State meteorological service takes over full operational control from British service.

1 May Draft Constitution published.

28 May P.M. Stanley Baldwin resigns; succeeded by Neville Chamberlain (Conservative).

8 June Executive Powers (Consequential Provision) Act transfers all functions of the Crown representative (Governor-General) to Free State Executive Council; confers on former Governor-General Domhnall Ua Buachalla a gratuity of £2,000 and a pension of £500 p.a. for life.

14 June De Valera's Constitution approved by the Dáil.

1 July General election and referendum in Free State on the new Constitution. Fianna Fáil, 69; Fine Gael, 48; Labour, 13; Independents, 8. For Constitution: 685,105; against: 526,945 (*see* 29 Dec.).

4 July Imperial Airways' *Caledonia,* captained by Capt. A. S. Wilcockson, becomes the first flying-boat on a transatlantic journey to land at Foynes, Co. Limerick; return flight to Port Botwood, U.S.A., takes 15 hours and 9 minutes.

5 July Pan-Am's *Clipper III* leaves Port Washington harbour, Long

Island, for Ireland; arrives at Foynes on 6th after journey of 12 hours and 31 minutes.

8 July Col. Charles Lindbergh examines on-going work at the Rineanna transatlantic airport, Co. Clare (later known as Shannon Airport) (*see* 18 May 1939).

22 Aug. Dr Pat O'Callaghan, twice Olympic gold medallist, sets a world record by throwing the hammer 195 ft 4⅞ in. at Fermoy, Co. Cork.

27 Aug. Flying-boat *Cambria* flies Foynes to Port Botwood, U.S.A., in 14 hours and 24 minutes, then a record for west-bound transatlantic flight.

Ireland's earliest traffic lights installed at Merrion Square/Clare Street junction, Dublin.

28 Sept. On her final survey flight flying-boat *Cambria* arrives at Foynes, Co. Limerick, from Canada in 10 hours and 57 minutes, a new record.

29 Dec. Constitution of Éire comes into force.

Census of population in Northern Ireland: 1,279,745 (increase of 1.8 per cent since 1926).

Pub. *The Irish Republic* by Dorothy Macardle.

Pub. *The Irish Countryman,* anthropological study of Clare by Conrad Arensberg.

1938

17 Jan. Anglo-Irish negotiations to end the Economic War start (*see* 25 Apr.).

9 Feb. General election in N.I.: Unionists, 39; Independent Unionists, 3; Nationalists, 8; Labour, 1; Independent Labour, 1. Craigavon continues as P.M.

1 Mar. Pub. first issue of *Irish Historical Studies,* ed. R. Dudley Edwards and T. W. Moody.

22 Mar. North Atlantic Air Route Conference held in Dublin, attended by Free State, Great Britain, Canada and U.S.A.; leads to Transatlantic Air Service Safety Organisation (T.A.S.S.O.).

24 Mar. Irish Committee for Historical Sciences founded by the Irish Historical Society and the Ulster Society for Irish Historical Studies.

25 Apr. Anglo-Irish Agreements ending the Economic War signed by de Valera and Chamberlain in London: (i) handover of 'Treaty ports' to Éire; (ii) financial agreement under which Éire pays £10 million 'as a final settlement of all financial claims of either of the two governments against the other'; (iii) a trade agreement under which tariffs are withdrawn by each side, allowing provision for protection of certain goods. The British market becomes once more open to cattle from Éire, and the return of the ports enables Éire to remain neutral during the Second World War.

26 Apr. P.M. Craigavon announces that 'step by step' policy in regard to Northern Ireland social services applies—U.K. will maintain Northern Ireland services at U.K. level if Northern Ireland revenues are insufficient.

27 Apr. Seanad Éireann, as reorganised under Constitution of 1937, meets for the first time.

1 May Park at Merrion Square, Dublin, becomes the property of the R.C. Archbishop of Dublin (*see* 1 May 1791 *and* 5 Apr. 1974).

27 May Dáil dissolved following government defeat on compulsory arbitration for civil servants.

17 June General election in Éire: Fianna Fáil, 77; Fine Gael, 45; Labour, 9; Independents and others, 7.

25 June Dr Douglas Hyde, elected unopposed, inaugurated as first President of Éire in St Patrick's Hall, Dublin Castle.

11 July De Valera hoists tricolour in Cork harbour when Éire takes possession of Spike Island, Fort Camden and Fort Carlisle under the agreement of 25 Apr. (*see* 29 Sept.).

15 Aug. Clann na Talmhan formed in Athenry, Co. Galway, by Michael Donnellan.

12 Sept. De Valera elected President of the Assembly of the League of Nations.

29 Sept. Berehaven handed over to Éire by British navy.

3 Oct. Lough Swilly handed over to Éire by British navy.

12 Dec. d. James MacNeill (69), Governor-General of the Free State (1928–32).

22 Dec. Northern Ireland again introduces internment under the Special Powers Act.

Pub. *Ploughman and Other Poems* and *The Green Fool* by Patrick Kavanagh.

Pub. *A Servant of the Queen*, autobiography of Maud Gonne MacBride.

1939

12 Jan. I.R.A. ultimatum signed by Patrick Fleming, secretary of the Army Council, calls upon British Foreign Secretary, Lord Halifax, to withdraw British troops from Northern Ireland within the four days and Crown representatives from 'every part of Ireland' or face the reprisals which will result.

16 Jan. I.R.A. bombing campaign in England starts with seven targets bombed (*see* 25 Aug.).

19 Jan. Small explosion in vicinity of Tralee, Co. Kerry, hotel where Francis Chamberlain, son of the British P.M., is staying; de Valera expresses 'sincere regrets'.

28 Jan. d. W. B. Yeats (74), poet, at Rocquebrune, overlooking Monaco (*see* 14 Sept. 1948).

1 Feb. German agent Oskar Pfaus arrives to liaise between I.R.A. and Abwehr II.

19 Feb. De Valera states that the aim of his government is to preserve the neutrality of Éire.

13 Mar. Pub. *At Swim-Two-Birds* by Flann O'Brien (Brian O'Nolan).

1 Apr. Capt. J. C. Kelly-Rogers test flies *Connemara* over Dún Laoghaire and Dalkey, Co. Dublin.

11 Apr. Pan-Am Boeing 314 flying-boat *Yankee Clipper*, captained by Harold Gray, lands at Foynes from Southampton, England; precursor of transatlantic mail and passenger traffic (*see* 28 June).

1 May Six R.C. bishops whose dioceses lie within Northern Ireland, led by Cardinal MacRory, state that in their opinion any attempt to introduce conscription will be 'an outrage on the national feeling and an aggression upon our national rights' (*see* 4 May).

2 May De Valera announces that the government has 'protested to the British government in the strongest terms against the threatened imposition of conscription' in Northern Ireland.

4 May P.M. Chamberlain announces that conscription will not extend to Northern Ireland.

Pub. *Finnegans Wake* by James Joyce.

18 May First aircraft lands on the new airfield at Rineanna, Co. Clare (later known as Shannon Airport); an Air Corps Anson Mark I serial 43, after one-hour flight from Baldonnell, Co. Dublin.

30 May Treason Act (Éire) provides death penalty for acts of treason.

14 June Offences Against the State Act (Éire), introduced in response to I.R.A. campaign, empowers government to declare any organisation unlawful and provides for the establishment of special criminal court (*see* 24 Aug.).

23 June Unlawful Organisation (Suppression) Order (Éire) outlaws the I.R.A.; Garda Commissioner bans the customary march to Wolfe Tone's grave at Bodenstown, Co. Kildare.

24 June Central London rocked by I.R.A. explosions; no casualties reported.

27 June Mrs Kathleen Clarke (Caitlín Bean Uí Chléirigh, widow of Tom Clarke, executed in 1916 for his part in the Easter Rising) elected Lord Mayor of Dublin; first woman ever to hold such an office in Ireland.

28 June *Yankee Clipper* flying-boat greeted by de Valera and Seán Lemass at Foynes; commanded by Capt. Harold Gray, it contains 18 passengers and 11 crew and 14 bags of mail; start of weekly New York – Foynes flights (cancelled in Oct. because of the war).

1 July Irish Red Cross established by act of the Oireachtas.

4 July Éire's Interdepartmental Committee on Emergency Measures meets for the first time.

24 July Prevention of Violence Bill introduced by British Home Secretary, Sir Samuel Hoare, in effort to curb I.R.A. activity; authorises registration of all Irish living in Britain and the right of deportation (six Irish citizens deported on 2 Aug.).

5 Aug. Imperial Airways' *Cambria*, captained by J. C. Kelly-Rogers, the first scheduled service from Foynes to U.S.A., carries 1,000 lb of mail.

8 Aug. Charles Bewley, Éire's representative in Berlin, recalled by de Valera, who is embarrassed by Bewley's pro-fascism (*see* 1 Feb. 1969).

22 Aug. Éire government invokes Parts V and VI of the Offences Against the State Act (internment).

23 Aug. Germany and the U.S.S.R. sign non-aggression pact.

24 Aug. Special criminal court consisting of five army officers established in Éire under the Offences Against the State Act to try political suspects.

25 Aug. Explosion at Broadgate, Coventry, kills five and injures 70; two Irishmen, James McCormack and Peter Barnes, executed for it on 7 Feb. 1940.

30 Aug. Irish Air Corps occupies airfield at Rineanna, Co. Clare (later known as Shannon Airport) for duration of the war.

31 Aug. Taoiseach de Valera informs German Ambassador in Dublin, Dr Edouard Hempel, that although Éire desires peace with all nations, including Germany, the government will have to show a certain consideration to Britain for geographical and economic reasons.

1 Sept. Germany invades Poland; start of Second World War.

2–3 Sept. Dáil and Senate meet in emergency session to enact two bills which postulate neutrality (both pass without division): (i) extends the phrase 'time of war' to mean a time when there is taking place an armed

KILKENNY COUNTY LIBRARY

conflict in which the state of Éire is not a participant; (ii) Emergency Powers Bill.

3 Sept. Great Britain and France declare war on Germany.

Under Emergency Powers Act a state of emergency is declared in Éire; start of 'the Emergency'.

8 Sept. Emergency Powers (No. 4) Order made by Éire government.

9 Sept. Special Branch officers raid I.R.A. H.Q. at Rathmines, Dublin; several arrests and confiscation of documents and some $8,000, severely curtailing I.R.A. activity.

18 Sept. Emergency Powers (Finance) (No. 1) Order made by Éire government.

23 Sept. Petrol rationed in Éire.

16 Oct. Myles Heffernan becomes first I.R.A. member to be sentenced by the military tribunal (three months' imprisonment for possession of documents).

20 Oct. The London *Times*, commenting on the sinking of the *Courageous* and *Royal Oak* at Scapa Flow, states: 'The casualty lists so far published in London have contained a high proportion of Irish names.'

8 Nov. Supplementary budget in Éire raises the standard rate of income tax to 7s in the £.

23 Dec. I.R.A. loot the Army Magazine Fort in Phoenix Park, Dublin, seizing over 1 million rounds of ammunition, bulk of which is subsequently recovered.

29 Dec. Gardaí seize I.R.A. transmitter used for communicating with the German Abwehr II; radio communication not re-established.

1940

3 Jan. Éire government introduces Emergency Powers (Amendment) Bill and Offences Against the State (Amendment) Bill.

8 Jan. Food rationing introduced in Northern Ireland.

d. Fr Thomas Finlay (92), founder-editor of *Lyceum* (1887); Professor of Political Economy, U.C.D. (1908–30).

25 Feb. I.R.A. prisoners in Éire start hunger-strike; ends following deaths of two prisoners (16 and 19 Apr.).

5 May Herman Goertz, sent by the Abwehr secret service to make contact with the I.R.A., lands by parachute in Co. Meath (captured on 27 Nov. and interned).

10 May P.M. Chamberlain resigns; succeeded by Winston Churchill (Conservative), whose coalition lasts until 23 May 1945.

5 June Minister for Defence introduces second reading of Defence Forces Temporary Provisions Bill (passes the Dáil in two days); regulates enlistment for the duration of the Emergency.

19 June Institute for Advanced Studies Act (Éire).

14 Aug. d. Seán Russell (47), I.R.A. Chief of Staff, on board a German submarine off the Galway coast (Frank Ryan taken back to Germany; *see* 10 June 1944).

26 Aug. Three women killed in creamery at Campile, Co. Wexford, struck by a German bomb.

Oct. Pub. first issue of *The Bell*, literary magazine founded and edited by Seán O'Faolain (later edited by his assistant, Peadar O'Donnell; runs until Dec. 1954).

24 Nov. d. James Craig (69), 1st Viscount Craigavon (69); replaced as leader of the Unionist Party and P.M. of Northern Ireland by John Miller Andrews.

3 Dec. Hitler orders Admiral Raeder to investigate the possibility of invading Ireland, but 'only if Ireland requests help'.

27 Dec. John Charles McQuaid consecrated R.C. Archbishop of Dublin.

1941

Local Defence Force (L.D.F.) established (*see* 6 Feb. 1946).

10 Jan. Further rationing of petrol in Éire.

d. Sir John Lavery (84), artist (portrait of his wife Hazel used on Irish paper currency).

13 Jan. d. James Joyce (58), novelist.

16 Jan. Outbreak of foot-and-mouth disease confirmed in Eglinton, Co. Londonderry; spreads to Éire on 20th, to become the worst recorded outbreak: 41,947 livestock slaughtered before it ends on 22 Sept.

23 Mar. Formation of Irish Shipping Ltd announced.

7–8 Apr. First German bombing of Northern Ireland kills 13.

15–16 Apr. Nearly 300 German bombs drop on Belfast, killing 745, injuring 1,500; 1,600 houses completely destroyed, and over 28,000 severely damaged; 40,000 accommodated in rest centres, and 70,000 fed in emergency centres. De Valera dispatches 13 fire-engines from Dublin, Dún Laoghaire, Drogheda and Dundalk to aid Belfast.

4–5 May Belfast again bombed by German planes; shipyards and Short's aircraft factory badly damaged, as are Harbour Power Station and York Street railway station; 150 killed and 157 seriously injured.

7 May Wages Standstill Order freezes wages in Éire.

26 May Political party leaders protest in Dáil at British proposal to extend conscription to Northern Ireland.

30–31 May 500-pound German bomb lands in the North Strand area of Dublin, killing over 30 and injuring 90; two 25-pounders fall on the North Circular Road and Summerhill Parade; Áras an Uachtaráin and the American Embassy are damaged when a 250-pound bomb lands in Phoenix Park (German government expresses regret in June and pays £327,000 compensation in 1958).

6 June d. John Hughes (76), sculptor (works include Charles Kickham monument in Tipperary).

22 June Germany invades U.S.S.R.

30 June Stephen Hayes, former I.R.A. Chief of Staff, kidnapped (*see* 18 Sept.).

4 July B.O.A.C. starts the first landplane service to Éire (Bristol–Collinstown, Co. Dublin) (*see* 21 Feb. 1942).

14 Sept. d. Oliver Sheppard (76), sculptor (works include 1916 memorial in G.P.O., Dublin, 'The Death of Cuchulain').

18 Sept. Seán McCaughey (*alias* Dunlop) convicted of kidnapping Stephen Hayes (*see* 30 June); sentence of death commuted on 25th (*see* 11 May 1946).

22 Sept. d. Michael Healy (68), stained-glass artist, with An Túr Gloine from 1903 (*see* 7 Aug. 1943).

23 Sept. Trade Union Act (Éire) sets up tribunal to license unions with largest number of workers as sole negotiators for workers in particular industries (Supreme Court finds it repugnant to the Constitution on 4 July 1946).

4 Dec. Harry Midgley (Labour) wins Belfast Willowfield by-election, traditionally a Unionist seat.

7 Dec. Japanese bomb Pearl Harbor in Hawaii; U.S.A. enters the war (8 Dec.).

Pub. *An Béal Bocht* by Myles na Gopaleen (Brian O'Nolan, usually known by his other pseudonym, Flann O'Brien); English translation, *The Poor Mouth*, by Patrick C. Power in 1973.

Pub. *The Land of Spices* by Kate O'Brien (banned in Éire).

1942

26 Jan. First U.S. troops arrive in Belfast (de Valera's protest the next day rejected by P.M. Andrews).

5 Feb. Base at Derry inaugurated as part of the U.S. Atlantic Fleet Command.

19 Feb. James Dillon, sole opponent in Dáil of Éire's policy of neutrality, resigns from Fine Gael.

21 Feb. B.O.A.C. inaugurates service from Bristol to Rineanna, Co. Clare.

3–4 Apr. Constable T. J. Forbes killed by the I.R.A. in Dungannon, Co. Tyrone; first policeman killed in Northern Ireland in a decade.

26 May Referendum Act (Éire) lays down procedure for referendums on amendments to the Constitution on bills referred by the President (under Article 27 of the Constitution).

28 May American Export airline survey flight by Capt. Charles F. Blair lands at Foynes, Co. Limerick.

4 Nov. Central Bank Act (Éire) dissolves the Currency Commission and establishes the Central Bank as currency authority (*see* 1 Feb. 1943).

24 Nov. d. Peadar Kearney (59), author of 'Amhrán na bhFiann' ('The Soldiers' Song'), the National Anthem.

2 Dec. Inaugural meeting of Éire cabinet Committee on Economic Planning.

Pub. *The Great Hunger*, poem by Patrick Kavanagh (banned in Éire).

Pub. *The Tailor and Ansty* by Eric Cross (banned in Éire).

1943

1 Feb. Central Bank opens in Dublin.

17 Mar. Pub. first issue of *Indiu*, Irish-language weekly (known as *Inniu* from 24 Sept. 1954).

25 Mar. d. Edmund Curtis, historian.

1 Apr. Office of Ulster King of Arms, Dublin Castle, abolished.

15 Apr. Supreme Court in Dublin rules that Section 4 of the School Attendance Act (empowering the minister to certify the standard of private education) is repugnant to the Constitution.

28 Apr. Having lost the confidence of the people and the Unionist Party, John Miller Andrews resigns from leadership of the party and post of P.M. of Northern Ireland; succeeded by Sir Basil Brooke on 1 May.

22 June General election in Éire: Fianna Fáil, 67; Fine Gael, 32; Labour, 17; Clann na Talmhan, 10; Farmers, 5; Independents and others, 7.

28 July Civilian plane, carrying mainly R.A.F. passengers, crashes at Slieveglas, Cloghane, on the slopes of Mount Brandon, Co. Kerry, having lost its bearing while travelling between Lisbon and Foynes; Capt. Thomas Alliott and nine killed; six crew and nine passengers survive; only civil aircraft accident during use of Foynes as seaplane airport.

7 Aug. d. Sarah Purser (95), portraitist and stained-glass artist; founder of An Túr Gloine ('The Tower of Glass') in 1903.

16 Sept. – 9 Oct. First Irish Exhibition of Living Art.

26 Oct. Comhdháil Náisiúnta na Gaeilge formed to co-ordinate Irish-language organisations.

1944

7 Jan. I.T.G.W.U. disaffiliates from the Labour Party.

14 Jan. The five I.T.G.W.U. members of the Labour Party in Éire secede to form the National Labour Party.

18 Jan. W. T. Cosgrave resigns leadership of Fine Gael; succeeded by Richard Mulcahy on 26th.

21 Jan. U.S. Ambassador to Ireland, David Gray, hands de Valera the 'American note' requesting him to have German and Japanese representatives recalled (de Valera refuses).

23 Feb. Children's Allowances Act (Éire) provides payments of 2s 6d per week for third and subsequent children under 16.

25 Feb. – 8 Apr. Harland & Wolff shipyard closed by strike.

13 Mar. d. Joseph Holloway (83), architect and diarist who recorded every first night at the Abbey Theatre, Dublin, for over 60 years.

12 May d. Edel Quinn (37), missionary of the Legion of Mary, in Nairobi (from T.B.).

30 May General election in Éire: Fianna Fáil, 76; Fine Gael, 30; Clann na Talmhan, 11; Labour, 8; National Labour, 4; Farmers, 2; Independents, 7.

10 June d. Frank Ryan (42), socialist Republican leader, who led Irish column in Spain, in Germany.

30 Sept. d. Gen. Eoin O'Duffy (52), Commissioner of the Garda Síochána (1922–33) and Blueshirt leader.

8 Dec. Transport Act amalgamates the Great Southern Railways Company and the Dublin United Tramway Company to form Córas Iompair Éireann (C.I.E.); comes into effect on 1 Jan. 1945.

1945

10 Jan. 23 killed in two-train collision at Ballymacarrett Junction, Belfast.

3 Feb. Shannon becomes compulsory stopover for American air traffic.

6 Feb. Northern Ireland Housing Trust established.

25 Apr. Split in Irish Trade Union Congress leads to formation of Congress of Irish Unions (C.I.U.).

2 May Taoiseach de Valera offers condolences to German Ambassador to Ireland, Edouard Hempel, upon news of the death of Adolf Hitler on 30 Apr.; widely criticised abroad for his action.

8 May VE Day: war in Europe ends.

13 May In his victory speech P.M. Churchill attacks de Valera for Éire's neutrality: 'His Majesty's government never laid a violent hand upon them . . . and we left the de Valera government to frolic with the Germans and later with the Japanese representatives to their hearts' content'; de Valera's reply (16 May) highly regarded in Éire.

23 May P.M. Churchill resigns from coalition government, but remains head of caretaker administration until general election of 5 July when Labour is victorious.

14 June General election in N.I.: Unionists, 33; Independent Unionists, 2; Nationalists, 10; Labour, 2; Independent Labour, 1; Commonwealth Labour, 1; Socialist Republican, 1; Independents, 2.

16 June Seán T. O'Kelly elected President of Éire (installed on 25 June);

succeeded as Tánaiste by Seán Lemass on 19th.

16 July 10 Nationalists returned in N.I. general election decide to take their seats at Stormont.

26 July Clement Attlee appointed P.M. of U.K.; leads the first Labour administration with an overall majority.

4 Aug. National Stud Act vests stud at Tully, Co. Kildare, in the Minister for Agriculture, to be run by a private company.

6 Sept. Duke of Abercorn, Governor of Northern Ireland since 1922, resigns; succeeded by Vice-Admiral the Earl of Granville.

16 Sept. d. John, Count McCormack (61), tenor.

15 Oct. d. Professor Eoin Mac Néill (78), politician (Cumann na nGaedheal) and historian; co-founder of the Gaelic League (1893) and Chief of Staff of the Irish Volunteers (1916).

24 Oct. American Export airline lands first transatlantic passenger flight to Shannon Airport, Co. Clare (Rineanna).

29 Oct. Pan-Am's last scheduled flying-boat service leaves Foynes, Co. Limerick (*see* 24 Mar. 1946).

14 Nov. Irish Anti-Partition League formed at Dungannon, Co. Tyrone.

19 Nov. Coastwatching service disbanded.

13 Dec. Family Allowances Act (N.I.) provides for payments of 5s per week for second and subsequent children.

1946

3 Jan. Pan-Am D.C. 4 lands at Shannon Airport, Co. Clare (Rineanna), following a record journey of 7 hours and 53 minutes from Gander (*see* 18 Jan. 1947).

16 Jan. d. Robin Flower (65), Celtic scholar (author of *The Western Island*, 1944).

3 Feb. Censorship of Publications Act (Éire) establishes an appeals board.

6 Feb. Fórsa Cosanta Áitiúil (F.C.A.) established as territorial force superseding the Local Defence Force.

7 Feb. First T.W.A. flight, Shannon – New York.

19 Feb. National Insurance Act (N.I.) extends to the state the British welfare system.

28 Feb. Public Health (Tuberculosis) Act (N.I.) establishes Tuberculosis Authority to supervise eradication of the disease (dissolved on 31 Mar. 1959).

Elections and Franchise Act (N.I.) stipulates that half of the aldermen and all of the councillors have to stand for re-election every third year; also increases to six the number of business votes to single occupier in local elections.

15 Mar. Marine Service established in Éire.

20 Mar. – 30 Oct. I.N.T.O. strike in Dublin (Archbishop McQuaid acts as mediator).

24 Mar. Last B.O.A.C. seaplane leaves Foynes, Co. Limerick, base; B.O.A.C., Pan-Am and American Export transfer their flights to Shannon Airport, Co. Clare (Rineanna).

11 May d. (hunger-strike) of Seán McCaughey in Portlaoise prison (*see* 18 Sept. 1941).

1 June Turf Development Act (Éire) establishes Bord na Móna.

6 July Clann na Poblachta political party founded by Seán MacBride, with Michael Kelly as secretary.

24 July Dáil agrees to apply for membership of the United Nations Organisation; U.S.S.R. vetoes application on 13 Aug. (*see* 14 Dec. 1955).

28 July Bread rationing introduced in Northern Ireland.

27 Aug. Institute for Industrial Research and Standards founded under Industrial Research and Standards Act (Éire) (abolished in 1988).

Industrial Relations Act (Éire) authorises establishment of a Labour Court.

15 Nov. Irish Naval Service formed.

24 Dec. Departments of Health and Social Welfare established in Éire.

Commencement of rural electrification scheme in Éire.

Census of population in Éire: 2,955,107 (decrease of 0.45 per cent since 1936).

1947

4 Jan. d. Forrest Reid (72), novelist and author of stories for boys.

18 Jan. Bread rationing introduced in Éire.

Pan-Am lands plane at Shannon Airport, Co. Clare, following a journey of 5 hours and 3 minutes, a record for the time.

22 Jan. De Valera announces that the state of emergency still exists: 'the possibility is that a period of even greater difficulty may occur'.

30 Jan. d. James ('Big Jim') Larkin (71), founder of the Labour Party, I.T.G.W.U. and W.U.I.

Feb. One of the worst winters on record; cold and fuel shortage cause industrial closedowns.

1 Mar. Éire begins negotiations with the International Monetary Fund and World Bank (joins in 1957).

27 Mar. Education Act (N.I.) provides secondary education for all from age 11; school-leaving age increased to 15; state provides 65 per cent of costs of building and maintaining voluntary schools (*see* 1 Apr. 1948).

9 Apr. d. Desmond FitzGerald, politician (Cumann na nGaedheal and Fine Gael), Minister for External Affairs (1922–27).

21 Apr. Shannon Airport becomes a duty-free area, the first in the world.

23–24 June Celtic Congress in Dublin.

28 June Éire ratifies Economic Cooperation Agreement (bilateral agreement with the U.S.A. as condition of participation in the Organisation for European Economic Co-operation (O.E.E.C.) and European Recovery Programme; *see* 28 Oct.).

12 July Éire represented at the Paris Conference on European Economic Co-operation.

31 July Act extends legislative power of Northern Ireland parliament to electricity and water schemes on both sides of the border.

13 Aug. Health Act in Éire extends responsibility of county councils in health and provides Mother-and-Child scheme (to which R.C. hierarchy objects privately to Taoiseach on 7 Oct.).

13 Oct. American International Airways' *Bermuda Sky Queen* leaves Foynes, Co. Limerick, carrying 61 passengers, the greatest number flown over the Atlantic in a flying-boat.

27 Oct. d. William Fay (75), actor-producer; co-founder of the Abbey Theatre (1904).

28 Oct. Éire signs European Recovery Programme loan agreement.

18 Nov. An Taisce, the National Trust for Éire, approved by the Dáil; appointed on 15 July 1948.

23 Dec. Safeguard of Employment Act imposes strict residence requirements on all eligible to work in Northern Ireland.

Report of the committee of Éire's Department of Education to the minister recommends that National Schools cater for pupils up to the age of 12 (instead of 14, as hitherto).

1948

19 Jan. Interdepartmental committee on Éire's participation in the European Recovery Programme meets.

4 Feb. General election in Éire: Fianna Fáil, 68; Fine Gael, 31; Labour, 14; National Labour, 5; Clann na Poblachta, 10; Clann na Talmhan, 7; Independents and others, 12.

18 Feb. John A. Costello (Fine Gael) elected Taoiseach and forms the first inter-party (coalition) government.

23 Feb. d. John Robert Gregg (80), inventor of system of shorthand writing.

11 Mar. Publication of first general wage agreement between the F.U.E., I.T.U.C. and the C.I.U.

1 Apr. Education Act (N.I.) (*see* 27 Mar. 1947) becomes operative, restructuring the primary and secondary system; releases teachers from the obligation to teach religion if called upon to do so.

16 Apr. Éire and U.K. founding members of the O.E.E.C. when Convention for European Economic Cooperation signed in Paris.

17–22 June Anglo-Irish economic discussions.

10 Aug. Ulster Transport Authority established under act.

7 Sept. Taoiseach Costello, visiting Canada, confirms in Ottawa that the External Relations Act (1936) is to be repealed and that Éire will become a republic (*see* 21 Dec.).

14 Sept. Remains of W. B. Yeats reinterred in C.I. graveyard at Drumcliff, Co. Sligo, in accordance with his last wish.

17 Oct. Anglo-Irish meeting to discuss implications of Éire's leaving the Commonwealth (another meeting occurs in Paris on 16 Nov.).

21 Dec. Republic of Ireland Act repeals the External Relations Act, 1936, providing for the declaration of an Irish Republic (*see* 18 Apr. 1949).

1949

1 Jan. Act governing peacetime national military service in the U.K. excludes Northern Ireland (although Stormont wishes to participate).

6 Jan. Northern Ireland ministers meet with British ministers to discuss the implications of the Republic of Ireland Act (*see* 21 Dec. 1948).

Jan. Éire's *Long-Term Recovery Programme* published as a government white paper, to be financed by £47 million of Marshall Aid.

27 Jan. All-party conference at the Mansion House, Dublin, leads to church-gate collection on 30th in support of the Anti-Partition League.

10 Feb. General election in N.I.: Unionists, 37; Independent Unionists, 2; Anti-Partition League, 9; Independent Labour, 1; Socialist Republican, 1; Independents, 2. Lord Brookeborough continues as P.M.

23 Feb. Seán MacBride, Éire's Minister for External Affairs, states that British claim to sovereignty in Northern Ireland makes it impossible for Éire to subscribe to N.A.T.O. (which comes into existence on 4 Apr.).

9 Apr. Northern Ireland Labour Party delegate conference votes (20,000–700) to 'maintain unbroken the connection between Great Britain and Northern Ireland as part of the Commonwealth'.

18 Apr. Éire leaves the Commonwealth and becomes a republic (known as the Republic of Ireland, but retaining the name Éire) (*see* 2 June).

5 May Republic becomes founder-member of the Council of Europe and the first state to accept the jurisdiction of the European Court of Human Rights.

2 June Ireland Act of the United Kingdom parliament recognises the Republic, but declares that although it is not part of the Commonwealth, it is not to be regarded as a foreign country, nor are its citizens aliens within the Commonwealth; also declares that Northern Ireland will remain within the United Kingdom so long as that is the wish of the Northern Ireland parliament.

10 July Last tram runs from Nelson's Pillar, O'Connell Street, Dublin, to Dalkey, Co. Dublin.

12 July d. Dr Douglas Hyde (89), scholar and first President of Éire (1938–45).

30 July Land Reclamation Act (R.I.) provides for state financing of undeveloped land: £40 million allocated over 10 years to bring 4 million acres of unused or uncultivated land into production.

18 Sept. Sterling devalued from $4.02 to $2.80; Republic follows suit to come into effect on 20th.

30 Sept. Giant's Causeway railway line, Co. Antrim, closes.

8 Oct. d. Edith Anna Œnone Somerville (91), creator, with 'Martin Ross' (Violet Martin), of the 'Irish R.M.' stories.

26 Nov. Bread again rationed in the Republic.

21 Dec. Irish News Agency Act provides for a propagandist news agency under the control of the Minister for External Affairs.

Pub. *Cré na Cille* by Máirtín Ó Cadhain (chosen by U.N.E.S.C.O. for translation into several European languages).

1950

19 Jan. Republic's first peat-fired electricity station, the only one in Europe outside the U.S.S.R., comes into operation, at Portarlington, Co. Laois.

21 Jan. Irish–American treaty of friendship, commerce and navigation.

4 Apr. Council on Education for the Republic appointed.

17 Apr. National Blood Transfusion Association starts operating under legislation enacted in 1948 (*see* 15 Apr. 1965).

3 May Republic's first capital budget introduced.

6 June Unification of Labour and National Labour parties agreed, to be led by William Norton (until 1960).

11 June d. Stephen Gwynn (86), author (works include *The Fair Hills of Ireland*, 1906).

June Erne Drainage and Development Acts (R.I., 13 June; N.I., 27 June) give effect to agreement between Republic and Northern Ireland for a joint scheme of drainage and electricity generation.

5 Aug. Supreme Court in Dublin, delivering judgment in Tilson case, rules that ante-nuptial promises about religious upbringing of children are valid, and that both parents constitutionally have equal rights in upbringing of children.

6 Sept. Alfred Chester Beatty presents collection of French paintings to the National Gallery of Ireland (presents collection of continental, English and Irish miniatures in 1951) (*see* 20 Jan. 1968).

13 Sept. d. Sara Allgood (67), actress.

19 Sept. Republic signs the European Payments Union agreement.

6 Oct. d. Osborn Bergin (77), Professor of Early Irish, U.C.D.; first Director of the School of Irish Studies at the Dublin Institute for Advanced Studies (1940).

10 Oct. R.C. bishops issue letter to Taoiseach Costello, condemning the Mother-and-Child scheme.

11 Oct. R.C. hierarchy informs Minister for Health, Dr Noel Browne, of the bishops' objections to his proposed Mother-and-Child scheme (*see* 4 Apr. 1951).

2 Nov. d. George Bernard Shaw (94), dramatist; bequest aids the National Gallery of Ireland.

20 Dec. Industrial Development Authority Act (R.I.) establishes I.D.A. as an agency of the Department of Industry and Commerce, to investigate areas of possible industrial development.

23 Dec. – 15 Feb. 1951 Bank strike in the Republic.

26 Dec. d. James Stephens (70), poet and novelist.

1951

9 Jan. Republic and Northern Ireland reach agreement on Great Northern Railway.

4 Apr. R.C. bishops condemn the Mother-and-Child scheme put forward by Dr Noel Browne.

10 Apr. Seán MacBride, by letter, requests Dr Noel Browne's resignation as Minister for Health.

11 Apr. Dr Noel Browne, no longer supported by his cabinet colleagues or his party's leader (Seán MacBride), resigns over the Mother-and-Child scheme controversy.

8 May Arts Act (R.I.) establishes the Arts Council.

30 May General election in R.I.: Fianna Fáil, 69; Fine Gael, 40; Labour, 16; Clann na Talmhan, 6; Clann na Poblachta, 2; Independents and others, 14.

13 June Eamon de Valera (Fianna Fáil) again appointed Taoiseach, with support of Independents (74 votes to 69).

16 June d. Louis Dalton (51), theatrical producer and dramatist.

18 July Abbey Theatre, Dublin, destroyed by fire (*see* 18 July 1966).

21 Oct. – 4 Nov. First Wexford Opera Festival.

24 Oct. Central Bank report for 1950–51 published; the first printed without approval of the Department of Finance, it expresses grave misgivings on the state of the Republic's economy.

10 Dec. Nobel Prize for Physics presented to Dr E. T. S. Walton, Professor of Natural and Experimental Philosophy, T.C.D. (shared with Sir John Cockcroft).

21 Dec. Córas Tráchtála (Irish Exports Board) incorporated.

Census of population in Republic: 2,960,593 (increase of 0.19 per cent since 1946).

Census of population in Northern Ireland: 1,370,921 (increase of 7.1 per cent since 1937).

1952

2 Apr. Seán MacEntee introduces budget; the earliest date for a budget up to then.

12 Apr. Pub. *Kavanagh's Weekly*, founded and edited by Patrick and Peter Kavanagh; last issue on 5 July.

18 Apr. d. Edward Conor O'Brien (71), first Irishman to sail around the world in his own yacht.

22 Apr. Act establishes Bord Iascaigh Mhara for regulation of Republic's sea fisheries.

14 June Social Welfare Act co-ordinates Republic's system of social insurance.

25 June Seán T. O'Kelly inaugurated as President for the second time.

3 July Act establishes Bord Fáilte to exploit and promote tourism in the Republic.

11 July – 29 Aug. Printing dispute in Dublin leads to non-appearance of newspapers.

2 Nov. d. Molly Allgood (65), actress under stage-name Máire O'Neill.

9 Dec. Irish Management Institute inaugurated.

13 Dec. Adoption Act (R.I.) stipulates that adopters have to be of the same religion as the adopted child and its parents; adopters of an illegitimate child must the same religion as mother of the child; married adopters must be of the same religion (some Protestant denominations grouped together) (*see* 13 May 1974).

Pub. *Eireaball Spideoige*, first collection of poems by Seán Ó Riordáin.

1953

31 Jan. Ferry, *Princess Victoria*, making from Stranraer for Larne, capsizes off Co. Down after wave bursts unsecured bulkhead doors in stern; Ireland's worst sea tragedy (128 killed, including Northern Ireland Minister of Finance, Major John Maynard Sinclair; 43 survive).

31 Mar. J. J. McElligott, Secretary of the Department of Finance, resigns after 25 years to become Governor of the Central Bank.

5–26 Apr. An Tóstal, a national period of festival throughout the Republic, launched as a tourist attraction.

27 Apr. d. Maud Gonne MacBride (87).

3 May Gael-Linn established to promote the Irish language.

5 May d. Robert Lloyd Praeger (87), botanist.

1–3 July Elizabeth II visits Northern Ireland.

8 Aug. Chester Beatty Library, Dublin, opens, specialising in oriental material.

1 Sept. Great Northern Railway begins operation under board appointed jointly by governments of Northern Ireland and the Republic.

3 Sept. National Development Committee established by Seán MacEntee; leads to National Development Fund (Mar. 1954).

27 Sept. 'Early Irish Society' (general editor, Professor Myles Dillon), first of the Thomas Davis series of lectures, starts on Radio Éireann; first lecture, 'The Irish Language', is delivered by Professor Dillon.

9 Oct. Committee of inquiry into Taxation on Industry appointed under chairmanship of Cearbhall Ó Dálaigh (reports in 1956).

22 Oct. General election in N.I.: Unionists, 38; Independent Unionist, 1; Anti-Partition League, 7; Independent Nationalists, 2; Independent Labour, 1; Irish Labour, 1; Republican Labour, 1; Independent, 1. Lord Brookeborough continues as P.M.

29 Oct. Health Act (R.I.) provides free Mother-and-Child scheme.

Last inhabitant taken off the Blasket Islands in *Naomh Lorcan* and settled by the government on the mainland.

1954

11 Mar. d. Margaret Cousins, *née* Gillespie, Irish suffragette leader; wife of James Cousins, educationist and author (d. 20 Sept. 1956).

6 Apr. Flags and Emblems (Display) Act (N.I.) empowers police to remove emblems other than the Union Jack.

20 Apr. Last execution at Mountjoy Jail, that of Michael Manning.

30 Apr. First Cork International Choral and Folk Dance Festival opens.

18 May General election in R.I.: Fianna Fáil, 65; Fine Gael, 50; Labour, 19; Clann na Talmhan, 5; Clann na Poblachta, 3; Independents and others, 5.

2 June John A. Costello (Fine Gael) again becomes Taoiseach in a coalition government.

12 June I.R.A. attack Gough Barracks, Armagh.

19 July First outbreak of myxomatosis in Ireland reported near Bagenalstown, Co. Carlow.

11 Sept. d. Robert Maire Smyllie (60), journalist; editor of *Irish Times* from 1934; wrote under pen-name 'Nichevo'.

17 Oct. I.R.A. attack Omagh military barracks.

19 Nov. *The Quare Fellow* by Brendan Behan opens at the Pike Theatre, Dublin, produced by Alan Simpson.

1955

6 Jan. National Farmers' Association formed in the Republic.

13 Mar. d. Evie Hone (60), stained-glass artist.

6 Apr. Sir Anthony Eden (Conservative) succeeds Winston Churchill (Conservative) as P.M.

21 July Regular television transmission starts in Northern Ireland.

26 Nov. Saor Uladh ('Free Ulster'), I.R.A. splinter group, attacks Rosslea police barracks, Co. Fermanagh.

29 Nov. Government of Northern Ireland announces ban on Saor Uladh.

2 Dec. Offences Against the State Act, 1939, applied in the Republic to prohibit newspaper publicity for illegal organisations.

12 Dec. Cork Opera House destroyed by fire.

14 Dec. Republic admitted to the United Nations Organisation.

1956

13 Mar. Emergency Imposition of Duties Act introduces 68 new taxes in an attempt to deal with worsening balance-of-payments deficit in the Republic.

d. Alfred (Alfie) Byrne (72), politician (Independent), Lord Mayor of Dublin (1930–39; 1954–55); former Home Rule M.P. (last surviving member of the Irish Parliamentary Party at Westminster).

21–27 May First Cork International Film Festival.

30 May Thomas Kenneth Whitaker succeeds Owen Joseph Redmond as Secretary of the Department of Finance (until 28 Feb. 1969).

17 July Irish Nationality and Citizenship Act (R.I.) permits persons born in Northern Ireland after 6 Dec. 1922 to be declared Irish citizens.

5 Aug. d. John Miller Andrews (85), Unionist leader, P.M. of Northern Ireland (1940–43).

1 Dec. Ronnie Delany wins gold medal for Ireland in the 1,500 metres at Olympic Games at Melbourne, Ireland's first since 1932; Delany's comment, reported worldwide: 'I've never felt so happy in all my life.'

12 Dec. I.R.A. campaign against Northern Ireland starts with 10 attacks (*see* 26 Feb. 1962).

14 Dec. Inaugural meeting of the Capital Investment Advisory Committee.

21 Dec. Brian Faulkner, Northern Ireland Minister of Home Affairs, uses Special Powers Act against I.R.A. and Saor Uladh.

Start of screenings of *Amharc Éireann* ('A View of Ireland'), newsreel on Irish life by Colm Ó Laoghaire (runs until 1965).

Census of population in Republic: 2,898,264 (decrease of 2.11 per cent since 1951).

1957

1 Jan. Seán South and Fergal O'Hanlon killed during I.R.A. attack on Brookeborough police barracks, Co. Fermanagh.

9 Jan. P.M. Eden (Conservative) resigns; succeeded by Harold Macmillan (Conservative) on 10th.

5 Mar. General election in R.I.: Fianna Fáil, 78; Fine Gael, 40; Labour, 12; Clann na Talmhan, 3; Clann na Poblachta, 1; Sinn Féin, 4; Independents and others, 9. De Valera becomes Taoiseach.

25 Mar. Treaty of Rome signed, establishing the European Economic Community (E.E.C.).

28 Mar. d. Jack Butler Yeats (85), artist, younger brother of William Butler Yeats.

13–27 May First Dublin International Theatre Festival; theatre director Alan Simpson arrested on 23rd for staging production of *The Rose Tattoo* by Tennessee Williams.

8 July Government order in the Republic invokes Part II of the Offences Against the State Act, 1940, to deal with I.R.A. campaign against Northern Ireland.

22 Sept. d. Oliver St John Gogarty (79), surgeon, Senator and author; original of Buck Mulligan in James Joyce's *Ulysses*.

25 Oct. d. Edward John M. D. Plunkett (79), 18th Baron Dunsany, dramatist and author of fantasy tales; patron of poet Francis Ledwidge (d. 1917).

18 Dec. Gaeltacht Industries Act establishes Gaeltarra Éireann to develop small industries in Irish-speaking parts of the Republic (effective from 1 Apr. 1958).

Republic becomes member of the International Monetary Fund (I.M.F.) and joins the World Bank.

1958

19 Feb. Act provides for the establishment of An Foras Talúntais (Agricultural Research Institute).

20 Mar. General election in N.I.: Unionists, 37; Nationalists, 7; Independent Nationalist, 1; Northern Ireland Labour Party, 4; Independent Labour, 1; Republican Labour, 1; Independent, 1. Lord Brookeborough continues as P.M.

23 Mar. Northern Ireland parliamentary Labour Party's new leader, T. W. Boyd, accepts the role of official opposition at Stormont when this role is turned down by the Nationalists.

24 Mar. d. James Sullivan Starkey (79) (pen-name Séamus O'Sullivan); founder and editor of *Dublin Magazine* (1923–58).

28 Apr. Aer Lingus service to North America inaugurated.

12 May Official opening of Ardmore Film Studios, built by Emmet Dalton and Louis Elliman (goes into receivership in 1963; bought by R.T.E. in 1973 on behalf of the Minister for Industry and Commerce, Justin Keating; renamed National Film Studios of Ireland in 1975; again placed in receivership in Apr. 1982 by the Minister for Industry and Commerce, Albert Reynolds; bought by Irish-American consortium in Sept. 1986).

21 May Meeting in Sligo called by Nora Niland forms Yeats Society to organise the first Yeats Summer School.

29 May Government of Republic presented with first draft of T. K. Whitaker's *Economic Development* (*see* 11 Nov.).

27 June Five Irish army officers depart for the Lebanon as U.N. observers; first Irish U.N. soldiers.

2 July Industrial Development (Encouragement of External Investment) Act (R.I.) removes restrictions on foreign ownership in manufacturing industry.

2–9 Aug. Social Study Conference at Garron Tower, Co. Antrim: 'The Citizen and the Community'.

8 Sept. Pan-Am's Boeing 707–121 *Clipper America* becomes the first commercial jet plane to Europe when it lands at Shannon Airport on proving flight from Gander (3 hours and 47 minutes) (*see* 3 June 1960).

23 Sept. Republic votes with communist bloc in favour of the admission of the People's Republic of China to membership of the U.N. General Assembly.

9 Oct. Flag at half-mast on Belfast City Hall to mark death of Pope Pius XII rouses anger of some Protestants.

14 Oct. d. Lennox Robinson (72), dramatist and manager of the Abbey Theatre (1910–23).

11 Nov. *Programme for Economic Expansion,* white paper laid before the Dáil and the Senate to 'redefine the objectives of national economic policy'; based on *Economic Development* by T. K. Whitaker, Secretary of the Department of Finance and others (pub. 22 Nov.); leads to the First Programme for Economic Expansion, 1959–63).

23 Dec. d. Dorothy Macardle (59), historian.

1959

10 Feb. Congress of Irish Unions and Irish Trade Union Congress vote (separately) to unify in Irish Congress of Trade Unions (I.C.T.U.).

7 Mar. d. Thomas Cornelius Murray (82), dramatist (author of *Maurice Harte,* 1912, and *Autumn Fire,* 1924).

17 June Eamon de Valera elected third President of the Republic.

Electorate in Republic rejects referendum proposal to abolish P.R.

23 June Seán Lemass succeeds de Valera as leader of Fianna Fáil and Taoiseach.

9 July First bangharda (female member of Garda Síochána) (Mary Margaret Browne, Castlerea, Co. Roscommon).

21 Aug. d. Denis Devlin (51), poet and diplomat.

22–24 Sept. I.C.T.U. holds inaugural conference in Dublin.

25 Sept. d. Richard Irvine Best, Celtic scholar; Director of the National Library of Ireland (1924–40).

30 Sept. Première at the Fourth Cork International Film Festival of *Mise Éire* ('I Am Ireland'), film documentary on Irish history, the first feature-length film in the Irish language; music by Seán Ó Riada; *Saoirse?* ('Freedom?'), a companion film, is released in 1961.

21 Oct. James Dillon succeeds Richard Mulcahy as leader of Fine Gael.

1960

2 Mar. Brendan Corish succeeds William Norton as leader of the Labour Party.

16 Mar. P. & O. liner *Canberra* launched at Belfast shipyards; 20,000 watch the last large liner (45,000 tons) built in Belfast enter Belfast Lough; the end of the post-war shipbuilding boom.

12 Apr. Broadcasting Authority Act establishes an authority of nine members to oversee radio and television services in the Republic.

27 May Last barge on the Grand Canal leaves James's Street Harbour, Dublin, carrying Guinness to Limerick; the end of a tradition 156 years old.

3 June Pan-Am introduces jet service to Shannon Airport (*see* 3 July).

5 June d. Monsignor Pádraig de Brún (71), scholar and President of U.C.G. since 1945.

3 July Pan-Am D.C.–8 becomes the first airliner to take off from the new Shannon runway, and the first jet to fly Shannon – U.S.A. on scheduled passenger flight.

27 July Battalion of Irish defence forces leaves for the Congo (*see* 8 Nov.).

Sept. Commission appointed under Chief Justice Cearbhall Ó Dálaigh to inquire into higher education in the Republic.

20 Sept. Frederick H. Boland elected President of the General Assembly of the U.N.

23 Oct. d. Séamus MacManus (91), poet and novelist.

25 Oct. d. Harry Ferguson (75), inventor and engineer who made his fortune from the Ferguson tractor (*see* 31 Dec. 1909).

8 Nov. Nine Irish soldiers of an 11-man patrol of the 33rd Battalion killed in ambush at Niemba in the Congo by Baluba tribesmen.

13 Dec. Inaugural flight of first Aer Lingus jet, the Boeing-built *St Patrick*.

31 Dec. Last train runs on the Waterford–Tramore line, which in its earlier years had yielded a $7\frac{1}{2}$ per cent dividend.

1961

4 Jan. d. Barry Fitzgerald (stage-name of William Joseph Shields) (71), Abbey actor and film star.

16 Jan. Dairy Produce Marketing Act (R.I.) sets up Bord Bainne (Milk Board).

31 Jan. West Clare Railway runs its last train (*see* 27 Jan. 1885 *and* 2 July 1887).

4 Feb. d. Edward Pakenham (58), 6th Lord Longford, theatre producer, dramatist and Senator.

25 Apr. Last I.R.A. internees in the Republic released.

9 May d. William Kirkpatrick Magee (91), essayist under the pen-name John Eglinton; assistant librarian, National Library (1898–1921).

1 Aug. Republic applies for full membership of the E.E.C.

3 Oct. Republic joins U.N.E.S.C.O.

4 Oct. General election in R.I.: Fianna Fáil, 70; Fine Gael, 47; Labour, 16; Clann na Talmhan, 2; National Progressive Democrats, 2; Clann na Poblachta, 1; Independents and others, 6. Seán Lemass (Fianna Fáil) forms a minority government.

31 Dec. Television services of Radio Éireann (Radio Telefís Éireann) commence.

Census of population in Republic: 2,818,341 (decrease of 2.7 per cent since 1956).

Census of population in Northern Ireland: 1,425,042 (increase of 3.9 per cent since 1951).

1962

26 Feb. I.R.A. calls off campaign directed against Northern Ireland since 1956.

2 Mar. Government announced to have compulsorily acquired mineral rights at Tynagh, Co. Galway (copper, zinc and lead-silver ore).

8 May d. Rev. Stephen James Brown (81), founder of the Central Catholic Library (1922).

12 May Foundation stone laid for new Liberty Hall; architect Desmond Rea O'Kelly.

31 May General election in N.I.: Unionists, 34; Nationalists, 9; Northern Ireland Labour Party, 4; Independent Labour, 1; Republican Labour, 1; Irish Labour, 1; Independent, 1. Lord Brookeborough continues as P.M.

July d. Frank Gallagher, journalist, first editor of the *Irish Press* (1931); Director of Government Information Services (1939–48); author under pen-name David Hogan.

6 July Gay Byrne hosts his first 'Late Late Show'.

10 July Initial section of first motorway in Northern Ireland opens (Belfast to Lisburn).

24 Aug. d. Anew MacMaster (68), actor-manager, brother-in-law of Mícheál Mac Liammóir.

Patrick Lynch heads a survey team to examine the needs of Irish education and how to satisfy them in the future (in association with the O.E.C.D.) (*see* Nov. 1963).

1963

1 Feb. d. John, Cardinal D'Alton (80), R.C. Archbishop of Armagh and Primate since 1946.

18 Mar. d. Sir Hubert de la Poer Gough (93), leader of British army officers in the 'Curragh Incident' (*see* 20 Mar. 1914).

25 Mar. Lord Brookeborough retires as P.M. of Northern Ireland and leader of the Unionist Party; succeeded by Capt. Terence O'Neill.

12 May d. George Fitzmaurice (85), dramatist.

20 May Dr Patrick Hillery, R.I. Minister for Education, announces government plans for a system of comprehensive secondary schools and Regional Technical Colleges.

4 June Rev. Ian Paisley leads march to Belfast City Hall to protest at tributes to the late Pope John XXIII (d. 3 June).

26–29 June U.S. President John F. Kennedy in Ireland; addresses Oireachtas (*see* 22 Nov.).

22 Aug. Pub. *Second Programme for Economic Expansion,* Part I (Part II appears in July 1965).

3 Sept. Foundation stone for the new Abbey Theatre laid by President de Valera.

10 Sept. William Conway appointed R.C. Archbishop of Armagh and Primate in succession to John D'Alton (d. 1 Feb.); created cardinal on 22 Feb. 1965.

9 Oct. National Industrial Economic Council (N.I.E.C.) holds its first meeting.

19 Oct. Harold Macmillan (Conservative) retires as P.M.; succeeded by Sir Alec Douglas-Home (Conservative) (until 16 Oct. 1964).

30 Oct. d. Domhnall Ua Buachalla (97), who filled post of Governor-General under title of Seanascal (1932–37).

1 Nov. Turnover tax of 2½ per cent on retail sales and services becomes effective in the Republic.

20 Nov. Sir John Lockwood appointed to head committee to review higher education facilities in Northern Ireland.

22 Nov. U.S. President John F. Kennedy assassinated in Dallas, Texas.

Nov. Patrick Lynch heads survey team to estimate technological needs in the Republic over the next two decades (in association with the O.E.C.D.).

1964

Jan. Campaign for Social Justice founded in Dungannon, Co. Tyrone, by Dr Con and Patricia McCluskey 'to collect data on all injustices done against all creeds and political opinions'; 12 attend initial meeting.

13 Feb. d. Patrick Ryan (80), winner of Olympic gold and silver medals for hammer-throwing at Antwerp in 1920 for U.S.A.; he set world record of 189 ft 6½ in. in 1913 at Celtic Park (lasts until 1937).

18 Feb. d. Maurice Walsh (84), novelist, whose story was the basis for the film *The Quiet Man*.

20 Mar. d. Brendan Behan (41), dramatist, author of autobiographical best-seller *Borstal Boy*.

26 Mar. An Foras Forbartha (National Institute for Physical Planning and Construction Research) incorporated (abolished in 1987).

4 Apr. d. Seán O'Sullivan (57), painter; youngest artist elected to R.H.A. (at age 21).

15 May d. Pádraig Ó Caoimh (67), general secretary of the G.A.A. since 1929.

2 June Eddie McAteer elected leader of the Nationalist Party at Stormont (*see* 2 Feb. 1965).

2 July Ulster Folk Museum, Cultra, Co. Down, opens.

8 Aug. First rescue by Helicopter Rescue service (operated by Air Corps) when man and boy are rescued from a drifting boat in Dublin Bay.

18 Sept. d. Seán O'Casey (84), dramatist.

16 Oct. Harold Wilson (Labour) succeeds Sir Alec Douglas-Home (Conservative) as P.M.

11 Nov. d. Pádraig Ó Siochfhradha (81), writer in Irish under pen-name 'An Seabhac'.

12 Nov. d. Robert Brennan (83), Republican, journalist and diplomat.

23 Dec. d. Desmond Ryan (71), historian and journalist.

31 Dec. d. Daniel Corkery (86), teacher and author.

KILKENNY COUNTY LIBRARY

1965

1 Jan. New Ministry of Development in Northern Ireland under William Craig comes into existence.

7 Jan. d. Jimmy O'Dea (65), comedian, creator of 'Biddy Mulligan'.

14 Jan. Taoiseach Seán Lemass and Northern Ireland P.M. O'Neill lunch at Stormont; statement says that their talks did not include constitutional or political issues (*see* 9 Feb.).

16 Jan. *Athbheochan na Gaeilge; The Restoration of the Irish Language*, government white paper, promulgates a 10-year plan to make the Irish language a popular medium of communication in the Republic.

2 Feb. Nationalist Party in Northern Ireland, led by Eddie McAteer, assumes role of official opposition at Stormont.

9 Feb. P.M. O'Neill and Taoiseach Lemass meet in Dublin.

15 Feb. Northern Ireland Economic Council meets for the first time.

Mar. Report of the commission of inquiry on mentally handicapped in Republic.

1 Mar. Following a state funeral, the remains of Roger Casement are reinterred in Glasnevin cemetery, Dublin (*see* 3 Aug. 1916).

7 Apr. General election in R.I.: Fianna Fáil, 72; Fine Gael, 47; Labour, 22; Clann na Poblachta, 1; Independents and others, 2. Seán Lemass remains Taoiseach.

15 Apr. Blood Transfusion Service Board replaces the National Blood Transfusion Association (Cork incorporated in 1975).

21 Apr. Liam Cosgrave succeeds James Dillon as leader of Fine Gael.

22 June d. Piaras Béaslaí (84), revolutionary and author.

2 July – 12 Sept. Strike by printers closes newspapers and Dublin commercial printing houses.

16 Sept. Clann na Poblachta announces its dissolution.

16 Nov. d. William Thomas Cosgrave (85), politician (leader of Cumann na nGaedheal, 1922–33, Fine Gael, 1934–44); first President of the Executive Council of the Free State (1922–32).

25 Nov. General election in N.I.: Unionists, 36; Nationalists, 9; Northern Ireland Labour Party, 2; National Democratic Party, 1; Republican Labour, 2; Liberal, 1; Independent, 1.

27 Nov. d. Francis MacManus (56), author and broadcaster, responsible for the Thomas Davis lectures on Radio Éireann.

14 Dec. Anglo-Irish Free Trade Area Agreement signed by Harold Wilson and Seán Lemass: most British duties on goods from the Republic entering U.K. abolished; effective from 1 July 1966.

d. Mary Ellen O'Donoghue, Ireland's first schoolmistress.

World's longest laminated wooden bridge opens at Ballycastle, Co. Antrim.

Pub. *Towards a Just Society*, Fine Gael policy document.

Pub. *Manuscript Sources for the History of Irish Civilisation* (11 vols) by Richard Hayes, Director of the National Library of Ireland.

Pub. *Investment in Education* (Vol. I), report of survey on educational needs in the Republic (Vol. II pub. 8 Aug. 1966).

1966

4 Mar. Capital punishment abolished in Northern Ireland except for political murders.

8 Mar. Nelson's Pillar in O'Connell Street, Dublin, demolished by explosion.

10 Mar. d. Frank O'Connor (62), pen-name of Michael O'Donovan, short-story-writer.

31 Mar. In U.K. general election Gerry Fitt (Republican Labour, 26,292 votes) wins West Belfast from James Kilfedder (Unionist, 24,281).

1 Apr. d. Brian O'Nolan (55) ('Myles na Gopaleen' of the *Irish Times* and novelist under pen-name Flann O'Brien).

10–17 Apr. Commemoration of the Easter Rising of 1916; passes without incident in Northern Ireland.

27 Apr. First of a series of farmers' demonstrations leads to arrest of 28 members of the Irish Creamery Milk Suppliers' Association under the Offences Against the State Act for picketing Dáil and the Department of Agriculture.

6 May Bank strike through action of junior officials (banks reopen in Northern Ireland on 21 June and in Republic on 5 Aug.).

1 June Eamon de Valera re-elected President of the Republic.

6 June Rev. Ian Paisley demonstrates in Belfast, protesting at 'Romeward' trend in the Presbyterian General Assembly, provoking unrest when he marches through Cromac Street in the Catholic Markets area of Belfast; Paisley arrested and jailed for three months when he refuses to be bound over (19 July).

26 June A barman killed and two other Catholics shot in Malvern Street on the Shankill Road; Augustus ('Gusty') Spence and two other members of the Ulster Volunteer Force sentenced to life imprisonment for the crime on 14 Oct.

28 June P.M. O'Neill announces banning of Ulster Volunteer Force.

July Department of Labour established in the Republic.

1 July Anglo-Irish Free Trade Area Agreement comes into effect, allowing for gradual removal of protectionist tariffs between U.K. and the Republic.

18 July Abbey Theatre reopens (*see* 18 July 1951).

22 Aug. Munster and Leinster Bank, Provincial Bank and the Royal Bank form the Allied Irish Banks.

First three comprehensive secondary schools open at Carraroe, Co. Galway; Shannon, Co. Clare; and Cootehill, Co. Cavan.

10 Sept. Addressing the National Union of Journalists at Dún Laoghaire, Co. Dublin, the Republic's Minister for Education, Donogh O'Malley, announces that free post-primary education will be available throughout the state from 1967/68 onwards.

7 Oct. National Farmers' Association sets off on march from Bantry, Co. Cork, to Dublin to protest at loss of a proposed increase of one penny on a gallon of milk.

24 Oct. Opening of Ireland's longest sea-bridge, the 498-yard-long Cork–Haulbowline link, costing £250,000 and taking two years to build.

10 Nov. Seán Lemass resigns as leader of Fianna Fáil and Taoiseach; succeeded by Jack Lynch.

23 Nov. d. Seán Thomas O'Kelly (84), President of Éire/Republic (1945–59).

National Bank of Ireland taken over by the Bank of Ireland.

Census of population in Republic: 2,884,002 (increase of 2.33 per cent since 1961).

Census of population in Northern Ireland: 1,484,775 (increase of 4.2 per cent since 1961).

Pub. *Death of a Naturalist,* first collection of poems by Séamus Heaney.

1967

16 Jan. Public inquiry into bread and flour prices opens in Dublin.

28 Jan. d. Helena Molony (82), former President of the I.C.T.U.

1 Feb. Northern Ireland Civil Rights Association (N.I.C.R.A.) founded at Belfast's International Hotel; Noel Harris elected chairman of committee of 15.

21 Feb. Landlord and Tenant (Ground Rents) Act (R.I.) facilitates purchase of ground rents by tenants.

27 Feb. O'Hanrahan Bridge across the River Barrow at New Ross, Co. Wexford, officially opened.

7 Mar. William Craig, Minister of Home Affairs, bans celebrations in Northern Ireland to mark the centenary of the 1867 Fenian rising; also bans Republican Clubs, which he describes as a front for the I.R.A.

Industrial Training Act (R.I.) establishes An Comhairle Oiliúna (AnCO) as a training body.

16 Mar. d. Thomas MacGreevy (74), Chevalier of the Legion of Honour, scholar, poet, critic; Director of the National Gallery of Ireland (1950–64).

3 Apr. Communications Centre, Booterstown, Dublin, opens.

18 Apr. Donogh O'Malley, Minister for Education, announces the government's intention to unite T.C.D. and U.C.D. in one University of Dublin (plan abandoned in favour of a scheme for co-operation between the two universities in 1970).

22 Apr. d. Walter Macken (51), actor, dramatist and novelist.

26 Apr. Harry West, Northern Ireland Minister for Agriculture, dismissed on ground that private land purchase conflicted with his position.

3 May I.T.G.W.U. resolves at its annual conference in Limerick to affiliate its 150,000 members to the Labour Party.

11 May Republic again unsuccessfully applies for E.E.C. membership.

12 June First fatal crash at Dublin Airport when an Aer Turas cargo plane crashes, killing crew members.

14 June d. Seán Sáirséal Ó hÉigheartaigh (50), civil servant and publisher, founder of Sáirséal & Dill (1945).

22 June Aer Lingus Viscount crashes near Ashbourne, Co. Meath, killing three.

11 July Censorship of Publications Amendment Act (R.I.) removes ban from works banned for more than 12 years (over 5,000 works).

20 Aug. Derrynane Abbey, Co. Kerry, home of Daniel O'Connell, becomes museum.

14 Sept. d. Rupert Edward Cecil Lee Guinness (93), 2nd Lord Iveagh, brewer and philanthropist; Chancellor of T.C.D. (1927–63).

5 Oct. Republic and Northern Ireland agree to link their electricity systems (Maynooth, Co. Kildare, to Tandragee, Co. Armagh).

6 Oct. Donogh O'Malley, Minister for Education, abolishes primary certificate examination for National Schools in the Republic.

12 Nov. First Rosc Art Exhibition at Royal Dublin Society's H.Q., Ballsbridge.

18 Nov. Edward Delany's sculpture of Wolfe Tone unveiled in St Stephen's Green, Dublin (damaged by explosion on 8 Feb. 1971).

30 Nov. d. Patrick Kavanagh (63), poet.

7 Dec. Daily immigration to the Republic restricted to 2,000 to prevent spread of Foot and Mouth disease from Britain.

11 Dec. Taoiseach Lynch visits P.M. O'Neill at Stormont (*see* 8 Jan. 1968).

12 Dec. Opinion poll in Northern Ireland reveals that given a choice between Capt. Terence O'Neill and Rev. Ian Paisley for P.M., 90 per cent favour O'Neill.

18 Dec. d. James Everett (77), who as Minister for Posts and Telegraphs played a central role in the so-called 'Battle of Baltinglass' (1950).

Employment Appeals Tribunal established in the Republic under Redundancy Act.

Pub. *Diaries* of Joseph Holloway, a unique record of Abbey Theatre performances since its foundation.

Pub. *Commission on Higher Education, 1960–67, Presentation and Summary of Report* (R.I.).

1968

1 Jan. d. Donagh MacDonagh (55), poet, dramatist and jurist.

8 Jan. P.M. O'Neill visits Taoiseach Lynch in Dublin.

20 Jan. d. Sir Alfred Chester Beatty (93), philanthropist and art collector; first honorary citizen of Ireland, given state funeral (*see* 6 Sept. 1950).

6 Feb. d. William Conor (83), artist specialising in Ulster themes.

21 Feb. Debate in Stormont on reorganisation of local government.

10 Mar. d. Donogh O'Malley (47), R.I. Minister for Education.

24 Mar. 61 people die when Aer Lingus Viscount *St Phelim* plunges into the sea near Tuskar Rock, Co. Wexford (cause of crash never established).

29 May President de Valera opens the John F. Kennedy Memoral Park at Slieve Coillte, Co. Wexford.

10 June T.C.D. breaks a 350-year tradition when creating five female teaching staff Fellows of the college.

20 June Austin Currie, M.P. (Nationalist), occupies house in Caledon, Co. Tyrone, which has been allocated to a single Protestant woman.

22 June d. Capt. Patrick J. Saul (74), aviator.

27 June Kevin Street College of Technology, Dublin, opens.

1 July Frank Aiken, R.I. Minister for External Affairs, among the U.N. signatories to the Treaty for the Non-Proliferation of Nuclear Weapons, in Moscow.

5 July Brian Lenihan, R.I. Minister for Education, announces that N.U.I. is to be dissolved, with U.C.C. and U.C.G. becoming separate universities.

12 July U. Thant, Secretary-General of the U.N.O., addresses the International Bar Association Conference in Dublin; receives honorary degree from T.C.D.

New Library building at T.C.D. opened by President de Valera.

16 July Archaeological team discovers passage and buried chamber at Knowth, Co. Meath.

22 July Fr James McDyer opens folk village at Glencolumbkille, Co. Donegal.

12 Aug. Kilkenny Castle purchased for restoration from the Marquis of Ormond for nominal fee of £50.

15 Aug. Higher Education Authority established in the Republic as *ad hoc* body (statutory powers conferred in 1977).

24 Aug. Northern Ireland Civil Rights Association marches from Coalisland to Dungannon, Co. Tyrone; R.U.C. separate N.I.C.R.A. and U.V.F. demonstrators.

Sept. Pub. (in *Studies*) 'Post-Primary Education: Now and in the Future' by Seán O'Connor, Secretary of the Department of Education.

13 Sept. First Merriman School opens, at Ennis, Co. Clare.

28 Sept. Lord Mayor of Belfast entertains All-Ireland Gaelic football champions, Down.

1 Oct. 400 students of the New University of Ulster at Coleraine (Ireland's first new university for over 50 years) attend an ecumenical service; university officially opens on 25 Oct.

3–5 Oct. William Craig, Minister of Home Affairs, bans N.I.C.R.A. march in Derry, organised by Eamonn McCann in support of the Derry housing action campaign; march takes place, followed by violence on 5 Oct., when 88 are injured, including 11 police.

8 Oct. Republic's first traffic wardens, 20 in number, start work in Dublin.

9 Oct. Students at Queen's University form what becomes People's Democracy (11th) to seek reform in Northern Ireland; Derry Citizens' Action Committee formed; Loyal Citizens of Ulster is set up in opposition on 18 Oct.

15 Oct. Nationalist Party withdraws from role of official opposition at Stormont.

16 Oct. Referendum in Republic on abolition of P.R. again defeated.

20 Oct. d. Paul Vincent Carroll (68), dramatist.

30 Oct. d. William O'Brien (87), trade unionist; general secretary of the I.T.G.W.U. (1924–46).

5 Nov. British P.M. Harold Wilson demands reforms in Northern Ireland at meeting with P.M. O'Neill, William Craig and Brian Faulkner.

7 Nov. d. Senator Margaret Pearse (90), sister of Patrick and William Pearse; accorded state funeral.

8 Nov. Londonderry Corporation accepts Nationalist motion to adopt points system for allocation of council housing.

16 Nov. 16,000 civil rights supporters defy ban to march in Derry; march passes without incident.

22 Nov. Northern Ireland P.M. O'Neill announces a series of reforms, including the abolition of Londonderry Corporation, abolition of business vote in local government, reform of local government within three years, fair allocation of local authority housing, establishment of post of Ombudsman, review of the Special Powers Act.

30 Nov. Civil rights march in Armagh.

3 Dec. British peer Lord Ratheaven calls for British troops to be sent to Northern Ireland, claiming that followers of Rev. Ian Paisley are 400 years behind the times.

Lord Grey of Naunton sworn in as (last) Governor of Northern Ireland.

6 Dec. Papers of John M. Synge purchased by T.C.D. for £50,000.

9 Dec. Northern Ireland P.M. O'Neill delivers his 'Ulster at the Crossroads' speech on television which brings him a huge measure of support (over 150,000 letters and telegrams); criticised by Minister for Home Affairs,

William Craig, who is dismissed on 11th.

12 Dec. Unionist parliamentary party passes vote of confidence in P.M. O'Neill (4 abstentions).

14 Dec. Rev. Ian Paisley greets Larne gun-running ship *Clydevalley* (*see* 24–25 Apr. 1914) at Larne on her arrival from Nova Scotia (*see* 21 Aug. 1974).

29 Dec. Capt. Terence O'Neill named 'Man of the Year' by the *Sunday Independent* in Dublin.

Report of the Consultative Council of the General Hospitals Services, Outline of the Future Hospital System (R.I.).

1969

1–4 Jan. People's Democracy marches from Belfast to Derry; ambushed by militant Unionists at Burntollet Bridge, near Claudy, Co. Londonderry; the approximately 80 R.U.C. officers in attendance make no effort to interfere; events are widely reported on television.

5 Jan. Following night of violence in the Catholic Bogside of Derry, in which members of the R.U.C. are injured, a citizens' army is formed.

8 Jan. Ulster Defence Force (U.D.F.), consisting of ex-servicemen founded to protect Protestant lives and property.

11 Jan. People's Democracy demonstration in Newry, Co. Down; 10 policemen and 28 others injured and 24 arrested.

21 Jan. Fiftieth anniversary of the First Dáil celebrated in the Mansion House, Dublin.

23 Jan. Brian Faulkner, Northern Ireland Minister of Commerce, resigns; succeeded by Roy Bradford.

24 Jan. d. Patrick Hogan (82), Ceann Comhairle, Dáil Éireann (1951–67).

30 Jan. 12 dissident Unionist M.P.s sign document seeking change in leadership; P.M. O'Neill responds: 'I will not back down. I will not trim my sails. I will do my duty.'

31 Jan. Deerpark colliery, last remaining in Castlecomer coalfield, Co. Kilkenny, closes.

1 Feb. d. Charles Bewley, lawyer and diplomat; first Irish Minister to the Holy See (1929) and to Berlin (1933–39) (*see* 8 Aug. 1939).

4 Feb. Seán Bourke wins appeal against extradition to Britain, where he faces charges of complicity in connection with the escape of spy George Blake from Wormwood Scrubs Prison (22 Oct. 1966).

5 Feb. New Ulster Movement formed to support P.M. O'Neill.

Anthony Peacocke takes office as R.U.C. Inspector-General.

18 Feb. d. James Larkin (jun.) (64), trade unionist; first T.U.C. official to present case in the Labour Court (1947).

24 Feb. General election in N.I.: Unionists, 36 (of whom 24 are pro-O'Neill and 12 anti-O'Neill); Independent O'Neill Unionists, 3; Nationalists, 6; Northern Ireland Labour Party, 2; Republican Labour, 2; Independents, 3. John Hume wins Foyle seat from Eddie McAteer (leader of the Nationalist Party); P.M. O'Neill defeats Rev. Ian Paisley at Bannside (7,745 votes to 6,331).

Secondary schools reopen in the Republic, following teachers' strike which closed 600 schools from 1 Feb.

1 Mar. Dr T. K. Whitaker becomes Governor of the Central Bank.

3 Mar. Lord Cameron appointed to head commission to investigate the causes of recent outbreaks of violence in N.I. (report published on 12 Sept.).

Mar. Pub. *Third Programme, Economic and Social Development, 1969–72* (R.I.).

26 Mar. Electoral Amendment Act increases the number of Dáil constituencies from 138 to 142.

30 Mar. Electricity sub-station at Castlereagh, near Belfast, destroyed by explosion, causing £500,000 worth of damage.

17 Apr. Bernadette Devlin (Unity (anti-Unionist alliance), 33,648 votes) elected Westminster M.P. for Mid-Ulster, defeating Mrs Anna Forrest (Unionist, 29,437); the youngest-ever M.P. in the U.K. parliament.

19–20 Apr. 200 N.I.C.R.A. supporters organise protest and sit in in the centre of Derry, where they are attacked by mob which drives them into the Bogside; barricades set up against police; Samuel Devenny, 42-year-old Catholic in the Bogside is kicked and batoned by police (dies on 17 July from the injuries); petrol bombs used for the first time in Derry.

20 Apr. In Belfast nine post-offices are burnt and two buses in depot on the Falls Road set on fire.

Explosion at Silent Valley reservoir, Co. Down, damages main pipe carrying water supply to Belfast; another damages electricity pylon at Annaboe, Kilmore, Co. Armagh.

22 Apr. Bernadette Devlin's maiden speech in House of Commons widely reported: 'I am not speaking of one night of broken glass, but of fifty years of human misery.'

25 Apr. 500 British troops arrive in Northern Ireland.

Dublin City Council dissolved by the Minister for Local Government for failing to strike a sufficient rate.

28 Apr. Capt. Terence O'Neill resigns as Unionist leader and P.M.; succeeded by his cousin, Major James Chichester-Clark (1 May), who defeats Brian Faulkner (17 votes to 16).

7 May Gulf Oil's terminal on Whiddy Island in Bantry Bay, Co. Cork, opened by Taoiseach Jack Lynch (*see* 8 Jan. 1979).

23 May First nature trail in the Republic opens in the grounds of Johnstown Castle, Co. Wexford.

d. Robert Briscoe (75), politician (Fianna Fáil); the first Jewish Lord Mayor of Dublin (1956 and 1961).

9 June Following London talks at Swiss Embassy on his banning from Switzerland during the forthcoming papal visit, Rev. Ian Paisley proclaims that the Swiss are 'dimwits' whose only contribution to the twentieth century has been the invention of the cuckoo clock.

17 June President de Gaulle of France commences official state visit to the Republic.

18 June General election in R.I.: Fianna Fáil, 75; Fine Gael, 50; Labour, 18; Independent, 1. Jack Lynch remains Taoiseach.

22 June d. Thomas J. O'Connell (87), leader of the Labour Party (1927–32).

30 June Six Zambians, the first foreign officers to be trained by the Irish army, graduate from the Irish Military Academy.

1 July Sir Edmund Compton takes up office as Ombudsman for Northern Ireland.

2 July *The Reshaping of Local Government: Further Proposals*, white paper, reveals plans for local government reforms in the Republic.

9 July Lt-Gen. Sir Ian Freeland takes up duties as G.O.C. Northern Ireland.

13–14 July Rioting in Dungiven, Co. Londonderry, where Orange Hall is burnt out and first death in the new disturbances occurs (14th).

17 July George Otto Simms succeeds James McCann as C.I. Archbishop of Armagh and Primate.

Fr Eamonn Casey, Director of the Catholic Housing Aid Society in London, appointed R.C. Bishop of Kerry.

20 July Derry Citizens' Defence Association founded to supersede Derry Citizens' Action Committee.

29 July Finance Act in Republic includes exemption from paying income tax to creators of works of 'cultural or artistic merit'.

1 Aug. Farthings and halfpennies no longer legal tender in the Republic.

2 Aug. d. Professor Alfred O'Rahilly (85), scholar.

5 Aug. Ulster Volunteer Force explode bomb at R.T.E. studios at Montrose, Donnybrook, Dublin.

12 Aug. Apprentice Boys' march in Derry triggers three days of rioting between police and Catholic inhabitants in the 'Siege of the Bogside'; 'Free Derry' comes into being; rioting ends with arrival of troops at 5 p.m. on 14th.

C.S. gas used for the first time in Northern Ireland.

13 Aug. Taoiseach Lynch in television broadcast says that 'the Irish government can no longer stand by and see innocent people injured'; calls for an end to partition of Ireland and announces movement of troops and field hospitals to the border; asks British government to seek dispatch of U.N. peacekeeping force to Northern Ireland.

P.M. Chichester-Clark responds to Lynch's broadcast, stating that he will hold Lynch 'personally responsible' for any worsening of feeling 'which those inflammatory and ill-considered remarks' might cause.

14 Aug. British troops move into the Bogside to separate opposing sides; five civilians shot dead.

15 Aug. Rioting in Belfast and several killed as clashes between Catholics and Protestants occur at Bombay Street in Clonard, Ardoyne, Divis Flats and the Falls Road, where Catholics erect barricades; British troops who move in to keep Catholics and Protestants apart are welcomed and fed by Catholics; Taoiseach Lynch mobilises Republic's first-line reserve as Catholic refugees flee from Northern Ireland to the Republic.

16 Aug. Garda baton-charge breaks up violent anti-British demonstration outside the British Embassy in Dublin; over 50 injured.

British troops feted as they enter Catholic Ardoyne area in Belfast.

19 Aug. Meeting between Northern Ireland government representatives and the British government in London: 'Downing Street Declaration' announces that Northern Ireland will remain part of the U.K. while a majority so wish; that Northern Ireland is a British concern; that British government welcomes reforms in Northern Ireland and wishes to see them continue; that the two governments are determined to restore normality in Northern Ireland.

20 Aug. U.N. adjourns consideration of the Republic's request for intervention in Northern Ireland.

25 Aug. Bernadette Devlin, M.P., on fund-raising trip to the U.S.A. claims to have raised $650,000 on two-hour radio phone-in programme.

26 Aug. Review body established under Lord Hunt to inquire into the R.U.C. and Special Constabulary (reports on 10 Oct.).

KILKENNY COUNTY LIBRARY

27 Aug. Tribunal established under Sir Leslie Scarman to inquire into recent disturbances in Northern Ireland (*see* 6 Apr. 1972).

27–29 Aug. James Callaghan, British Home Secretary, in Northern Ireland; welcomed to the Bogside in Derry on 28th; announces immediate grant of £250,000 for alleviation of distress.

28 Aug. Oliver Wright installed as first U.K. government representative in Northern Ireland to monitor Northern Ireland government's reform programme.

31 Aug. Figures published reveal 10 deaths, 154 gunshot wounds and 745 other reported injuries during rioting of July and August.

1 Sept. 5p and 10p coins introduced in the Republic.

2 Sept. Northern Ireland government announces three-week amnesty during which no action will be taken against individuals surrendering arms or ammunition.

3 Sept. R.U.C. Inspector-General Anthony Peacocke announces disciplinary charges against 16 constables as a result of inquiry into events at Burntollet and Derry city on 4–5 Jan.

10 Sept. British army establishes peace-line, 1½ miles in extent, in Belfast.

Sept. First Regional Technical Colleges open in the Republic at Athlone, Carlow, Dundalk, Sligo and Waterford.

12 Sept. Report of the Cameron Commission places much of the blame for current disturbances on Stormont and the R.U.C.

16 Sept. Northern Ireland Public Protection Authority reveals that it has received almost 600 complaints of threats and intimidation within a week of formation by Home Affairs Minister, Robert Porter.

21 Sept. Rev. Ian Paisley claims to have received admissions from British troops that they are there to 'keep the Catholics happy'.

22 Sept. All barricades taken down in Belfast.

White lines replace barricades in the Bogside and Creggan areas of Derry city.

Scarman Tribunal opens in Derry.

24 Sept. Pub. *Report of Public Services Organisation; Review Group, 1966–1969* (Devlin Report); calls for widespread reorganisation of the public services in the Republic.

2 Oct. 100,000 loyalists petition P.M. Chichester-Clark, protesting at proposed disarming of the 'B' Special Constabulary.

4 Oct. An estimated 6,000 are present in congregation when Rev. Ian Paisley opens his Martyrs Memorial Free Presbyterian Church in Belfast.

d. Cathal O'Shannon (80), trade unionist.

9 Oct. Higher Education Authority (R.I.) issues its first report.

10 Oct. Report of the Hunt Committee of inquiry on policing in Northern Ireland published: R.U.C. to be deprived of guns on normal duties; 'B' Specials to be disbanded and replaced by new forces; greeted with anger among Unionists.

Sir Arthur Young, head of the City of London police, replaces Anthony Peacocke as Inspector-General of R.U.C.

11–12 Oct. 3,000 Unionists march from Shankill Road district to Unity Flats; troops move in; guns and petrol bombs used.

Constable Victor Arbuckle becomes the first member of the R.U.C. killed in the new violence in Northern Ireland when shot in Shankill Road, Belfast (11th).

12 Oct. d. Louise Gavan Duffy (85), pioneering educationist; one of the first women to enter U.C.D.; founder of Scoil Bhríde, the first all-Irish school for girls in Dublin (1917).

13 Oct. James Callaghan, U.K. Home Secretary, informs House of Commons that rioting in Belfast on the 11th had reached a critical turning-point; states that firearms had been freely used and troops forced to respond; advises the House that the only remaining barricades in Derry are three Protestant ones; gives current garrison strength in Northern Ireland as 9,000 including permanently posted R.A.F. personnel.

Over 100 'B' Specials at Newtownards, Co. Down, resign in protest at Hunt Report's recommendation to disband the force (rejoin on 20th.).

17 Oct. 250 'B' Specials at Ballymena, Co. Antrim, resign in protest at Hunt Report.

23 Oct. Samuel Beckett announced winner of the Nobel Prize for Literature.

24 Oct. H.M.S. *Maidstone* berths in Belfast harbour to provide additional accommodation for British troops (later used as prison ship).

25 Oct. Rent-an-Irish-Cottage Scheme inaugurated by Bord Fáilte at Ballyvaughan, Co. Clare.

26 Oct. Speaking on BBC radio, Denis Healey, U.K. Secretary for Defence, says that a four-month tour of duty is the desired maximum for troops 'in present conditions'; he adds: 'In Northern Ireland it is just not a riot. We are preventing a civil war.'

28 Oct. Minesweeper H.M.S. *Kellingham* deployed to prevent smuggled arms from entering Northern Ireland.

30 Oct. Government in the Republic authorises the use of troops to protect generating stations.

3 Nov. Breathalyser introduced in the Republic.

As the army in Northern Ireland reports incident-free weekend, the government lifts restrictions on weekend drinking (the sale of alcohol had been prohibited from 7 p.m. on the weekend of 17 Oct.).

7 Nov. Over 3,000 Viking artifacts discovered on side of proposed Dublin city civic offices at Wood Quay.

20 Nov. d. Josephine MacNeill (74), first Irish woman diplomatic representative abroad (1949).

23 Nov. First annual conference of the People's Democracy reveals that the weekly circulation of the *Free Citizen* newspaper is 6,000 copies.

24 Nov. Car ferry between Portaferry and Strangford, Co. Down, begins operations.

25 Nov. Electoral Law Act (N.I.) introduces reforms: qualifying age for franchise reduced to 18; local government franchise extended to all parliamentary electors; local government elections postponed to 1971.

Under the Special Powers Act the N.I. Minister for Home Affairs bans the proposed Ulster *v.* Springboks (South African touring side) rugby match scheduled for 29 Nov.

27 Nov. N.I. Minister for Development announces that £600,000 has been made available to assist families who have been burnt out of their homes.

28 Nov. Pub. first issue of *Loyalist News*.

9 Dec. National Gallery of Ireland purchases Goya's 'The Dream' for £145,000.

17 Dec. Review body on reorganisation of local government in Northern Ireland appointed under Patrick Macrory (report submitted on 29 May 1970 and adopted by Stormont in Jan. 1971).

18 Dec. U.K. Ulster Defence Regiment Act to establish part-time force under army control.

27 Dec. d. Dan Breen (75), I.R.A. veteran and politician (Fianna Fáil); first Republican to take the oath of allegiance (Apr. 1927).

28 Dec. *Sunday Press* in Dublin discloses split in the I.R.A. over proposal to contest elections; Provisional Army Council formed (*see* 11 Jan. 1970).

Bernadette Devlin, M.P., named 'Man of the Year' by the *Sunday Independent* in Dublin.

Pub. *The Price of My Soul*, autobiography of Bernadette Devlin.

1970

1 Jan. Terence O'Neill created life peer in New Year Honours List (takes title Lord O'Neill of the Maine).

6 Jan. Tribunal of inquiry opens at Dublin's Four Courts into illegal money-lending following exposé on R.T.E.'s 'Seven Days' programme; ends on 8 Apr., longest inquiry to date.

11 Jan. Split in Sinn Féin on issue of parliamentary abstention results in formation of Official and Provisional Sinn Féin, with headquarters at Gardiner Place and Kevin Street respectively; corresponding split in the I.R.A.

28 Jan. d. Gerard Sweetman (61), politician (Fine Gael), Minister for Finance (1954–57).

8 Feb. d. Cahir Healy (93), politician (Nationalist).

15 Feb. d. Eoin ('The Pope') O'Mahony (66), barrister and genealogist.

17 Feb. 50p coin introduced in the Republic.

24 Feb. Health Act (R.I.) provides for establishment of eight registered Health Boards and hospitals authority (Comhairle na hOispidéal).

15 Mar. Republic and Northern Ireland Communist Parties unite to form the Communist Party of Ireland (general secretary Michael O'Riordan).

21 Mar. 'Dana' (Rosemary Brown) wins the Eurovision Song Contest with song 'All Kinds of Everything'.

26 Mar. Police authority, association, advisory board and R.U.C. reserve established in Northern Ireland under the Police Act.

31 Mar. – 1 Apr. Phased disbandment of the 'B' Special Constabulary starts (*see* 30 Apr.).

16 Apr. Rev. Ian Paisley (Bannside) and Rev. William Beattie (South Antrim) returned in by-elections to Northern Ireland parliament.

18 Apr. Speech by Stephen Coughlan, Mayor of Limerick, widely attacked for its anti-semitism.

21 Apr. Alliance Party formed in Northern Ireland as a moderate platform for Catholics and Protestants; Oliver Napier, Robert Cooper and David Corkery among founder-members.

23 Apr. St Enda's, Rathfarnham, school founded by Patrick Pearse, presented to the nation as a Patrick Pearse Museum.

27 Apr. d. Arthur Shields (74), actor, brother of Barry Fitzgerald.

28 Apr. Capt. James Kelly, personal assistant to the Director of Army Intelligence, relieved of his post and transferred to training depot; resigns his commission on 29 Apr. (*see* 1 May).

30 Apr. – 17 Nov. Bank strike in the Republic.

30 Apr. Ulster Defence Regiment (U.D.R.) assumes duties of the Ulster Special Constabulary (now officially stood down).

Industrial Development Authority (I.D.A.), established in 1950, becomes autonomous state-sponsored body.

1 May Capt. James Kelly and Belgian-born Albert Luykx arrested under Offences Against the State Act; released within 24 hours.

4 May Mícheál Ó Moráin, R.I. Minister for Justice, resigns for health reasons.

6 May Taoiseach Jack Lynch dismisses from cabinet Charles J. Haughey, Minister for Finance, and Neil T. Blaney, Minister for Agriculture; Kevin Boland, Minister for Local Government, resigns (*see* 28 May).

8 May 37½-hour debate in Dáil on allegations of arms smuggling; ends, in what is effectively a confidence motion, with government victory (73 votes to 66) on approval for new ministerial appointments; James Gibbons replaces Neil Blaney at Agriculture, and George Colley replaces Charles Haughey at Finance.

22 May Employer–Labour Conference established under chairmanship of Professor Basil Chubb.

28 May Ex-ministers Charles J. Haughey and Neil T. Blaney arrested and charged with conspiring to import arms and ammunition, as are Capt. Kelly and Albert Luykx; Blaney discharged on 2 July (*see* 22 Sept.).

31 May Champion steeplechaser Arkle put down.

3 June Ex-minister Kevin Boland expelled from Fianna Fáil parliamentary party following his refusal to withdraw remarks about Taoiseach Lynch's 'unparalleled treachery'; Boland resigns from the Fianna Fáil organisation on 22 June.

7 June d. Dr Owen Sheehy-Skeffington (61), humanist and academic.

10 June Tarbert, Co. Kerry, generating station opened by Taoiseach Lynch; its 120,000 kw capacity is 1.5 times that of Shannon Scheme at Ardnacrusha.

18 June British general election; Edward Heath (Conservative) appointed P.M. on 19th; Rev. Ian Paisley returned in Northern Ireland, as is Frank McManus (Unity).

25 June Catholic hierarchy announces removal of restrictions on Catholics attending T.C.D.

27 June Provisional I.R.A. in action for the first time during rioting in Short Strand area of Belfast when six people are killed; 550 extra British troops airlifted to Belfast.

3–5 July Gen. Sir Ian Freeland, G.O.C. Northern Ireland, declares a curfew in the Lower Falls Road from 10 p.m. while British troops carry out house-to-house searches; curfew lifted after 35 hours, during which many houses are totally without food; over 1,000 women from other Catholic areas bring food to Falls Road residents; the search by the army yields over 100 guns and rifles, 100 home-made bombs, 250 lb of explosives, 8 two-way radio sets and over 20,000 rounds of ammunition; six civilians die during rioting.

6 July Dr Patrick Hillery, R.I. Minister for External Affairs, visits the Falls Road, Belfast; his visit is criticised by British Foreign Secretary, Sir Alec Douglas-Home, as 'an error of judgment and a serious diplomatic discourtesy'.

12 July Over 1,000 'refugees' from Northern Ireland arrive in the Republic during preceding 48 hours.

23 July Two C.S. gas containers thrown from Strangers' Gallery force evacuation of the House of Commons; James A. Roche is subsequently imprisoned for 18 months for the crime.

2 Aug. Robert Porter, N.I. Minister of Home Affairs, increases the reward for information leading to convictions for illegal use of explosives (from £10,000 to £50,000).

10 Aug. Horse Industry Act (R.I.) provides for establishment of Bord na gCapall.

12 Aug. Two R.U.C. men killed by bomb in south Armagh; first policemen killed in a Catholic area in the present disturbances.

17 Aug. Unapproved roads at the border in south Armagh 'spiked' by troops.

21 Aug. Social Democratic and Labour Party (S.D.L.P.) formed in Belfast; led by Gerry Fitt, includes Paddy Devlin, John Hume, Austin Currie, Ivan Cooper and Senator Patrick Wilson.

23 Aug. Soviet news agency Tass opens its first office in Ireland in Dublin.

16 Sept. National Institute for Higher Education, Limerick, opens for student enrolment (*see* 27 Sept. 1972); director Dr Edward M. Walsh (renamed University of Limerick in 1989).

20 Sept. d. Leo Rowsome (70), musician, known as 'king of the Irish pipers'; co-founder of Comhaltas Ceoltóirí Éireann (1951).

22 Sept. Trials of Charles J. Haughey, Capt. James Kelly and Albert Luykx on charges of conspiring to import arms to the Republic; jury discharged on 29 Sept. (*see* 6 Oct.).

23 Sept. Sir Arthur Young announces resignation as chief of the R.U.C.; succeeded by Deputy Chief Constable Graham Shillington.

25 Sept. d. Dr James Ryan (78), politician (Fianna Fáil), Minister for Finance (1957–65).

Oct. Department of Education in Republic announces creation of community school system (free schooling of a comprehensive nature to all within a catchment area without selection procedures for pupils).

3 Oct. The *Esso Ulidia*, 253,000-ton tanker, largest ship ever built by Harland & Wolff, commences sea trials.

5 Oct. U.S. President Richard M. Nixon arrives in the Republic; visits Timahoe, Co. Laois, reputed burial place of a Quaker ancestor.

6 Oct. New trials of Charles J. Haughey and others on charges of conspiring to import arms to the Republic, starts under Justice Seámus Henchy; defendants acquitted on 23 Oct.

18 Oct. d. Máirtín Ó Cadhain (63), short-story-writer in Irish; whose novel *Cré na Cille* (1949) was chosen by U.N.E.S.C.O. for translation into several European languages.

31 Oct. Remains of three Connaught Rangers, Privates Daly, Miranda and Smith, returned to Ireland for reburial (*see* 28 June 1920).

21 Nov. Republic's largest Protestant school, with 310 pupils, opens in Dundrum, Co. Dublin.

26 Nov. N.I. Minister of Defence places strength of U.D.R. at 201 officers and 3,668 other ranks, of whom about 15 per cent are Catholics; states that 'rather more' than one-third of force is authorised to hold weapons at home.

28 Dec. Pat Taaffe, one of Ireland's most celebrated steeplechase jockeys, announces retirement.

30 Dec. N.I. Auditor-General puts cost of 1969–70 disturbances at £5½ million.

1971

17 Jan. Official Sinn Féin votes to end abstentionist policy from Dáil, Stormont and Westminster (*see* 3 Aug.).

24 Jan. d. St John Ervine (87), dramatist, novelist and critic.

2 Feb. Fr Robert Murphy becomes the first Catholic chaplain to read prayers to Stormont parliament.

3–6 Feb. Rioting in Catholic areas of Belfast; Gunner Robert Curtis becomes first soldier killed in Northern Ireland disturbances when shot by the Provisional I.R.A. at New Lodge Road on 6th.

4 Feb. Lt-Gen. Erskine Crum succeeds Lt-Gen. Sir Ian Freeland as G.O.C. Northern Ireland (*see* 18 Feb.).

12 Feb. d. Delia Murphy (69), ballad-singer and song-writer.

15 Feb. 'D Day': decimal currency officially introduced in Ireland.

18 Feb. Lt-Gen. Harry Tuzo appointed G.O.C. Northern Ireland in succession to Lt-Gen. Crum, who suffers a fatal heart-attack (*see* 4 Feb.).

25 Feb. Housing Executive established in Northern Ireland to take over housing functions of local authorities and the Northern Ireland Housing Trust.

1 Mar. Taoiseach Jack Lynch states on B.B.C.'s *Panorama* that the Republic's constitutional claim to jurisdiction over the six-county Northern Ireland state is fundamental and cannot be abandoned.

10 Mar. Three off-duty soldiers found shot dead near Belfast.

Outbreak of fighting between Official and Provisional I.R.A.

12 Mar. Lord Carrington, British Secretary of State for Defence, announces that in future no soldiers aged under 18 will serve in Northern Ireland; immediate recall of 170 under that age serving in the province.

20 Mar. Major James Chichester-Clark resigns as Northern Ireland P.M.; succeeded by Brian Faulkner, who defeats William Craig (26 votes to 4) on 23 Mar.

27 Mar. 2,000 attend the first annual conference of the Alliance Party under the chairmanship of Basil Glass at the Ulster Hall.

29 Mar. A detective sergeant reveals to Belfast Crown Court that sales of guns have taken place between the I.R.A. and the U.V.F.

9 Apr. End of nine-day arms amnesty in Northern Ireland, during which 446 revolvers, 47 automatics, 585 rifles, 240 shot-guns, 300 air-guns, 99,440 rounds of ammunition and 64 grenades handed over to authorities; 85 per cent of the arms were illegally held.

11 Apr. At annual conference in Belfast G.A.A. removes the ban on 'foreign games' (Rule 27).

15 Apr. d. Muiris ('Kruger') Kavanagh (77), Kerry adventurer and publican at Dún Chaoin.

20 Apr. Two British naval launches in Baltimore harbour, Co. Cork, destroyed by the Official I.R.A.

10 May d. Archie Heron (77), trade union organiser.

11 May d. Seán Lemass (72), politician (Fianna Fáil), Taoiseach (1959–66).

14 May Ulster '71 Exhibition opens in Belfast; over 700,000 attend in 17 weeks.

15 May d. Sir Tyrone Guthrie, theatre producer, whose home, Annaghmakerrig House, Co. Monaghan, is bequeathed to the nation as a retreat for Irish artists and writers.

12 June James Chichester-Clark created life peer in Queen's Birthday Honours List.

5 July Nuclear Energy Act (R.I.) provides for Nuclear Energy Board.

10 July Explosion destroys offices of the British Legion in Dublin.

16 July S.D.L.P. withdraws from Stormont in protest at refusal of inquiry into shooting of two men in Derry by troops on 8 July.

20 July 200 Derry ex-servicemen burn their medals and ex-service documents in protest against army harassment of people in the Catholic Bogside.

22 July Northern Ireland unemployment figures at 15.5 per cent are the highest for 19 years.

1 Aug. Figures released in Northern Ireland show drop of £5 million from tourist revenue.

3 Aug. Sinn Féin (Gardiner Place) registers in Dublin as a political party, now eligible to contest elections.

9–10 Aug. Internment introduced in Northern Ireland under Section 12 of the Special Powers Act: 342 picked up (mainly Catholics), of whom 116 are released within 48 hours; remainder held either at Crumlin Road jail or on the *Maidstone*, a converted troopship (*see* 19 Sept.); number of internees reaches 1,576 by Dec. In a reaction to internment two soldiers and 10 civilians are killed; rioting continues throughout the day and night. Among those killed is a Catholic priest, Fr Hugh Mullan, in Ballymurphy, while administering last rites; 240 houses in Ardoyne are destroyed; Catholics flee south to the Republic.

10 Aug. Mrs Sarah Worthington, 50-year-old widow, becomes first female victim of Northern Ireland disturbances when she is accidentally shot by member of the Green Howard regiment during search of her home.

People's Democracy newspaper changes name from *Free Citizen* to *Unfree Citizen*.

18 Aug. 24 Catholic members resign from the U.D.R. in protest against internment.

25 Aug. Provisional I.R.A. bomb at the electricity supply office in Malone Road, Belfast, kills one and injures 16.

Gerry Fitt, leader of the S.D.L.P., acquaints U.N. Secretary-General U Thant in New York with details of ill-treatment of detainees in Northern Ireland.

31 Aug. Radio Free Derry begins transmission.

Sept. New primary school curriculum introduced in Republic.

National College of Art reconstituted as the National College of Art and Design.

2 Sept. 18-month-old Angela Gallagher killed by stray bullet during Provisional I.R.A. ambush in Belfast.

6 Sept. 14-year-old girl shot dead in the Derry Bogside becomes the 100th victim of Northern Ireland violence since 1969.

6–7 Sept. Taoiseach Lynch meets with P.M. Heath at Chequers to discuss Northern Ireland disturbances (*see* 27–28 Sept.).

8 Sept. Joe Cahill, member of Provisional Sinn Féin executive, on fund-raising tour for the I.R.A., deported from U.S.A.

14 Sept. Rev. Ian Paisley and Desmond Boal form the Democratic Unionist Party.

15 Sept. N.I. Minister of Development announces that the civil disobedience campaign is costing local authorities £65,000 per week (*see* 21 Oct.).

19 Sept. Inaugural meeting of Aontacht Éireann (Unity of Ireland) Party founded by Kevin Boland, formerly of Fianna Fáil.

Most of the internees (*see* 9 Aug.) transferred to Long Kesh, near Lisburn, Co. Antrim (later called the Maze prison).

24 Sept. *Daily Mail* opinion poll indicates that 59 per cent of people in Britain want troops withdrawn from Northern Ireland.

26 Sept. David Bleakley, N.I. Minister of Community Relations, resigns in protest at internment; succeeded by W. B. McIvor.

d. Conor Maguire (82), Chief Justice in Republic (1946–61).

27–28 Sept. Talks at Chequers between British P.M. Heath, Taoiseach Lynch and Northern Ireland P.M. Faulkner.

1 Oct. Section 31 of the Broadcasting Act, 1960, invoked to prevent R.T.E. from reporting the activities of illegal organisations.

Dublin and London linked by S.T.D. dialling.

3 Oct. d. Seán Ó Riada (40), musician and composer.

17 Oct. *Sunday Times* carries allegations of use of brainwashing techniques on internees at Hollywood police barracks, near Belfast.

20 Oct. U.S. Senator Edward Kennedy speaks in Congress in support of motion calling for immediate withdrawal of British troops from Northern Ireland for the purpose of establishing a united Ireland.

21 Oct. In effort to counteract civil disobedience campaign Northern Ireland government enacts Payment for Debt (Emergency Provisions) Act with powers of attachment or deductions from state salaries of amounts outstanding in respect of rent and rates.

National Prices Commission in the Republic meets for the first time.

22 Oct. An additional £11,600,000 is required to fund military operations in Northern Ireland for the current financial year, according to the British Under-Secretary for the Army.

27 Oct. Dr Gerard B. Newe becomes the only Catholic appointed to the Northern Ireland cabinet (as a minister of state).

6 Nov. British government releases figures on internment, showing that since introduction on 9 Aug. 476 of the 882 arrested have been released; 278 are interned, 112 held under detention orders, and 16 held under Section 10 of the Special Powers Act.

7 Nov. Marathon Petroleum (Ireland) Ltd announces a gas-strike off the Old Head of Kinsale, Co. Cork.

16 Nov. Compton Committee reports that while there was ill-treatment of detainees during and after 9 Aug., there was no brutality or torture.

British government appoints committee of three Privy Councillors, led by Lord Parker, to examine methods of interrogating suspected terrorists (*see* 2 Mar. 1972).

Nine prisoners escape from Crumlin Road prison, Belfast, during a football game; two recaptured within 48 hours.

23 Nov. Northern Ireland tourist revenue down by £1,800,000 in 1970, a decline of 7.3 per cent.

25 Nov. Lord Balniel at Westminster states that Catholic membership of the U.D.R. has fallen from 15 per cent to 8 per cent.

Seven escapees still at large from Crumlin Road jail-break (*see* 16 Nov.) give a press conference in Dublin.

2 Dec. John Taylor, N.I. Minister of State for Home Affairs, announces that violence in Northern Ireland for the past two years has cost an estimated £16 million.

4 Dec. Explosion at McGurk's public house in North Queen Street, Belfast, kills 15 and injures 13 in loyalist attack; Belfast's worst explosion to date; reponsibility claimed by 'Empire Loyalists'.

16 Dec. d. Gen. Richard Mulcahy (85), politician (Fine Gael), who, although leader of the majority party in government, was not acceptable to coalition partners and stepped aside to permit John A. Costello to become Taoiseach (1948–51; 1954–57).

Census of population in Republic: 2,978,248 (increase of 3.27 per cent since 1966).

Census of population in Northern Ireland: 1,536,065 (increase of 3.5 per cent since 1966).

1972

1 Jan. Farmers' organisations in the Republic, including the National Farmers' Association, amalgamate to form the Irish Farmers' Association (I.F.A.).

11 Jan. d. Pádraic Colum (90), poet.

17 Jan. Seven internees escape from prison ship *Maidstone* in Belfast Lough.

22 Jan. d. Col. Eamonn Broy (84), Commissioner of Garda Síochána (1933–38); formed 'Broy Harriers' (1933).

30 Jan. 'Bloody Sunday': 13 demonstrators shot dead by soldiers of the 1st Parachute Regiment following a banned civil rights march in Derry; Taoiseach Lynch recalls Republic's Ambassador, Dr Donal O'Sullivan, from London and declares 2 Feb. a national day of mourning.

2 Feb. Following the biggest demonstration in Dublin in over 50 years, the British Embassy is burned in Dublin during national day of mourning for 'Bloody Sunday'.

British government appoints Lord Widgery to lead tribunal of inquiry into events of 30 Jan. in Derry; opens on 14 Feb. and closes on 20 Mar. (*see* 19 Apr.).

12 Feb. Ex-Minister William Craig leads Ulster Vanguard in its first rally at Lisburn, Co. Antrim.

13 Feb. Dermot Ryan consecrated R.C. Archbishop of Dublin by Pope Paul VI.

17 Feb. Scottish rugby officials advise the Irish Rugby Football Union that they cannot fulfil Lansdowne Road fixture on 26 Feb. as they fear for players' safety; Wales cancels its match for 11 Mar. for same reason.

22 Feb. Official I.R.A. kill six civilians and an army chaplain when bombing officers' mess of 16th Parachute Brigade H.Q. at Aldershot, Hants, England.

24 Feb. U.K. parliament passes Northern Ireland Act conferring retrospective powers on Northern Ireland government to give orders to the army.

25 Feb. John Taylor, N.I. Minister of State for Home Affairs, seriously wounded in Official I.R.A. assassination attempt in Armagh.

2 Mar. Methods of interrogation used in Northern Ireland condemned in minority report signed by Lord Gardiner of the Parker Committee; P.M. Heath announces that such methods will no longer be used.

4 Mar. Abercorn Restaurant, Belfast, bombed on a crowded Saturday; two killed and 136 injured.

20 Mar. Explosion in Belfast's Donegall Street kills two policemen and four civilians.

22 Mar. Northern Ireland P.M. Faulkner flies to London to meet with British P.M. Heath; returns to Belfast and flies back to London for another meeting the next day; Faulkner refuses to accept transfer of security to Whitehall (*see* 24 Mar.).

24 Mar. British P.M. Heath announces suspension of Northern Ireland government, to be replaced by direct rule from Westminster through a Secretary of State for Northern Ireland (*see* 30 Mar.).

27 Mar. Eight people lose their lives in fire at Noyek's timber-merchant warehouse, Parnell Street, Dublin.

28 Mar. Last sitting of Stormont parliament, Northern Ireland (*see* 18 July 1973).

30 Mar. U.K. Northern Ireland (Temporary Provisions) Act suspends Stormont for one year; P.M. Brian Faulkner has held office for 366 days, the shortest term of Northern Ireland's six premiers; William Whitelaw takes up office as Secretary of State for Northern Ireland on 1 Apr.

2 Apr. Radio na Gaeltachta inaugurated.

6 Apr. Report of the Scarman tribunal exonerates R.U.C. of acting in partisan manner; finds no evidence of planned insurrection, but finds that there was deliberate violence by extremists on both sides.

7 Apr. Internees (47) and detainees (26) released in Northern Ireland; *Maidstone* prison ship closed.

15 Apr. Official I.R.A. leader Joe McCann killed by British troops.

19 Apr. Widgery tribunal of inquiry into events of 30 Jan. exonerates the army, laying blame on N.I.C.R.A. for organising the march.

27 Apr. Ban lifted on marches in Northern Ireland; amnesty for those who participated in illegal marches since 25 Dec. 1971.

E.S.B. workers' strike ends after 15 days.

29 Apr. French rugby team receives tumultuous welcome as the only international side to play 'home' international series in Republic at Lansdowne Road (Ireland wins by 24 points to 14).

3 May d. Jimmy Bruen (51), golfer, first Irishman to win the British Amateur title (1946).

10 May Referendum in Republic on entry to European Economic Community: for, 1,041,890; against, 211,891.

26 May Government of the Republic declares establishment of Special Criminal Court under Part V of the Offences Against the State Act, 1939; three judges to sit without jury.

28 May Eight killed when I.R.A. bomb explodes prematurely in Short Strand, Belfast.

29 May Official I.R.A. orders cessation of hostilities following killing of Ranger William Best while visiting his family in Derry.

8 June Special Criminal Court (*see* 26 May) sits for the first time.

12 June Leading Irish businessmen among the 118 victims of B.E.A. Trident crash (Britain's worst air disaster to date).

18 June d. Myles Dillon (72), scholar, Director of School of Celtic Studies, Dublin Institute for Advanced Studies (1960–68).

19 June First native craft, L.E. *Deirdre,* commissioned for Irish naval service.

20 June N.I. Secretary of State William Whitelaw announces special category status for certain prisoners, ending republican hunger-strike in Belfast.

27 June Danny McAlinden becomes first Irishman to win the British heavyweight boxing championship when he knocks out Jack Bodell.

1 July School-leaving age in the Republic raised from 14 to 15.

7 July N.I. Secretary of State Whitelaw meets Provisional I.R.A. leaders in London.

21 July 'Bloody Friday': 22 bombs, for which Provisional I.R.A. accepts responsibility, explode in Belfast; 11 killed and 130 injured.

31 July Over 36,000 members of the British army, the R.U.C. and the U.D.R. dismantle barricades in Catholic areas of Belfast and Derry in 'Operation Motorman'.

Three car-bombs kill six and injure over 30 (two of whom later die) at Claudy, Co. Londonderry.

7 Aug. Shooting of U.D.R. soldier brings Northern Ireland death toll to 500 since 1969.

15 Aug. Chief Justice Cearbhall Ó Dálaigh appointed Irish member of the European Court of Justice.

22 Aug. Nine die in Newry customs office bombing.

23 Aug. Lord Killanin becomes the first Irishman to be elected President of the International Olympics Commission.

1 Sept. Radio licences abolished in the Republic.

3 Sept. Mary Peters of Belfast wins gold medal in Pentathlon at the Munich Olympic Games.

20 Sept. Pub. *Towards a New Ireland* by S.D.L.P., proposing joint Anglo-Irish sovereignty for Northern Ireland, British declaration in favour of the eventual unification of Ireland, a Northern Ireland assembly with increased powers, and an all-Ireland senate.

25–27 Sept. Unionist Party, Alliance and the Northern Ireland Labour Party attend conference called by Secretary of State Whitelaw, meeting at Darlington, Co. Durham; Nationalist Party, S.D.L.P., D.U.P. and Republican Labour refuse invitations.

27 Sept. National Institute of Higher Education, Limerick, opened by Taoiseach Jack Lynch.

6 Oct. Sinn Féin's Kevin Street, Dublin, H.Q. closed down by gardaí under the Offences Against the State Act.

29 Oct. Seven escape from the Curragh, Co. Kildare, military detention camp.

1 Nov. Value Added Tax (V.A.T.) replaces turnover and wholesale taxes.

5 Nov. Dermot Ryan becomes the first R.C. archbishop to attend a service in Dublin's Christ Church Cathedral (C.I.) since the Reformation.

24 Nov. R.T.E. Authority replaced by government after radio interview with Provisional I.R.A. Chief of Staff, Seán Mac Stiofáin; Gerard Collins, Minister for Posts and Telegraphs, deems interview to be in breach of Section 31 of the Broadcasting Act.

Taoiseach Lynch and P.M. Heath meet in London.

25 Nov. Seán Mac Stiofáin, Provisional I.R.A. Chief of Staff, receives six months' sentence for membership of an illegal organisation; Kevin O'Kelly, radio reporter, sentenced to three months for contempt when he refuses to identify Mac Stiofáin as his interviewee (*see* 24 Nov.).

27 Nov. Seán Mac Stiofáin admitted to the Curragh Military Hospital for observation during hunger-strike (ends on 16 Jan. 1973).

1 Dec. As Dáil debates the Offences Against the State (Amendment) Bill, two are killed and 127 injured by two explosions in Dublin. Fine Gael drops opposition to the bill, which passes (69 votes to 22, Fine Gael abstaining) on 3 Dec.; act enables a Garda superintendent in the Republic to secure a conviction by swearing that he believes an accused to be a member of the I.R.A.

7 Dec. Referendum in Republic: (i) lowers minimum age for voting from 21 to 18; (ii) deletes from Constitution reference to the special position of the Catholic Church (50.7 per cent poll).

20 Dec. Pub. report of the Diplock Commission, which recommends giving soldiers powers to arrest and detain suspects, and trial without jury.

28 Dec. Teenage boy and girl killed and nine injured by car-bomb in Belturbet, Co. Cavan.

1973

1 Jan. Republic becomes a member of the E.E.C., along with United Kingdom and Denmark.

3 Jan. d. Ria Mooney (68), actress, chosen by Seán O'Casey to play Rosie Redmond in first production of *The Plough and the Stars* (*see* 8 Feb. 1926).

5 Jan. d. Gerald Boland (87), politician (Fianna Fáil), minister in various departments (1933–57).

6 Jan. Dr Patrick Hillery appointed Irish Commissioner in the E.E.C.; receives portfolio for Social Affairs (*see* 26 Nov. 1976).

11 Jan. Ruairí Ó Brádaigh, President of Provisional Sinn Féin, imprisoned for six months under Offences Against the State Act.

20 Jan. One killed and 13 injured when car-bomb explodes in Dublin.

24 Jan. d. Willie Clancy (51), traditional musician and folklorist; commemorated in Willie Clancy Festival, Milltown Malbay, Co. Clare.

5 Feb. Two Protestants become first loyalists to be detained under Special Powers Act; Loyalist Association of Workers (L.A.W.) holds one-day strike in protest on 7th; loyalist attacks on Catholic homes and businesses lead to five deaths following gun-battle with army.

22 Feb. d. Elizabeth Bowen (73), novelist.

Sir Arthur Galsworthy replaces Sir John Peck as British Ambassador to the Republic.

26 Feb. Pub. report of the R.I. Commission on Status of Women, recommending an end to sex discrimination in employment, equal pay, maternity leave, day-care for children, marriage counselling and family-planning advice.

28 Feb. General election in R.I.: Fianna Fáil, 69; Fine Gael, 54; Labour, 19; Independents, 2. Fine Gael and Labour form a coalition government: Liam Cosgrave (Fine Gael) Taoiseach and Brendan Corish (Labour) Tánaiste.

8 Mar. Referendum in Northern Ireland on remaining within U.K.: for, 591,820; against, 6,463. Low poll (59 per cent) reflects republican campaign to discourage voting.

Car-bomb explosions in central London kill one and injure over 240; 10 arrested waiting to board plane for Belfast (*see* 15 Nov.).

28 Mar. *Claudia* intercepted off Waterford, found to be running guns; six arrested, including Joe Cahill of Provisional I.R.A. (*see* 21 May).

30 Mar. William Craig forms Vanguard Unionist Progressive Party (V.U.P.P.) to challenge Unionist Party leadership of Northern Ireland loyalists.

5 Apr. Richard Burke, R.I. Minister for Education, announces that while Irish is no longer required for a pass in either the Intermediate or Leaving Certificate examinations, it will remain a compulsory subject in the primary and post-primary curriculums.

7 Apr. d. John Charles McQuaid (77), R.C. Archbishop of Dublin (1940–72).

13 Apr. National Gallery purchases David's 'The Funeral of Patroclus', using £250,000 from the Shaw Bequest.

19 Apr. Mount Melleray secondary boarding college closes, ending 130-year tradition at the Co. Waterford Cistercian abbey.

25 Apr. Dr Garret FitzGerald, R.I. Minister for Foreign Affairs, visits Catholic areas of Belfast.

21 May Joe Cahill of Provisional I.R.A. sentenced to three years' penal servitude (*see* 28 Mar.).

30 May District council elections in Northern Ireland held under P.R. for the first time since 1922: Unionists, 201; S.D.L.P., 76; Democratic Unionist Party and Vanguard Unionist Progressive Party, 74; Alliance Party, 59.

Erskine Hamilton Childers (Fianna Fáil) elected President of the Republic, defeating T. F. O'Higgins (Fine Gael) (635,867 votes to 587,771); inaugurated on 25 June.

2 June Rosslare – Le Havre ferry service opens (Irish Continental Line).

11 June d. Seán Kenny (40), stage designer.

12 June Six killed and 33 injured when car-bomb explodes in Coleraine, Co. Londonderry.

Dr Raymond McClear becomes Derry's second Catholic mayor (following Hugh O'Doherty, 1920).

26 June S.D.L.P. Senator Paddy Wilson and Irene Andrews stabbed to death by Ulster Freedom Fighters (U.F.F.).

28 June General election to Northern Ireland Assembly: Official Unionists, 23; 'Unpledged' Unionists, 10; S.D.L.P., 19; Alliance, 8; D.U.P., 8; Vanguard Unionist Progressive Party, 7; West Belfast Loyalist Coalition, 2; Northern Ireland Labour Party, 1.

Lough Key Forest Park, Co. Roscommon, opens.

7 July d. Gen. Seán Mac Eoin (79), veteran of War of Independence ('Blacksmith of Ballinalee', *see* 2–9 Nov. 1920); politician (Fine Gael).

18 July Northern Ireland Constitution Act abolishes the parliament of Northern Ireland and the office of Governor; empowers the Secretary of State to appoint an executive; reiterates promise that Northern Ireland will remain part of the U.K. so long as a majority desire it.

25 July Northern Ireland (Emergency Provisions) Act repeals the Special Powers Act, abolishes the death penalty, and provides for trial by one judge sitting without jury for offences of a 'terrorist' nature.

31 July First meeting of Northern Ireland Assembly; ends in disorder when 26 loyalist members refuse to accept ruling that the House adjourn.

Act (R.I.) abolishes bar against continued employment of women civil servants who marry while in the service.

18 Aug. d. Basil Brooke (85), 1st Viscount Brookeborough, Unionist leader and P.M. of Northern Ireland (1943–63).

21 Aug. British army paratroopers accused by Derry city coroner, Major Hubert O'Neill, of 'sheer unadulterated murder' (*see* 30 Jan. 1972 *and* 19 Apr. 1972).

Sept. First community schools open in the Republic.

1 Sept. In deepest maritime rescue in Irish history, two men trapped in miniature submarine *Pisces II* while cable-laying 90 miles off the Cork coast are brought to safety.

16 Sept. Tommy Herron of the U.D.A. shot dead at Drumbo, Co. Down.

17 Sept. Edward Heath becomes the first British P.M. to visit the 26-county state since independence, when he meets with Taoiseach Cosgrave at Baldonnell, Co. Dublin, to discuss setting up Council of Ireland.

24 Sept. Having moved from the G.P.O. building, O'Connell Street, Dublin, R.T.E. begins live radio broadcasts from the new radio studios at Montrose H.Q.

26 Sept. First of the ecumenical conferences held at Ballymascanlon, Co. Louth, presided over by Cardinal Conway and the C.I. Archbishop of Armagh, G. O. Simms; representatives of all the main churches attend.

2 Oct. Irish Republic's case against British government for torturing republican internees opens in Strasbourg before the European Commission of Human Rights; Irish case presented by Declan Costello (Attorney-General); report of the commission pub. on 2 Sept. 1976 finds U.K. guilty of torture.

11 Oct. Ireland's first woman ambassador, Mary Catherine Tinney, appointed to Sweden and Finland.

31 Oct. Three I.R.A. prisoners (Kevin Mallon, J. B. O'Hagan and Séamus Twomey) escape from Mountjoy Jail, Dublin, by helicopter.

1 Nov. James Flanagan becomes first Catholic to hold the post when he succeeds Sir Graham Shillington as Chief Constable of the R.U.C.

9 Nov. All I.R.A. prisoners in the Republic convicted under the Offences Against the State Act moved to Portlaoise prison.

15 Nov. Eight Irish people receive life sentences for car-bomb explosions on 8 Mar. in London; include sisters Marion and Dolours Price (*see* 18 Mar. 1975).

22 Nov. Unionist Party, S.D.L.P. and Alliance Party agree to form power-sharing Executive for Northern Ireland, following six weeks of negotiations (*see* 1 Jan. 1974).

2 Dec. Francis Pym succeeds William Whitelaw as Secretary of State for Northern Ireland.

6 Dec. Unionists outside the Faulkner-led Unionist Party meet in Ulster Hall, Belfast; Vanguard Unionists, D.U.P. and Orange Order decide to form United Ulster Unionist Council (U.U.U.C.), opposed to power-sharing.

6–9 Dec. Sunningdale Conference: Republic and British governments and Northern Ireland Executive represented; agreement reached that unification of Ireland can only be with the consent of the majority in Northern Ireland; a Council of Ireland to be established to promote North–South economic co-operation (*see* 4 Jan. 1974).

19 Dec. In majority decision Supreme Court of the Republic rules that it is unconstitutional to prohibit the importation of contraceptives (judgment in case taken by Mrs Mary McGee against the state).

20 Dec. 13 letter bombs bearing British and Northern Ireland postmarks are discovered in Dublin (all safely detonated by army).

27 Dec. Thomas Niedermeyer, managing director of Grundig, kidnapped in Belfast (his body found on 11 Mar. 1980; had died of heart-attack).

1974

1 Jan. Power-sharing Executive of Northern Ireland takes up office; Chief Executive, Brian Faulkner (*see* 22 Jan.).

4 Jan. Sunningdale Agreement repudiated by U.U.U.C.

Ireland's worst storm for 70 years: 2 killed, 30,000 subscribers without electricity, and over 10,000 telephones affected.

16 Jan. Northern Ireland Chief Executive Faulkner meets with Taoiseach Cosgrave at Baldonnell Aerodrome, Co. Dublin.

22 Jan. Northern Ireland Assembly meets at Stormont; anti-power-sharing loyalists disrupt proceedings, which end when police remove 18 of them.

23 Jan. Official Unionists, D.U.P. and Vanguard Unionists withdraw from Assembly.

d. James J. McElligott (80), civil servant; Secretary of the Department of Finance (1927–53); Governor of the Central Bank (1953–60).

24 Jan. Four Provisional I.R.A. members, including Dr Rose Dugdale, make unsuccessful attempt to bomb Strabane, Co. Tyrone, police barracks from a helicopter (*see* 27 Nov.).

1 Feb. Taoiseach Cosgrave and P.M. Faulkner meet at Hillsborough, Co. Down, to discuss law enforcement and the proposed Council of Ireland.

28 Feb. United Ulster Unionist Council (coalition of anti-power-sharing loyalists) win 11 out of 12 Ulster seats in the U.K. general election in Northern Ireland; Gerry Fitt holds West Belfast for the S.D.L.P.

4 Mar. Harold Wilson (Labour) appointed P.M. of U.K.

5 Mar. Merlyn Rees succeeds Francis Pym as Secretary of State for Northern Ireland.

11 Mar. Senator Billy Fox (Fine Gael) killed in Co. Monaghan by I.R.A., first member of the Oireachtas to be killed since Kevin O'Higgins (1927); five receive life sentences for the crime on 7 June.

Mother, father and 10 children die in fire tragedy in Dalkey, Co. Dublin.

13 Mar. Taoiseach Cosgrave in the Dáil accepts that the status of Northern Ireland can only be altered with the consent of the majority in that state.

20 Mar. d. Austin Clarke (78), poet.

25 Mar. Dr Edward Brennan nominated Republic's first Ambassador to the U.S.S.R.

5 Apr. R.C. Archbishop of Dublin leases land at Merrion Square to Dublin Corporation at a nominal rent for use as a public park.

17 Apr. Following three-day public hearing, the Minister for Local Government, James Tully, rules that Dublin's new Central Bank building (designed by Sam Stephenson) in Dame Street, Dublin, will have to be reduced in height by 30 feet; a compromise is reached on 30 Jan. 1975 when the government accepts a plan for copper-encased roof with steel 'umbrella' exceeding planning authority regulation by 17 feet.

26 Apr. 19 paintings stolen from the Blessington, Co. Wicklow, home of Sir Alfred and Lady Beit (recovered by gardaí on 4 May; *see* 25 June).

1 May E.E.C. farm retirement scheme comes into effect.

2 May Bomb explodes at the Rose and Crown public house in Ormeau Road, Belfast, killing five and injuring 17, many seriously.

13 May Dublin couple successfully challenge a section of the Adoption Act, 1952, in the High Court (section prohibited husband's adoption of wife's illegitimate son because his religion differed from that of his wife) (*see* 13 July 1976).

14 May Motion before the Northern Ireland Assembly condemning the Sunningdale Agreement rejected (44 votes to 28); Ulster Workers' Council starts general strike as protest (decision by electricity workers is crucial to the success of the strike).

17 May Loyalist bombs explode in Monaghan town and in Dublin; 25 killed and over 100 wounded in Dublin, six killed in Monaghan.

18 May Continual power blackouts in Belfast.

19 May Ulster Workers' Council set up roadblocks around Belfast inner city; state of emergency declared.

20 May Hijacked lorries and cars seal off main routes to Belfast city centre (except for the Falls Road and Andersonstown).

21 May Len Murray, general secretary of the Belfast T.U.C., fails to get the workers to return to Harland & Wolff shipyard, Belfast.

24 May First official strike in 215 years at Guinness's brewery (ends on 14 June).

25 May During a broadcast P.M. Harold Wilson alienates loyalist public opinion in Northern Ireland when, denouncing the strike, he describes the U.W.C. strikers as 'people who spend their lives sponging on Westminster and British democracy and then systematically assault democratic methods'.

27 May Troops in Belfast take over main petrol stations; U.W.C. reduces electricity to 10 per cent capacity.

28 May Chief Executive Brian Faulkner and five other Unionists resign when he is refused support to negotiate with the strikers; the Executive falls; the strike ends.

29 May Northern Ireland Prorogation Order enacted, resuming direct rule from Westminster.

3 June Michael Gaughan, I.R.A., dies in Parkhurst prison, Isle of

Wight, following 65-day hunger-strike (first known Irish hunger-striker to die in an English prison since Terence MacSwiney in 1920).

12 June Monsignor Tomás Ó Fiaich replaces Monsignor Jeremiah Newman (created Bishop of Limerick) as President of St Patrick's College, Maynooth.

14 June First Soviet Ambassador to Ireland, Anatoli Kaplan, presents his credentials to President Childers.

17 June Seven injured when I.R.A. bomb explodes at the Houses of Parliament and damages Westminster Hall.

25 June Dr Rose Dugdale sentenced to nine years' imprisonment for receiving paintings stolen from Sir Alfred Beit (*see* 26 Apr.).

8 July Dublin's nine-week bus strike ends.

16 July Taoiseach Cosgrave votes against his own government's bill for regulation of contraception (defeated by 75 votes to 61).

11 Aug. d. Professor Liam Ó Briain (86), scholar, philologist.

13 Aug. d. Kate O'Brien (77), novelist.

18 Aug. 19 I.R.A. prisoners escape by blowing open the gates of Portlaoise jail.

21 Aug. The *Clydevalley* sails from Larne to England for scrapping (*see* 14 Dec. 1968).

9 Sept. Green paper reveals £313 million in direct aid from British Exchequer granted to Northern Ireland in last financial year.

11–12 Sept. Taoiseach Cosgrave and P.M. Wilson meet in London.

16 Sept. Rory Conaghan and Martin McBirney, members of the Northern Ireland judiciary, shot dead by the I.R.A.

23 Sept. d. Denis Ireland (80), Ulster Presbyterian, member of the Senate of Éire in 1948.

27 Sept. £74,000 taken from a post office van at Tralee, Co. Kerry, in the country's biggest-ever armed robbery to date (until 31 Mar. 1976).

5 Oct. Explosions at two public houses in Guildford, Surrey, kill five and injure 65 (four Irish people later imprisoned).

8 Oct. Seán MacBride becomes first Irish citizen to be awarded Nobel Prize for Peace when he is jointly nominated with former premier of Japan, Sato.

9 Oct. d. Pádraic Fallon (69), poet and dramatist.

10 Oct. Labour win British general election; Official Unionist Party leader Harry West is unseated by Frank Maguire (Independent) and is succeeded as U.U.U.C. leader by James Molyneaux.

21 Oct. 650,000-gallon oil spillage from tanker *Universal I* poses major pollution threat to Glengarriff, Co. Cork, and other scenic areas.

23 Oct. T. F. O'Higgins succeeds the late William O'Brien Fitzgerald as Chief Justice in the Republic.

4 Nov. Powerscourt House, Enniskerry, Co. Wicklow, destroyed by fire.

6 Nov. 33 republican prisoners escape by tunnel from the Maze prison; one shot dead during attempt, and all others recaptured within 12 hours.

7 Nov. Government announces that Irish will no longer be compulsory for entry to the civil service in the Republic.

17 Nov. d. Erskine Hamilton Childers (68), President of the Republic since 25 June 1973 (first President to die in office).

21 Nov. Two bombs in Birmingham kill 21 and injure over 180; six Irishmen later convicted and sentenced. Despite many doubts about the soundness of their convictions, the verdicts were confirmed on appeal in 1988.

27 Nov. Dr Rose Dugdale, already serving nine years for receiving stolen Beit paintings, is sentenced to additional nine years for role in the Provisional I.R.A. helicopter attack on 24 Jan.

28 Nov. Republic's yearly exports break the billion-pound barrier for the first time.

29 Nov. U.K. Prevention of Terrorism (Temporary Provisions) Act provides for deportation from or prohibition of entry to Great Britain; renewed for six months on 10 Apr. 1975.

3 Dec. Cearbhall Ó Dálaigh becomes fifth President of the Republic (unopposed); inaugurated on 19 Dec.

8 Dec. Irish Republican Socialist Party (I.R.S.P.) and the Irish National Liberation Army (I.N.L.A.) formed in Dublin; breakaway from Official Sinn Féin and Official I.R.A. respectively.

10 Dec. Four Protestant clergymen meet with Provisional I.R.A. leaders in Feakle, Co. Clare; the clergymen meet with N.I. Secretary Merlyn Rees a week later to report on the talks; I.R.A. cease-fire operates from 22 Dec. to 16 Jan. 1975.

28 Dec. d. Stephen Hayes (78), former Chief of Staff of the I.R.A.

National Committee on National Schemes to Combat Poverty established in Republic (government ceases to fund it in 1980).

1975

7 Jan. Six Burtonport, Co. Donegal, fishermen lost when their trawler, the *Evelyn Marie*, strikes submerged rock off Donegal coast.

d. Sinéad Bean de Valera (96), author, wife of Eamon de Valera.

8 Jan. Eamon Barnes becomes the Republic's first Director of Public Prosecutions.

10 Jan. 115,000 tons of heavy fuel-oil discharged into Bantry Bay, Co. Cork, in collision between tanker *African Zodiac* and a tug.

19 Jan. Bord na Gaeilge established under chairmanship of Dr T. K. Whitaker.

27 Jan. d. Mother Mary Martin (82), founder of the Medical Missionaries of Mary (1937).

28 Jan. Colm Ó Briain appointed first full-time director of the Arts Council.

31 Jan. Unemployment in Northern Ireland exceeds 100,000 for the first time in over 30 years.

Gardiner Report recommends continuation of detention without trial in Northern Ireland as 'short-term necessity' and the abolition of 'special category' or political status.

3 Feb. Health Education Bureau established in Republic under chairmanship of Bunny Carr (abolished in 1988).

10 Feb. I.R.A. start cease-fire after talks with British officials; 'incident centres' set up by government (*see* 12 Nov.).

16 Feb. Republican prisoner Patrick Ward, seriously ill in Jervis Street Hospital, Dublin, ends his 45-day hunger-strike.

23 Feb. d. Ernest Blythe (86), politician (Cumann na nGaedheal and

Fine Gael), minister in various departments (1918–32); manager of the Abbey Theatre (1941–67).

7 Mar. Freedom of the city of Dublin conferred on retired political leaders Eamon de Valera and John A. Costello.

10 Mar. Project Arts Centre, Dublin, opened by President Ó Dálaigh.

10–11 Mar. Heads of E.E.C. governments meet in Dublin, with Taoiseach Liam Cosgrave presiding.

17 Mar. One prisoner shot dead and two injured in attempted escape from Portlaoise prison.

18 Mar. Price sisters transferred to Armagh prison from Durham prison in England.

19 Mar. Israel's first Ambassador to the Republic, Gideon Raphael, presents his credentials to President Ó Dálaigh.

5–6 Apr. 10 killed and 75 injured in Belfast violence.

28 Apr. Billy McMillen, Official I.R.A. commander in Belfast, killed, allegedly in feud with the I.N.L.A.

1 May General election to the Northern Ireland Constitutional Convention: Official Unionists, 19; Vanguard Unionists, 14; D.U.P., 12; Independent Loyalist, 1; S.D.L.P., 17; Alliance, 8; Unionist Party of Northern Ireland, 5; Northern Ireland Labour Party, 1; Independent, 1.

8 May Northern Ireland Constitutional Convention meets for first time.

3 June Three Protestants returning to Northern Ireland from dog show in Co. Cork killed at the border.

24 June d. Frank MacDermot (89), founder of the National Centre Party (1932).

3 July Druid Theatre opens with a production of Synge's *The Playboy of the Western World* at the Jesuit Hall, Galway.

16 July Edmund Garvey appointed Garda Commissioner in succession to Patrick Malone.

17 July Four British soldiers killed and one seriously wounded in ambush near the border in Co. Armagh.

30 July Finance (No. 2) Act (R.I.) abolishes death duties (*see* 31 Mar. 1976).

31 July Three members of the Miami showband killed; two of the U.V.F. killers die in premature bomb explosion.

5 Aug. Capital Gains Tax Act (R.I.) provides for taxes on inheritance and gifts to replace death duties (abolished on 30 July).

9 Aug. d. Maurice Gorham (73), journalist and author; Director of Radio Éireann (1953–59).

10 Aug. d. Robert Barton (94), longest surviving signatory of the Treaty of 1921.

13 Aug. Bomb explosion at Baynardo Bar in Shankill Road, Belfast, kills five and injures 40.

22 Aug. Bomb explodes in Armagh public house, killing three and injuring 12.

28 Aug. Irish rugby international Willie John McBride, world record holder of 63 caps as a forward, announces his retirement from the international game.

29 Aug. d. Eamon de Valera (92); state funeral to Glasnevin on day of national mourning.

1 Sept. Five killed and 12 wounded in attack on Orange hall in Tullyvallen, Co. Armagh (for which South Armagh Republican Action Force claims responsibility).

8 Sept. U.U.U.C. convention members vote to reject power-sharing at cabinet level; William Craig resigns leadership of Vanguard Unionist Progressive Party (expelled from U.U.U.C. on 24 Oct.).

2 Oct. 11 killed in wave of U.V.F. violence in Northern Ireland.

d. Séamus Murphy (68), sculptor.

3 Oct. Dr Tiede Herrema, Dutch managing director of Ferenka Ltd, Limerick, kidnapped by republicans who seek release of imprisoned Dr Rose Dugdale (*see* 7 Nov.).

5 Oct. Holy Cross Abbey, Co. Tipperary, reopened; restored as a contribution to European Architectural Heritage Year.

12 Oct. Blessed Oliver Plunkett becomes first Irish saint to be canonised since St Laurence O'Toole in 1226.

29 Oct. Ashford Castle, Cong, Co. Mayo, becomes first Irish hotel to win an Egon Ronay gold plate award.

7 Nov. Dr Tiede Herrema freed when his captors, Eddie Gallagher and Marion Coyle, surrender to gardaí after 18-day siege in housing estate at Monasterevin, Co. Kildare (*see* 11 Dec. 1975 *and* 11 Mar. 1976 *and* 27 Sept. 1985).

12 Nov. 'Incident centres' in Northern Ireland close (*see* 10 Feb.).

29 Nov. One killed and five injured in explosions at Dublin Airport for which U.D.A. claim responsibility.

5 Dec. Internment ends in Northern Ireland.

11 Dec. Dr Tiede Herrema and his wife Elizabeth receive honorary Irish citizenship.

19 Dec. Four killed and 25 injured in pub bombings in Dundalk, Co. Louth, and Silverbridge, Co. Armagh.

30 Dec. Five killed and 30 injured in C.I.E.'s worst disaster to date at Clogh Bridge, Tubberneering, Co. Wexford.

Release of *Caoineadh Airt Uí Laoire* (*Lament for Art O'Leary*), first independently produced feature film in the Irish language; directed by Bob Quinn.

1976

4 Jan. Five Catholics killed in two separate incidents near Whitecross, Co. Armagh.

5 Jan. Ten Protestants shot dead in ambush at Kingsmill, Co. Armagh, by Republican Action Force.

d. John A. Costello (84), lawyer and politician (Fine Gael), Taoiseach (1948–51 and 1954–57).

12 Feb. Frank Stagg, I.R.A., dies in Wakefield prison, following 60-day hunger-strike; in resulting violence in Northern Ireland a reserve constable is shot dead.

5 Mar. Taoiseach Cosgrave and P.M. Wilson meet in London.

10 Mar. Republic refers test case alleging torture of prisoners in Northern Ireland to the European Court of Human Rights (*see* 2 Sept.).

11 Mar. Eddie Gallagher and Marion Coyle sentenced to 20 and 15 years' imprisonment respectively for their roles in the kidnapping of Tiede Herrema (*see* 7 Nov. 1975).

26 Mar. Secretary of State Merlyn Rees announces abolition of special category status in Northern Ireland jails, starting on 31 Mar.

30 Mar. Rent and rate strike in Northern Ireland (begun in 1971) called off by N.I.C.R.A.

31 Mar. Capital Acquisitions Tax Act (R.I.) imposes duties on gifts and inheritance (*see* 30 July 1975).

Cork–Dublin mail train robbed of £150,000 near Sallins, Co. Dublin (*see* 17 July 1984).

5 Apr. P.M. Harold Wilson (Labour) resigns; succeeded by James Callaghan (Labour).

8 Apr. Prison Officer O. C. Dillon becomes first warder to be shot in Northern Ireland, killed outside his home in Omagh, Co. Tyrone.

12 Apr. Committee established under chairmanship of W. G. H. Quigley to inquire into economy of Northern Ireland (report on 15 Oct. recommends capital investment of £100 million).

14 Apr. During four-hour peace vigil in St Anne's Cathedral, Belfast, the names of 1,289 victims of violence in Northern Ireland are read; total does not include 208 names of those suspected of terrorist activity.

25 Apr. Provisional I.R.A. defies government order banning their Easter Rising commemorative demonstration at G.P.O., Dublin; some 10,000 attend. Dr David Thornley expelled on 28th from the parliamentary Labour Party for appearing on Sinn Féin platform.

5 May Nine I.R.S.P. prisoners escape through Maze prison tunnel.

6 May President Ó Dálaigh signs Criminal Law (Jurisdiction) Bill which he had referred to the Supreme Court on 10 Mar.

8 June d. Dominic O'Riordan (53), broadcaster and film critic.

28 June – 6 Sept. Bank strike in the Republic.

3 July Bomb explosions in Dublin, Killarney, Limerick and Rosslare, for which responsibility is claimed by Ulster Freedom Fighters.

11 July d. Michael Hayes (87), scholar and politician (Cumann na nGaedheal); Ceann Comhairle (Speaker) of the First Dáil.

13 July Adoption Act (R.I.) permits adoptions in which adoptive and natural parents are not of the same religion (*see* 13 May 1974).

15 July Five prisoners escape from cells in Special Criminal Court, Dublin, when bomb explodes within building; four recaptured.

21 July Christopher Ewart-Biggs, British Ambassador to the Republic, and Judith Cooke, a civil servant, killed in a landmine explosion near his official residence at Sandyford, Co. Dublin (*see* 29 July).

22 July Fair Employment (Northern Ireland) Act establishes equal opportunity agency; comes into force on 1 Dec.

29 July Inauguration of the Christopher Ewart-Biggs Memorial Fund Committee to promote peace and understanding in Ireland and the strengthening of ties between the British and Irish peoples (*see* 21 July).

6 Aug. Republic claims jurisdiction over 200-mile area of the continental shelf, including Rockall Island.

10 Aug. Three Maguire children killed and their mother, Anne, injured when car driven by Provisional I.R.A. member who is shot by troops, crashes into them; Máiréad Corrigan, sister of Mrs Anne Maguire, and Mrs Betty Williams form the Peace People movement the next day; first peace rally held in Belfast on 14th.

18 Aug. Former Northern Ireland P.M. Brian Faulkner announces his retirement from public life.

1 Sept. Oireachtas declares state of national emergency coinciding with second reading of Emergency Powers Bill.

2 Sept. European Court of Human Rights finds U.K. guilty of torture of republican prisoners in Northern Ireland, but not guilty of discrimination in operation of internment during Aug. 1971.

10 Sept. Roy Mason replaces Merlyn Rees as Secretary of State for Northern Ireland.

15 Sept. Mrs Anne Dickson becomes first woman to lead an Irish political party when elected leader of the Unionist Party of Northern Ireland.

Ciarán Nugent signals start of H-Block 'blanket protest' by going 'on the blanket' as a protest against removal of special category status.

24 Sept. President Ó Dálaigh refers the Emergency Powers Bill to the Supreme Court (*see* 18 Oct.); signs bill on 16 Oct.

8 Oct. Richie Ryan, R.I. Minister for Finance, appointed chairman of the International Monetary Fund and of the World Bank.

15 Oct. Garda Michael Clerkin killed and five colleagues injured in booby-trap explosion at Garryhinch, Co. Laois.

18 Oct. Patrick Donegan, Minister for Defence, while addressing members of the army during function at Columb Barracks, Mullingar, Co. Westmeath, reportedly refers to President Ó Dálaigh as 'a thundering disgrace' for referring Emergency Powers Bill to Supreme Court.

22 Oct. Following failure of the government to deal with crisis precipitated by Patrick Donegan's remarks on 18 Oct., President Ó Dálaigh resigns 'to protect the dignity of the office' (*see* 9 Nov.).

27 Oct. In absence of a President, the Canadian Ambassador to Ireland, Edgar Ritchie, presents credentials to the Presidential Commission (first time the Commission carried out such a function).

d. Edward Roth (54), who as first Director-General of Telefís Éireann (later R.T.E.) set up the television station in 1960.

28 Oct. Máire Drumm, former Vice-President of Provisional Sinn Féin, shot dead in the Mater Hospital, Belfast.

2 Nov. d. Walter Starkie (82), scholar, author and authority on Romany gypsies; director of the Abbey Theatre (1927–42).

3 Nov. E.E.C. report shows that the Republic has the highest inflation rate in the community (18.9 per cent).

9 Nov. Dr Patrick Hillery becomes sixth President of the Republic (unopposed) (*see* 22 Oct.); inaugurated on 3 Dec.

26 Nov. Richard Burke, Minister for Education, nominated as the Republic's E.E.C. Commissioner in succession to Dr Patrick Hillery.

30 Nov. Máiréad Corrigan and Betty Williams, founders of the Peace People movement, receive the Nobel Prize for Peace (£200,000).

9 Dec. Provisional I.R.A. fire-bomb blitz in Derry causes over £1 million worth of damage.

14 Dec. Dr Garret FitzGerald commences first-ever visit to U.S.S.R. by an Irish Minister for Foreign Affairs.

1977

21 Jan. d. Seán Ó Riordáin (61), poet.

3 Mar. d. (in hunting accident) Brian Faulkner (56), Baron Faulkner of Downpatrick, politician (Unionist), P.M. of Northern Ireland (1971–72).

7–8 Mar. Eight S.A.S. soldiers found armed south of the border on 5th fined £100 each.

10 Mar. Barretstown Castle, Co. Kildare, with 507-acre demesne, presented to the nation by the Canadian businessman Garfield Weston.

4 Apr. Workers' Participation (State Enterprises) Act (R.I.) allows worker-directorships on semi-state boards.

6 Apr. Unfair Dismissals Act (R.I.) provides redress for employees unfairly dismissed.

17 Apr. d. William, Cardinal Conway (64), R.C. Archbishop of Armagh and Primate.

22 Apr. Following intervention of James Kavanagh, Auxiliary Bishop of Dublin, I.R.A. prisoners in the Curragh end 47-day hunger-strike.

3 May Ulster Unionist Action Council begins strike as protest against security policy in Northern Ireland and demands return to majority government; strike called off 10 days later when it fails to involve the power workers.

9 May Ireland's first horse museum opens at the H.Q. of the National Stud, Co. Kildare, with Mary McGrath as curator.

26 May Five soldiers killed in training accident on the army's artillery range in the Glen of Imaal, Co. Wicklow.

16 June General election in R.I.: Fianna Fáil, 84; Fine Gael, 43; Labour, 17; Independents and others, 4. Fianna Fáil return to power; Jack Lynch appointed Taoiseach on 5 July.

19 June New Zealand's P.M., Robert Muldoon, meets Máiréad Corrigan and Betty Williams in Belfast to discuss the possibility of former terrorists being allowed to emigrate to New Zealand.

23 June Former Taoiseach Liam Cosgrave announces his resignation from leadership of Fine Gael; succeeded by Dr Garret FitzGerald on 1 July.

27 June Four killed and 18 injured in Belfast I.R.A. feud.

1 July Brendan Corish resigns leadership of the Labour Party; succeeded by Frank Cluskey.

Employment Equality Agency set up in Republic under chairperson Sylvia Meehan.

14 July European Court of Justice orders government of the Republic to suspend its unilateral fisheries conservation measures from 18 July.

5 Oct. Séamus Costello, leader of the I.R.S.P., killed (first Irish party leader to be assassinated).

16 Nov. National Board for Science and Technology to be established in Republic under act.

18 Nov. National Institute for Higher Education and Thomond College in Limerick withdraw from N.U.I.; degrees to be conferred by National Council for Education Awards.

26 Nov. William Craig announces disbandment of Vanguard organisations.

28 Nov. Ferenka factory, Annacotty, Co. Limerick, strike-bound since 3 Oct., closes, with loss of 1,400 jobs.

21 Dec. d. Seán Keating (88), artist; President of the R.H.A. (1949–62).

1978

18 Jan. European Court of Human Rights rules that interrogation methods used in Northern Ireland on internees were 'inhuman and degrading' but not torture; case brought by the Republic.

19 Jan. Garda Commissioner Edmund Garvey dismissed by the government following his refusal to resign; dismissal subsequently declared null and void by the Supreme Court, which awards him damages and costs; his resignation is accepted by the government on 15 May, and he is succeeded by Patrick McLoughlin.

10 Feb. Cuspóir supersedes Cosac as official sports body.

14 Feb. Matt Talbot Memorial Bridge officially opened; the first new bridge over Dublin's River Liffey for almost a century.

17 Feb. 12 killed instantly and four others die later when bomb explodes at La Mon Hotel, Comber, Co. Down (largest single death toll resulting from explosion since disturbances began in 1969).

4 Mar. d. Gen. Emmet Dalton (80), aide to Michael Collins; later a film producer.

6 Mar. d. Mícheál Mac Liammóir (79), actor, writer, designer, cofounder of the Gate Theatre (1928).

21 Mar. d. Cearbhall Ó Dálaigh (66), jurist; President of the Republic (1974–76).

25 Mar. John Treacy wins the World Cross-Country Championship at Ballyhouston Park, Glasgow.

2 May David Cooke (Alliance Party) becomes Belfast's first non-Unionist Lord Mayor.

2 Nov. R.T.E. 2, a second national television channel, inaugurated from Opera House, Cork.

26 Nov. Albert Miles, deputy governor of the Maze prison, shot dead by the I.R.A.

13 Dec. d. Jack Doyle (66), boxer and entertainer.

Dublin Institute of Technology established by City of Dublin Vocational Education Committee, from amalgamation of Bolton Street and Kevin Street Colleges of Technology; College of Commerce, Rathmines; College of Music, Chatham Row; College of Marketing and Design, Parnell Square; and College of Catering, Cathal Brugha Street.

1979

8 Jan. Explosion on Whiddy Island, Bantry Bay, Co. Cork, kills 50 and destroys French tanker *Betelgeuse* (*see* 25 July 1980).

31 Jan. d. Maurice MacGonigal (79), artist; Keeper of R.H.A. since 1950.

2 Mar. d. Christy Ring (58), outstanding Cork hurler.

13 Mar. Republic joins European Monetary System (E.M.S), breaking parity with sterling.

19 Mar. Údarás na Gaeltachta established by Oireachtas as statutory body (containing elected representatives and nominated members) to oversee development of Irish-speaking areas.

28 Mar. Northern Ireland M.P.s play crucial role in defeat of British minority Labour government on confidence motion, when the Unionists vote with the Conservative Party and Gerry Fitt (S.D.L.P.) and Frank Maguire (Independent) abstain.

30 Mar. Airey Neave, Conservative spokesman on Northern Ireland, killed by the I.N.L.A.

26 Apr. Gráinne Cronin, Aer Lingus's first woman pilot completes her first scheduled flight, from Frankfurt to Shannon.

3 May Conservatives return to power in U.K. general election; D.U.P. gain two seats from the O.U.P. in Northern Ireland; Margaret Thatcher appointed P.M. on 4th.

4 May d. Jack Cruise (63), entertainer.

KILKENNY COUNTY LIBRARY

5 May Humphrey Atkins replaces Roy Mason as Secretary of State for Northern Ireland.

31 May R.T.E. Radio 2 officially launched.

7 June First direct elections to the European Parliament: Republic (15 seats)—Fianna Fáil, 5; Fine Gael, 4; Labour, 4; Independents, 2. Northern Ireland (3 seats)—Rev. Ian Paisley (D.U.P.), John Hume (S.D.L.P.) and John Taylor (Official Unionist).

10 June d. Séamus Kelly (67), drama critic and columnist ('Quidnunc' of the *Irish Times*).

15 June Statue of James Larkin unveiled in O'Connell Street, Dublin; sculptor Oisín Kelly.

22 June Body of republican socialist Frank Ryan, who fought in the International Brigade in Spain (1936–39), reinterred in Glasnevin, Dublin.

25 June End of first national postal strike (started on 17 Feb.).

30 June Tomás Ó Fiaich, Archbishop of Armagh, created cardinal.

5 July Two amendments to the Constitution, on adoption (Sixth Amendment) and university representation in Seanad Éireann (Seventh Amendment) carried in referendum; poll less than 28 per cent.

10 July Francis and Mary Murphy successfully challenge section of the Income Tax Act pertaining to married couples, in the High Court, Dublin, which finds it repugnant to the Constitution.

9 Aug. 59 Vietnamese refugees ('boat-people') arrive in Ireland.

26 Aug. Eddie Macken has record-breaking fourth successive win in British show-jumping derby at Hickstead.

27 Aug. Lord Mountbatten, the Dowager Lady Brabourne and two teenagers killed at Mullaghmore, Co. Sligo by I.R.A. bomb (*see* 23 Nov.).

18 soldiers killed in explosion near Warrenpoint, Co. Down; greatest number of fatal casualties suffered by the British army in a single incident in Northern Ireland.

29 Sept. First papal visit to Ireland: Pope John Paul II arrives on three-day visit and celebrates mass in Phoenix Park before a crowd in excess of 1,000,000; makes an impassioned plea at Drogheda for an end to violence; also visits Limerick, Galway, and Knock, Co. Mayo.

2 Oct. Provisional I.R.A. rejects the Pope's call for peace.

12 Oct. £500,000 stolen in raid at Trinity Bank, Dublin.

15 Nov. d. Patrick McGilligan (90), last surviving member of the first Free State government.

23 Nov. Thomas McMahon found guilty of the murder of Lord Mountbatten and sentenced to penal servitude for life; Francis McGirl acquitted.

28 Nov. John Hume, M.E.P., chosen as S.D.L.P. leader in succession to Gerry Fitt.

7 Dec. Charles J. Haughey defeats George Colley (44 votes to 38) for leadership of Fianna Fáil; elected Taoiseach on 11 Dec.

28 Dec. 1979 is proclaimed the worst year for industrial disputes in the history of the 26-county state.

National Council for Educational Awards, established on an *ad hoc* basis in 1972, receives statutory authority.

Census of population in Republic: 3,364,881 (increase of 13 per cent since 1971).

1980

6 Jan. Landmine explosion near Castlewellan, Co. Down, kills three

U.D.R. members and injures four others; Northern Ireland death toll reaches 2,000 since 1969.

7 Jan. Constitutional conference opens at Stormont; boycotted by Unionists and adjourned indefinitely on 24 Mar.

22 Jan. Estimated 700,000 P.A.Y.E. employees march in demonstrations throughout Republic against inequities in tax system.

26 Jan. d. Michael McInerney (74), author and journalist.

7 Feb. d. Michael Browne (84), retired Bishop of Galway.

11 Feb. George Otto Simms, C.I. Archbishop of Armagh, retires; succeeded by John Ward Armstrong on 25th.

17 Feb. Derrynaflan treasure hoard (chalice and other ancient ecclesiastical objects) discovered near Killenaule, Co. Tipperary, with the aid of metal detectors by Michael Webb and his son (*see* 6 Mar. 1980 *and* 29 July 1986).

27 Feb. Dr David Rosen becomes Chief Rabbi to the Jewish community in Ireland.

6 Mar. Derrynaflan chalice goes on display at the National Museum, Dublin.

7 Mar. Donal Cashman succeeds Paddy Lane as President of the Irish Farmers' Association.

18 Apr. Two unarmed Irish soldiers of U.N. peace-keeping force in the Lebanon are shot dead, and colleagues seriously wounded, during capture by Christian Militia.

25 Apr. Electoral commission report recommending 18 additional Dáil seats and more than double the number of five-seat constituencies accepted by Dáil Éireann.

30 Apr. Marion Price, convicted with sister Dolours for involvement in 1973 London car-bombing, released on humanitarian grounds from Armagh prison (*see* 22 Apr. 1981).

1 May d. John D. Sheridan (77), humorist.

15 May Former Taoiseach Jack Lynch announces intention to resign from politics on dissolution of current Dáil.

d. Alan Simpson (60), theatre director; co-founder with wife, Carolyn Swift, of the Pike Theatre.

21 May P.M. Margaret Thatcher and Taoiseach Charles Haughey meet at Downing Street; communiqué stresses 'unique relationship' and anticipates closer political co-operation.

19 June European Commission on Human Rights rejects submission by H-Block prisoners, but criticises British government's handling of the H-Block protest.

20 June d. Paddy Prendergast (68), racehorse trainer; leading trainer under Jockey Club rules (1963–65).

2 July d. Gen. Tom Barry (83), republican soldier and guerrilla tactician who defeated Crown forces at Kilmichael and Crossbarry, Co. Cork, during the War of Independence.

5 July d. A. J. (Archie) Potter (62), composer.

7 July Criminal Law Jurisdiction Act, 1976, used for the first time when three Co. Monaghan men face charges in Republic of murdering U.D.R. soldier in Northern Ireland.

9 July Northern Ireland internment law, unused since 1975, repealed.

25 July Mr Justice Declan Costello, chairman of the Whiddy tribunal, indicts both Gulf Oil and Total in his report, holding them responsible for the *Betelgeuse* explosion (*see* 8 Jan. 1979).

8 Aug. Five adults and five children die in fire at the Central Hotel, Bundoran, Co. Donegal.

5 Sept. d. Eric Cross (77), author (*The Tailor and Ansty*, 1942, the subject of bitter controversy and a four-day debate in the Senate of Éire).

12 Sept. Republic of Ireland and the People's Republic of China exchange ambassadors for the first time (John Campbell is posted to Peking; Madame Gong Pusheng takes up residence in Dublin).

3 Oct. Dubliner Mella Carroll becomes first female High Court judge in the Republic.

11 Oct. Dr Rose Dugdale released from Limerick jail, having served six years of her sentence (*see* 25 June *and* 27 Nov. 1974).

27 Oct. Seven H-Block prisoners commence hunger-strike over the right to wear their own clothing (*see* 15 *and* 18 Dec.).

29 Oct. Central Fisheries Board established in Republic, with seven regional boards.

7 Nov. d. Frank Duff (91), founder of the Legion of Mary (1921).

3 Dec. Republic's National Council for Educational Awards formally inaugurated.

8 Dec. Taoiseach Haughey and P.M. Thatcher hold summit meeting at Dublin Castle; agree to examine 'the totality of relationships' between U.K. and Ireland, and to establish an Anglo-Irish Committee.

15 Dec. H-Block crisis deepens when 23 additional republican prisoners join the hunger-strikers of 27 Oct.

18 Dec. First H-Block hunger-strike for return of political status ends, following intervention of Cardinal Ó Fiaich (*see* 1 Mar. 1981).

1981

16 Jan. Bernadette Devlin McAliskey and husband Michael seriously wounded in gun attack on their home at Derrylaughan, Co. Tyrone.

20 Jan. d. Charles E. Kelly (78), artist; co-founder (with Tom Collins and Arthur Booth) of *Dublin Opinion* (1922).

21 Jan. Former Speaker of the Northern Ireland House of Commons, Sir Norman Stronge, and his son killed at their home, Tynan Abbey, Co. Armagh.

30 Jan. Inflation rate in the Republic stands at 18.2 per cent, according to E.E.C. report.

6 Feb. British coal-boat *Nellie M* sunk by Provisional I.R.A. off Moville, Co. Donegal.

14 Feb. 48 die and almost 200 are injured in fire at the Stardust Ballroom, Artane, Dublin, during St Valentine's Night dance (*see* 5 July 1982).

1 Mar. Second hunger-strike for political status by republicans in H-Blocks at the Maze prison, led by Bobby Sands.

5 Mar. Taoiseach Charles Haughey announces establishment of Aosdana to help provide guaranteed income for certain creative artists.

d. Frank Maguire (52), Independent M.P. for Fermanagh and South Tyrone (*see* 9 Apr.).

17 Mar. 'Friends of Ireland' launched by leading members of the U.S. Congress (*see* 29 May 1982).

24 Mar. Geoffrey Armstrong, British Leyland executive, shot and wounded by pro-H-Block supporters as he addresses conference at T.C.D.

9 Apr. Bobby Sands, H-Block prisoner (30,493 votes), elected M.P. for Fermanagh and South Tyrone in U.K. by-election, defeating Harry West (O.U.P., 29,046) (*see* 5 May).

Former Taoiseach Liam Cosgrave, leader of Fine Gael (1965–77), announces his retirement from active politics when current Dáil is dissolved.

22 Apr. Dolours Price released from Armagh jail suffering from *anorexia nervosa* (*see* 30 Apr. 1980).

27 Apr. First female cadets (eight) in the history of the 26-county state commissioned.

2 May Laurence Downey, former Cistercian monk, arrested at Le Touquet airport in hijack attempt on Aer Lingus plane.

5 May Bobby Sands, M.P. for Fermanagh and South Tyrone, dies after hunger strike of 66 days in the Maze prison (*see* 20 Aug.); his funeral on 7 May attended by over 50,000.

12 May Francis Hughes, once described as 'the North's most wanted man' dies after hunger-strike of 59 days in the Maze prison.

13 May Whitegate, Co. Cork, oil refinery closes (*see* 1 Mar. 1982).

19 May Gerry Fitt loses Belfast Council seat which he has held for 23 years to Fergus O'Hare, prominent H-Block campaigner.

Five British soldiers killed in armoured car by a landmine near Bessbrook, Co. Armagh.

21 May Patsy O'Hara and Raymond McCreesh die after hunger-strike of 61 days in the Maze prison.

8 June Joseph McDonnell dies after hunger-strike of 61 days in the Maze prison.

11 June General election in R.I.: Fianna Fáil, 78; Fine Gael, 65; Labour, 15; Workers' Party, 1; Independents and others, 6 (including two I.R.A. prisoners in the Maze; *see* 2–3 Aug.).

Frank Cluskey, having lost his Dáil seat, resigns as leader of the Labour Party; succeeded by Michael O'Leary.

Eight Provisional I.R.A. prisoners escape from Belfast prison while awaiting sentencing.

30 June Dr Garret FitzGerald (Fine Gael) elected Taoiseach and forms a coalition government with the Labour Party.

7 July d. Donal Foley (59), journalist (compiler of satirical column 'Man Bites Dog' in the *Irish Times*).

13 July Martin Hurson dies after hunger-strike of 46 days in the Maze prison.

31 July Family of Pat Quinn intervenes on 47th day of his hunger-strike.

1 Aug. Kevin Lynch dies after hunger-strike of 71 days in the Maze prison.

2–3 Aug. Kieran Doherty, T.D. for Cavan–Monaghan, dies after hunger-strike of 73 days in the Maze prison.

8 Aug. Thomas McElwee dies after hunger-strike of 65 days in the Maze prison.

20 Aug. Owen Carron (Anti H-Block Proxy Political Prisoner, 31,278 votes) defeats Ken Maginnis (O.U.P., 29,048) in Fermanagh and South Tyrone by-election (*see* 5 May).

Michael Devine dies after hunger-strike of 60 days in the Maze prison; tenth and last death resulting from republican hunger-strike (*see* 3 Oct.).

21 Aug. Family of Pat McGeown seeks medical intervention to save his life on 42nd day of his hunger-strike.

4 Sept. Family of Matthew Devlin seeks medical intervention on the 52nd day of his hunger-strike.

6 Sept. Family of Laurence McKeown instructs medical staff to intervene on the 70th day of his hunger-strike.

d. Christy Brown (49), artist, novelist and poet (author of *Down All the Days*, 1970).

7 Sept. Two R.U.C. officers die in Provisional I.R.A. landmine explosion at Pomeroy, Co. Tyrone.

10 Sept. National Concert Hall, Dublin, opens.

13 Sept. James Prior replaces Humphrey Atkins as Secretary of State for Northern Ireland.

27 Sept. Taoiseach Garret FitzGerald announces a 'constitutional crusade' to abolish 'sectarian elements' in the law and Constitution of the Republic.

28 Sept. d. Joe Linnane (71), broadcaster and entertainer.

3 Oct. Following the deaths of 10 republicans in H-Block hunger-strike, and further intervention by relatives, the Provisionals call off the hunger-strike; it has had widespread repercussions in political terms and in associated violence (61 people, including 30 members of the armed forces, died during the campaign).

6 Oct. As a result of ending of H-Block protest, it is announced that all prisoners will now be allowed to wear their own clothing at all times.

12 Oct. d. Oisín Kelly (66), sculptor of 'The Children of Lir' in Dublin's Garden of Remembrance and the monument to James Larkin in O'Connell Street, Dublin.

13 Oct. Pub. *An Bíobla Naofa,* first Irish-language version of the Bible for over 200 years.

2 Nov. d. The O'Conor Don (Rev. Charles O'Conor, S.J.), last direct descendant of Toirdhealbhach Ó Conchobhair, High-King of Ireland (d. 1156) (O'Conor Don family said to be able to trace its descent through more generations of legitimate ancestors than any family in Europe).

5 Nov. d. Daniel Morrissey (84), politician (Fine Gael) who established I.D.A. as instrument of his department (1949).

6 Nov. Following talks in London, P.M. Margaret Thatcher and Taoiseach Garret FitzGerald agree to setting up of Intergovernmental Council.

14 Nov. Rev. Robert Bradford, M.P. for South Belfast, assassinated at a constituency clinic in Finaghy; the caretaker of the building is also killed.

16 Nov. 'Third Force', a D.U.P.-supported vigilante organisation, marches in Enniskillen, Co. Fermanagh.

3 Dec. Rev. Ian Paisley claims membership of 15,000–20,000 for his 'Third Force' (*see* 16 Nov.); N.I. Secretary James Prior says that private armies will not be tolerated.

Census of population in Northern Ireland: 1,481,959 (decrease of 2.8 per cent since 1971); figure revised in 1985 to 1,532,198 (revision necessitated by the killing of an enumerator during the census).

1982

22 Jan. E.E.C. survey names Dublin the community's most polluted capital.

26 Jan. d. Seán Bourke, who claimed a major role in the escape of spy

George Blake from Wormwood Scrubs.

1 Feb. Corporal punishment banned in schools in the Republic.

4 Feb. Rev. Martin Smyth (O.U.P., 17,123 votes) defeats David Cook (Alliance, 11,726) in South Belfast by-election (*see* 14 Nov. 1981).

12 Feb. Hearing into allegations concerning the Kincora Boys' Home in Belfast collapses when three of the five-member inquiry team resign.

16 Feb. d. Major Vivion de Valera (71), politician (Fianna Fáil), eldest son of Eamon de Valera; managing and controlling director of Irish Press Group since 1959.

18 Feb. General election in Republic: Fianna Fáil, 81; Fine Gael, 63; Labour, 15; Workers' Party, 3; Independents and others, 3. Charles J. Haughey elected Taoiseach on 9 Mar. and forms a Fianna Fáil government.

21 Feb. Ireland wins rugby Triple Crown for the first time since 1949, beating Scotland (21 points to 12).

23 Feb. Poland accuses Britain at European conference of using torture in Northern Ireland.

24 Feb. Heroin worth £300,000 seized by gardaí near Ballymun, Dublin.

25 Feb. Challenge to C. J. Haughey's leadership of Fianna Fáil dissipates when Desmond O'Malley withdraws opposition.

1 Mar. Government announces that it is to take over Whitegate refinery, Co. Cork (*see* 13 May 1981).

Michael O'Kennedy resigns as E.E.C. Commissioner and is replaced by Richard Burke; Burke appointed Vice-President of the European Commission on 16 Dec.

27 Mar. I.R.A. offers amnesty to informers as 'supergrasses' give evidence.

18 Apr. Irish trawler *Sheralga* dragged to bottom by British submarine in Irish Sea; no lives are lost.

4 May Following sinking of Argentinian ship *General Belgrano* by British forces in the Falklands War, with loss of over 500 lives, Republic calls on U.N. to meet in emergency session and to seek cessation of hostilities in the south Atlantic.

10 May Séamus Mallon, deputy leader of the S.D.L.P., and John Robb, a surgeon at the Royal Victoria Hospital, Belfast, appointed to Senate by Taoiseach Haughey (*see* 16 Sept.).

13 May European Parliament calls for ban on plastic bullets throughout U.K.

Treas Honan (Fianna Fáil) becomes first female Cathaoirleach (Chairman) of the Senate.

29 May U.S. Congress 'Friends of Ireland' group arrives on fact-finding mission in Northern Ireland.

23 June *Sunday Journal* (Dublin) ceases publication.

5 July Tribunal of inquiry into Stardust fire (*see* 14 Feb. 1981) concludes that fire was probably started deliberately; owners severely criticised, and Dublin Corporation and Department of the Environment are also censured.

13 July Irish legal history is made when Gerard Anthony Tuite is sentenced to ten years' imprisonment on explosives charges (the first Irish citizen to be tried in the Republic for a crime allegedly committed outside the state).

20 July Eight British soldiers killed and 51 people injured (of whom three later die) in two bomb attacks by I.R.A. in London – one near Household Cavalry barracks at Knightsbridge, London, and the other at Regent's Park, where army band is playing.

19 Aug. President Hillery opens permanent John McCormack exhibition of memorabilia in the National Concert Hall, Dublin.

22 Aug. Restoration work on Bank of Ireland head office at College Green, Dublin (old Parliament House) completed after eleven years.

24 Aug. d. Eoghan Ó Tuairisc (63), writer.

4 Sept. Flint mace-head, over 5,000 years old and regarded by experts as one of the greatest treasures of Ireland, unearthed at Knowth, Co. Meath, by Liam O'Connor.

13 Sept. d. Mick Mackey (70), outstanding Limerick hurler.

16 Sept. New Ireland Group founded by Senator John Robb.

20 Sept. Radar station at Schull, Co. Cork, blown up by the I.N.L.A.

Phoenix Park racecourse purchased by consortium headed by Ballydoyle, Co. Tipperary, trainer Vincent O'Brien.

24 Sept. d. Cornelius Lucey (80), retired R.C. Bishop of Cork and Ross.

25 Sept. Commdt Michael Nestor of Irish U.N. peacekeeping force killed with three other U.N. soldiers by a mine near Beirut.

6 Oct. Challenge to C. J. Haughey's leadership of Fianna Fáil on motion proposed by Charles McCreevey ends in victory for Haughey (58 votes to 22); Desmond O'Malley and Martin O'Donoghue resign from the cabinet before the vote is taken.

7 Oct. d. Séamus Ennis, seminal figure in modern Irish uilleann piping.

20 Oct. General election to new Northern Ireland Assembly: Official Unionists, 26; D.U.P., 21; S.D.L.P., 14; Alliance, 10; Sinn Féin, 5 (with 10 per cent of the vote).

28 Oct. Michael O'Leary, T.D., resigns leadership of the Labour Party (joins Fine Gael); succeeded by Dick Spring.

1 Nov. d. Michael Mullen, general secretary of the I.T.G.W.U. (while visiting Frankfurt).

10 Nov. Leonard Murphy, leader of the notorious 'Shankill Butchers' gang, shot dead by Provisional I.R.A.

11 Nov. Seán Burns, Gervaise McKerr and Eugene Toman, unarmed I.R.A. members, shot dead by R.U.C. H.Q. mobile support units near Lurgan, Co. Armagh, when they allegedly drove through a checkpoint; this incident, with others, leads to allegation of R.U.C. 'shoot to kill' policy (later investigated inconclusively by John Stalker); inquest opens on 14 Nov. 1988 at Craigavon and is adjourned.

James Kilfedder (O.U.P.) elected first Speaker of the Northern Ireland Assembly; his salary as Speaker, together with his salary as Westminster M.P., makes him U.K.'s highest-paid politician.

Assembly boycotted by S.D.L.P. and Sinn Féin.

18 Nov. d. Hilton Edwards (79), co-founder with Mícheál Mac Liammóir of the Gate Theatre.

24 Nov. General election in R.I.: Fianna Fáil, 75; Fine Gael, 69; Labour, 16; Workers' Party, 2; Independents and others, 3. Fine Gael enters into coalition with Labour; Garret FitzGerald elected Taoiseach.

6 Dec. 17 people, including 11 British soldiers, killed by I.N.L.A. bomb at

Droppin' Well public house, Ballykelly, Co. Londonderry.

16 Dec. In an action brought by Harold McCusker, M.P. (O.U.P.), at Armagh election petitions court, Séamus Mallon (S.D.L.P.) is deprived of his Assembly seat—his membership of Seanad Éireann (*see* 10 May) makes him ineligible to sit in the Northern Ireland Assembly.

20 Dec. *Stubbs' Weekly* reports an increase of over 50 per cent (to 700 in number) in firms in the Republic which went out of business during 1982.

1983

5 Jan. I.N.L.A. proscribed in the Republic.

19 Jan. Michael Noonan, R.I. Minister for Justice, publicly announces that the previous (Fianna Fáil) administration was involved in unauthorised 'bugging' of phones of political journalists (Bruce Arnold and Geraldine Kennedy) (*see* 16 Feb.).

21 Jan. Ranks (Ireland) announces nationwide closure.

2 Feb. B. & I. announces closure of Cork–Pembroke ferry service.

7 Feb. Taoiseach Garret Fitzgerald's nominees to the Senate include Bríd Rodgers, general secretary of the S.D.L.P., John Robb, Belfast surgeon (previously a member through nomination by Charles Haughey), and Stephen McGonagle, Northern Ireland trade unionist.

Challenge to Charles J. Haughey's leadership of Fianna Fáil on motion of Ben Briscoe ends in victory for Haughey (40 votes to 33).

8 Feb. Shergar, outstanding racehorse (1981 Derby winner), kidnapped from Ballymany Stud, Newbridge, Co. Kildare (never found) (*see* 20 Nov.).

16 Feb. Fianna Fáil parliamentary party condemns bugging of journalists' phones (*see* 19 Jan.) and the recording of private conversation by Ray MacSharry, T.D., between himself and Senator Martin O'Donoghue (who resigns from Fianna Fáil).

21 Mar. Punt (Irish £) devalued by approximately 5 per cent.

P.M. Margaret Thatcher's meeting with Taoiseach Garret FitzGerald at E.E.C. summit bridges 16-month gap in meetings between the leaders of the two countries.

23 Mar. d. Constantine Fitzgibbon (64), novelist, journalist and translator.

25 Mar. Senior prison officer at Portlaoise jail seriously wounded in shooting near Dublin's National (Boxing) Stadium (d. 30 Sept. 1984).

4 Apr. Mercer's Hospital, Dublin, closed (building purchased by Royal College of Surgeons for £1 million in Jan. 1984).

11 Apr. 14 U.V.F. members jailed on evidence of 'supergrass' Joseph Bennett, a former U.V.F. battalion commander who had been granted immunity in respect of terrorist offences involving at least two murders.

21 Apr. Irish women's hockey team wins Intercontinental Cup in Malaysia, defeating Spain (2 goals to 1) in the final.

27 Apr. Government defeated on proposed wording of 'Pro-Life' amendment regarding abortion; original wording proposed by Fianna Fáil passes and is used in referendum (*see* 7 Sept.).

18 May d. Frank Aiken (85), politician (Fianna Fáil), holder of five different portfolios in Fianna Fáil administrations.

24 May 1,000 lb Provisional I.R.A. bomb explodes outside Andersonstown police station, West Belfast, causing an estimated £1 million damage.

30 May First meeting of New Ireland Forum at Dublin Castle under chairmanship of Colm Ó hEocha; representatives of Fianna Fáil, Fine Gael, Labour and S.D.L.P. attend; D.U.P., O.U.P. and the Workers' Party decline invitations.

9 June Conservatives win U.K. general election; Gerry Adams (Provisional Sinn Féin) takes Gerry Fitt's West Belfast seat; Ken Maginnis (O.U.P.) takes Fermanagh and South Tyrone from Owen Carron (Provisional Sinn Féin).

21 June £70 million E.E.C. aid for Belfast approved.

8 July Northern Ireland Assembly votes (35 votes to 11) for death penalty in cases of terrorist murder (Northern Ireland Catholic bishops have advised against this).

13 July Four U.D.R. members killed by I.R.A. landmine in Co. Tyrone (U.D.R.'s heaviest loss in a single incident).

U.K. House of Commons rejects death penalty in terrorist-related murder by 116 majority.

21 July Gerry Fitt created life peer (takes title Lord Fitt of Bell's Hill).

5 Aug. End of 120-day trial of 38 implicated by 'supergrass' Christopher Black; 22 convictions, involving sentences totalling in excess of 4,000 years passed by Mr Justice Kelly (*see* 17 July 1986).

680 jobs lost when Dunlop closes its Cork plant.

14 Aug. Eamonn Coughlan wins world 5,000 metres championship at Helsinki.

22 Aug. Eight die and over 30 are injured in head-on train crash at Cherryville Junction near Kildare station.

3 Sept. Very Rev. Dominic Byrne becomes second Irishman to be elected Master of the Dominican order (first was Cardinal Browne); Very Rev. Martin Nolan becomes the first Irishman to be elected Father-General of the Augustinian order.

7 Sept. 'Pro-Life' amendment to the Constitution (*see* 27 Apr.) carried (841,233 votes to 416,136).

17 Sept. d. George Colley (57), politician (Fianna Fáil), former Tánaiste.

19 Sept. d. Con Lehane, founder-member of Clann na Poblachta.

21 Sept. d. F. S. L. Lyons, historian (author of *Ireland since the Famine*, 1971), Provost of T.C.D.

25 Sept. 39 I.R.A. members in mass breakout from Maze prison, during which a warder is killed; 19 escape (*see* 27 Apr. 1988).

4 Oct. Naas bypass, Republic's first motorway, officially opened.

19 Oct. P.M.P.A., Republic's largest insurance company, founded by Joseph Moore, to be run by state-appointed liquidator, Kevin O'Kelly; debts of over £200 million.

21 Oct. President Hillery returned unopposed for a second term as President of the Republic.

24 Oct. Government abolishes the term 'illegitimacy' as a legal definition in the Republic.

28 Oct. Aughinish Alumina plant in Shannon estuary, between Askeaton and Foynes, Co. Limerick, commences production; with investment of £600 million, it is the largest private enterprise investment in an industrial undertaking in the Republic.

1 Nov. 19 per cent pay increase announced for the members of the Oireachtas and the judiciary.

3 Nov. New Ireland Forum told that the cost of violence in Northern Ireland since 1970 is in the region of £11,900 million.

7 Nov. First meeting of the Anglo-Irish Intergovernmental Council.

8 Nov. Frank Cluskey (Labour), Minister for Trade, Commerce and Tourism, resigns from government because of disagreement over Dublin Gas takeover; succeeded by John Bruton (Fine Gael).

13 Nov. Irish army participates for the first time in the Remembrance Day (Poppy Day) ceremony in Dublin.

20 Nov. Three killed when gunmen open fire on congregation in Darkley Pentecostal Hall in Co. Armagh.

A foal of kidnapped Shergar (*see* 8 Feb.) fetches 260,000 guineas at Goff's Bloodstock Sales.

16 Dec. Supermarket executive Don Tidey rescued from I.R.A. kidnappers who seek £5 million ransom; a garda and a soldier killed during rescue in a wood near Ballinamore, Co. Leitrim, when two of the six kidnappers are arrested.

17 Dec. Five killed by I.R.A. bomb in Harrods of London.

27 Dec. Book of Kells valued at £15 million by Sothebys.

1984

1 Jan. An Post (to operate the postal service) and Telecom Éireann (to operate telecommunications services) established as statutory companies (both services formerly under the control of the Department of Post and Telegraphs).

3 Jan. Michael Mills, former political correspondent of the *Irish Press*, takes office as Republic's first Ombudsman.

9 Jan. d. Seán MacEntee (95), politician (Fianna Fáil), minister in all Fianna Fáil governments between 1932 and 1965.

17 Jan. Ford plant in Cork (since 1917) announces closure.

30 Jan. d. Luke Kelly (43), ballad-singer with the group 'The Dubliners'.

11 Feb. Royal Hibernian Hotel, Dawson Street, Dublin, closes (opened in 1751); demolished in Sept.

d. T. W. Moody (77), historian (co-editor with F. X. Martin of *The Course of Irish History*, 1967).

3 Mar. d. 'Rinty' Monaghan (65), first world flyweight boxing champion to retire undefeated; noted for renderings of 'When Irish Eyes Are Smiling' after his fights.

17 Mar. G.A.A.'s centenary year celebrations commence.

18 Mar. I.N.L.A. leader Dominic McGlinchey extradited to Northern Ireland on charge of murder.

31 Mar. Super-levy of 93p per gallon of milk in Republic (in excess of quota imposed by E.E.C. Council of Ministers).

6 Apr. d. Jimmy Kennedy (81), song-writer ('Red Sails in the Sunset', 'South of the Border', 'Teddy Bears' Picnic' and the 'Hokey-Cokey').

7 Apr. Orbiting space satellite 'Challenger' has aboard first large-scale Irish 'pay-load' from Dublin Institute for Advanced Studies, conducting experiment into origin and evolution of matter in the galaxy.

9 Apr. d. Leslie Bean de Barra (91), widow of Gen. Tom Barry, leader in foundation of Irish Red Cross (1939).

Dermot Ryan, Archbishop of Dublin, appointed Pro-Prefect of Propaganda Fide in Rome, where he d. 21 Feb. 1985 (*see* 20 Jan. 1985).

2 May Pub. report of the New Ireland Forum after discussion at Dublin Castle over 11 months; Taoiseach FitzGerald and opposition leader, Charles Haughey, differ in interpretation.

3 May d. Seosamh Ó hÉanaí (Joe Heaney) (64), *sean-nós* (traditional) singer, in U.S.A. (buried at Muighreas, Carna, Co. Galway, on 8th).

21 May First home in Dublin city converted to natural gas.

24 May U.S. House of Representatives adopts resolutions welcoming work of New Ireland Forum (Senate adopted similar resolution on 22nd).

1 June U.S. President Ronald Reagan, accompanied by his wife Nancy, arrives on four-day official visit to the Republic.

14 June Second direct elections to the European Parliament: Republic—Fianna Fáil, 8; Fine Gael, 6; Independent, 1 (T. J. Maher). Northern Ireland—Rev. Ian Paisley (D.U.P.), John Hume (S.D.L.P.) and John Taylor (O.U.P.) retain their seats.

Referendum on Ninth Amendment to the Constitution of the Republic, extending voting rights to non-citizens, carried (828,483 votes to 270,250).

28 June Veteran actor Noel Purcell and comedienne Maureen Potter receive freedom of the city of Dublin.

13 July Fr Niall O'Brien released from prison in the Philippines.

17 July Nicky Kelly, jailed in 1976 for Sallins mail-train robbery (*see* 31 Mar. 1976), freed from Portlaoise jail on humanitarian grounds.

5 Aug. Irish team winners of six gold medals, return from paralympics at Stoke Mandeville, England.

8 Aug. d. (William) Denis Johnston (83), dramatist.

12 Aug. John Treacy wins silver medal behind Carlos Lopez in marathon at the Olympic Games in Los Angeles.

7 Sept. d. Liam O'Flaherty (88), novelist and short-story-writer.

Royal Hospital, Kilmainham, restored by Office of Public Works, is officially handed back to the state.

10 Sept. Douglas Hurd succeeds James Prior as Secretary of State for Northern Ireland.

12 Sept. Wang Laboratories, Europe's largest factory for production of office automation units, is officially opened in Limerick by the Taoiseach, Garret FitzGerald.

15 Sept. d. Charles Lynch (78), concert pianist.

29 Sept. Trawler *Marita Ann* arrested by navy at Fenit, off Kerry; found to be carrying arms from U.S.A.; over seven tons of arms and ammunition seized by authorities; the *Valhalla*, suspected of involvement, is impounded in Boston on 17 Oct.

12 Oct. Five killed and many injured (including U.K. Industry Secretary Norman Tebbit and his wife) when I.R.A. bomb explodes in Grand Hotel, Brighton, during the Conservative Party conference (P.M. Thatcher and cabinet members present in hotel).

21 Oct. Ireland's first toll bridge for motorists, the East Link Bridge, opens in Dublin (at cost of £8 million).

Liffey Ferry service closes with the opening of toll bridge linking Fairview and Ringsend.

1 Nov. President Hillery attends function at Hayes's Hotel, Thurles, where G.A.A. was formed one hundred years before to the day.

13 Nov. Four well-known Irish journalists among nine people killed when plane crashes in Sussex *en route* between Dublin and Paris in annual Beaujolais race.

14 Nov. Jim Mitchell, R.I. Minister for Transport, announces liquidation of Irish Shipping Co.

19 Nov. Following London meeting with Taoiseach FitzGerald, P.M. Thatcher rejects the three options of the New Ireland Forum in her 'Out! Out! Out!' speech.

13 Dec. Government decides against additional funding for Knock Airport, Co. Mayo, and passes the project over to private developer.

1985

1 Jan. Cork city commences 'Cork 800' celebrations, commemorating 800th anniversary of the city's foundation.

6 Jan. Peter Sutherland, R.I. Attorney-General, succeeds Richard Burke as member of the European Commission; John Rogers appointed new Attorney-General.

16 Jan. Chief Justice T. F. O'Higgins awarded new post in European Court of Justice; succeeded as Chief Justice by Thomas Finlay.

19 Jan. d. Shelah Richards (82), actress and producer.

20 Jan. Kevin McNamara enthroned as R.C. Archbishop of Dublin.

29 Jan. Patrick McEntee, S.C., becomes first Q.C. from the South, since partition, to be admitted to Northern Ireland's Inner Bar.

30 Jan. A Mazda 323 assembled in Dublin is the last car made in Ireland, closing a 60-year-old chapter in Irish car industry.

15 Feb. Government in Republic intervenes to avoid crash of the Insurance Corporation of Ireland (owned by Allied Irish Banks).

19 Feb. Government rushes bill through Oireachtas to freeze alleged I.R.A. funds and seizes £1¾ million from bank account.

28 Feb. Seven policemen and two policewomen die in Provisional I.R.A. mortar-bomb attack on Newry R.U.C. station.

3 Mar. d. Noel Purcell (84), actor.

13 Mar. 'Tip' O'Neill, Speaker of the U.S. House of Representatives, arrives in the Republic on six-day visit.

14 Mar. Two schoolchildren at Asdee, Co. Kerry, claim to have seen a statue of the Virgin and Child 'move' in their local church (followed by similar claims throughout the south of Ireland until the end of the year; *see* 22 July).

30 Mar. Ireland wins rugby Triple Crown by defeating England at Lansdowne Road, Dublin.

19 Apr. Ireland's first human liver transplant carried out at St Vincent's Hospital, Dublin (patient dies within 48 hours).

Revenue Commissioners in Republic release names of evaders for the first time (over 800 names feature).

18 May Wreck of vessel from the Spanish Armada discovered off the coast of Mayo by a team of English and Scottish divers.

4 June Sinn Féin councillor Paul Corrigan elected chairman of Fermanagh County Council.

5 June d. Diarmuid Ó Súilleabháin (53), republican and writer.

8 June Barry McGuigan defeats Eusabio Pedroza to become World Boxing Association featherweight champion.

20 June d. George Gilmore (87), republican socialist, co-founder with Frank Ryan and Peadar O'Donnell of the Republican Congress (1934).

23 June Air India Boeing 747 crashes some 80 miles off the Kerry coast in the world's worst aviation disaster to date, killing 329 passengers and crew.

29 June d. Máire Ní Scolaí, traditional singer.

summer Very heavy flooding.

1 July Over 2,000 athletes participate at European Special Olympic Games for mentally handicapped at R.D.S., Dublin.

13 July Live Aid organised by Dublin-born Bob Geldof raises an estimated £45 million for famine victims in the Third World; the Republic contributes some £8 million.

16 July Viking artifacts found during excavation at Wood Quay, Dublin, on display at the National Museum.

22 July Claire O'Mahony reports seeing a movement of the statue of the Virgin Mary at Ballinspittle, Co. Cork which quickly becomes a place of pilgrimage (*see* 14 Mar.).

11 Aug. d. Hector Grey (trading name of Alexander Thompson Scott) (81), who traded for almost 50 years in Middle Abbey Street, Dublin.

22 Aug. Government announces closure of Irish Steel plant in Cork, with loss of 650 jobs.

26 Aug. d. John O'Donovan (64), presenter of almost 1,000 issues of the popular radio programme 'Dear Sir or Madam'.

10 Sept. Ireland's first human heart transplant performed at the Mater Hospital, Dublin, on Edward Kelly, by a team led by Maurice Neligan and Freddie Woods.

27 Sept. Marion Coyle, having served ten years of her 15-year sentence, is released from Limerick jail (*see* 11 Mar. 1976).

11 Oct. d. C. S. ('Tod') Andrews (84), former chairman of Bord na Móna (1946), C.I.E. (1958–66) and R.T.E. Authority (1966–70).

25 Oct. First commercial flight from Connaught Regional Airport, Knock, Co. Mayo, to Rome.

6 Nov. d. Breandán Breathnach (73), leading expert on Irish traditional music and folklore.

15 Nov. Republic and U.K. sign Hillsborough Agreement; approved by Dáil (88 votes to 75) on 21 Nov.

4 Dec. d. Frederick H. Boland (81), diplomat; Republic's permanent representative to the U.N. (1956–64), President of the General Assembly (1960–61).

5 Dec. Whiddy Island oil terminal, Co. Cork, transferred to state ownership, with government receiving $44 million from former lessees.

11 Dec. First meeting of the Anglo-Irish Intergovernmental Conference at Stormont Castle.

17 Dec. All 15 Unionist M.P.s resign their Westminster seats in protest at Anglo-Irish Agreement (*see* 23 Jan. 1986).

17 Dec. d. Leo Maguire, composer and broadcaster.

21 Dec. Progressive Democratic (P.D.) Party founded by Desmond O'Malley; first public meeting on 8 Jan. 1986 in Dublin.

31 Dec. Republic's national debt stands at £20,417 million.

1986

1 Jan. Galway city becomes county borough; the first Irish city to receive the status in this century.

4 Jan. d. Phil Lynott (35), rock star/ writer/singer/guitarist.

23 Jan. By-elections in Northern Ireland (*see* 17 Dec. 1985); 14 of the 15 Unionists regain their seats; Séamus Mallon wins seat for S.D.L.P.

27 Jan. Margaret Heckler takes up post as U.S. Ambassador to the Republic.

5 Feb. d. Ruaidhrí Roberts (69), former general secretary of the I.C.T.U.

10 Feb. d. James Dillon (83), politician, leader of Fine Gael (1959–64).

4 Mar. d. Edward McLysaght (99), historian and genealogist; last surviving member of the Irish Convention (1917–18).

26 Mar. Australian artist Sidney Nolan announces bequest of some 50 of his paintings to the Irish nation.

25 Mar. d. Eddie McAteer (72), leader of the Nationalist Party in Northern Ireland (1953–70).

8 Apr. Ireland's first successful liver transplant operation performed on Maureen Nowlan (aged 3) at Our Lady's Hospital, Crumlin, Dublin (she leaves hospital on 10 July).

16 Apr. Jennifer Guinness rescued by gardaí from house in Ballsbridge, Dublin, after eight-day kidnap ordeal; two Dublin brothers subsequently sentenced to a total of 31 years' imprisonment for the crime.

21 Apr. Robert Eames enthroned as C.I. Archbishop of Armagh and Primate.

13 May d. Peadar O'Donnell (93), revolutionary, agitator and novelist.

17 May A white marble panda, tribute to President Cearbhall Ó Dálaigh (d. 1978) from the People's Republic of China, unveiled at Sneem, Co. Kerry.

21 May £10 million art robbery at Russborough House, Co. Wicklow, home of Sir Alfred Beit.

30 May Connaught Regional Airport (Knock Airport) officially opened by Fianna Fáil leader Charles Haughey (*see* 1 Aug.).

2 June Six nuns die in fire at Loreto Convent, St Stephen's Green, Dublin.

6 June John Stalker, Deputy Chief Constable of Greater Manchester, removed from his inquiry into an apparent 'shoot to kill' policy by the R.U.C. directed against the I.R.A. in Co. Armagh.

19 June Kilmainham jail, run as a museum by voluntary committee since 1960, reverts to state control.

26 June Divorce referendum (Tenth Amendment to the Constitution) in the Republic: against, 935,843; for, 538,279 (62.5 per cent poll).

27 June Dawn Run, champion Irish racehorse, killed in fall at Auteuil in French Champion Hurdle.

30 June King Juan Carlos and Queen Sofia of Spain commence four-day state visit to Republic.

1 July C.I.E. formally hands over control of canals to the Commissioner of Public Works.

3 July Only V.C. to be awarded to an Ulsterman in Second World War (to Leading Seaman James Magennis) sold by Sothebys for £31,900 (six V.C.s were awarded to service members living in or with connections with Éire).

13 July First National Day of Commemoration to honour all Irish people who died in war or on U.N. service.

17 July 18 men found guilty on evidence of Northern Ireland 'supergrass' Christopher Black released by Appeals Court, Belfast (*see* 5 Aug. 1983).

23 July Northern Ireland Assembly dissolved; loyalist members evicted by police.

24 July Bob Geldof awarded British honorary knighthood for services to African famine relief (*see* 13 July 1985).

29 July High Court, Dublin, rules that Derrynaflan hoard, valued at £8 million, should be returned to the finders by the National Museum (*see* 17 Feb. 1980).

First transatlantic flight arrives at Connaught Regional Airport, Knock, Co. Mayo.

1 Aug. d. Monsignor James Horan (74) while visiting Lourdes; originator of Connaught Regional Airport (popularly known as Knock Aiport); airport subsequently renamed Horan International Airport.

2 Aug. Punt (Irish £) devalued within the E.M.S. by 8 per cent.

6 Aug. N.I. Department of Agriculture announces that owing to afforestation the pine marten has again become common after almost total absence for 200 years.

7 Aug. Peter Robinson, deputy leader of the Democratic Unionist Party, arrested in Co. Monaghan during loyalist incursion; released on bail.

25 Aug. Ireland hit by Hurricane Charlie; widespread damage.

4 Sept. Government lends Bord na Móna £25 million to help overcome the consequences of disastrous harvest.

18 Sept. At separate Dublin and London ceremonies agreement is signed between Ireland and Britain for international fund to channel U.S. and foreign financial aid to Northern Ireland (*see* 26 Sept.).

26 Sept. Agreement signed in Washington, D.C., allowing release of first $50 million in U.S. aid for Northern Ireland (*see* 18 Sept.).

20 Oct. d. Gen. Michael Joseph Costello (82), soldier and public servant; general manager of the Irish Sugar Company (1945–66).

28 Oct. 'Big Bang Day' as Dublin's stockmarket is computerised.

2 Nov. Sinn Féin votes to end policy of abstention from the Dáil.

16 Nov. d. Siobhán McKenna (63), actress.

23 Nov. 100-ton iron-ore vessel *Kowloon Bridge* is abandoned by her crew off west Cork coast; later runs aground, causing severe pollution to beaches in the scenic south-west.

11 Dec. Transport (Reorganisation of Córas Iompair Éireann) Act permits restructuring of the company into three major operating companies of Iarnród Éireann (Irish Rail), Bus Éireann (Irish Bus) and Bus Átha Cliath (Dublin Bus).

19 Dec. High Court, Dublin, rules that it is illegal for family planning clinics to give advice concerning abortion facilities.

24 Dec. Single European Act signed by the President, but, as a result of a judicial ruling, referendum is ordered for 26 May 1987.

Pub. *Against the Tide*, autobiography of Dr Noel Browne.

Census of population in Republic: 3,537,195 (increase of 5 per cent since 1979).

1987

2 Jan. d. Roger McHugh (81), Professor of English, U.C.D.

18 Jan. d. T. D. Williams (66), Professor of Modern History, U.C.D. (1949–85).

20 Jan. Labour Party members withdraw from coalition government.

14 Feb. General election in R.I.: Fianna Fáil, 81; Fine Gael, 51; Progressive Democrats, 14; Labour, 12; Workers' Party, 4; Independents and others, 3. Fianna Fáil return to power; Charles Haughey appointed Taoiseach on 10 Mar.

11 Mar. Dr Garret FitzGerald announces his resignation from the leadership of Fine Gael; succeeded by Alan Dukes.

12 Mar. d. Niall Montgomery (73), architect and poet; involved in design of Dublin Airport buildings and the Kilkenny Design Centre.

27 Mar. New Fianna Fáil government introduces 'fiscal rectitude' budget, deflationary in impact, involving severe cutbacks in expenditure.

7 Apr. Figures issued by the Republic's Department of Finance on revenue show: P.A.Y.E. sector contributing £1,987 million; self-employed £172.7 million; farmers £37 million (but they receive back V.A.T. repayments of £79.4 million).

8 Apr. Sir Patrick Dun's Hospital, Dublin, purchased for £1½ million by the Institute of Clinical Pharmacology.

25 Apr. Lord Justice Gibson (of Northern Ireland judiciary) and his wife Cecily are killed by I.R.A. carbomb as they cross the border to link up with R.U.C. escort; rugby internationals Nigel Carr, David Irwin and Philip Rainey are injured in the explosion.

28 Apr. d. Oliver J. Flanagan (66), recently retired Fine Gael T.D. for Laois–Offaly (1943–87), Knight of St Gregory.

8 May Eight I.R.A. members shot dead by security forces during raid on Loughgall R.U.C. station, Co. Armagh.

17 May d. Liam Miller (63), founder of the Dolmen Press (1951).

18 May Dolmen remains with jewellery and pottery fragments from c. 2500 B.C. uncovered in the Burren, Co. Clare, by archaeologists from Office of Public Works.

26 May Referendum in Republic on Single European Act: for, 755,423; against, 324,977.

28 May Ireland's last manual telephone exchange, at Mountshannon, Co. Clare, closes (postmistress Florence Bugler).

12 June General election in U.K.; Enoch Powell (O.U.P.) loses his South Down seat to Eddie McGrady (S.D.L.P.).

National Heritage Park, Ferrycarrig, Co. Wexford, opens.

26 July Stephen Roche becomes first Irish rider to win the Tour de France (*see* 6 Sept.).

29 July Air Corps helicopter crew makes first night-time rescue, of three Mayo fishermen on sandbank in Rossport harbour (until now night-time rescue was performed by R.A.F.).

31 July Albert Reynolds, R.I. Minister for Industry and Commerce, announces that the Shannon Free Airport Development Company (S.F.A.D.Co.) is to have responsibility for tourism and all industrial development in the Mid-West region, assuming the functions of Bord Fáilte and the I.D.A. for that region.

6 Sept. At Villich, Austria, Stephen Roche becomes the first Irish rider to win the World Professional Road Race Championship (*see* 26 July).

14 Oct. John O'Grady kidnapped in Dublin by I.N.L.A. group led by Dessie O'Hare (*see* 27 Nov.).

30 Oct. French customs authorities seize *Eksund*, ship carrying 150 tons of armaments, believed to be for the I.R.A.

8 Nov. 11 killed when I.R.A. bomb explodes at War Memorial in the centre of Enniskillen, Co. Fermanagh, during Remembrance Day celebrations.

23 Nov. National search in Republic for I.R.A. arms and equipment.

25 Nov. d. Canon James McDyer (76), whose work in Glencolumbkille, Co. Donegal, 1951–71, revitalised the area through co-operative enterprises.

27 Nov. Dessie O'Hare wounded and captured in Co. Kilkenny in a joint Garda/army operation.

22 Dec. U.D.A. leader John McMichael killed by I.R.A. car-bomb.

31 Dec. Republic's national debt stands at £26,345 million.

R.N.L.I. lifeboat crews rescue 89 people on 265 missions of mercy during 1987.

1988

1 Jan. Dublin commences celebration of its 'Millennium'.

Release of British cabinet papers of Oct. 1957 reveals plans to construct nuclear plant on Lough Neagh.

d. Joe Keohane, outstanding Kerry Gaelic footballer.

7 Jan. Announcement of £200 million major road development project under E.E.C. Regional Fund.

8 Jan. Following major loyalist arms find, R.U.C. raid Belfast H.Q. of U.D.A. and arrest three.

11 Jan. John Hume, S.D.L.P. leader, and Gerry Adams, Sinn Féin leader, have surprise Belfast meeting which is condemned by other parties; further meetings on 21 Jan. and 3 Mar. (*see* 23 Mar.).

13 Jan. Progressive Democrats draft constitution of Ireland, dropping constitutional claim to jurisdiction by Republic over Northern Ireland, and deleting reference to God (reference to God restored on 2 June).

15 Jan. Christopher Nolan wins Whitbread Book Prize (£18,750) for *Under the Eye of the Clock*.

d. Seán MacBride (83), Chief of Staff, I.R.A. (1936–38); founder of Clann na Poblachta (1946); Nobel Prize for Peace (1974); Lenin Peace Prize (1977); American Medal for Justice (1978).

16 Jan. Conradh na Gaeilge (Gaelic League) branch founded in Montmartre, Paris (only branch on European mainland).

21 Jan. Monsignor Desmond Connell announced to succeed Kevin McNamara as R.C. Archbishop of Dublin.

27 Jan. In introducing Republic's budget, Ray MacSharry, Minister for Finance, reduces exchequer borrowing by over £300 million (down from 10.3 per cent G.N.P. to 8.2 per cent).

28 Jan. Birmingham Six appeal rejected by Court of Appeal in London.

1 Feb. Meteorological Service announces the wettest Jan. in over 30 years.

3 Feb. Aer Rianta wins multi-million-pound contract to provide and maintain fleet of ground-service vehicles in partnership with Aeroflot; joint running of duty-free shops at Moscow (and later Leningrad) is also announced.

6 Feb. d. P. V. Doyle (65), hotelier and chairman of Bord Fáilte.

9 Feb. Four die as 107 m.p.h. gales are recorded, causing widespread disruption.

21 Feb. Aidan McAnespie shot at Aughnacloy, Co. Tyrone, checkpoint on way to Gaelic football match; government of Republic announces inquiry under Deputy Garda Commissioner (later Commissioner) Eugene Crowley. 18-year-old Grenadier Guardsman subsequently charged in Northern Ireland; hearing finds that his gun was accidentally discharged.

24 Feb. d. Tommy O'Brien (83), opera enthusiast whose Radio Éireann programme 'Your Choice and Mine' ran for over 40 years.

25 Feb. President Mitterand begins first official visit to Republic by a French head of state; addresses both Houses of the Oireachtas on 26th.

28 Feb. Tailors' Hall, Dublin, last surviving guild hall in the capital, opened as an An Taisce office by Taoiseach Charles Haughey.

6 Mar. Three members of an I.R.A. active service unit shot dead in Gibraltar by S.A.S. unit; coroner's inquest jury on 30 Sept. finds (by 9 votes to 2) that they were 'lawfully killed'.

13 Mar. Seán Kelly wins Paris–Nice cycle race for the seventh time.

16 Mar. Three mourners killed when funeral of I.R.A. members is attacked by loyalist gunman in Milltown cemetery; loyalist Michael Stone is charged with six murders (22nd), including those at the cemetery.

19 Mar. Two British soldiers attacked and killed by members of I.R.A. during a funeral procession in Belfast.

23 Mar. Delegates of the S.D.L.P. and Sinn Féin start talks 'to find out and seek agreement in which peace and justice can be established'; meetings close on 11 July, followed by publication of position papers.

27 Apr. 18 Maze escapers of 25 Sept. 1983 jailed.

1 May Three killed in I.R.A. attack on R.A.F. base in Holland.

5 June d. Robin Dudley Edwards, historian, Professor of History at U.C.D.

15 June Six British soldiers killed by I.R.A. bomb in Lisburn, Co. Antrim, following a 'fun run'.

17 June 'Anna Livia' sculpture, sponsored for the Dublin Millennium by Jefferson Smurfit Ltd, unveiled in O'Connell Street.

30 June Fr Patrick Ryan detained in Belgium; following three-week hunger-strike deported to Ireland on 25 Nov.

4 July 20 R.U.C. officers to be disciplined over 1982 shootings.

10 July Taoiseach Charles Haughey, on official visit to Australia for its bicentennial celebrations, presents P.M. Bob Hawke with microfilm record of Irish emigration to Australia.

21 July £2 million award to Grange Development after Dublin County Council refuses planning permission (money paid on 22 Mar. 1989, when a receiver is appointed to the County Council).

20 Aug. Eight British soldiers killed in landmine attack on bus near Ballygawley, Co. Tyrone.

1–30 Sept. About £500 million in unpaid taxes collected under tax amnesty.

12 Sept. Dermot Clifford enthroned as R.C. Archbishop of Cashel and Emly in succession to Thomas Morris (retired).

14 Sept. I.R.A. training camp found at Rossmore, Co. Monaghan.

20 Sept. R.I. Minister for Education launches new Junior Certificate programme to replace the Intermediate Certificate, to become effective from Sept. 1989.

16 Oct. Ireland wins Dunhill Nations Golf Cup Tournament at St Andrew's (Scotland).

19 Oct. d. Martin Quirke, Irish champion jockey (1923), with 86 winners, a record which stood until 1972, when broken by Johnny Roe.

30 Nov. The Irish entry for the Whitbread Round the World Yacht Race, *N.C.B. Ireland*, custom-built at a cost of £4 million, is launched for its trials.

1989

8 Jan. 45 people killed as a London–Belfast Dan-Air Boeing 737 crashes at East Midlands airport.

27 Jan. Johnston, Mooney and O'Brien, Dublin's oldest bakery, announces closure.

20 Mar. Two senior R.U.C. officers returning from top-level meeting with Gardai at Dundalk, Co. Louth, killed by I.R.A. at Edenknappa, Co. Armagh.

2 Apr. Mikhail Gorbachev becomes the first Soviet leader to visit Ireland when, en route to Cuba, he meets Taoiseach Charles Haughey and government ministers at Shannon. Mrs Raisa Gorbachev tours nearby Bunratty Folk Park.

18 Apr. Shannon-based aircraft-leasing company G.P.A. announces the placing of a record thirty-billion dollar order with World's leading aircraft manufacturers.

1 June Hugh Annesley succeeds Sir John Hermon as Chief Constable of the R.U.C.

15 June General election in R.I.: Fianna Fáil, 77; Fine Gael, 55; Labour, 15; Workers' Party, 7; Progressive Democrats, 6; Independents and others, 6 (*see* 29 June).

Third direct elections to the European Parliament: Republic—Fianna Fáil, 6; Fine Gael, 4; Labour, 1; Progressive Democrats, 1; Workers' Party, 1; Independents, 2. Northern Ireland—Rev. Ian Paisley (D.U.P.); John Hume (S.D.L.P.); Jim Nicholson (O.U.P.).

d. Ray McAnally, stage, film and television actor.

29 June Dáil assembles and fails to elect a Taoiseach; Charles J. Haughey resigns office and becomes acting Taoiseach of a caretaker Fianna Fáil government; Dáil adjourns while Mr Haughey enters into negotiations with the main parties.

3 July Dáil reassembles and fails to elect a Taoiseach; adjourns again while Mr Haughey negotiates with other parties.

6 July Dáil reassembles and Acting Taoiseach Haughey asks for adjournment so that talks between Fianna Fáil and others can continue.

6–12 July Negotiations proceed between Fianna Fáil and the Progressive Democrats: Bertie Ahern and Albert Reynolds (Fianna Fáil) negotiate with Pat Cox and Bobby Molloy (Progressive Democrats), while there are also meetings between Acting Taoiseach Haughey and Desmond O'Malley, leader of the Progressive Democrats.

12 July Dáil reassembles; Fianna Fáil enters into its first coalition when Charles J. Haughey is elected Taoiseach with the support of the Progressive Democrats; Desmond O'Malley and Bobby Molloy of the Progressive Democrats enter the cabinet (Mary Harney of the Progressive Democrats receives junior ministry a week later).

18 July Mr Justice Donal Barrington of the High Court appointed the Republic's first member of the new Court of First Instance of the European Communities (assuming duties on 1 Sept.).

27 July Reprints of 19th-century large-scale Ordnance Survey maps (selling at £5 each) launched.

28 July Following U.K. cabinet reshuffle, Peter Brooke replaces Tom King as Secretary of State for Northern Ireland.

4 Sept. Century Radio, Republic's first licensed commercial national radio station begins broadcasting in Dublin.

14 Sept. Inauguration of University of Limerick (formerly N.I.H.E.), first university opened since foundation of state (1922).

John Stevens, Deputy Chief Constable of the Cambridgeshire Constabulary, appointed to investigate leaks of security documents in Northern Ireland.

22 Sept. Nine army bandsmen and one civilian killed when I.R.A. bomb explodes at Royal Marine barracks in the Kent town of Deal.

30 Nov. Publication of J. E. Doherty and D. J. Hickey, *A Chronology of Irish History since 1500*.

Index

B

D

F

G

K

L

M

N

P

Q

R

KILKENNY COUNTY LIBRARY